ADVANCED
BLUEWATER
CRUISING

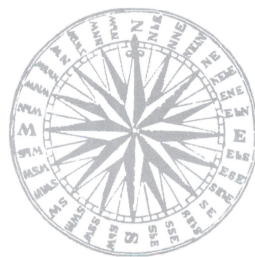

D0222668

What you need to know for safe, comfortable passages under sail

by HAL SUTPHEN

Published by Cruising Rally Association

Published by Cruising Rally Association
2 Canonicus Avenue
Newport, RI 02840

ISBN 0-9704560-0-X

Library of Congress Control Number: 2001126827

Printed by R.R. Donnelley & Sons Company

Manufactured in the United States of America

CONTENTS

INTRODUCTION

Our first reason for doing this book was to make portable the information in the CRUISING RALLY ASSOCIATION's Passagemaker Seminars. Along the way, it became clear that a book would also let us delve into topics touched on only briefly in a weekend seminar. So this book supplements the seminars, whose agenda has evolved based on lessons learned over a decade of cruising rallies, to both the Caribbean (West Marine Caribbean 1500) and Bermuda (West Marine Bermuda Cruising Rally), as well as over thousands of sea miles sailed elsewhere.

You'll find two general parts:

1. Strategies you can use to increase the probability that an ocean passage will be successful (safe, reasonably swift and enjoyable); and

2. Tactics to help cope with the more common difficulties that can arise offshore, despite applying these preventive strategies.

I want to take this opportunity to thank the hundreds of sailors with whom I have sailed over many years of involvement with boats, seamanship, navigation and safety at sea. Few concepts or techniques here are original. Most are skills, ideas or knowledge acquired by working with others or by reading their writings. And there is rarely a passage or seminar from which I do not gain some new insight or useful idea. To all who have helped in my learning process, I am indebted. If this book manages to enlighten and to convey some of the knowledge I have inherited, and so helps others become successful passagemakers, it will have fulfilled its goal.

This book is truly a living document. Your suggestions, criticisms and comments are welcome, and will make it a more useful resource for a prospective passagemaker, whether novice or seasoned salt.

Hal Sutphen
Kilmarnock, Virginia
May, 2001

ABOUT THE AUTHOR

Hal Sutphen is educational director for the Cruising Rally Association, which conducts the West Marine Caribbean 1500 and Passagemaker Seminars. He is a frequent contributor to *Blue Water Sailing, Ocean Navigator* and *Cruising World,* and is one of a small group of experts authorized to moderate Safety at Sea Seminars under the auspices of *Cruising World* and US Sailing. His thousands of sea miles include seven passages to the Caribbean and five to Bermuda.

He discovered sailboats as a boy summering at the New Jersey shore. Everything about them captivated him, and - after attending Brown University on a Navy ROTC scholarship – he pursued a career as a Navy surface warfare officer. His sea assignments included command of an experimental patrol craft, an ocean minesweeper and a 19,000-ton ammunition ship. While teaching Naval Science at NROTC Unit Hampton Roads, he skippered the unit's 50' sail training ketch on a 5,000 mile training voyage, participating in Tall Ships events in Quebec, Toronto, and Rochester, New York.

Subsequently, Captain Sutphen was Director of Navy Sailing, overseeing the Navy's professional and recreational sailing programs worldwide.

Hal met rally organizer Steve Black while taking a friend's boat in the first Caribbean 1500 Cruising Rally. Since that time, he has participated in all the Cruising Rally Association's rallies and seminars. Three of his passages south in West Marine Caribbean 1500 Rallies have been aboard his Pearson 424 ketch, Sea Duty. He and his wife, Helen, also enjoy cruising on Chesapeake Bay from their home outside Kilmarnock, on Virginia's Northern Neck.

ACKNOWLEDGEMENTS

We wish to thank the following for their contributions:

Steve Black for the chapters on fear and leadership

Michael Carr on the weather sections

Charles Oman on seasickness medications

Dave Flynn on the sail chapters

Dr. Rob Amsler and Dr. Dan Carlin on the medical chapters

Dr. Fred Botta on the dental section

John Bonds on the boat inspection chapter

Ken Kroth on amateur radio material and for text review

Ralph Naranjo for text review and commentary

Cruising World Magazine for permission to reprint material from several articles

West Marine for use of their electrical power calculation form

CHAPTER 1

PASSAGEMAKING AND COASTAL CRUISING

The urge to make an extended passage – to distant and perhaps romantic destinations – motivates many a sailor. Though passagemaking may appear to be a simple extension of coastal cruising, there are some important differences. What are those differences and their implications? Once these are clear, subsequent chapters will assess passagemaking in detail; the strategies that can increase your prospects for a successful passage, and tactics you can adopt to cope with adversity should it arise.

While we're discussing sailboats, many issues are equally applicable to powerboats. The powerboat skipper doesn't have to worry about trimming and changing sails, but must pay greater attention to engine condition and fuel consumption. Travelling a more direct route will often make a motor passage shorter, but the underlying characteristics of the voyage are similar.

Crew routine – coastal vs. offshore. The most obvious difference between coastal cruising and passagemaking is the duration of the voyage. Coastal sailors grow used to a routine in which the whole crew lives on the same time schedule. Everyone arises in the morning; they get the boat underway and sail through the day to their destination. Then they moor for the night, and everyone rests before the next day's transit. Even when a coastal trip runs longer – 24-36 hours – human endurance allows the crew to operate in a similar mode.

For longer passages, voyagers must adapt to a plan that enables the crew to sail the boat continuously, for days and perhaps weeks without a common "rest stop." This has implications for both crew and boat.

The offshore crew must be organized to operate around the clock. At any given point in the 24-hour day, part of the crew must be running the boat and part must be getting rest. There must be a watch schedule that allocates each crew member's working and resting times. On Caribbean 1500 rallies, we've seen crews that tried to get by without any set schedule, and boats on which one person (usually the skipper) tried to stay up 22 hours a day. Neither approach has been successful, leading to unhappy crews, poor boat performance and ill-considered decisions by fatigued skippers.

With different people running the boat at different times, there must be standard routines for daily activities such as standing watch, recording information in the log and navigating, and for emergencies such as fighting a fire or recovering a crew overboard. Without set routines, there will be confusion, misunderstandings and overlooked responsibilities. Even a minor difference, such as the way halyard tails are coiled and secured, could seriously affect the safety of boat and crew – say, when a sail must be quickly reefed in the night. Not only should there be an agreed way to do things, every crew member must be trained to do each thing the same way.

Sailing at night. The crew must also adjust to the demands of sailing at night. Trimming sails, steering and moving around the boat at night can be quite challenging for those who have sailed primarily by day. With about 50% of any long passage taking place at night, crew must be able to find equipment and sail the boat in darkness as well as they can in daylight. Many new passagemakers find it difficult to get enough rest. Some find it tough to sleep during daylight. For others, the motion and noise created by the boat's movement interfere with sleep. One rally participant, who had lived aboard her boat for two years, complained several days into her first ocean passage that she couldn't sleep with all that water rushing past the hull a few inches away. She'd been told voyaging was like camping, but no one had warned her it would be "like camping in a washing machine!"

Demands on boat and equipment. Demands of a long passage also require more of a boat's design and construction. It must be strong enough to cope with adverse weather, because when a boat is 500 miles offshore, there are no harbors to nip into, to hide from a storm. The layout must facilitate operation in rough weather as well as fine, and secure accommodations must permit off-watch crew to rest comfortably, whichever tack the boat is on, motoring in a calm or fore-reaching in a gale.

An extended passage – such as the Caribbean 1500 – lasting for 11-15 days imposes as much stress on most of the boats (and every piece of equipment) as they would normally encounter in a year of weekend cruising. Chafe occurs at an astonishing rate: A jib sheet that would look fine after a season of daysailing can chafe through overnight if the same 3" section has been rubbing against a tiny rough spot on a shroud. Steering systems, electrical equipment, plumbing systems, galley gear: all are placed under sustained heavier loads than on shorter journeys, and so are more prone to failure.

Effects of time and distance. A second basic difference between passagemaking and coastal cruising involves the time and distance scales. A few hours' delay on a coastal passage can seriously impact its safe completion (crew fatigue, tide/current shifts, arrival before or after darkness, etc.). Adding four hours to a 12-hour journey is an increase of 33%. However, when the passage is measured in days or weeks, a few hours won't make much difference. (The exception is at the end when landfall introduces considerations similar to coastal passages.) For the passagemaker, minor changes in sail trim and boat speed that might be crucial on a coastal trip diminish in importance. For instance, the 650-mile passage to Bermuda might take five days. Sustaining the concentrated effort needed for perfect sail trim might require three people on watch. This could improve speed by 5-10 seconds per mile – for less than two hours' difference in arrival time. Even a four-hour delay represents an increase in the voyage's length of just over 3%. Most passagemakers would consider a smaller, more relaxed watch well worth a few extra hours under way.

Though time plays a controlling role in coastal trips, it's a commodity the passagemaker can spend more liberally. Rather than pressing on to make a deadline, the passagemaker can slow down and adjust arrival to coincide with a rising tide or an early morning landfall and daytime entry. Changing course by 30° may add a few miles, but if a smoother ride puts less strain on boat and crew, hours added to the passage are a worthwhile investment.

Navigation – far from the hard stuff. The larger distance scale on a passage mainly impacts navigation. On coastal trips, the boat stays relatively close to the ocean's greatest navigational risks: the hard stuff around the edges. Along the coast, a prudent skipper keeps track of the boat's position with a high level of accuracy, since a few hundred yards may make the difference between delight and disaster. That position must be updated frequently, with fixes plotted usually at intervals of under an hour.

When you are hundreds of miles offshore, the hard spots are far away. Knowing the boat's location by dead reckoning within a few miles is perfectly adequate, and verifying that position with a fix, by electronic or celestial means, at 6-12 hour intervals is sufficient.

Whereas coastal waters are cluttered with outlying ledges and rocks, buoys, fishing craft and coastal shipping, aside from an occasional merchant ship the high seas have few such obstructions. All the water is deep. While a continuous alert watch is required, both by the Rules of the Road and by the tenets of good seamanship, the situation is far less demanding. At sea, going below for five minutes to make cocoa does not entail the same risk it might closer to shore.

Self-sufficiency – far from the 7-Eleven. A third difference between passagemaking and coastal cruising may be the most important: the level of self-sufficiency required. There seems to be a food/fuel/convenience store within 10 minutes of any place in the coastal United States, and major chandlery chains such as West Marine seem to have outlets springing up like mushrooms. While the coastal sailor has regular contact with support facilities on land, the passagemaker can't expect to find unexpectedly needed supplies or outside assistance until the end of the voyage.

For offshore, a boat must have storage for provisions, spare parts, tools, fuel, water and other consumables needed, not only for the planned trip – but also for any extensions caused by weather or a change of destination. The menu-planning that precedes food provisioning will balance short-lived fresh and refrigerated stores with dry and canned foods for the longer haul. To spare parts, fuel, etc., you'll add necessities such as toilet paper, books and deodorant.

There must also be some place to stow trash. International treaties prohibit disposal of plastics at sea, and other materials are subject to specific limitations. Good steward-ship of planet Earth and Neptune's Domain requires passagemakers to keep any overboard disposal to an absolute minimum. My personal rule is to keep onboard for disposal ashore anything that is not as readily biodegradable as food scraps. A few years ago on a rally, during the daily radio chat, the communication coordinator surveyed the boats about their evening meal. One boat crewed by several young men replied by naming a popular pastry product intended to be heated in a toaster or eaten cold. A sim-ilar survey several nights later elicited the same response. A few days before arrival, the boats were asked how much trash they had for disposal when they arrived, and where it was stowed. The young men replied that they had no trash. When questioned further, they claimed they'd gotten so tired of eating the pastry product that they'd eaten their trash instead! No one is expected to go that far in controlling trash disposal, but trash must be taken into account in voyage planning.

The need for self-sufficiency offshore has many ramifications. It puts a premium on engine reliability - not only for propulsion, but also as the main source of all-important electrical power needed for lights, communication and navigation. While self-sufficient, you'll also be isolated from the usual telephone service, mail and other links to friends, families and creditors, many of whom seem unable to understand why the passage-maker can't respond as swiftly as folks ashore can.

A simpler lifestyle. Both limited storage and the need to be self-sufficient cause most voyagers to adopt a simpler lifestyle on passages. It's like stepping backward 30+ years to the days before there was an electrical or electronic device to ease boring or unpleasant tasks, such as washing clothes or dishes. Repairs are a matter of doing it yourself with the tools on hand rather than calling in a professional, and leisure time centers on games, reading and handicrafts instead of watching TV or surfing the net. Contact with friends and family is not as simple as picking up the telephone. To fully enjoy passagemaking, all crew members must willingly accept compromises entailed in this simpler lifestyle. Men, in particular, must realize that some aspects of the minimum social and physical comfort level for women might be quite different from theirs, and may require accommodations for a mutually enjoyable resolution.

The requirement for self-sufficiency during a passage cannot be overlooked. As David Burch nicely put it in his introduction to *Emergency Navigation*:

"At sea we must accept that everything can get wet, turned upside down, and dropped. Any piece of equipment, no matter how well guarded, can fail or be lost – somehow we could end up without it. There's no way around this; it's part of the challenge we accept when we go to sea. We must be self-reliant. If equipment fails, we must go on or go back, one mile or a thousand miles, without it."

The level of hazards. A final distinction between coastal and offshore passage-making is really a product of time and distance. This is the higher level of hazards the passagemaker must be prepared to face. The clearest of these is the weather. With no safe harbors close at hand, the offshore voyager must be ready to face a full spectrum of wind and sea conditions. It means paying much greater attention to weather forecasts and making onboard observations that will enable the voyager to anticipate weather changes. It means knowing how to cope with deteriorating conditions and being ready to make sail changes, heave to or deploy a sea anchor.

The different level of hazards also affects the equipment needs of the passage-making boat. While the coastal cruiser can be quite safe without some of these, no prudent offshore voyager should go without a life raft, a modern 406 MHz EPIRB, and a well-considered abandon-ship kit. Other equipment highly recommended for an offshore passage includes: HF single sideband radio, drogue, sea anchor, radar detector and high quality distress signals. And the whole crew must know how and when to use these items.

Ups and downs – staying positive. Greater risks make the cruising life less consistent in joys and disappointments, victories and defeats, than is life ashore or on shorter passages. Less time is spent in a "normal" routine when everything goes more or less as expected. In its place is a pattern of alternating higher highs (a 12-hour spinnaker reach across a flat blue sea, a sparkling green flash in a spectacular sunset, a snug cove with crystal clear water and tree-lined shore) and deeper lows (reefer failure just after provisioning and two hours before six guests arrive, a sail that rips during heavy weather in the Gulf Stream, a deck leak that saturates your best clothes and favorite books before shorting out the primary bilge pump). The passagemaker learns to stay positive, to remember that the trying times always end eventually, and that a deeper low makes the succeeding high more rewarding.

Fatigue. Last but not least, the duration of longer ocean passages and the sometimes demanding conditions encountered increases the risk of fatigue for both boat and crew. For the boat, fatigue can mean breakage of vital components - spars, running rigging, steering systems. For the crew it can mean flawed decision making, deteriorating morale, physical discomfort, increased risk of injury. Fatigue can be insidious - and the longer the passage, the greater the effort required to prevent it.

In summary, offshore passagemaking differs from coastal cruising in its continuity, its scale of time and distance, its requirement for self-sufficiency, and its exposure to greater levels of hazards. There are ways to cope with these differences, and strategies the passagemaker can use to reduce their effect. We'll address all these points specifically in later chapters. But first let's examine a basic element of any passage: the boat in which it is made.

CHAPTER 2

BOAT SELECTION

What's the "best" boat for passagemaking? It's a highly individualized choice. But there are some generally accepted guidelines about what makes a good offshore boat. If you have not yet chosen a boat, this chapter can be a helpful checklist. If you already have a boat, you may find some ways to improve its offshore suitability.

As any naval architect will be quick to point out, every boat is a compromise. The best we can expect is an acceptable balance, with some boats longer on certain criteria (such as speed and maneuverability) and some stronger on others (stability, internal space). Each cruising skipper must define those preferences individually. Some will prefer small, inexpensive boats with the simplest accommodations and anyone-can-fix-it systems. Others can't conceive of a long passage without three cabins, plenty of hot and cold pressure water, sail and engine power to average eight+ knots, power winches, roller furling and all the latest in electronic wizardry.

Broad spectrum of yacht designs. In a broad spectrum of yacht designs, the lightweight, go-fast racers would be at one end and heavy, can't-get-out-of-their-own-way sea slugs at the other. The best choices for passagemaking would occupy the vast midsection. Those closer to the light racer (this includes the ex-racers, often considered by the cruising skipper looking for a bargain boat) have serious disadvantages. Most were built to a purpose – to sail swiftly around a race course for a few seasons without falling apart – and nothing brawnier than necessary has been included. Their durability over an ocean passage is suspect. The racer was probably designed for six or more crew to be camped on the weather rail in winds over 12 knots, and the boat needs that weight to give it stability. In a cruising environment, this design will have to reef early and deeply, eliminating much of its speed advantage. Because the race boat has Spartan accommodations, life onboard is seldom pleasant (just read any account of a Whitbread Race!). Backfitting an ex-racer with nicer facilities adds weight that encroaches on the boat's speed, as does the ton or more of spares, provisions, etc. that every cruising sailor seems to accumulate.

At the heavyweight end, the drawbacks are perhaps less hazardous, but just as signif-

icant. These boats often boast great stability, near indestructible strength, and great creature comforts; unfortunately, it takes a gale of wind to make them sail. Their passages
tend to be slow, which takes much of the joy out of passagemaking.

Seaworthiness – the #1 priority. What should the passagemaker look for in that
vast middle ground of the design spectrum? Topping the list must be seaworthiness – a
combination of stability, strength of hull, deck and rig, crew accommodations and
protection, and durability of sail handling, steering and auxiliary systems.

What is stability? Stability is complex, but two aspects are relevant. The first is a
boat's ability to carry sails - its ability to resist heeling as wind increases. Some designs
achieve this partly through form stability, based on the hull shape. By making a hull
beamy and shallow, a naval architect can create a boat with a strong initial righting
moment – the force that wants to bring the boat back to level flotation at small to
moderate angles of heel. Unfortunately, as the heel angle exceeds some moderate
amount, righting moment decreases rapidly, so small additional increases in wind can
push the boat much further over. These designs can carry full sail and make impressive
speeds while heel can be controlled. But as heel increases, rapid reduction of sail may be
needed to keep the boat under control. The general shape of these boats, particularly in
cross section, resembles that of a sailing dinghy. Anyone who has sailed a dinghy in gusty
winds appreciates that excessive heel can cause knockdowns, broaching and capsizing.
Their bigger counterparts face similar difficulties.

Another approach is to make the hull narrow and deep and to include significant
ballast low in the bilges or keel. Such a boat may heel easily in light winds, but as wind
and heel increase, so does the righting effect of the ballast, making the boat more and
more resistant to further heeling. These designs may carry less sail initially but will be
able to carry it longer as winds build and they are less vulnerable to broaching and capsize than are their shallower, beamier cousins.

A second aspect of a boat's stability is its ultimate stability: how far it can heel and still
have a positive righting force tending to return it to level flotation with the mast pointed
upward. At some point, virtually any design will develop negative righting force, meaning
the boat will tend to continue heeling further, until the mast points downward. Having
reached this negative area of its stability curve, a boat will tend to stay inverted until some
outside force (an ocean swell or rolling wave) heels it enough to return to the positive section of the curve, at which point the boat will regain its tendency to float right side up.
From a passagemaker's standpoint, the larger the angle to which a boat can heel before
losing its positive stability, the better. This means the boat can stand being rolled to a large
angle of heel by wind or (more likely) sea before it's in danger of capsize. A small negative
area means the boat is relatively easy to return to positive stability, and suggests that the
boat will not remain inverted very long before being righted (Figure 2.1).

A boat for passagemaking should have positive stability through at least 110°, preferably as much as 120°. That is, it should be capable of being rolled until the mast is

Figure 2.1 - Ultimate Stability for Different Hull Types

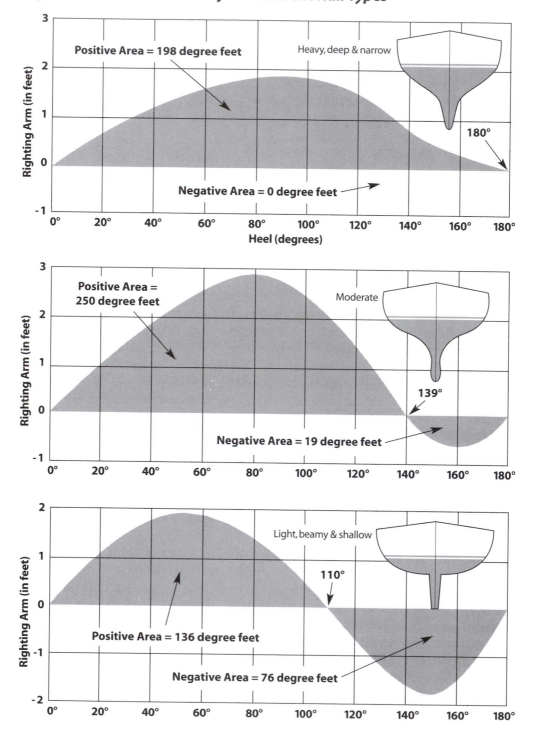

20°-30° below horizontal, and still tend to return to upright. Many passages have been made in boats that don't meet this criterion, but the sailor who selects such a boat must take extra precautions in terms of planning (season, routes) and readiness to handle adverse conditions.

A joint committee of the Society of Naval Architects and Marine Engineers (SNAME) and US SAILING (then U. S. Yacht Racing Union) developed a capsize screening formula that serves as a rough indicator of a boat's vulnerability to capsize. In its simplest form, this formula has been described as follows:

1. *Start with the gross weight of the boat (in pounds)*
2. *Divide it by 64 to determine the volume of seawater it displaces*
3. *Take the cube root of this number*
4. *Divide it into the boat's maximum beam (in feet).*

If applying this formula to a given design results in a number greater than 2.0, a closer assessment of the boat's stability is warranted, and special precautions might be needed for a long passage.

Hull, deck and rig strength. The strength of the boat's hull, deck and rig are key components of seaworthiness. The hull must be stiff enough to resist twisting or flexing under stress, and strong enough to withstand impact loads that could be imposed by high seas, pounding, floating debris or grounding. Internal structural components must be securely fastened to the hull; and heavy equipment, ballast and cabinetry must be held firmly in place. The deck must be strong, and deck-mounted equipment must be solidly fastened, with through-bolts and backing plates to spread the loads. The hull-deck joint must be strong (for structural reasons) and watertight, to prevent leakage that impairs comfort and endangers equipment. The rig must be strong. This includes adequate dimensions for the spars and standing rigging, proper tuning to prevent misalignment of the mast column or stress in a single component, and connection to the hull with secure, watertight chainplates strong enough to handle any severe weather loads.

A seaworthy design will also avoid features that could leave a boat vulnerable to severe flooding in a knockdown. Hatches and ports will be no larger than necessary, and they will be fitted with strong, easily operated watertight closures. Off-center companionways and cockpit lockers that offer access to the interior of the hull must be easily closed and secured to prevent inflow of water.

Crew accommodations. Crew accommodations must provide space and facilities for daily living functions, including cooking, eating, sleeping and personal hygiene. These accommodations must be adequate when the boat is heeled (on either tack) and pounding, as well as when on an even keel. A surprising number of boats advertised as being intended for offshore lack decent sea berths; others have berths usable only on one tack. Good ventilation in the cabin is also important. A seagoing design will include Dorade vents to permit interior air flow even when hatches and ports are dogged tight. Crew protection in the form of a dodger or pilothouse, plus weather cloths if freeboard is low, are priceless when it's rainy or when sloppy seas put green water across the decks. When the wind dies and the sun bakes every exposed surface, an awning or bimini can be a lifesaver. Exposure to the elements radically increases crew fatigue, so good crew protection becomes an important offshore safety consideration.

Operating systems. Just as the hull, deck and rig must be strong, so must the boat's principal operating systems. Sail handling systems – sheeting, reefing, furling – must work smoothly under all conditions and be able to take sustained loading on long passages. The steering system and its components (from the wheel/tiller to the rudder blade) must have the brawn to cope with loading for weeks on end, and must be capable of adjustment, lubrication and easy maintenance to keep them operating with minimum friction. A seaworthy boat must also have reliable and adequate auxiliary systems: manual and electric bilge pumps, electrical generating and distribution systems, fresh water, salt water and sewage systems, fire protection and extinguishing equipment, communication equipment and emergency gear (life raft, EPIRB, etc.).

Seakindliness – the "comfort ratio". Closely related to seaworthiness is seakindliness. Seakindliness extends not just to a boat's absolute ability to handle severe conditions, but also to the ease with which it does so. A boat can be built strongly enough to endure the stress of pounding into a seaway – making it seaworthy in the technical sense – but that is hardly a pleasant way to make a passage. A seakindly boat is one that rides the seas easily, without severe jolts, violent rolling or "runaway elevator" pitching. Naval architect Ted Brewer has devised this "comfort ratio":

1. *Multiply waterline length by 0.7 and length overall by 0.3 and add them*
2. *Multiply the sum by 0.65*
3. *Multiply the product by the beam (in feet) raised to the 1.333 power ($B^{1.333}$)*
4. *Divide this number into the boat's displacement, measured in pounds.*

Applying this formula will yield a number that ranges from under 10 for boats that move like a day sailer to over 50 for boats approaching the "sea slug" category. Good cruising designs produce numbers in the mid-30s.

Boat size – and why one size doesn't fit all. Boat size is a criterion that is hotly debated. Some cruising sailors prefer smaller boats, under 30 feet in many cases, on the grounds that they're less costly, simpler, have lighter sailing loads and less complex systems, and ride atop heavy seas like a cork. Others are convinced that "bigger is better", citing creature comforts and faster passages (since speed is generally a function of waterline length), while relying more on power-assistance to handle heavier loads. The USYRU/SNAME capsize study, which originated in the wake of the disastrous 1979 Fastnet Race, confirmed that larger boats are less likely to be rolled by high seas but also found that size alone does not assure protection. Ultimately, a passagemaker's boat choice is usually driven by cost of acquisition and maintenance as well as handling ability by the anticipated crew, rather than by length and beam dimensions.

An aspect of boat size that's less frequently mentioned is the vertical dimension: draft and mast height. While deeper draft usually implies better performance, especially upwind, shallow water effectively closes many wonderful destinations to boats drawing more than about six feet. If the cruising plan includes areas such as the Bahamas, draft limitations can constrain boat choices. Similarly, if plans include waters crossed by bridges, such as the Atlantic Intracoastal Waterway (AICW), maximum mast height comes into play. While the standard minimum high-water clearance under fixed bridges on the AICW is 65', several bridges have less than that, and boats with masthead sensors and antennas in the 64-65' range may encounter difficulties.

As a practical matter, balancing cost, comfort and performance brings most passage-makers to the 35-50' range. Rally experience confirms this. Smaller seaworthy boats tend to be significantly slower, while larger boats involve purchase and maintenance costs beyond the affordability of the typical passagemaker. Within this range, there is a wide array of styles and designs from which a prospective voyager can choose. Appendix A lists the models of boats that have participated in rallies managed by the Cruising Rally Association from 1990 to 2000.

Sloop, cutter or ketch? There is a similar choice among rigs, with the most popular being the sloop, cutter and ketch (Figure 2.2). The sloop rig, with its single headsail, is probably the simplest to sail, with the minimum number of controls. It is also the quickest rig, other factors being equal, especially going to windward. The sloop, with its single mast, is also very strong. One disadvantage is its lack of sail-plan flexibility. Major sail area changes can be made only by changing or reefing the headsail or reefing the main.

The contemporary cutter is a single-masted rig having the mast stepped further aft in the hull than a sloop and with two or more headsails. Nearly as speedy as the sloop to weather, the cutter has added standing rigging that may make it even stronger. The cutter's second headsail gives it flexibility, because the staysail supplements the jib on

Figure 2.2 - Popular Cruising Rigs

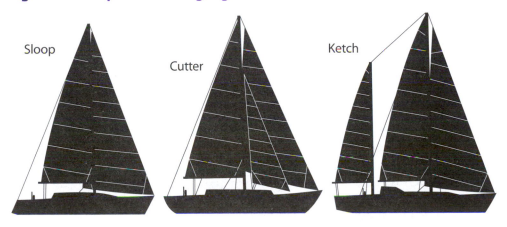

Sloop

Cutter

Ketch

reaches and acts as its smaller replacement when winds pick up. Shifting from the jib to the staysail and reefing the main tends to keep the sail plan's center of effort closer to the mast as well as lowering it, both of which are desirable results of reducing sail.

Of the dual-mast rigs (schooner, ketch, yawl), the ketch is clearly the most popular today. The ketch rig may be less efficient than the sloop or cutter when beating to windward, but it offers noteworthy advantages. It has a much greater array of sail combinations to cope with changing conditions, and the sails are smaller, for easier handling. With more rigging and control lines, the ketch is more complicated to operate, but having two masts lends a safety factor – especially if the two spars are completely independent of one another (no triatic stay between mastheads).

Performance – what makes it or breaks it? Related to size is the question of speed, since for displacement craft – which includes most cruising monohulls – the hull speed at which wave-making resistance increases sharply (hence limiting further speed) is a function of waterline length. While passagemaking should be enjoyable, most cruising sailors would prefer a fast passage to a slow one. The longer the boat is en route, the greater its exposure to stress and to potential adverse weather, and the greater the risk of crew fatigue. Thus performance, in speed or ability to go to weather, is a desirable feature.

Performance tends to be inversely related to displacement, so the desire for performance must be balanced against capacity – stowage for provisions, parts, tools and other baggage most passagemakers want to take along. Adequate stowage volume can be crucial, but other aspects of stowage are equally important. It must be secure, so stowed objects don't become unguided missiles in the event of a knockdown, yet it must allow easy access. Stowage space needs to be distributed, so supplies and equipment can be kept close to their area of use (food near the galley, tools near the engine). To maximize usable volume in the boat's midsection, stowage is often pushed toward the bow and stern, but concentrating weight at the ends adversely impacts performance and comfort. Ideally, heavy items should be stored low in the boat on or near its center, where they will contribute to stability.

Cockpit – aft or center? Cockpit location is another feature in which all alternatives have merits, and the choice becomes one of preference. Aft cockpits usually give a better view of the sails, permit the hull to have lower freeboard, and leave the central section available for living space. They may be wetter, and having the entire boat in front of you sometimes obstructs vision from the helm. Center cockpits usually require higher freeboard, which can detract from overall appearance, and they split the interior into two areas separated by the cockpit and engine room, which occupy the boat's spacious midsection. The benefits include a cockpit less likely to take on water, room for a larger and more accessible (hence maintainable) auxiliary/propulsion plant, and a spacious aft cabin. Regardless of its location, remember that the bigger the cockpit, the bigger the drainage system it needs.

Monohull or multihull? Another debate with no single answer rages between monohull and multihull enthusiasts. Multihull supporters emphasize the comfort that comes from sailing a boat that heels much less than a monohull. Monohull fans point out that when a multihull does heel, it becomes unstable much more quickly than a monohull, and has an inverted stability as great as its upright stability, making capsize recovery doubtful. The multihull sailor replies that while a capsize is highly unlikely, most unballasted multihulls will float when damaged, even when inverted, and provide a safe survival space for the crew, unlike the typical monohull whose heavy keel is constantly trying to take the boat to the bottom. Modern construction and design techniques have eliminated the old argument that multihulls are not strong enough to cope with sea passages, but seakindliness remains an issue. Every multihull has some finite clearance under the bridge between its hulls, and as seas build, there is an increasing vulnerability to slamming as waves strike the underside of the bridge. Though these blows may not be dangerous structurally, they can make the quality of life onboard deteriorate.

An issue that must be examined with great care when assessing a multihull for passagemaking is the question of speed and performance. These are touted as evidence of multihull superiority, but the data are usually drawn from other than passagemaking situations. Multihulls can be swift, indeed, but their performance is greatly influenced by their loading status. Adding a ton of provisions to a monohull may increase its draft by an inch or two, but the changes to its performance will be marginal. Adding a ton of load to a multihull can transform a brilliant performer into a sea slug. Any assessment of a multihull for passagemaking must be based on the boat's performance when loaded for a passage.

Selecting the right boat for passagemaking is a compromise on almost every front except seaworthiness; even there, differences of degree are possible. Beyond that, almost every feature is open to choice. Subjective preferences will play a leading role as the prospective passagemaker balances seakindliness and storage capacity and performance, determines the acceptable levels of crew comfort, opts for a given rig and cockpit location, chooses monohull or multihull. Successful passages have been made by boats of virtually every size and shape, though not with comparable speed and comfort.

For the prospective passagemaker who already has a boat, the considerations above should serve as a checklist to identify possible modifications that might help that boat become a safe, comfortable and tolerably swift ocean voyager.

REFERENCES:
USYRU (now US SAILING), *Final Report of the Directors, USYRU SNAME Joint Committee on Safety from Capsizing,* June 1985
Ted Brewer, *Understanding Yacht Design,* 4th edition. Comfort Ratio, page 8.
Dave Gerr, *The Nature of Boats*
C. W. Marchaj, *Seaworthiness: The Forgotten Factor*
John Rousmaniere, (Ed) *Desirable and Undesirable Characteristics of Offshore Yachts*
United States Sailing Association, *Safety Recommendations for Cruising Sailboats*

CHAPTER 3

OUTFITTING THE BOAT

Outfitting a boat for passagemaking starts with essential equipment, which is then supplemented in accord with the owner's interests, skills and pocketbook. Aside from safety equipment (see Chapter 16), a boat intended for a long voyage could slip by with little more than a good compass, a portable GPS receiver, a lead line for determining depth and a stove. Few passagemakers will be satisfied with such Spartan arrangements, however. (The trip is supposed to be fun, remember?) Generally, the *"minimum essential list"* will include: an auxiliary engine (preferably diesel for safety and reliability), a radio (VHF, possibly HF single sideband), simple instrumentation (speed-distance log, depth sounder, wind speed/direction), 12 volt DC electrical system (for lighting, bilge pump, electronics), and an electronic navigation system that includes at least an installed GPS receiver and perhaps much more.

Adding these systems greatly improves the onboard lifestyle and the likelihood of a safe, enjoyable passage. Many a passagemaker will consider this basic list satisfactory. If the bank balance allows, most will include systems to make operating the boat easier, safer and more comfortable. Keep in mind that each system increases complexity, and creates opportunities for breakdowns. As Santa Cruz Yacht founder Bill Lee likes to point out, the reliability of any machine is inversely proportional to the number of moving parts it contains. Each system also increases the maintenance load and the parts requirement. At some point, adding more gear becomes counterproductive, and the logic of the KISS principle (Keep It Simple, Sailor) prevails. Getting the benefit of any system involves knowing how to use it properly, so installing additional equipment demands additional training for skipper and crew.

Electronics – the "gee-whiz" stuff. Electronics are the focal point for the "gee whiz" technology in sailing today, and many passagemakers have embraced electronic aids with a passion. Instrumentation packages include components that report both true and apparent wind speed and direction, water temperature, incremental boat and wind speed changes, average and maximum boat speed, and other performance variables. Installations now include integrated navigation systems that link navigation devices, electronic position plotting displays and steering systems. They actually enable a boat to go directly from point A to point B without human intervention (provided, of course, the direct path from A to B does not lie across rock X and there are no collisions with other vessels along the way!). Radar is increasingly common. With proper training, it offers invaluable help for collision avoidance as well as being a splendid aid for coastal navigation. Unfortunately, without training, it often induces a false sense of security. Communications equipment is proliferating, with installed and handheld VHF transceivers augmented by amateur and marine single sideband systems, cellular telephones and satellite communication systems. The latter promise to grow rapidly, and systems for transmitting and receiving digitized data such as e-mail, voice and graphic images are coming within reach of cruising budgets. Digital selective calling features, which will become common as the global maritime distress and safety system (GMDSS) is developed over the next few years, are already available in some VHF radios.

Computers at sea. Many cruising folk now take computers to sea. Their applications include keeping an inventory of supplies, monitoring boat performance and location, displaying satellite photos and weather data, plotting celestial observations, and providing instant access to worldwide tidal data. The computer options are limitless. Some boats carry permanently installed, continuously operating computers hard wired into the ship's electrical system. Others carry a laptop/notebook and turn it on to perform a specific function. A computer can be a very productive crewmember, one that works long hours without rest and doesn't expect food three times a day (though it constantly nibbles on the electrical supply).

The major risk with computers afloat is their incompatibility with water – especially salt water. In the seagoing environment, salt and humidity can combine to quickly damage the mechanical and electrical components of a computer. Computers designed to survive the oceanic environment are available, but most boats carry non-marinized models that require careful protection from the elements. The second vulnerability of the cruising computer is its absolute dependence on a stable power supply. If power is lost, as a result of broken/corroded connections or low voltage on the ship's batteries, the computer can no longer function. Prudent seamanship dictates having a manual backup to perform any vital computer function in the event the machine decides to crash.

Water – and watermakers. For centuries, one constraint on passagemaking – whether in a private yacht or a Royal Navy ship of the line – has been the ability to carry an adequate supply of drinking water. While humans can survive for astonishingly long periods without food, life cannot be sustained for more than a few days without water. Voyages have long been planned around the opportunities to replenish water, sometimes by visiting friendly ports, sometimes by collecting tropical downpours, occasionally by stopping at remote islands blessed with streams or springs.

Today, reverse osmosis desalination systems can largely free a voyager from this limitation. High pressure pumps, filters and permeable membranes now permit the passagemaker to obtain fresh, safe potable water from the seawater through which the boat sails. In many cases, water produced by a desalination system is purer than that obtainable ashore, even from public water sources in developed cities. A boon not only to a long passage, but also to local cruising in areas short of natural water supplies, reverse osmosis systems nevertheless have their weaknesses. Like computers, they are vulnerable to power supply problems, and their multiple components, high pressures and sensitive operating parameters create many opportunities for breakdowns. The expensive membranes require regular operation and maintenance to prevent biofouling and most have a finite lifetime, necessitating periodic replacement. They are susceptible to permanent damage if contaminated by petroleum products, so making water in harbor, where fuel leakage and oil slicks are common (and where most cruising boats spend the majority of their time), is a risky proposition.

Above all, prospective passagemakers should resist the temptation to reduce water tankage and rely on the watermaker to meet daily needs. With adequate tankage and prudent fresh water consumption, voyages of surprising length are possible, but if storage is reduced and the watermaker quits, the crew faces an immediate emergency that will demand draconian conservation measures and strong leadership.

Refrigeration – the cold truth. Another system that can affect voyage planning, crew morale, comfort, maintenance needs and daily operating routine is the refrigeration plant. While a number of voyagers opt for a well insulated icebox, most choose to install mechanical refrigeration. A low cost option, the icebox is not a bad choice if it's very well insulated, long passages are infrequent and ice is readily available.

Selecting a mechanical refrigeration system involves several choices. One concerns the method for driving the refrigerating compressor. A second is between systems that operate almost continuously and those that use holdover plates and intermittent operating cycles. The usual power sources for the compressor are the main engine or the boat's battery banks. (Either can include a 110-volt AC drive motor that can be used when on shore power or when an onboard AC generator is running.) Because the engine drive system provides more power, these systems can use larger compressors to refrigerate more quickly. The disadvantage is that keeping the refrigerator box cold entails running the main engine–with all its noise and heat–once or twice a day. Engine driven compressors work best with systems that use large holdover plates, which act like a block of super-cold ice to keep the temperature relatively steady between running times.

Systems that drive the compressor with 12-volt DC power from battery banks generally use smaller compressors to reduce the power drain, and are correspondingly slower cooling. The efficiency of these systems has improved greatly, and modern 12-volt DC refrigeration units offer significant advantages. Since power is available continuously, they can use smaller cooling plates that chill the box directly, somewhat like a household refrigerator, rather than using large holdover plates. Because they increase the total electrical load, these systems are especially suited to boats that have wind and solar electrical generators to replenish batteries without operating the main engine. Such DC refrigeration systems can provide a quiet and efficient means for preserving food for an extended passage.

All refrigeration systems need maintenance, and the skipper is well advised to learn about the system. Repairs often entail special tools (refrigeration gauge set, leak detector) whose use requires special training. With environmental constraints forcing manufacturers to abandon the Freon long used in boats, the cost of repairing, recharging and maintaining Freon systems is increasing. New, environmentally friendly refrigerants have been developed, but most have operating characteristics incompatible with Freon. It is rarely feasible to switch a Freon system to a new refrigerant, so older systems often must be replaced.

Having a good refrigeration system, particularly one that can keep food frozen and make ice to chill the crew's beverage of choice, can make life afloat more civilized and boost morale. But it comes at a real cost, and the cost-benefit equation deserves very careful assessment.

Galley fuels – their pros & cons. Another galley-related outfitting issue concerns the choice of fuel for the galley stove. Factors include safety, efficiency and availability. For safety, *compressed natural gas (CNG)* is a clear leader. Being lighter than air, any CNG leakage disperses upward and safely out of the boat. It has a relatively high heat value, so it cooks efficiently. CNG has two distinct drawbacks. First, it is stored at extremely high pressure (as much as 2250 psi at ambient temperatures in the tropics), uses very large cylinders and requires a special reducing valve to deliver fuel at low service pressures. Service for that valve, should it malfunction, will be extremely difficult to find. Though a full CNG cylinder fuels the stove for a long time, CNG's second disadvantage is the limited number of suppliers, especially beyond the US or other industrialized countries. Few distribution points can actually refill a CNG tank. Empty tanks are usually exchanged for replacements that have been refilled at a central point where the special and very expensive natural gas compressor is located. Thus, in the Caribbean and other popular cruising destinations, CNG refill points are rare, and even if you find one, it may be out of recharged cylinders. This lack of availability is serious enough to virtually disqualify CNG for extended voyages.

Liquified propane gas (LPG) scores high marks for efficiency and availability. It's among the hottest of common fuels, so it cooks quickly. It is stored at lower pressure (130-150 psi) than CNG, uses a simple pressure reducer that can be serviced or replaced almost anywhere, and it is widely available, even in remoter parts of popular cruising grounds. The principal objection to LPG relates to the danger it presents if not handled correctly. Propane (like its European counterpart, butane) is heavier than air, so any leakage tends to settle to the lowest point in the boat. It can lie in an invisible pool in the bilge, awaiting a tiny spark to ignite it explosively.

Safe use of LPG demands scrupulous observation of good operating procedures. The tanks must be kept in isolated lockers that absolutely preclude leaked gas from flowing into the interior of the boat. Airtight lockers, with gasketed lids and drains from the low point of the locker downward to an overboard outlet, are best. Secure the gas supply at the bottle whenever the stove is not in use. When preparing to use the stove, first open the valve at the bottle, then open the remotely operated solenoid valve. Next light the match with which the burner will be ignited (or activate the electronic spark generator, if the stove has one). Then open the burner gas control valve. Never open the valve without having a flame or active igniter at the burner. Never leave a propane stove unwatched. Should a fitful puff of wind blow the flame out, unless the stove is fitted with a thermocouple valve the gas will continue to flow, creating an extremely hazardous situation. The proper sequence for securing the stove is to leave one burner lit, trip the solenoid valve, and observe that the flame goes out. This tests the solenoid system and also removes excess gas from the supply line. After the flame is out, secure the burner valve and the valve at the LPG cylinder.

Test the propane system for leaks on a weekly basis. It is an easy, 10-minute chore that can avoid a disaster and provide peace of mind for the whole crew. Simply close all appliance valves. Energize the solenoid valve, then open the tank valve to pressurize the system. Close the tank valve and carefully note the exact reading on the system pressure gauge. Wait 5-10 minutes and check the gauge again. If there has been any drop in pressure, the system has a leak that must be repaired before it's safe to use it again. While the system is still at least partially pressurized, locate any leaks by swabbing all joints, fittings, hoses and, if necessary, the burner valves with soapy water. Leaks will generate foamy bubbles.

Any LPG system should be installed in strict compliance with the guidelines published by the American Boat and Yacht Council (ABYC). The system should be fitted with sensors to warn of propane gas accumulating in the bilge, and should have a bilge ventilation system like those used with gasoline engines: ignition-protected blowers drawing air from the deepest part of the bilge and discharging it overboard. Handled with care and respect, LPG has proven to be an excellent cooking fuel, and its wide acceptance afloat and ashore makes it a practical choice, as well.

Alcohol was long considered a safe and inexpensive fuel, but it has fallen from use, for good reasons. The cost of alcohol has risen sharply, and its availability is uncertain in many areas. It has a very low heat value, so it takes a long time and a lot of fuel to cook even a simple meal. Alcohol burns with a flame that is very difficult to see, especially in bright sunlight, so it's not easy to see when a burner has gone out. Pressurized alcohol stoves require preheating of the burner element to convert the liquid alcohol into vapor before it is burned. This is usually achieved by allowing a small amount of liquid alcohol to flow into a priming cup beneath the burner, then lighting it so it warms the burner itself. It's very easy to let too much of the clear alcohol into the cup, producing a sometimes spectacular and hazardous flare-up when it is ignited. If a burner goes out or the stove runs out of fuel, the unit must be allowed to cool off before the priming process can be safely repeated. Alcohol's high safety rating was based on the fact that it mixes with water and that water can therefore be used to extinguish an alcohol fire. This is true, but with qualifiers: It takes a relatively large amount of water to be effective, and it takes time. Alcohol is lighter than water, and applying small quantities to a puddle of burning alcohol will simply cause the alcohol to spread out as it floats atop the water's surface. Even with larger volumes, it will take a few seconds for the alcohol and water to mix, cool and cease producing the vapors that feed the flame. Those few seconds can be enough to allow the fire to spread to nearby materials such as curtains or paper products commonly found in the galley. Even when a kettle or large pot of water is put over the burner during the preheat process to absorb heat and function as a ready extinguishing agent, alcohol remains an undesirable choice for galley fuel.

For a similar reason – the need to preheat – *kerosene* is not a good fuel choice. Although it has the highest heat value, it is also dirty, often producing smoke and soot, particularly when using the low quality fuel often encountered in cruising areas. Like alcohol, its odor is repugnant to many, with persistent exposure often inducing nausea.

Regardless of the fuel used or the stove model, clear, readable instructions for operating the stove should be posted where they are easily visible to the person using the stove. They should specify both operating procedures and safety precautions, and the crew should self-police to make sure they are observed.

Autopilots/wind vanes – the extra crew. At the end of their initial offshore passage, rally participants are virtually unanimous in identifying their autopilot or wind vane as their most important equipment. By relieving the crew from the drudgery of steering, these systems have a remarkable impact. By acting as an extra crew member, they may permit a reduced number of crew on watch. They free the watch-keeping crew to maintain a lookout, keep logs up to date, and inspect the boat and its equipment for incipient failures. In all but the most demanding circumstances, these systems can steer a more accurate course than most human helmsmen, while reducing crew fatigue.

Whether a cruising skipper installs an autopilot, wind vane or both is a choice that may be influenced by the boat's design and power availability. Mizzen booms on ketches and yawls can create obstructions that complicate vane installations on the stern. An autopilot uses a boat's power system to control the rudder, usually in response to guidance signals received from a fluxgate compass. It steers the boat in a given compass direction, though some can also use a vane sensor to steer by wind direction. By contrast, a vane uses only the apparent wind; if wind direction or speed changes, the compass course will also change. Since winds offshore tend to be more consistent in direction and, to a lesser extent, speed, than coastal winds, this is not a significant problem.

Vane systems differ in their method for translating wind-direction guidance information into rudder movements, but all are independent of the boat's electrical power system, a major advantage for vanes. While autopilots require a power supply, their advantage is that they will operate when motoring, in light airs and with the wind well aft, all situations in which vanes are useless or marginal.

Whichever self-steering is selected, it will be efficient under sail only if the sails are trimmed properly. Vanes simply will not keep the boat going in the desired direction if incorrectly trimmed sails want to drive it in some other direction. The vane functions like a trim tab, intended to compensate for small variations of heading. It is not effective as a brute system that will overcome significantly unbalanced sails. While an autopilot can cope more successfully with larger sail imbalances, it does so at great cost in terms of system wear, power use and rudder drag.

Radar – and detectors & reflectors. Radar has a great deal to offer, but it also takes money, maintenance and training. At a lower price, other equipment can fill some radar functions. A radar detector can contribute significantly to collision avoidance. Most large ships operate their radars continuously, regardless of weather or visibility. The frequency with which an operator looks at the radar is less predictable. Radar-equipped ships have been known to hit boats simply because no one observed their radar image. The Collision Avoidance Radar Detector manufactured by Survival Safety Engineering, in Norfolk, VA, combines a directional antenna, sensitive to shipboard radar frequencies (9330-9420 MHz for 10 cm radar, 3020-3120 for 3 cm), with a display showing the relative direction from which a radar signal is coming. It also indicates the strength of the signal, and changing strength can reveal whether the source is getting closer or farther away. By alerting a voyager to the presence of a radar-operating vessel, this system provides time to assess the situation and act.

Every passagemaking boat should carry a radar reflector to enhance the signal it reflects back to an operating radar. Small craft, especially those made of fiberglass, are notoriously poor reflectors of radar energy. They may not show up on a ship's radar display at all; at best they appear as weak and intermittent targets. A fixed reflector mounted well up in the rigging provides better radar visibility at longer distances, and in high seas it substantially improves the size of a boat's radar image. This improves the probability it will be detected and provides large ships with greater opportunity to avoid a dangerous situation. A number of very effective omni-directional radar reflectors are on the market, ranging from simple single open tri-plane reflectors to multiple tri-plane units housed inside aerodynamically shaped plastic or vinyl coverings. Other devices, such as flags with metallic fibers, are far less effective, especially when the radar beam strikes them edge-on, rather than broadside to the maximum area of fabric.

Power sail handling – pros & cons. Also increasingly common aboard cruising boats are power-assisted sail handling systems. As boat size and sail area grow, the loads on halyards and sheets increase sharply. They can quickly exceed the forces that can be handled comfortably with manual systems, especially by a limited crew. One solution has been to add power-driven winches to do the hard work. Power assistance, usually electrical but occasionally hydraulic, has also been incorporated into roller furling systems for headsails and mainsails. These systems certainly make life afloat much less demanding, with sail setting and trimming reduced to pushing a button. They also increase costs. If they fail at a crucial moment (when most systems quit) they could leave the boat in a very dangerous position, with insufficient human strength to cope with high loads generated by large sails or strong winds. On an offshore passage, the sail handling situations in which these systems are most advantageous occur much less frequently than in coastal sailing. Tacking or jibing may occur once or twice a day, rather than every 20 minutes; sails may be reefed/unreefed repeatedly, but not changed for days. If boat and sails are so large that the crew can't handle them easily, it's time to reconsider the choice of boat and crew.

While all these systems can contribute to the ease of passagemaking, with a few exceptions such as communications systems and radar reflectors/detectors, they are optional items. There is no need to delay a departure until a boat has been outfitted with every bell and whistle. Remember, each system means purchase cost and maintenance time and money. Before adding major systems such as sophisticated electronics, watermakers, radar or power-assisted sail handling systems, be sure they are really needed, preferably by accumulating passage time without them before making the decision to buy.

How much electrical power do you need? Electrical power, like fresh water, is a commodity the passagemaker must be prepared to ration. Electricity is usually a renewable resource, but generating sufficient power for a well equipped boat can be a challenge, and every method for augmenting the electrical supply involves cost of some sort.

Begin by calculating the daily demand for electrical power. Determine the current drawn by each electrical consumer: autopilot, nav lights, GPS, galley accessories, radio transceivers, stereo systems, and bilge, shower sump and fresh water pumps. If possible, use a digital ammeter to measure current used by each device (turn everything else off, verify that battery output is zero amps, turn the device on and record the current draw). If AC devices are run off an inverter, it's best to measure the DC draw created by the inverter when the appliance is used, because this takes inverter inefficiency into account. Alternatively, read the power requirement (in watts) on the AC device's label and multiply that number by 10 to determine amps at 12 volts. Once the load created by each device has been measured, estimate the hours (or decimal parts of an hour, with .1 hour = 6 minutes) each device will operate in a typical day during the passage. Multiplying the amps each unit draws by the time it will operate yields the daily load, in amp-hours, of each device. The sum of these loads gives a clear indication of two key aspects of the boat's electrical system: the minimum storage capacity needed in the batteries and the generating capacity needed to recharge them. West Marine has developed a handy worksheet for determining not only the demand but also the associated battery, alternator, charger and inverter capacities required (Figure 3.1).

Taking the time needed to perform such an assessment is very important, especially in an older boat. Original equipment alternators and batteries are seldom large enough to service much beyond the engine starting battery and a basic load of electrical services (interior and navigation lights, pumps, VHF radio). When the electrical demands grow to include autopilots, SSB radio, radar, fans, entertainment systems and integrated electronic navigation suites, the small alternator and battery that made up the original installation just can't handle it. Corrective measures will be needed. They include installation of more and/or larger batteries, replacing the old alternator with a larger one or adding a second alternator dedicated to supplying the service batteries, and supplementing the engine-driven system with a separate generator.

Batteries – their care and feeding. Storage batteries are rated in many ways, but the most useful is a battery's amp-hour rating. This reflects the amount of electrical power that can be drawn from the battery before it is fully discharged (i.e., when its open circuit voltage drops to 10.5 volts). Maximum battery life results if batteries are routinely kept between 50 and 85% charged. They should not be drawn down below 50%, and routine charging should restore them to at least 85%. (Getting the last 15% in can take inordinate charging time, since charging occurs at a progressively slower rate as the batteries approach full charge.) To achieve this, the service battery bank should have a total amp-hour capacity equal to at least three times daily consumption.

Common wisdom holds that batteries should be allowed a rest period between being recharged and going back into service. If a passagemaker wants to do this while charging once a day, it means alternating between two banks of batteries, each with a capacity twice the daily power consumption. Some battery experts prefer using a single large-capacity bank that will require less frequent charging cycles.

Since starting the engine can be crucial, most passagemakers carry a separate, dedicated *starting battery*. Whereas the house batteries that provide daily electricity should be deep-cycle batteries, designed to endure extended discharge periods, the starter battery can be an automotive type, for heavy but short-lived loads, with rapid recharge following each discharge.

Selection of the *house batteries* requires a comparison of cost, performance, safety, and physical dimensions. Opinions differ on the best balance. Wet cell batteries have long been the standard source of electrical power. They often have a lower price, but getting their full lifetime of service requires careful maintenance (checking water level and specific gravity, assuring purity of any water added, and conducting periodic equalization charging). They also present serious safety risks if they develop a leak or if a capsize causes battery acid to drain from the vented access caps. Ongoing research, driven largely by efforts to develop economical electrically powered automobiles, may lead to production of new types of wet cell batteries with higher capacity, greater efficiency, reduced maintenance and extended life.

Gel cell batteries often cost more, but their sealed cases provide protection against

Figure 3.1 - West Marine Electrical System Worksheet

There are two basic methods for sizing components for any electrical systems upgrade. Each requires the determination of your "load" between charge cycles. This can be accomplished either by using this worksheet to estimate electrical consumption, or by installing an amp-hour meter and actually using your boat under normal conditions for a "real" number.

12V DC Demand over a 24 hour period

Device	Current Draw (amps)	Time Used (hours)	Consumption (amp-hours)
Refrigeration (duty cycle?)			
Interior Lights			
Instrumentation			
Stereo			
Anchor Light			
Other DC Load #1			
Other DC Load #2			
Other DC Load #3			
(A) Inverter (from below) *enter total at right* ▶			
12V DC CONSUMPTION TOTAL:			

120V AC Demand supplied by an inverter

Device	Power (watts)	Time Used (hours)	Consumption (watt-hours)	12V Consum. (÷ 10 = amp-hr)
Microwave				
TV/VCR				
Coffeemaker				
Hair Dryer				
Other AC Load #1				
Other AC Load #2				
Other AC Load #3				
INVERTER TOTAL DC CONSUMPTION: *transfer to line (A) of table above:*				

Transfer 12V DC consumption total to next page ▶

Figure 3.1 - West Marine Electrical System Worksheet (continued)

The number of amp-hours consumed in a day allows you to select the correct batteries, alternator, charger, and inverter. Charging intervals greater than 24 hours will require larger batteries. Here are our general recommendations:

Daily 12V DC consumption (from prev. page) = ⬚ **Amp-hrs.**

Batteries
Daily Consumption _____ amp-hours x 3 = _____ amp-hour battery capacity necessary to conform to the Mid-Capacity Rule (batteries are normally cycled between 50% and 85% of capacity).

Alternator
Total Consumption _____ amp-hours = output of an alternator (in amps) necessary to replenish batteries in approx. 80 min. (assumes smart regulation). *EXCEPTIONS:* A powerboat which utilizes the engine more often can generally use a smaller alternator, unless it spends the majority of its time at low engine RPMs.

Battery Charger
Battery size amp-hours ÷ 10 = the size of a smart charger (in amps) necessary to replenish your batteries in under 8 hours. Battery size _____ amp-hours ÷ 20 should still allow batteries to be charged in less than 16 hours.

Inverter
Review your Inverter Load Demand table. The recommended inverter size will depend on the combined consumption of those appliances used simultaneously. An inverter should draw on a bank of batteries that has 20% as many amp-hours as the inverter has watts (Inverter watts ÷ 5 = minimum battery amp hours).

Examples for Given Amp-Hour Consumptions:

Amp-hr Use	House Bank Batteries	Alternator	Smart Charger	Inverter
50	1 - 4D (150 AH)	50 amp	15 amp	to 750w
75	1 - 8D (220 AH)	75 amp	20 amp	to 1000w
100	2- 4D (300 AH)	100 amp	30 amp	to 1500w
150	2- 8D (440 AH)	150 amp	40 amp	to 2500w
200	3- 8D (660 AH)	150 amp	60 amp	to 3000w

rollover leakage, and they offer long life with minimal maintenance. Since they have different charging characteristics, wet cell and gel cell batteries should never be combined in a single system. The newly-introduced *absorbed glass mat (AGM) battery* technology offers advantages such as rapid recharging capacity and the ability to sustain high loads over a long life of charge/discharge cycles. On the downside, they cost more (twice the price of gel cells) and are vulnerable to damage through overcharging by regulators not set to a specific AGM algorithm.

Limitations on the batteries' physical characteristics (dimensions, weight) may influence your choice. Increased total capacity can be achieved with larger individual batteries or a number of smaller batteries wired in parallel. The size and weight of batteries at the 4D size and larger present serious handling problems. In replacing old batteries, the size of installed battery boxes may play a decisive role. Where space permits, many voyagers find that using high capacity, deep cycle batteries designed for driving golf carts and wheelchairs is an effective solution, even if they have to use a group of 6-volt cells and connect them in series to get 12-volt power.

Many boats now carry a rechargeable, portable *jump-start battery*. These also provide a clean DC power supply for accessories and voltage-sensitive equipment, such as computers.

When it comes to recharging the battery system, there are a number of alternatives. The most common is to use the propulsion engine, equipped with an alternator. This option will usually benefit from two modifications to the system provided by most boat builders. The first is to install a higher output alternator, the second is to change the regulator system that controls the alternator's output.

Alternators. Virtually all stock boats have alternators designed to do little more than recharge the engine starting battery. They have nominal outputs in the 30-60 amp range, but at engine-room operating temperatures, actual output will be far less. Replacing 100 amp-hours of consumed electricity (not an uncommon daily usage) with such a system will take hours of engine operation, consume a lot of fuel, create noise, and decrease engine life. Upgrading to an alternator that can produce 100 amps or more on a sustained basis will speed up the charging process and reduce the costs and headaches. In many cases, it is possible to mount a high output alternator on the engine for recharging the house battery bank, while leaving the original unit in place and dedicating its output to keeping the starting battery fully charged.

Regulators. The alternator's output is controlled by a regulating device whose function is to avoid sending more current to the battery than it can accept. This prevents overheating that could damage the battery or even cause it to catch fire or explode. Most original installations employ automotive-type regulators which err on the side of safety: They reduce the charging level quickly, often dropping it well below the rate at which a good deep cycle marine battery can accept charging current. These regulators take longer than necessary to recharge the battery and place little load on the engine while doing so. Since running a diesel under light load is inefficient and contributes to carbon buildup within the cylinders, such charging systems carry high hidden costs.

Improvements to the regulator system range from manually operated versions to highly sophisticated, electronically controlled "smart" regulators. The manual systems simply transfer control of the alternator's output (actually, control of the voltage in the alternator's field circuit) from the internal components of the regulator to a manually adjustable knob. By keeping field voltage high, output stays high instead of tapering off, and the battery is charged much more rapidly. The danger is that the battery can be overcharged and damaged by overheating if the manual system is not properly monitored to reduce field voltage as the battery approaches full charge. Hence the next step in regulator complexity: a manual controller with a built-in timer to limit the period of high alternator output.

Modern "smart" regulator systems go several steps further. They use sensors to determine not only the battery voltage (hence the need for recharging), but also the rate of current flow into the battery and the battery temperature. Using these factors and applying a complex algorithm defining battery state and charge acceptance, the "smart" systems charge the battery at the maximum safe rate. Most "smart" systems include features such as equalization cycles, which enhance wet cell battery condition and life expectancy by periodically giving them an extended, higher voltage charging. They also provide digital readouts of data such as battery voltage, current draw, and amp-hours consumed. The latter information is particularly useful as an indicator of when battery charging is needed. With a "smart" regulator system and a high output alternator whose nominal output equals daily amp-hour consumption, most batteries can be brought from the 50% level to the 85% level with 60-80 minutes of charging.

Generators – diesel, wind, water. Many voyagers complement the auxiliary engine with other systems for generating electrical energy. One is a generator independent of the propulsion engine. Modern technology has made these power plants smaller and quieter than ever. They offer the benefit of not only recharging the 12-volt system but also providing an ample supply of 110-volt AC power, enabling the voyager to use appliances, tools and heavy load systems (such as air-conditioning) built for use with household electrical service. Running at higher speeds (usually 1800 or 3600 rpm) the generator's small diesel is stingy with fuel, and the system's principal drawback is its noise level (often more noticeable and annoying for those on nearby boats than for those onboard, thanks to efficient acoustic insulation). Other electricity sources in common use include wind- and water-driven generators. Wind generators can be a very efficient source of power as long as wind speeds are sufficiently strong. They come in many sizes and styles and offer a number of alternative locations (e.g., aloft on a mast platform, on a dedicated pole, or suspended in rigging). Most generators have a maximum wind speed limitation, but incorporating automatic braking and control systems permits some to operate unattended in winds up to hurricane force. Aside from possible requirements to shut them down in high winds, the principal disadvantages of most wind generators are the whirring noise produced by their rotating blades and the vibration that accompanies minute blade imbalances. Design improvements have made some new models exceedingly quiet in wind speeds as high as 25 knots.

Water-driven generators, towed astern, are less popular than wind-driven systems. Their output tends to be low until boat speeds exceed 4 or 5 knots, limiting their usefulness aboard many cruising sailboats. Like patent logs towed astern to measure speed and distance, water-driven generators use spinners that seem to attract fish and seaweed, either of which can cause rotation–and electrical output–to stop. These systems are quiet but, like anything dragged through the water, they detract somewhat from boat speed.

Solar panels. A final source of electricity usable at sea is a solar panel, which converts sunlight to electrical energy. Quiet, clean and relatively simple (no moving parts!), solar panels may be an ideal source of power. Their shortcomings include a low efficiency (it takes a lot of light to get a little power) and the cells' need to be oriented directly toward the sun to produce full output. Low efficiency of individual cells is compensated for by increasing the number of cells used and the size of the resulting panel. The orientation problem can be resolved in part by making the panels adjustable so they can be tilted or pointed to get full sunlight. Often, this shortcoming is simply accepted, with the panels mounted horizontally on cabin or dodger for the best average exposure with minimum time in shadows from the rig above.

These alternative electrical sources must also be managed by a regulator system to prevent damaging batteries by overcharging. Most "smart" systems can accept power generated by these sources, regulate the flow to the batteries, and keep track of their contributions to the total power supply.

Important word! One word of warning applies to all the above outfitting options. It is highly inadvisable to delay any installation until immediately before departure on a passage. It's easy to postpone acquiring new gear, especially if it's expensive, until late in the preparations, but that is a serious error. New equipment should be completely installed at least a month before setting out on an offshore passage. That provides time to give it a full shakedown aboard and to learn how to use it properly. In virtually every rally, a few boats report that one or more pieces of newly installed equipment will not function, usually early in the passage. Sometimes these difficulties reflect hardware, software or wiring errors overlooked during the hurried post-installation checkout. Others have been a result of operator error, due to insufficient experience with the new equipment (compounded by reluctance to spend the time required to read the instruction manual, if it's aboard). A prudent passagemaker will ensure that all major modifications have been completed well before departure, that every new piece of gear has been thoroughly tested, and that crewmembers have a comfortable working knowledge of it.

Ground Tackle. One outfitting unit is of minor importance during a passage, but becomes highly significant on arriving at the destination. That is the ground tackle – the anchors and rodes and the system for handling them On the high seas, any anchor left topside must be fastened securely. Most voyagers prefer to stow them below if possible, for reduced weight topside and at bow and stern.

A voyager's ground tackle outfit should include at least two anchors of suitable holding capacity and of different types for different bottoms. Plow- and Bruce-type anchors are popular, backed up by Danforth-style or lightweight anchors. A light "lunch hook" for temporary stops or for use as a stern anchor to keep a boat headed into a chop, and a serious heavyweight storm anchor round out the set. Several rodes are desirable, all in the 250-350' range. One may be all chain, while all others should be fitted with 40-80' of chain to enhance catenary and withstand abrasion from rocky, coral or other rough bottoms. An anchor windlass, either manual or power (usually electric, occasionally hydraulic) can greatly facilitate recovering anchor and rode. Assuring a perfect size match between the chain and the windlass gypsy is essential to prevent jammed or disengaged, free-running chain. Chain hooks and riding pendants or bridles which transfer anchorage loads from the windlass to mooring cleats or a samson post complete the ground tackle package.

Weapons? It's a bit of a stretch to consider this part of "outfitting" but one topic that arises at almost every Passagemaker Seminar is that of carrying weapons aboard. It's a sensitive issue, about which many people have strong sentiments. In approaching it, one must remember that few countries other than the United States view possession of firearms as a "natural right." In most places, weapon ownership is strictly regulated. Occupants of visiting vessels must comply with local laws or face potentially severe penalties.

Any decision to carry weapons must be preceded by an analysis of the reasons for doing so, and the benefits weighed against the disadvantages. If weapons are intended to protect a boat from attack at sea by "pirates" of some type, it is more than likely that the pirates will be much better armed and organized than the voyager. Introducing firearms may be counterproductive and only escalate the situation well beyond the cruising sailor's ability to control it.

Protection against break-ins in port is often offered as the reason for having a weapon aboard. Unfortunately, local authorities frequently take temporary custody of a boat's weapons or require them to be sealed in a secure locker while in port. In such cases, they are of no use should a break-in occur. Even if not removed or sealed, weapons stored in a concealed location are unlikely to be accessible quickly, defeating the express reason for their possession. Weapons openly available may serve their purpose, but there's an equal possibility that they will actually wind up in the wrong hands–those of the intruder. Since most intruders prefer to do their mischief in unoccupied boats, an owner is likely to return to find the weapon's "protection" being enjoyed by the thief rather than the victim.

If a weapon is carried, the owner must be sure he or she is really prepared to use it and to face the consequences of doing so. Consider the guilt that will be carried by the person who shoots an "intruder" only to discover it was an inebriated cruising sailor who got aboard the wrong boat. Contemplate the implications of shooting a "robber" in an anchorage off a remote village, when the victim turns out to be the son or nephew of the local chief of police or mayor. These risks can counter most of a weapon's purported advantages.

The case against carrying guns is strengthened by the fact that there are non-lethal devices that can perform with equal effectiveness in most situations for which guns are justified. Pepper sprays and "Mace" (especially in the large spray cans carried by hunters for chasing bears) can disable an intruder without doing permanent bodily injury. So can some hair sprays. Even oven cleaner has been used, although it can in fact inflict serious injury, especially to the eyes.

Over the years, many rally participants have chosen to carry weapons during their cruise. I know of none who have ever had occasion to use them for defensive or protective purposes. They have uniformly proven to be a headache during visits to foreign ports. Declaring their presence leads to red tape and inconvenience (inventory by serial number and a count of the number of bullets, protective custody ashore that means returning to the entry port at a time convenient to local authorities, etc.). Failing to declare them leaves one open to serious penalties, extending to imprisonment and confiscation of not only the weapon, but also the boat. More than one weapon-carrying cruising skipper has reported that, short of dropping them over the side, there is no way to get rid of a weapon that has become more of a problem than a value. It is easier to leave the guns at home and avoid cruising in waters that have a poor reputation for security.

Having selected the equipment that suits lifestyle preferences and budget constraints, and arranged for an adequate power source to operate the systems that need it, you'll have established the basic framework for voyaging. Before exploring the strategies to improve the likelihood of success, it's necessary to explore, in greater detail, the boat that will make the voyage possible. As will be seen, nothing – absolutely nothing – will be more important to you – the passagemaker – than a thorough, up close, head-down/heels-up familiarity with every nook, cranny, valve, fastening, wire, opening and piece of equipment in the boat. Getting that familiarity is the next topic on our agenda.

REFERENCES:
David Burch, *Emergency Navigation*
Steve and Linda Dashew, *Offshore Cruising Encyclopedia*
Jim Howard, *Handbook of Offshore Cruising*
Beth A. Leonard, *The Voyager's Handbook*
West Marine Advisor – discussions of batteries, battery systems, and alternators/regulators in the *West Marine Catalog*

CHAPTER 4

INSPECTING THE BOAT

This chapter owes much to the work of Captain John B. Bonds USN.

The best way to gain complete familiarity with any boat is to examine it very closely. A thorough inspection is a time-consuming, sometimes dirty job, but it will pay dividends many times over. This job is too important to delegate to someone who will not be making the passage, but the assistance of a meticulous professional or a knowledgeable crew member can increase the valuable firsthand knowledge you will derive from the task.

The inspection should be orderly, with minimum duplication or backtracking. Let's follow such an inspection as it starts from the bow and works aft inside the boat, then moves topside and goes aloft.

Start in the forepeak. Equipped with a good flashlight, some rags and a notebook or tape recorder to log significant findings, we start in the forepeak. Look at the forestay chainplate and stemhead fittings. Are they corroded? Are there signs of leakage or loose bolts? Is the grounding strap securely fastened? Check all electrical wiring, looking for loose or corroded connections and bights of slack wire that can get tangled in the rode or other gear stowed here. Wiring to the navigation lights frequently runs through this space. Find and identify it. Remove enough rode to see down into the chain locker, which should be free of debris and fitted with a drain at the bottom. Check the condition of hull and deck for damage, delamination or moisture penetration. Check the hull-deck joint, which should be tight, with no signs of leakage, and fastened with mechanical fasteners in addition to glue, sealant or bonding. Be sure the foredeck cleats and fittings are tightly through-bolted with ample backing plates to distribute the stress, again with no signs of leakage. Is the rode marked with length indicators, free of rust on the chain, without fraying or kinking in the line, and securely fastened at the bitter end? Is the bulkhead that separates this locker from the forward cabin securely fastened to the hull, all the way around, with no rot or delamination? Take a look at the gear stowed here: Remove any flammables (teak oil, solvents, spray paints, ether), which should be kept in topside lockers. Get rid of wet rags or haphazardly stowed gear. Start now to enforce the rule, "A place for everything and everything in its place."

The head. The head is often the next compartment aft. Make sure the toilet operates and that clear instructions are posted where users can easily read them. Check around the pump shaft for leaks, and inspect the shaft itself for corrosion or pitting. Make sure the whole toilet is firmly fastened with clean, tight hold-down bolts and that the seat is secure on the bowl. Follow the intake hose from the toilet to its through-hull valve, looking for cracks, deterioration and kinks. Check the hose clamps at the valve connection. Unless the valve has a very short nipple that does not allow room for fitting more than one clamp, there should be two and they should be of all-stainless construction. Here and throughout, be alert for automotive-type clamps that use stainless bands but mild steel tightening screws which will rust and lose their grip. Cycle the through-hull valve to assure easy operation. Trace the discharge hose as well, and make sure the anti-siphon loop is in place above the waterline and that the vacuum-breaker valve in that loop is open to let air into the line. Check clamps at any Y-valves and other connection points, and cycle all valves to verify smooth and leak-free operation.

In the head and elsewhere, take advantage of this opportunity to *label the valves* that control boat systems. This is especially true for through-hull valves, which should be top quality sea cocks or ball valves. Gate valves are notoriously unreliable and so are unacceptable for through-hulls. Every through-hull fitting must have an appropriate size soft wood plug stowed immediately adjacent to it, ready to use if the fitting should break.

If the sewage system includes a holding tank, make sure it's securely fastened to the boat, all hose connections are secure, and the vent line is clear. Test any manual or electric pumps fitted for dumping the holding tank.

Back in the head itself, check the freshwater system. Make sure the faucets don't leak, and trace the hot and cold water lines as far as possible. Look for loose hoses and clamps, leaks, kinks and chafing – especially where they pass through bulkheads or deck panels. Inspect any valves for leakage or corrosion. Check that the wash basin drain plug works and trace the drain line, checking all clamps and through-hull valves. Be sure the head ventilation port seals tightly, with no leakage, and check for a closure plate that can be used to close Dorade-type vents in heavy weather. If there is a shower, check all its freshwater lines, valves, faucets and drains. If the shower drains into a sump, make sure that the sump pump operates and that the overboard discharge line is well secured, has a functioning anti-siphon loop, and includes a proper sea cock or through-hull valve.

Before leaving the head, check for adequate space to stow personal toilet gear and a reliable way to keep toilet paper from getting wet. Head cabinets often provide an opportunity to check another section of the hull-deck joint and to see the way electrical wires are run through the boat. Any 110-v AC outlets here (and in the galley) should be equipped with ground-fault interruption circuits to protect against shock hazard. Test them by pressing the "test" and "reset" buttons. Take every opportunity here and elsewhere to *examine the connection between bulkheads and the hull,* looking for broken fiberglass tabbing or movement of bulkhead panels. Look at the tops of bulkheads for any deterioration or movement relative to the headliner or deck structure, and examine the lower edges for decay, delamination or moisture damage. Finally, check the head door to be sure it opens and closes easily and that the latch works.

Lockers and cabinets. Look inside storage lockers and cabinets adjacent to the head, checking hull-deck joint, bulkheads, wiring, drainage and ventilation. All doors and drawers should have positive latches to prevent accidental opening in a seaway. Be alert for improperly stowed items, and look behind and beneath drawers for gear gone adrift (these nooks may also offer storage).

Main cabin. The next space aft is usually the saloon, or main cabin, and we'll start in the bilges, working our way aft from the head. Check all *through-hulls* beneath the cabin sole: Be sure they are tightly fastened to the hull, free of corrosion, easily operable, labeled, and fastened to hoses with double stainless steel clamps. Make sure each valve has its wood plug. If metal through-hulls are bonded, check the condition of the bonding wire and the tightness of its connection.

Since most offshore boats have keel-stepped masts, the *mast step* will be under the cabin sole. Look for evidence of step fatigue or collapse, including cracking of the laminate, bending of metal beams and cracked welds. Both the step and the butt of the mast should be free of corrosion, and preferably protected by a layer of epoxy sealant. The mast should be mechanically fastened to the step with a bolt or pin to prevent its loss in the event of rigging failure. The foot of the mast should be notched or drilled to permit drainage of any condensation or spray from inside the spar, and the mast should be fitted with an ample grounding wire, preferably run to a keel bolt when the keel is mounted externally. Inspect all wiring running into the mast. It should be neatly bundled, without any fraying or chafe, and labeled for troubleshooting. All connections must be above reach of bilge water and covered with tape and/or sealant to impede corrosion.

Tankage is often located in the cabin bilge area. Look for solid mounting to the hull, with no sign of movement, cracks or leakage. Inlet, outlet and vent hoses should be in good condition, properly labeled and securely clamped. Each tank should have large access plates for cleaning, secured with uncorroded fasteners and watertight gaskets.

While in the bilge, check all accessible *keel bolts* (some may be hidden beneath tanks) by tapping with a hammer. A sound bolt will give a clear metallic "clack" while a dull "clunk" implies trouble that could range from looseness to a deteriorated bolt. Examine each bolt for seepage around the shaft, which signals leakage and suggests corrosion. Look for signs of movement produced by a sharp impact such as grounding or striking a heavy object. Check for symmetrical damage: A downward push at one end of the keel is usually matched by an upward one at the other end; a similar port/starboard relationship occurs with lateral impact.

Examine *electrical wiring* runs, looking for neatness, clean and protected connections, and fastening at frequent intervals to prevent the wiring from drooping into bilge water. The electrical grounding system for lightning protection should use at least #8 AWG copper cable and be corrosion-free at all connections. Inspect the general bilge area for cleanliness, since debris and small objects that accumulate here are likely to clog bilge pumps later. Check for easy operation of all through-hull fittings and check for their soft wood damage-control plugs. Speed and depth sensors often found here should get equal attention to ensure watertight fitting and tight, clean wiring connections.

Continuing aft through the bilges toward the galley, check *freshwater lines* for condition and security; they should be held in place at frequent intervals to prevent movement in a seaway. Examine any clamps and connections for tightness. They often go unobserved until after one has come loose and allowed all the freshwater to be pumped into the bilge. Troubleshooting will go more easily if each line is labeled to show direction of flow and destination ("hot water to head" or "cold water to galley sink").

Test manual and electric *bilge pumps*. Check for screens or strainers that will keep pumps from becoming clogged. Be sure pumps discharge individually overboard, not into a common line or into cockpit or galley drains. Get a better feel for pump capacity and the effort needed to operate them by dumping a sizable quantity of water (10 gallons or so) into the bilge and checking how long it takes the electric pump to remove it. Repeat for each manual pump, noting both time and amount of work involved. The result may suggest that an extra pump or larger capacity pumps are needed.

After looking all through the saloon bilge, check the fit of each deck plate that gives access to the bilge. They should be tight enough to stay in place in a knockdown and not float free in a flood, preferably secured with positive latch mechanisms.

In the saloon, check for a snug fit of the tension strut adjacent to a keel-stepped mast. Its function is to prevent the coach roof from flexing upward in response to shroud/stay loads. If the mast is deck-stepped, check the compression post beneath the mast. It should sit on a solid foundation at keel or cabin sole level, and the upper end should support a strong plate somewhat larger than the mast extrusion. If mast loads are taken by bulkheads rather than a compression post, inspect those bulkheads at top and bottom for any weakening, delamination or compression damage.

Next inspect the shroud *chainplates* and their attachment to the hull. Are there signs of water seepage or plate movement? All nuts and bolts should be tight and corrosion-free (check with the hammer test used on keel bolts). The chainplates should be electrically bonded to the keel and the lightning protection system. Look for any signs that the transverse bulkheads, especially those carrying chainplates, have moved or separated from the hull.

Unless there are signs of a problem, it is seldom necessary to disassemble interior cabinetry, but use every access point to explore the areas normally hidden by furnishings. Look under and behind cushions, bins and drawers and inside lockers. Check any visible wiring runs for careful bundling and securing. Examine *hoses and piping* for security and padding to avoid chafe. Look for unprotected hull penetrations, and label and cycle any valves that are not easily accessible (and hence seldom operated). Use every opportunity to inspect the *hull-deck joint*. Any leakage calls for corrective action before heading offshore.

Look for positive closures on all lockers, and check for stowage of heavy items that could go adrift and cause injury or damage in heavy weather. Check all cabin lights. Are there dim red lights that will illuminate the cabin without destroying the crew's night vision? Are seat cushions fitted with covers to protect them from water damage offshore? Each bunk should be fitted with a strong lee cloth or lee board for use at sea with the boat heeled over.

Inspect the saloon overhead to be sure the headliner is tight and secure. Look for leakage from topside hardware, examining backing plates if they are visible. Check the hatches and ports – whether opening or fixed, on deck or cabin-side – for watertightness. If in doubt, test them with a solid stream from a large garden hose. This will reveal loose seals, but it will not match the ability of a deck-sweeping sea to cause leakage. The saloon should have adequate grab rails and handholds, securely fastened, for safe movement in rough weather. Check that the dining table is solidly mounted and able to withstand the impact of a heavy crew member thrown off balance by an unexpected wave. If the table folds up against the bulkhead, are its latches tight? Check for plates or plugs to permit closing Dorade vents from below. Look for any leakage around the mast collar. Make sure all doors open and close freely and that their latches work.

Navigation station. Moving to the navigation station, check that each piece of equipment is firmly attached. Make sure that every piece works, including actual radio checks with as distant a station as possible. Wiring behind equipment should be neatly bundled and attached to supporting structures. Inventory publications to be sure the following are included: Selected Worldwide Marine Broadcasts, International Code of Signals (HO Pub 102), nautical almanac and associated sight reduction tables, tide and current tables, appropriate light lists and *Coast Pilot* volumes, and a copy of *Dutton's*, *Bowditch* or equivalent reference book. Review charts for area coverage and up-to-date corrections (Notices to Mariners or automated summaries of chart corrections should be on hand). The nav station should include a second compass with a deviation table, and the navigation gear should include binoculars, a hand-bearing compass, dividers, drafting compass, parallel rules, nautical slide rule, universal plotting sheets, maneuvering boards, plenty of pencils and good erasers. Inspect the sextant for cleanliness and freedom of movement, and check its alignment (It backs up your GPS). What timepiece will be used for celestial navigation, and has its accuracy been determined? Review the logbook for accuracy and adequacy of information recorded, keeping in mind its role as the primary legal record of the boat's operation.

Electrical panel. The electrical panel is often near the nav station. Check all the meters, switches and circuit breakers, looking particularly for jury rigs and jumpers that lack proper overload protection and create a fire hazard. Despite suggestions from some electronics manufacturers to wire their equipment directly to the battery to minimize voltage drops, all leads should come off "downstream" of the main battery switch to ensure that power can be cut off quickly in an emergency. If possible, look at the rear of the electrical panel to assess the quality of the installation. Wires should be bundled, labeled, color coded and fastened to terminal boards with ring rather than fork terminal fittings. Solder connections are preferable to crimped, which eventually corrode if not sealed; "wire nuts" commonly used ashore and "twist and tape" connections are never acceptable. Inspect the back side of the main battery switch if possible, to ensure its contacts are protected against shorting by metal objects stowed nearby. If circuits are protected by fuses, be sure there's an adequate stock of spares. If AC and DC circuitry share a common panel (undesirable but often unavoidable), the two systems should be separated as clearly as possible. Covers to prevent accidental contact with 110-volt AC components while working on 12-volt DC elements are highly desirable.

The galley. The galley is next on our agenda. Start by inspecting the *refrigerator/icebox*. It should be free of cracks, broken racks or weak shelf supports, clean and odor-free. Test the drain by pouring a glass of water down it. The drain should run to a sump, not directly into the bilge. (The latter is a guaranteed source of foul bilges!) If a mechanical refrigeration system is installed, check the temperature it maintains: The chill side should be just above freezing (34-38°), while a freezer area should be down around 10° or less. Check the condition of seals on the reefer access opening, and make sure the opening can be latched closed to prevent dumping the contents in a knockdown.

Assessing the stove and its installation is significantly influenced by the type of fuel involved. Advantages and disadvantages of the various choices will be addressed later (see Chapter 15), but many common precautions apply. The *fuel tanks* should be firmly mounted in vented and drained lockers located to prevent fuel vapors from accumulating inside the cockpit or hull. Tanks should rest on hardwood chocks that keep the tanks dry on the bottom. Compressed gas fuels must have an accessible cutoff valve at the tank, then a pressure reducing valve, a pressure gauge and a remotely-operated solenoid valve leading to approved marine piping, firmly mounted and supported, that carries the gas to the stove.

The *stove* should be fitted with gimbals mounted on a fore-and-aft axis to compensate for rolling movement, and have a short length of approved flexible hose linking it to the fuel supply line. Check the flexible hose for cracks or splitting, especially at the ends, and test the security of any clamps. Clear and understandable instructions for operating the stove should be posted, and the warning plates specified by the American Boat and Yacht Council (ABYC) should be mounted at the tanks as well as at each appliance. Be sure the operating procedures follow the steps listed in Chapter 15, and follow those instructions to test each burner, including the broiler and oven if installed. Regardless of the stove type, be sure the tray beneath the burners is scrupulously clean and that all elements of the stove are as clean and free of rust/corrosion as possible. Check the knobs and burner valves for smooth movement, absence of slack or play and abrasion. The gimbaling brackets must latch to prevent the stove from lifting out of the gimbals in a capsize, and the stove must have a lock to provide fixed, rather than gimbaled, positioning. The stove needs a set of fiddles or brackets to keep pots in place on the cooking surface in a seaway. There should be a bar across the front to prevent the cook from being thrown against the stove, and a strap to give the cook support when heeling tends to push him or her away from the stove. When going offshore, it's also prudent to fit the galley with a "Sea Swing"-type stove (one burner with fitted pot and a fuel canister) for use in storm conditions. Check for operating instructions for such a stove, and be sure they address procedures for installing and changing the fuel canisters. Check safe stowage for spare canisters.

Protection from flare-ups and fires at the galley is essential. Fire-fighting materials (extinguishers, blankets) must be readily available and stowed to allow access without reaching across the stove, the most likely source of fire. An extinguishing agent that leaves no contaminating mess, such as CO_2 or Halon, is the best choice for the galley area.

Check all galley storage racks and cabinets for security and positive latches. Is there a sanitary cutting board/chopping block? Is there safe storage for knives and other sharp galley tools? There should be adequate stowage for galley gear and food, with sufficient working counter space for meal preparation. Look for any signs of rodent or insect infestation; plan both preventive and corrective measures to counter unwanted critters. Check for a cookbook and a food stowage plan.

At the *galley sink,* inspect all freshwater lines, faucets, valves, connections and drains for leaks, loose clamps and deterioration. Foot pumps for both salt- and freshwater are helpful for water conservation.

Before leaving the main cabin, check for tight hatches and scuttles, *protected instruments,* safe movement for crew, alternate access/escape routes in event of a midships fire, and safe footing on cabin sole – especially when wet. Assess ventilation throughout. Ample ports and hatches are a starting point, but good Dorades are needed for rough/wet weather. Consider internal air flow, which is enhanced by installing louvers or screens in solid doors, using mesh curtains instead of tight closures, and leaving air gaps at the back of shelves. Fans must be securely mounted, safely positioned and properly wired to the power supply. Note any parts of the hull that are concealed behind permanent cabinetry or hull liners, and determine the simplest way to gain access to those areas in an emergency (e.g., a holed hull behind the fiberglass shower stall). Identify any special tools, such as a wrecking bar, that might be needed to get to concealed areas quickly.

At the companionway, be sure the ladder is firmly mounted and cannot move in a seaway or fall out in a knockdown. Are there convenient grab rails for a person on the ladder? Can a crew member easily clip to a secure fitting or a safety line in the cockpit before leaving the protection of the cabin?

If there's an aft cabin and head, they should get the same scrutiny given forward spaces: bilges, bunks and lockers, stowage, ports and hatches, chainplates, piping and wiring runs, hoses and valves, faucets and drains, and hull-deck joint access.

Aft bilge. Before moving topside, inspect the boat's vital operating systems that are located below. While in the aft cabin bilge, check the stern tube for leakage. Dripless shaft seals should be tight and corrosion-free, with clean clamps and a flexible bellows. Traditional stuffing boxes can drip slightly when the shaft is stopped, but not more than a few drips per minute. Check bilges for transmission fluid, which would indicate leaking seals.

Steering system. Also while aft, examine the steering system. (On aft cockpit boats, this may be best done from the cockpit.) The cables of mechanical systems must be in good condition, the adjustment nuts tight, and fairlead sheaves firmly mounted to strong structural members. Guards should prevent fouling of cables. Proper stowage is essential to keep loose gear from entangling in the wires. The cable tension should be adjusted to remove slack that could let the wire jump out of a sheave in heavy weather, but not so tight that the cable and fairleads are under stress. Look for evidence that fairlead sheaves have been lubricated. Look beneath sheaves for telltale grit and metal shavings that would indicate misalignment and excessive wear. Examine the rudder post for galls and burrs, and check the packing gland that prevents leakage around the post. Be sure there are rudder stops and that they are solidly mounted and padded to reduce impact damage. Have someone move the helm from maximum rudder on one side to max on the other and observe the rudder post, cables and sheaves for signs of wobble, play or sticky movement. Check cable turnbuckles for lubrication and for cotter pins that will keep the barrel from turning. Be sure at least two cable clamps are properly installed (U-bolt on dead end side of the wire eye) on the cable eye (Figure 4.1); if swage fittings are used, examine them closely for cracks, corrosion and looseness. Also make

Figure 4.1 - Cable clamps

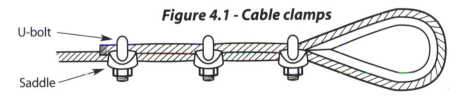

U-bolt

Saddle

sure the quadrant is securely fastened to the rudder post with snug bolts and a fitted key.

For hydraulic systems, check the full run of hydraulic lines for leaks while at rest and under pressure. Check the pressure gauge on the reservoir, and be sure a pump is available to pressurize the system. Hydraulic rams must be fitted with dust-cover boots to protect the ram surface from scoring. Can the hydraulic system linkage to the rudder be disconnected quickly to permit hand steering?

Fit the emergency tiller and observe its operation. If operated from belowdecks, is there a compass available for the helmsman, or are rudder angles marked to help in steering with the emergency rig? Are access plates leading to the top of the rudder post lubricated and easy to open? Is the tiller itself strong and in good condition? Is it stowed in a readily accessible place?

The engine room. In the engine room, the most effective and thorough technique is to examine one system at a time. The *raw water cooling system* is a good starting point. Begin at the intake sea cock, which should be labeled, lubricated for easy operation, and leak-free. The hose leading to the strainer should be in good condition, without kinks or crimps, and fastened with double clamps at both ends. The strainer should be mounted securely and accessible for cleaning. The basket should be clean, and closure mechanisms should be well gasketed and corrosion-free. A good-condition hose, double clamped, should lead to the raw water circulating pump. Check for leakage at the pump and around its shaft. Does the shaft wobble when turned by hand? When in place, the drive belt should be tight enough to prevent turning the pump by hand. Is there evidence that the flexible impeller inside the pump has been checked or replaced recently (a job much easier to do at dockside than at sea!)? A good, double clamped hose should take cooling water from the circulating pump to the heat exchange system. Check the exchangers (there may be separate units for engine water, lube oil and transmission fluid) for leaks and corrosion. Remove and inspect the zinc pencils necessary to preclude heat exchanger failure due to electrolytic corrosion. Good double clamped hose should carry the cooling water to the exhaust manifold where it is injected into the exhaust stream for discharge overboard.

Now turn to the *exhaust system,* and trace it from the engine manifold to the muffler, looking for leaks and cracks, often revealed by carbon spots. Be sure hot, dry exhaust lines between the manifold and the cooling water injection elbow are adequately lagged with insulation. Are there any signs of exhaust or cooling water leakage from beneath the lagging on the exhaust elbow (a common failure point)? Inspect the muffler for corrosion and leaks and check that there's a working drain at the lowest point in the system. Follow the exhaust line aft, checking for leaks, abrasion and potential chafe. The line should be equipped with an anti-siphon loop 3-4 feet above the waterline to avoid water back-flooding into the manifold in following seas. (An alternative is a large stop valve between the muffler and the overboard discharge point.)

Back at the engine, examine the *freshwater cooling system.* All hoses should be in good condition – not mushy, collapsed, crimped or cracked – and securely clamped at the ends (double clamps not necessary here). Check the water pump for leaks, adequate belt tension and absence of shaft wobble. Locate the thermostat housing, usually near the raw water pump, and check for leaks. Check the level of coolant in the expansion tank reservoir and ensure that the coolant includes 50% antifreeze solution (for its preservative qualities more than low temperature protection). Look at the water fill cap, which should be corrosion-free, well gasketed and fitted with a spring-loaded over-pressure relief mechanism. If the fill cap opening is fitted with a drain line, be sure it's not clogged with corrosion debris or salts.

Trace the *fuel system* from the tank(s) to the primary filter/separator, checking for leaks, solidly attached and supported lines, and freely operating valves. This line may include a solenoid valve linked to the engine starting circuit, and should also include at least one manual valve that will cut off all fuel to the engine. Check the primary filter for cleanliness of the filter element (when was it last changed?). Draw a sample from the bottom of the separator section: Severe discoloration, water droplets and fine muddy sediment are indications of contaminated fuel tanks that should be cleaned before heading onto the high seas. All non-machine-made connectors in the fuel system should be double clamped with all-stainless clamps. Trace the line from the primary filter to the lift pump (normally flexible tubing), then to the secondary filter unit and the main injection pump, and finally to the injectors (hard lines handling extremely high pressure). Check for leaks at every joint and connection. Cycle the lift pump manually to check smooth operation. When was the secondary filter element last changed? Check the fuel system bleed points (on filter assembly, injector pump and at injectors themselves) for evidence of over-tightening (rounded shoulders on hex fittings) or frequent use (implying chronic air leakage into the system). The injector pump controls should be firmly fastened – usually wired to prevent movement. Be sure the throttle and fuel shutoff (engine stop) linkages are securely fastened and that they operate smoothly. Finally, trace the fuel return lines from injectors back to the fuel tank, looking for leaks and damage.

Other engine features to check include the air filter, if installed, for cleanliness. Instrument sensor wires (oil pressure, water temperature, alarms) should be firmly attached, corrosion-free and bundled for protection. Check the oil level and condition of the oil: Brown froth indicates water or coolant in the oil; thin, watery oil suggests dilution by fuel. Check the oil filter for leakage, and determine when it was last changed. Have you sufficient spare oil and filters aboard for at least one complete change? Look for oil leaks around the valve cover, timing gear cover and fuel pump. Look for corrosion buildup and signs of overheating (scorched and discolored paint, softened or partially melted plastic fittings). Examine the engine mounts to be sure nuts are tight (double or lock nuts are best to prevent vibration-induced loosening). The vibration damper must have live rubber (not hard, dried or cracked), and the spider arms extending from the engine block must be free of cracks and distortions.

Check the *transmission* cover for corrosion. The housing should include a vent with a cap to keep salt, dirt, dust and foreign objects out of the unit. Look for signs of leaks from the transmission, and make sure there's a supply of extra transmission fluid. The transmission normally connects to the propeller shaft with flanges whose bolts should be safety-wired or double-nutted to prevent loosening. Examine the *prop shaft* inside the hull. It should be well secured to the collar linking it to the transmission, with a keyway in the shaft to prevent slipping. (Set screws in the collar are insufficient by themselves.) The shaft should have a couple of hose clamps or a spare zinc installed just forward of the stuffing box to prevent the shaft from slipping aft if it breaks or gets uncoupled from the transmission. If there's a line shaft bearing between the transmission and the stuffing box, it should be fitted with lubrication points (recently serviced?) and show no signs of misalignment.

Next follow the *electrical system,* starting at the batteries. Both service and engine-start batteries must have tightly connected cables well protected from corrosion. They should be color-coded (red = positive, black = negative) and in good condition. The batteries must be in a container that will contain acid in the event of a broken case, securely fastened to prevent movement even in a 180° knockdown, and shielded to prevent accidental shorting across the terminals. The negative cable usually runs to the ground connection on the engine, which must be clean, tight and corrosion-free. Trace the cables to the starter, where the connections should be clean, tight and protected with a light coating of grease. Tap bolts with a wrench to check that they're sound and snug. All cable runs and harnesses should be banded and secured to prevent damage. Sight along the plane of the alternator belt to be sure the alternator is properly aligned, and look for dust accumulations caused by excessive belt wear. Check for proper size of engine drive belts: The outer edge of the belt should be flush with the lips of the sheave, not riding above it or sunk down in the groove (Figure 4.2). The alternator drive belt(s) should be tight enough to prevent turning the alternator by hand. Check the alternator wiring and its labeling. Trace the field, ground and output leads and make sure all connections are tight.

Figure 4.2 - Drive Belts

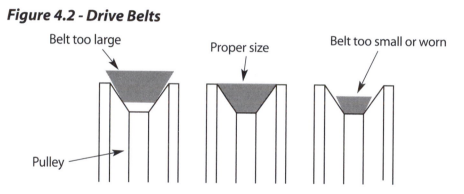

While in the engine area, check the *ventilation system*. Diesels need a good supply of air to operate properly. Unlike gasoline engine installations, which always have the exhaust blower arranged to draw heavy, explosive vapors from the lowest part of the bilge, diesel installations sometimes draw from the top of the space to remove unpleasant but nonexplosive fumes; other diesel installations have no exhaust blower. If the boat uses LPG to fuel a cooking or heating system, however, a powered exhaust that draws from the lowest point in the boat is *essential*.

Check all tanks, wires, fuses, instruments, switches and other equipment in and around the engine space. Look for loose or deteriorated connections, exposed contacts or other dangerous conditions. Check the condition of any installed fire extinguisher, preferably an automatic unit with a thermostatic valve. Check the engine area bilges and remove any oil in an environmentally sound manner. If oil is present, determine its source and correct the situation. Inspect the cockpit drains which often run through the engine space to be sure hoses are in good shape, connections are tight, sea cocks operate freely and wood plugs are on station.

Before leaving the engine area, check the whole space for hazards such as exposed light bulbs, frayed wires, unsecured items, flammables, objects that could catch in the shaft or foul engine belts, leaks from the overhead and loose deck plates.

Moving topside. Moving topside, check the companionway hatches and washboards for fit, ease of operation and accessible stowage. For heavy weather, they should be able to be secured from either side, and there should be a positive method to prevent loss of the boards in a knockdown.

Run the engine blower system and confirm air flow, then start the engine, listen for alarms and watch the gauges. The oil pressure alarm should sound until pressure rises (quickly) to operating pressure (usually 40-60 psi). The ammeter should show a high initial charge rate as the alternator replaces current drawn to start the engine, then taper off to a low maintenance rate. Make sure there's an adequate flow of engine cooling water in the exhaust stream; check throttle and gear shift operation in forward and reverse. Look for excessive play in the linkages and stiffness of movement. Before securing the engine, duck below and watch it operate. Check for heavy vibration, signs of belt misalignment, wobble of pump shafts or alternator pulleys, and exhaust, water or fuel leaks. Check the shaft stuffing box to see if rotating the shaft has caused increased water leakage (drips should be at least ten seconds apart). Then secure the engine, checking alarms again.

Touring the deck, check every stanchion and bow and stern pulpits for looseness; look at the fastenings at the deck for corrosion, stress fractures and leakage. Check side lights and stern light. Check lifeline tension; they should be neither sloppily slack nor bar tight. Check lifelines at the end fittings for rust. If in doubt, peel back the plastic covering and examine for broken strands and deteriorating swaged fittings.

Check all *standing rigging* at the deck level. Start by removing any tape and cleaning off residue. Turnbuckles should have clean, undamaged and lubricated threads. They should be straight and fitted with brass or stainless cotter pins to prevent movement. Each shroud and stay should be fitted with toggles to prevent lateral stresses on turnbuckles, chainplates and pins. Each leg of the standing rig should also have one clevis pin that is fitted with a cotter pin spread only 20° – to facilitate easy removal in an emergency. Check for clevis pins that have backed out and are placing strain on cotter pins. Check for cracks in every turnbuckle and end fitting, preferably with a dye penetrant, but at least with a magnifying glass to detect tiny cracks, particularly in swaged connections. Any signs of wire unlaying suggests broken strands inside the swage fitting. Any cracks or broken strands indicate serious impairment of rig strength. Remove cosmetic covers on shrouds and look for corrosion and wire deterioration. (Though these covers reduce chafe on sails and sheets, they keep the shrouds in a permanent salt-loaded environment that is detrimental to wire life.)

Examine the *roller furling* headsail installation, looking for condition and lubrication of the drum, swivels and foil, security of bolts, pins and connections, and smooth operation. The control pendant should have a fair lead aft, with minimum friction, be in good condition, and have at least five turns remaining on the drum when the sail has been fully rolled up under normal conditions. If the boat has a roller-furling main, make a similar check of its operating components.

At the *mast*, examine the collar and wedges for a snug fit and weather protection. Look for stress cracking in the partners and the mast. If the mast is deck-stepped, check for a mechanical fastening between the spar and the step, and inspect the wiring leading to the mast (watertight deck fitting, chafe protection at the mast entry, connections sealed against water entry?). Check all mast-mounted winches for free movement and muted clicks of the pawls, indicating lubrication (if there are loud metal clicks, when was the winch last overhauled?). Is there a convenient holder for winch handles? Examine all halyards to determine the condition of wires and fittings, looking for broken strands ("meat hooks"), kinks and twists (possibly

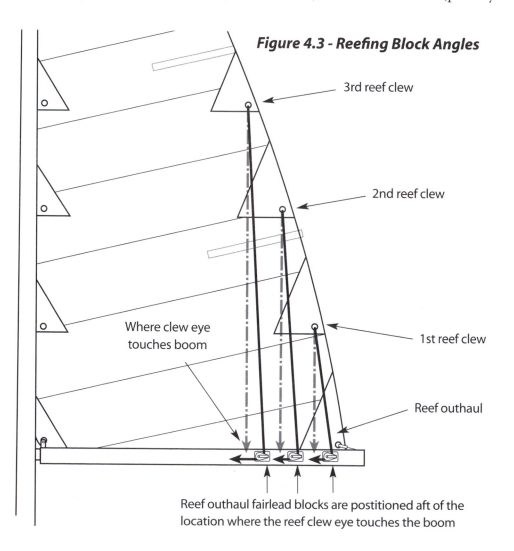

Figure 4.3 - Reefing Block Angles

3rd reef clew

2nd reef clew

Where clew eye touches boom

1st reef clew

Reef outhaul

Reef outhaul fairlead blocks are postitioned aft of the location where the reef clew eye touches the boom

signaling a roller furling wrap problem). If wire is in bad shape, consider replacing it with low-stretch synthetic fiber line of appropriate size and strength. Check spinnaker gear to ensure the pole attachment slides smoothly, adjustments lock easily and securely, and the pole itself operates properly.

The *gooseneck* should include sturdy, snugly-fitted clevis pins equipped with cotter pins, all clean and corrosion-free and lightly lubricated. Sail track up the mast and along the boom must be straight, and any junctions must be perfectly aligned to avoid having slides hang up. A light coating of silicone or "dry" lubricant will help free movement. It is very desirable to have a separate track on the mast on which the trysail can be mounted and stowed, with a switch to connect it to the main sail track above the boom. Examine the vang tackle for smooth operation, secure mountings, strong connecting fittings, and check the condition of all wires or lines. Check the reefing gear on the boom to be sure the outhaul fairlead blocks are securely attached at a point aft of the point at which the clew eye touches the boom (Figure 4.3). The halyard should be marked to indicate the proper position for each reef, and there should be a winch for hauling the reefing pendants tight. Check for free movement and lubrication of all blocks, sheaves and sliding parts on the mast and boom.

Checking aloft. Next, break out the bosun's chair, inspect it for condition and strength, and rig it for a ride aloft. Don't forget to run a safety line with a second halyard and take along a canvas bucket with a few basics (crescent wrench, pliers, Phillips and straight-blade screwdrivers, wire cutters, knife, sandpaper or small wire brush, rigging tape, stainless safety wire, spray detergent, a small can of oil, a couple of rags and paper towels). On the way up, check the standing rigging for broken strands and unlaying (wipe wire with paper towel to create "flags" of paper at broken strands). Pausing at the spreaders, check attachment of the lower shrouds: clevis pins all the way in, heads outboard, and fitted with nonferrous cotter pins. Be sure the bolt through the mast holding the tangs is tight and pinned to prevent loosening. Check the inboard ends of spreaders for wear, elongation of pin/bolt holes and security of fastenings. Examine wood spreaders for rot, especially on upper surface (must be replaced if any rot is found). Swing out to the spreader tip and check for equal angles between the spreader and shroud (Figure 4.4). Try to move spreader tip up and down to ensure tightness of seizings. Check condition of soft covering at tips to prevent headsail chafe.

Continuing upward, check the steaming

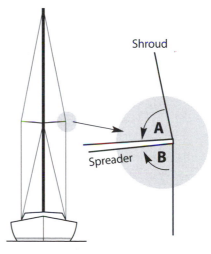

Figure 4.4 - Spreader Angle
Angle A = angle B to ensure load on spreaders is only compression

light and security of any mast fittings encountered along the way, including the radar antenna and platform. Repeat checks at upper spreaders, if present. At the masthead, check the mechanical wind direction indicator for free movement. Look at the halyard sheaves for wear, misalignment or seizing. Do they fit snugly, or are there gaps that could allow a halyard to jump out and jam between the sheave and cheeks? Check all clevis and cotter pins. Inspect tangs and standing rigging for fair alignment, cracks, rust stains or unlaying. Clean and examine swages. Look for cracks or fractured welds in the masthead box. Test tightness of instrument and antenna connections. Test the masthead tricolor and anchor lights. On split rigs, check the triatic stay for solid attachment and good tension (no slack). Check blocks and rigging for spinnaker gear. Ensure that all shackles aloft have safety wires to prevent accidental opening. Examine the upper end of roller furling gear for wear, misalignment, abrasion or fouling of the halyard.

Satisfied that everything at the masthead is tight and lubricated, come back down, checking the sail track or boltrope groove for alignment, soundness and cleanliness. Then repeat the entire process on deck and aloft for the mizzen, if any.

Back on deck. Back on deck, check all crew overboard gear for condition and readiness for deployment; a quick release system is desirable. On the foredeck, check how the anchor will be secured against movement in high seas. Look at mooring cleats, fairleads and chocks to be sure they're strong and free of sharp/rough edges. Check the topside decks and hatches for cracks, stress fractures, delamination. Make sure there are closure plates that actually fit each ventilator. Examine the fastening, alignment and condition of all deck-mounted hardware – handrails, blocks, tracks and padeyes. Is the companionway cover securely attached to its slides, and does it move freely? Is the steering pedestal firmly mounted, with a substantial backing plate? Does the compass light come on with the navigation lights? Review plans for rigging jacklines for crew safety tethers: They should be snug and not create a trip hazard, yet permit a crew member to clip on before leaving the cockpit and move all the way to the headstay and stern pulpit without having to unfasten. There should be a padeye or strong point for the helmsman to fasten his or her safety harness while at the wheel.

Check the condition of weather cloths and dodger (as well as any zippers or window). Make sure the shore power cable is in good condition and that its receptacle is corrosion-free and fitted with a watertight cover. Check cockpit lockers for secure stowage, and climb inside where possible to look at the hull-deck joint, through-hull valves, electrical wiring, and any machinery or equipment there (refrigeration units, generators, autopilot drive units, SSB radio tuners). Cockpit lockers should fit with gasketed lids and have positive latches to keep them from opening in a knockdown. Check the cockpit drainage, with a minimum of two 1" drains preferred.

A thorough inspection should include an inventory of kits assembled for use in medical situations, sail damage, rig failure and hull penetration. Contents of these kits will be discussed in following chapters.

Inspecting sails ashore. Because the engine that lives in the hull is only an auxiliary means of propulsion, any inspection must include a careful look at the primary source of driving power: the sails. There is seldom room on the boat for a thorough job, so the sails should be taken ashore, where they can be spread out fully. Start at one corner and work all the way around the sail, checking condition along the luff, foot and leech. Then examine each panel. Look for rips, cuts or holes, for chafing, and for broken, worn or loose stitching. At the head and along the foot, look closely for UV degradation (discoloration accompanied by crumbling of the resin that holds the threads in place in the fabric). At the leech, watch for damage at the hem caused by fluttering and by wear from the leech line. Look closely at the points where stress is concentrated: the tack, clew and head fittings and reefing tacks and outhauls. Examine hardware such as headboards, and tack, reef and clew rings for corrosion, cracks or deteriorating fastenings. Check batten pockets for signs of wear; be sure the battens fit snugly and are held in place securely. Inspect each sail slide and its attachment to the sail, and replace any that may be suspect.

Safety equipment. Last, but far from least important, inspect the safety equipment installation. Is the life raft stowed securely with as much weather/sea protection as possible, and is the painter/ operating lanyard secured to the boat with a weak link? Are there sufficient Coast Guard approved inherently buoyant PFDs? Are they supplemented by top quality inflatable flotation gear? Is there a safety harness and tether for each crew member? Is there an adequate abandon ship ditch-kit assembled? Are the distress signals – preferably SOLAS grade – within expiration dates? Is all this equipment stowed securely where it will be easily accessible in an emergency? Are there adequate fire extinguishers distributed around the boat, and have they been maintained for reliability? Another issue is as important as the equipment itself: Are there carefully considered plans for using the emergency equipment, assigning responsibility to specific crew members and ensuring that they know how to perform their duties?

Sources for construction standards. To help define how a boat should be constructed and outfitted, standards have been prepared by several national and international authorities charged with responsibility for such matters. Three of particular interest to passagemakers are compiled by the American Boat and Yacht Council (ABYC), National Fire Protection Association (NFPA) and the Offshore Racing Council (ORC).

The ABYC's "Standards" covers the installation of LPG systems, stoves, fire extinguishers, electrical systems, engine fuel tanks, engine-room ventilation and many other common systems. (See References.) For fire-fighting systems, the ABYC refers to Fire Protection Standard for Pleasure and Commercial Motor Craft, manual NFPA 302.

The ORC standards are internationally recognized minimum levels of design and outfitting for boats engaged in ocean racing at several different levels, from inshore races to extended ocean races. The publication includes sections on safety harness manufacture and life raft specifications. Copies of these regulations with supplementary recommendations from US SAILING can be obtained from US SAILING. Entitled *Recommendations for Offshore Sailing,* a new edition is published each year, usually in March. *Safety Recommendations for Cruising Sailboats* (see Chapter 2) is a modified version of this publication.

Years ago, a seagoing sage pointed out that when it comes to performance of equipment, you get not what you EXpect, but what you INspect. Our experience certainly supports this thesis. The skippers who know their boats thoroughly and take nothing for granted usually encounter few surprises during their passage. Those who assume that things will work the way they were intended, without testing or inspecting to make sure, tend to suffer one disconcerting surprise after another. A day or two devoted to a penetrating and comprehensive inspection of your boat may prove to be the best investment you can make toward a safe passage. If you find that everything is in top notch condition, you'll sleep better and enjoy the passage. If you find shortcomings, you'll have the opportunity to correct them or figure out how to live with them. At the very least, you'll avoid some unpleasant, middle-of-the-night, green-water-on-the-deck, screaming-wind surprises, such as learning five minutes after the steering cable parts that the emergency tiller doesn't fit the rudder post! The proverb about an ounce of prevention being worth a pound of cure may have been written by a landsman, but it applies ten times over to the passagemaking sailor.

REFERENCES:
ABYC, *Standards and Recommended Practices for Small Craft*
NFPA, *Fire Protection Standard for Pleasure and Commercial Motor Craft,* manual NFPA 302
US SAILING, *Recommendations for Offshore Sailing* and *Safety Recommendations for Cruising Sailboats*
Nigel Calder, *Boatowner's Mechanical and Electrical Manual*

CHAPTER 5

FEAR AND THE CRUISING SAILOR

This chapter is adapted from an article by Steve Black published in Cruising World *magazine.*

Like other four-letter words, fear is almost never mentioned in polite company. Each individual is left to cope with it in his or her own way. The truth is that fear is a healthy emotion which serves as our early warning system for situations that may be threatening to our property or well-being. Fear focuses our concern on those aspects of sailing that require most careful attention and preparedness. And sailors are not immune.

While helping sailors prepare for their Virginia-to-Virgin Gorda passage with the West Marine Caribbean 1500 cruising rally, we could clearly see that some of the less experienced among them were anxious about the potential hazards of such a trip. This brought home the realization that understanding and managing fear is a vital sailing skill, one that is rarely discussed or taught.

As a result, I've explored the subject with many experienced sailors in the hope that others could learn from them without having to do it the hard way. As you'll see from the firsthand stories that follow, fear often accompanies the *anticipation* of danger, yet it is an emotion that is strangely absent when the feared event actually takes place.

Fear exists in varying degrees, ranging from slight apprehension to full-blown terror. The object of the fear also varies widely, from vague fears of the unknown to specific fears, such as embarrassment while docking, storms, giant waves, falling overboard, or having your boat sink.

If I've just touched on one of your worst fears, please stay with me: there's a method here. As unpleasant as fear can be, it's only an emotion and it can't hurt you by itself. It is the mind's way of exploring the unknown.

When I first climbed aboard a sailboat, I worried that it would turn over – until I became accustomed to heeling. I worried the first time the wind blew 20 knots and again each time it blew harder than I'd seen it blow before. Now that I've experienced 70 knots of wind, I still find 50 knots unpleasant, but far less threatening. Clearly, experience determines the size of your envelope of comfort, and each time you go beyond your previous experience, new anxieties may well appear. To minimize apprehensions, take smaller steps to gain experience before taking on tougher challenges.

A two-step procedure. Anyone who has never experienced fear probably hasn't been paying attention. For the rest of us, there's a two-step procedure that is helpful for getting the upper hand in situations we find threatening. First, we must identify the things we fear. Once the source of the fear has been identified, you can take steps to do something about it. If you fear hitting the dock, put out more fenders. If you fear falling overboard, wear a harness and flotation device. If you fear drowning, sinking or being lost, get familiar with life jackets, life rafts, EPIRBs and radios. Simply knowing how to use all your safety gear and practicing crew-overboard drills will reduce the threat induced by many hazards.

The thing I feared most as a single-handed multihull racer was having the boat flip over. To cope with this fear, I confronted it directly. I lay on the floor of my boat with my feet in the air and I imagined the boat upside down. I located drier spaces, a place for my stove, storage spots where dry clothes would be found if my world turned upside down, and I even fastened flashlights near the floor where they would be accessible if I ever needed them. Understanding how I would function if the boat capsized greatly reduced my apprehensions about such an event. Remember: fear helps you identify situations for which you need to be prepared. It is a road sign to enjoyable passagemaking.

What we need to avoid is not fear, but panic, which is an irrational response to fear. We need to use fear to lead us to the proper corrective action. We must not let it push us into impulsive, possibly counterproductive responses that may only serve to make a difficult situation more dangerous. As an example, consider the panic-stricken crews during the 1979 Fastnet Race, who abandoned their damaged boats for the perceived "safety" of a life raft, only to die in the raft and have their boats found afloat and safe several days later. We must avoid panic by making a rational assessment of the source of our fear.

Thus, the second step in accommodating to fear is to ask ourselves, "What is the worst thing that can happen?" Use this technique when the situation looks bad and your apprehensions are mounting. To qualify the hazard, you must ask yourself if the situation is truly life-threatening. Fortunately, 99.9% of the time it is not, and with this realization, much of the fear will recede. With a storm at its peak and the waves towering around you, watch your boat rise and fall with the seas – just as it was designed to do. You'll soon realize that the waves aren't hurting the boat or crew, and that they are not objects to fear. This is one way in which you will learn the difference between conditions that are merely unpleasant and uncomfortable and those that are really life-threatening.

A good way to learn what might happen if your worst nightmares were to materialize is to hear from people who have encountered – and emerged unscathed from – some harrowing situations. In every case, thorough preparations resulted in happy endings.

On doing a 360° roll in the Southern Ocean: Australian Don McIntyre encountered tough conditions in the 1990-91 BOC Challenge, a single-handed race around the world.

"I was sitting at the chart table talking on the radio at the time. The boat went down and I went backward. I thought it was just another severe knockdown, but the boat just kept going. All of a sudden the lights went out – because all the ports were under water. There was this weird light and a huge amount of noise, with things being jumbled around in the lockers. When this happens, you are totally disoriented and wondering what the hell is going on. First you're on the cabin top and next you're diving over to the other side of the boat as you are recovering and you're saying, 'Hang on a minute, this doesn't make sense,' and halfway through the recovery you realize you've gone right through the whole sequence. It took about 25-30 seconds and you think, 'Wow, that was a rollover!' And then it's just a matter of getting on with the job. Four hours later when everything was cleaned up again, I got to thinking how serious it had been."

On being washed overboard: Don continues:

"I was washed over once on the Cape Town to Sydney leg, when I was at the mast. I wasn't really scared, but a lot of things flash through your mind, like 'Did I clip my harness onto a strong enough point?' But then you get back aboard and go on with hoisting the storm jib. It's when you're back below again that you say to yourself, 'Boy, that was a pretty interesting situation!'"

On being caught in a hurricane: Early in a circumnavigation aboard their 37' Black Watch, *Rabbit,* Rhode Islanders Dan and Mimi Dyer were buffeted by the tail end of a hurricane. Both of them found it unpleasant, but Mimi, as a much less experienced sailor, also found it terrifying. Would the boat fall apart? Would Dan fall overboard off the bow while changing headsails? Would the stove break loose? Would the mast stay up? "I'm frightened to death," her log reads. "It's very rough, with seas higher than I've ever seen." They were making six knots under the No. 4 jib alone – until the winds piped up and the seas got even nastier. Dan, realizing that the situation was not life-threatening, was able to put it in perspective for Mimi with a few well-chosen words: "It's amazing to think," he told her, "that we'll be becalmed tomorrow." Later she allowed that just having the assurance that it would soon be over, and that their boat was well-found and prepared for the conditions, made it tolerable.

On capsizing in a multihull: During an attempted record-breaking voyage aboard the 60' trimaran *Great American* from San Francisco to New York City in

November 1990, a massive low exploded out of Antarctica, catching *Great American* and her two-man crew just off Cape Horn with no place to go. Steve Pettingill described the conditions he and Rich Wilson encountered:

"The barograph had been off the paper for two days. We were running off, towing warps, with winds in the 70-knot range and seas around 50 feet. An occasional rogue wave would hit the boat at 90°, and one broke the blades off the wind generator. I figured we had things pretty well under control and went down to put on lunch. Suddenly the boat slid sideways on the face of a breaking wave and lifted up on her side. I thought she'd come back, but instead I found myself walking up the side of the cabin as she slowly continued to roll 180°. Richie and I both knew what to do and just went into motion."

They activated their EPIRB and gathered supplies on the underside of the cockpit sole where it was dry. Just as they were finishing this, the boat was picked up again and slammed upright, leaving the boat dismasted and the crew neck deep in water. "We each made sure the other was OK and talked it through again," said Steve. They found the sail locker forward of the main bulkhead to be relatively dry, and passed supplies along the deck and down through the forward hatch. They ate their Thanksgiving dinner out of cans and rested. "Things were going like clockwork," says Steve. "We planned out the next few days and went to sleep." They were awakened at 3:30 a.m. by the welcome sound of a 900' ship coming alongside, and they scrambled to safety, jumping to the ship's boarding ladder. Steve summarized the experience, saying "There are no 'time outs' in this kind of sailing. You just do the best you can with what's presented to you."

On making a first offshore passage: Tony Lush, now a veteran of three OSTARs and the first BOC Challenge, once sat alone for five days in the harbor at St.Pierre, a French island near Newfoundland, contemplating his first ocean passage. His home-built *One Hand Clapping* was his first boat – prior to her launch he had sailed only a dozen times and those outings were in dinghies. The fear of the unknown, combined with the certain knowledge of his inexperience, caused him to think long and hard about departing. The fear was resolved by taking time to attend to every detail possible for the crossing. Water was aboard. The log cable was replaced. Food stowed. Masthead fitting examined. Reefing lines checked. Charts updated. Sights practiced. Water topped up. Tools oiled, and food stowed again. Finally, the only thing left to do was confront the fear directly – by departing. It took another three days before his queasy stomach settled down, but Tony was finally off on his first grand adventure. Now, after many thousands of passagemaking miles, Tony says "I still confront fears each time I anticipate a departure. A little fear is a healthy thing and I still attend to it as on my first passage – by preparing boat and crew as thoroughly as I can for the unknowns ."

Nearly a century earlier, that experienced professional mariner and sailing ship captain, Joshua Slocum, experienced similar reservations about setting off on his history-making voyage around the world. He wrote that he headed for a cove near Gloucester "again to look the *Spray* over, and again to weigh the voyage, and my feelings, and all that." And he subsequently "sat and considered the matter all over again, and asked myself once more whether it were best to sail beyond the ledge and rocks at all." Slocum responded to his apprehensions in the same way Tony Lush did – by doing his best to be sure the boat and its crew were thoroughly prepared for the passage.

Most of us will sail for the rest of our lives and never experience the severe conditions and rare situations described in some of the previous accounts, but all of us will probably experience fear of some kind along the way. So it is reassuring to hear how real people have coped with the very situations we fear the most and succeeded through good planning, preparation and communication.

Put fear in its place. You, too, can avoid or overcome difficult situations and put fear in its place by following these simple steps. Prepare boat, crew, and equipment carefully before you set sail. Acknowledge the sources of your concerns and plan steps to minimize their threat. Inspect your boat daily while underway, including any item that is subject to chafe. When a situation occurs that raises fears in your mind, assess its seriousness. Is it really life-threatening or just very unpleasant? Next, take positive action to deal with the source of the worry. The following chapters will address the many strategies available to you for doing so. By taking positive steps to deal with problems, you will do much to restore your confidence in your boat and in yourself. Because fear alerts us to real dangers, it should not be suppressed, but rather used to identify hazards that careful preparation will help avoid. Being prepared will keep fears in perspective and ensure safe, enjoyable sailing.

CHAPTER 6

LEADERSHIP

This chapter is adapted from the article "The Skipper's Many Hats," by Steve Black, published in Cruising World *magazine.*

There's an old sailor's dice game called "Ship, Captain and Crew" that requires a player to roll a 6 (the ship) and a 5 (the captain) before finding out how many crew there will be. It's a logical sequence to follow, since the ship can't work without a captain and a captain can't accomplish much without a crew. Having looked closely at the passage-making boat, we now consider the role of the captain before turning to a consideration of the crew.

For many, involvement in sailing begins as a family event, joining parents or other relatives afloat. For others, it may begin with an invitation from a friend or neighbor. Regardless of how it starts, two things are happening for novice sailors: they are learning new skills and they are observing and absorbing the skipper's leadership techniques. What the novice learns and the way it's conveyed will exert a powerful influence on the way he or she handles the situation years later when, as a skipper, he or she introduces a new set of beginners to the mariner's skills. Every skipper bears many responsibilities as well as the opportunity to make first-rate crew and future skippers of those who are learning to enjoy the art of sailing.

To some degree, we all learn to be skippers by example, and we become better skippers through practice. Just as children learn parenting skills from the example (good or bad) of their own parents, we are strongly influenced by our first skippers, and we tend to adopt their leadership style. Once we're on our own, we get trial-and-error feedback that refines our style and determines our skill.

Other than parenthood, few leadership roles require as much of a person as being a good skipper. Whenever you take someone sailing, you assume a number of responsibilities and an obligation to carry them out in a way that will leave your crew happy and ready to sail with you again. Let's look first at the unique relationship with the crew that defines the skipper's responsibilities. Then we'll look at leadership styles, the human side of the relationship.

They're counting on you. As skipper, you are responsible for preparing and operating the boat in a safe, seamanlike manner, arriving at the destination with a crew that is unharmed, in good spirits, eager to sail with you again, and better trained than before you set sail. That's a sobering list, but the crew believe they can count on you to deliver it. That is why they agreed to sail with you in the first place!

To understand how this tacit (and reasonable) expectation fixes responsibility on the skipper, look at an outing – whether a day sail or an extended passage – from your crew's viewpoint. They assume you know your boat's equipment and workings better than anyone else. They take for granted your concern for their safety and enjoyment. These are implicit in your asking them to sail with you.

Since you are "the expert" in the eyes of your crew, they are unlikely to second-guess your preparations. In fact, it would be awkward for them (and perhaps distasteful for you) to "grill" you with checklists to assure that there's sufficient food, fuel and water, and so on. They are unlikely to count PFDs, check the inspection date on the life raft, or examine your chart stock to assure coverage of alternate harbors of refuge. (If they do, you either have very experienced crew from whom you may be able to learn a few things, or crew who for some reason lack full confidence in you – a situation that signals a need for prompt correction.) The crew usually trust in your preparedness, otherwise they would not have come along. If a needed piece of gear isn't aboard, it's the skipper's fault, even if the task had been delegated to someone else (in which case, the skipper should have checked to be sure the task was done properly). To some degree, every crewmember places blind faith in the skipper. This can be a weighty responsibility. At the same time, you never need wonder where the buck stops: It stops with the skipper!

The crew assumes you have selected an appropriate boat, one that is big enough, strong enough, with sound hull, sails and rigging and properly provisioned for the voyage. They believe you have verified the completeness of safety gear, with good PFDs, fresh distress signals, inspected life raft and adequate medical kit. They expect you to have the proper navigation equipment and up-to-date information, and they assume you've inspected all the boat's equipment to make sure it's working properly. It is the skipper's job to select a balanced, compatible crew with adequate skills to carry out all the tasks (see Chapter 7).

Last but certainly not least are the legal responsibilities. The skipper alone is responsible for the boat's papers, licenses, passports, customs clearance and for ensuring that the boat is drug-free.

The skipper's responsibilities under way. On the water, the skipper's first responsibility is the safety and well-being of all those on board. Boats can be replaced, but people cannot; even the safety of the boat must be viewed from the perspective of protecting the crew first. Remember the skipper's duty cited above: to get the crew safely to the destination. It's up to you to point out hazards, explain tasks before they are performed, provide instruction on the use and location of safety equipment, and assign duties. The skipper must make all the tough decisions during emergencies. Your personal style will influence your approach to these duties, but don't forget the importance of training your crew. Are they prepared, for example, to take over if you should be injured, get sick or fall overboard?

Leadership styles. How you carry out your responsibilities as skipper can be as important as what you do. A dictatorial style may get the job done but leave the crew wishing they had stayed home (and certain they'll never sail with you again). Even a "benevolent" dictator – often found on racing boats – will adversely affect the overall experience for the crew. The opposite situation, an attempt to have a democracy, is equally ineffective. It is usually perceived as a leadership vacuum, and it can easily turn into anarchy. Strange though it may seem, the most successful style of skippering has a great deal in common with good parenting, with a combination of listening and guiding, publicly commending good performance and privately counseling shortcomings, setting reasonable standards and enforcing them evenhandedly while adhering to the same or higher standards in your own conduct. There need not be anything patronizing involved, but everyone must feel fairly treated.

The crew looks up to you for your knowledge, puts their faith in you to protect their comfort and safety, and accepts your authority to make decisions. This relationship is essential to the well-being of boat and crew, since it permits quick, coordinated action in emergencies. The crew's acceptance of the skipper's leadership creates an obligation to lead: Failing to do so, the skipper would leave the crew without a functional decision-making process, and the result would surely be chaos, injuries and damage. The skipper should enjoy his or her role, but never forget those who make it possible.

For couples, sailing can place an enormous strain on a relationship, particularly if one person is a skilled, enthusiastic sailor and the other is not. The first step toward reconciling this is to recognize that you are partners before you are skipper and mate. You cannot expect your partner to share your enthusiasm for sailing unless you are willing to share some of the responsibility and some of the satisfaction that comes from meeting a challenge successfully.

It is easy to fall into fixed roles on a boat, often at the expense of enjoyment. Sail handling, navigation and steering are skills that should be taught and shared just as cooking, cleaning and maintenance are. Bellowing bullies, glued to the helm, shortchange themselves, their mates and their relationship. Successful cruising couples have learned to become contributing partners in every aspect of the sailing experience.

Couples spend more time together on a boat than they are likely to do on land. Being in close quarters for long periods can strain a relationship unless both partners work at showing consideration, practicing good manners, and communicating openly. Don't let boat roles get in the way of an otherwise good relationship.

8 steps to a happy crew. The care and maintenance of the crew is just as important as that required by the boat's mechanical systems. On longer trips, good food and adequate rest are necessary for an alert, smoothly operating crew, but it is the crew's mental well-being that can place the most challenging demands on the skipper. While not a comprehensive magic formula, here are eight suggestions for maintaining a happy crew.

1. Teach them all you can. The more each crewmember knows, the more he or she is able to help the overall effort. You will rest better as you develop confidence in the crew's skills, and the risk of injuries and mistakes will decrease. As they gain experience, crewmembers are better able to help one another, giving each the sense of being a valuable and valued member of a team.

2. Show, then ask. Demonstrate how you want each task performed before you ask a crewmember to do it. It's better to show someone how many turns you want on the genoa sheet winch and give them the chance to do it right the first time than to correct them while they're doing it "wrong."

3. Unless it's an emergency, *ask your crew to perform tasks rather than issuing orders.* This is not only more civil but also lends urgency to the rare case where an instant response is needed.

4. Yelling is for fight fans. On a boat, it's OK to yell "Duck!" but in most other situations, a normal voice will get your point across more effectively. Sailing is supposed to be fun! As the ship's morale officer, among other things, the skipper more than anyone else can see to it that the crew feels good about the day, themselves and each other.

5. Variety is the spice. Encourage everyone to learn new jobs. Give as many people as possible a turn at the helm. It's important for their understanding of the boat that they have a feel for the way she responds, and it will give you a fresh perspective as well. If the crew hasn't had plenty of practice on the helm in good conditions, they won't be ready to take over when the going gets rough and the autopilot packs it in. Learning new jobs will keep the crew interested.

6. Remember that there is more than one "right way" to perform many tasks. Being the skipper does not necessarily mean you are the ranking expert on all aspects of sailing. Be willing to learn from your crew.

7. Say "Cheese!" There may not be a camera aimed at you, but all eyes are on you, nevertheless. As skipper, you control crew morale to such a degree that their response to a situation is likely to mirror your own. As long as the skipper stays calm, the crew will believe the situation is under control, even as conditions become impressive or uncomfortable. Instill in yourself and your crew a sense of self-confidence and self-reliance. A bit of common sense, initiative and immediate practical action will usually save a situation. People have been making long passages in small boats for more than a thousand years, and most did so in craft that were less well built than ours and with far less knowledge than we enjoy.

8. Look on the bright side. No matter what, keep a positive attitude and find a way to see a light at the end of any tunnel that is something other than an oncoming train! Nothing will destroy morale quicker than a rancid outlook on the skipper's part. Be generous with your compliments, because the crew sees you as the only real judge of their success. Accept responsibility for things that go wrong, but share the rewards for jobs well done.

Leadership in tough times. Exercising strong and positive leadership is most difficult at the very times it's most needed: when weather and sea conditions deteriorate or a casualty to boat or crew creates an emergency. Bad weather, with violent boat motion, and a cold, wet environment creates physical demands that will wear down even the youngest and healthiest of bodies. Motion sickness degrades individual performance, and may be seen by tired fellow crewmembers as a poor excuse for evading work, leading to resentment and plummeting morale. Tired, discouraged, wet people are not easily motivated to perform, and effective leadership (by one who is seldom immune to ocean motion and fatigue) demands great strength of character in the skipper. Compound the situation with a casualty such as a parted halyard or a life raft gone adrift at 0300 on a black night, and the skipper's leadership challenge is multiplied several times over. Getting the right action, right away, will require the skipper to draw upon crew confidence that has been earned earlier in the passage.

A particularly tricky situation develops when a crewmember has been seriously injured. There is a tendency for the crew's attention to shift from sustaining the boat's seaworthiness to caring for the victim. Morale decays, mistakes lead to knockdowns or worse, leadership evaporates and the crew gives up. It may even lead to a hasty decision to abandon the boat in the mistaken belief that the injured person would be safer in a raft. If the victim is the skipper, and there is no command structure to replace his or her leadership, the situation has become what John Rousmaniere described as a "formula for disaster." Only well-earned crew confidence and a clear understanding of who is in charge can keep the crew focused on the real mission in such a circumstance: keeping the boat afloat.

While it is nearly impossible to define what it takes to produce leadership, or how to exercise it in any given scenario, it is clear that a skipper's leadership skills play a pivotal role in the success of any ocean passage. No skipper can afford to pass up an opportunity to hone his or her leadership skills and build in the crew the confidence necessary to insure their enthusiastic support, even in the toughest times.

A skipper's quiz. Here is a Skipper's Quiz that can be amusing for some and revealing for others:
1. Has the same person ever crewed for you twice?
2. Is PB&J an accepted acronym for a gourmet dinner?
3. If your passage will take five days and your crew can eat four cans of tuna per day, how many days will it take you to find a crew?
4. When weighing anchor, do you normally put the largest person on the helm and the smallest on the bow?
5. Are you ever hoarse after sailing?
6. Does talking about a bigger boat cause your spouse's eyes to roll?
7. Do you interpret mutiny as your crew's way of telling you to be more firm?
8. Does your crew usually hit the dock running the moment the boat is tied up? Do they ever try to get off before it is tied up?

9. Are boats the sole topic of conversation when you and your crew are sailing?
10. Do your sailing friends ever invite you to crew for them?

After asking yourself these questions, do you like the skipper you see? Would you like to crew for this person? If not, it's time to shape up, Skipper!

CHAPTER 7

CREW SELECTION AND ORGANIZATION

Too often, prospective passagemakers focus on preparing the boat, with too little consideration of the crew. A Navy friend observed that all a ship can do by itself is rust. To do anything more, a crew is required. Most sailboats don't rust, but without the crew, about all they can do is drift.

One of the first questions asked by those considering their first long passage concerns the number of people to take. Sometimes the issue is settled by an insurance company that makes its coverage contingent upon having some minimum number of people onboard (often three or four). In other cases, there may be a wider array of options.

Single-handing? While single-handed sailing has its advantages (no mutinies, no complaints about the cook), there are persuasive arguments against going it alone for safe, enjoyable passagemaking. First is the inability to maintain a proper lookout, an obligation imposed by international law (COLREGS) and nautical tradition. The solo sailor is exceedingly vulnerable to the effects of fatigue, which can cloud judgment and sharply impair physical and mental capabilities. With no human assistance, the lone sailor can face tasks that demand greater strength than one person can muster. Other tasks will require presence in two places at once. There are many happy and competent single-handed sailors, but – Joshua Slocum's achievements notwithstanding – having a crew of one is not the best way to assure a successful passage, especially if that one has limited offshore experience.

Double-handing. Many couples have racked up thousands of miles of eminently successful ocean passages with just two persons aboard. The legendary Hiscocks, Lin and Larry Pardey, and Hal and Margaret Roth are names that come quickly to mind. Most of the legendary sailing twosomes have enjoyed a signal advantage: both partners have had a relatively high level of sailing competence, and they have shared the passion for voyaging. Many of these couples acquired their knowledge and cultivated their ability to operate the boat together through many years of coastal cruising and short passages. Rally experience suggests that the typical couple contemplating their first major ocean passage is quite different these days. They often have highly unequal skill and experience levels, as well as significantly different interests and motivations. For this group, making that first ocean passage unassisted is probably not a prudent choice. They could sharply increase the prospects for success by recruiting additional crew, preferably people with ocean passage experience who can help keep otherwise worrisome situations in perspective.

Larger crews. When the crew grows to three, the opportunity for distributing responsibilities improves enormously. You can maintain a person on watch around the clock and still leave each crew member sufficient time to rest and to perform other functions – meal preparation, navigation, weather observation, boat maintenance. With a four-hour watch rotation, the watch stander can always get help from a fellow crewmember who has had between four and eight hours of rest. There is sufficient depth to allow individuals to specialize in the things they enjoy most or do best. A crew of three is probably the smallest that should be considered by novice passagemakers.

Larger crews mean greater opportunities to share the workload. More people on watch can make watch standing more enjoyable. Watches can be shortened or decreased in frequency. Greater specialization is possible, perhaps to the extent of having a dedicated cook. The upper limit for crew is a function of boat size and the number of sea berths. On some 36' boats, three can be comfortable while four are surprisingly crowded. A 60-footer may have ample living space for eight or more, but performance will suffer and morale will plummet like a lead line if there are only two decent sea berths. (With yacht design driven by marketing offices and boats sold on the basis of how many they will sleep at dockside, the latter is not uncommon.) Rally experience has shown that 6-8 people seems to be the largest practical crew size for happy passagemaking.

The crew as a team. Selecting the crew is one of the skipper's most important but least appreciated responsibilities. The crew must be able to function as a team. This means they must be able to get along, not just ashore but in the humid, confined environment of a boat, perhaps in conditions that would drive even the saintliest of sailors to speak ill of the deity. The group should include a balance of viewpoints, but everyone must be willing to accommodate differences. A boat full of pessimists could make even the nicest day of sailing distasteful, while a crew of determined optimists could ignore all but the most foreboding indicators of trouble. A boat needs an orderly command structure, and there must be agreement that the skipper's word is final. Still, good crew will participate in an interchange of ideas that gives the skipper the best basis for making choices, choices that everyone will implement with confidence.

Boswell quoted Dr. Samuel Johnson as observing that:

"No man will be a sailor who has contrivance enough to get himself into a jail; for being in a ship is being in a jail, with a chance of being drowned." Johnson further noted, "A man in jail has more room, better food, and commonly better company."

While conditions at the beginning of the 21st century may be substantially better, both afloat and in jails, there is nevertheless a germ of truth to be drawn from these statements. Many a novice's initial passage has gone sour, not because of broken gear or bad weather, but because of unrealistic expectations and a lack of readiness to deal with the interpersonal problems that can develop during a passage. *Prospective cruising skippers tend to focus on preparing their boat more than on preparing themselves and their crew for the stresses of a passage.*

Preparing the crew. Emotional preparation is vital, because in many cases the offshore sailor is about to do something he or she has never done before, and it is an undertaking that includes significant risk. The novice's evaluation of that risk may be exaggerated, but that is not important. What counts is that he or she is concerned about the hazards. Conversely, if the prospective voyager has no experience offshore, the risks may be greatly underestimated, creating the opportunity for nasty and possibly debilitating surprises. That's why it is best if the skipper has offshore experience as a crewmember aboard someone else's boat before venturing into blue waters as captain.

Crew must understand that interpersonal relations are much more complex and sensitive in the boat environment than they are ashore. Even a loving couple who have shared life harmoniously for years may find it difficult to cope with the stressful situations that develop aboard during a passage. In the past, sailors usually acquired an appreciation of this during the years they spent developing seamanship skills before undertaking a major passage. Today, advanced sail handling systems, electronic navigation and reliable autopilots have enticed people into voyaging before learning those traditional skills – or the organizational sense that was absorbed along with them. As a result, they sometimes jump into passagemaking without realizing that keeping the crew happy and working together is a major challenge, and without knowing how to handle interpersonal stress when it arises.

Consider the new environment into which a novice crewmember will be thrust. Patterns of sleeping, eating, working, relaxing, entertainment, washing, etc. will be radically different from shoreside patterns. These activities may well be more difficult and strenuous. With sleep patterns disrupted, little control over the environment (temperature and humidity), no privacy, little personal space and even drastically altered gravitational influences, the crewmember's performance will be evaluated mainly based on an ability to complete activities that he or she has seldom performed. The resulting tension, fatigue, sleep deprivation and anxiety could cause a new passagemaker to wonder what happened to the fun of sailing and to vow never to venture off dry land again.

Know your crew! As noted in Chapter 6, helping a new crewmember prepare for and cope with this environment is one of a skipper's most important duties. It can best be accomplished by getting to know prospective crewmembers well and establishing open two-way communication. Educating each crewmember in the "ways of the boat" is a vital component, to be addressed shortly. The objective is to ensure that each crewmember knows what to expect of the voyage and how the skipper manages the boat and crew. The skipper must use every chance to gain a good grasp of each crewmember's expectations, capabilities and limitations. Without this mutual understanding, an otherwise nice passage can become an ordeal and a difficult voyage a nightmare.

A good crew should have a blend of skills. It's better to have a seamstress, a shade tree auto mechanic and a ham radio enthusiast than to have three electrical engineers, though the latter may have more in common. It's nice to have a "night person" who enjoys standing watch when most of the world is asleep. For self-sufficient passagemaking, the crew's skills should cover as wide a spectrum as possible to cope with any contingency.

Crew health. Crew health is a key issue, with several important wrinkles. A passage-making boat is removed from ready access to outside medical help. The crew needs to be healthy and fit, both mentally and physically. It takes mental fitness to cope with the close quarters, grinding routine and limited contact with the "real world." Physical fitness is important because sailing offshore can be extremely demanding. A naval aviator friend described his flying career as "hours and hours of boredom interrupted by short intervals of sheer terror." Ocean voyaging often consists of hours and hours, perhaps days, of sedentary relaxation, interspersed with brief periods of vigorous and arduous physical activity. The crew must be capable of handling all that Mother Nature can dish out.

Saying the crew must be healthy does not exclude people who have medical problems, providing they can be managed successfully. Hypertension and diabetes come to mind. It is absolutely vital that the skipper and at least one other crewmember are aware of these conditions and know how to respond if a problem arises. The appropriate medications must be at hand, and someone must know how and when to administer them. Several years ago, a young man signed on to help sail a boat from Maine to the Chesapeake. Afraid he'd be rejected if the skipper knew he was a diabetic, he concealed that fact. For breakfast the second morning out, the skipper prepared pancakes with fresh-picked Maine blueberries. Both skipper and crew ate a full ration, with butter and syrup. A short time later, the skipper found his crewman semiconscious on the cabin sole. Through good fortune, quick action and medical guidance obtained by radio, the young man's life was saved, but it was a close call. He had given himself an insulin injection to help his body cope with the sugar in the syrup, unaware that the skipper had served a sugar-free variety. In insulin shock, the youngster was revived with a sweet soft drink and a candy bar. The whole incident could have been avoided had the diabetic condition been open knowledge.

Select crew carefully. While it's relatively easy to find suitable crew among friends and acquaintances around home, it can be challenging in less familiar surroundings. Any crew selection should include a long personal conversation, preferably in person rather than in writing or on the phone. Discuss personal background, sailing experience and capabilities, education and special skills, food/dietary preferences and restrictions, physical fitness and health, and pet peeves/passions (e.g., loud music, personal hygiene). It is important to reach clear understanding on issues such as smoking and alcohol onboard, possession/use of illegal "recreational" drugs, any financial contribution expected, and post-passage expectations (fly home? stay aboard for how long? seek another crew slot?). Definitely obtain references to verify prior sailing experience, and check with those references.

Obviously, this is a time-consuming process that cannot be left until the last minute. The sooner the crew is identified, the better. That leaves time for crewmembers to become familiar with the boat and participate in final preparations. It also gives the skipper the opportunity to start training the crew.

One word of warning regarding crew selection: Beware the enthusiastic shore-side friends (worse yet, cousins and brothers-in-law) who assure you they'll be happy to go along as crew "any time you need me." They usually don't understand what they are getting into. Worse, they have a distressing habit of dropping out (unexpected business demands, spousal opposition, sick grandmother) at the last minute, leaving the skipper in the lurch. Unless you're confident these prospects are really committed to making the voyage, until the docklines are taken in, view them as "additional" crewmembers.

Training the crew. Training can make the difference between a smoothly running team and a collection of individuals working at cross-purposes. As a minimum, any crew needs to be trained in basic emergency drills and in the standard onboard procedures. Emergency drills include assigning specific responsibilities and practicing the planned response in the event of a crew overboard, a fire onboard, or flooding. Individual tasks and the steps to be followed if it becomes necessary to abandon ship must also be assigned and practiced. These emergency procedures should be posted where they can be reviewed frequently.

Standard procedures require training to insure consistency. They include boat maneuvers such as tacking and jibing, log keeping, watch standing and watch turnover procedures, monitoring weather forecasts, engine starting/shutdown, and personal safety measures such as crew overboard prevention, going aloft and galley safety. Standardizing the way to coil halyard and sheet tails, where to keep binoculars, bearing compass and winch handles, and other simple shipkeeping can prevent a normal procedure from causing frustration or worse.

The crew also needs training with respect to onboard living routines. Each member should know the boat's freshwater capacity and the need to conserve it. Habits such as leisurely daily showers and allowing the water to run while washing hands or brushing teeth must be left ashore. This applies even when the boat is equipped with a water-maker, since they are mechanical devices and vulnerable to failure (at the least convenient moments). It's a good idea to leave pressure pumps turned off at the circuit breaker during a passage. This will prevent inadvertently pumping a whole tank of water into the bilge if a hose pops loose or a fitting breaks. It will also encourage the crew to use the more economical hand pumps at galley and head sinks. If there are no manual pumps, the crew should be trained to turn the pressure pump on, use the minimum amount of water, then secure the pump. An excellent reward for effective water conservation is an occasional shower/shampoo en route.

The crew must be trained to be similarly stingy with electricity, staying constantly on guard for unnecessary use of lights and other electrically operated appliances. We all need to break habits acquired ashore, where unlimited electricity is available, and treat electrical power as another scarce resource.

Stowage and boat cleanliness also require some crew indoctrination. Observing "a place for everything, and everything in its place" and "don't put it down, put it back" will pay dividends. The cabin will be more livable. There will be fewer incidents of damage as a result of loose gear dropping off countertops. Harnesses, tools, etc. will be easier to find, and preparing the boat for rough weather will be much easier. Messiness tends to feed upon itself, and one piece of gear left on the cabin sole or chart table will soon be accompanied by three more, until clutter makes the simplest task difficult.

From the very beginning, it's important to set high standards of cleanliness, and everyone should help with daily cleaning of the boat. The galley and head merit special attention. Thorough cleanup in the galley after every meal should be the norm, with clear assignment of responsibility. Meal preparation is a major responsibility that directly influences crew morale, readiness and health. It often entails working in challenging and uncomfortable conditions, so when possible it's nice to compensate the cook by observing the rule "the cook never cleans up." Galley cleaning can be assigned to the off-going watch or, if cooking duties rotate, to the person responsible for the next meal (so he/she will know where things are stowed). Freshwater conservation in the cleanup process deserves emphasis. Try washing dishes in detergent and seawater, with a quick freshwater rinse (some use a water-filled spray bottle).

The head calls for special training. Everyone must know exactly how the toilet operates and understand the rules about putting solid objects in the bowl. Generally, aside from small pieces of toilet tissue, nothing should go into the toilet unless it's been eaten first. A single exception might be soapy dishwater, which can be flushed through to help clean out the plumbing. The rule "he who clogs it, cleans it" helps motivate careful operation. If the system employs a holding tank, crew must be aware of any limitations it places on the amount of water flushed through the toilet. If a macerator/chlorinator is installed, each crewmember must know how and when to operate it.

Daily head cleaning is essential to prevent foul odors. If the head smells bad, a thorough scrub, with a bleach solution, will usually cure it. Using seawater is OK, but a final wipe with fresh water is necessary to remove microscopic marine life. Don't forget to look outside the head vent for sources of aroma detected inside. We once scrubbed the head twice in an unsuccessful effort to eliminate a rank, fishy odor, only to discover it was coming from a flying fish on deck just outside the head port!

It's wise to establish rules for using the head. On a passage, I require that the head be used for all eliminations. The masculine habit of urinating over the side (sometimes described as trolling for mermaids) creates an unacceptably high risk of crew overboard. We've all heard stories about the high percentage of male drowning victims found with their fly open, and there's no sense giving them credence. Another good offshore practice is to observe the "Gentlemen, be seated!" convention. A rocking boat and a confined space are not the place to demonstrate marksmanship skills, because somebody will have to clean up the misses. Whenever the sea roughs up, it is safest to perform all functions from the seated position and minimize the cleaning chores.

Watchstanding. On a passage, you'll need to establish a crew watch system, to share both the work and the sleep. The duties of watchstanders will be addressed in greater depth (see Chapter 10), so the focus here is on organization. Many factors will influence your choice of watch system. The first are crew size and minimum watch size. If there are four aboard and it takes two people per watch, options are limited to a "port and starboard" system. More people or smaller watches permit three or more watches and increase alternatives. Another factor is the duration of the passage. If a voyage is only a few days, crewmembers can stand long watches with short rest periods. For longer trips, the watch schedule must provide everyone with adequate rest daily.

Individual preferences and skills play a role in organizing watches. A system that satisfies preferences, teams up compatible crew and spreads skills evenly among the watches makes for a happier, smoother-running boat. Since people have different sleep-wake patterns (morning people and night people), you'll want to assign watches that complement those traits. If possible, follow the crew's consensus on a fixed or rotating system. A fixed plan yields the same watch pattern each day, while a rotating one cycles watch assignments. If there aren't strong preferences, we recommend a fixed pattern (Figure 7.1 on next page). Most people adapt better to a system that keeps waking and sleeping patterns the same for at least four or five days in a row. Anticipated weather also plays a role. Cold, wet, stormy weather argues for shorter watches with more frequent relief to warm up or dry off. Settled, fair weather far from shore and traffic may allow smaller watch sections and/or longer watches.

The *Port and Starboard* system with all watches of equal length is the simplest. Most use three- or four-hour watches, which yield a nonrotating pattern. Its major drawback is the lack of a long off-watch rest period. Research suggests people work best if they have at least one unbroken rest of six or more hours daily. Some cruising skippers use six-hour cycles, but maintaining an acceptably high level of vigilance for the six hours on watch is extremely difficult.

The *Traditional* system uses three watch sections, with each standing four-hour watches. This produces a four-on, eight-off pattern that provides good rest periods for the off-watches. The pattern does not rotate, but it does if watches are reduced to three hours, giving a three-on, six-off routine.

The *Swedish* systems are variations that set watches of unequal length. They extend daytime watches to five or six hours while cutting night watches to two or three hours. The premise is that day watches are less stressful (off-watch crew are often awake and

Figure 7.1 - Fixed Watch Patterns

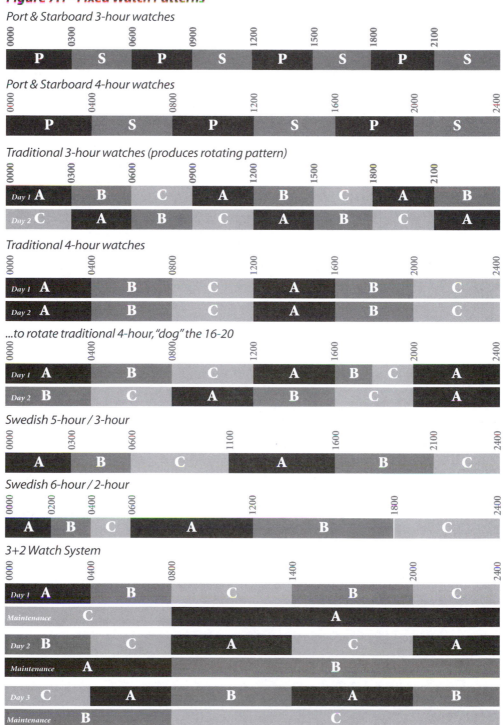

available) and night watches more demanding and difficult. Swedish systems can produce rotating or fixed patterns.

Overlapping watches require four or more sections, but a section can consist of just one person. This system uses two separate watch teams following the same watch pattern, but on different time schedules. The object is to have a new member, presumably fresh and rested, join the duty watch at the midpoint of each watch. Such a system also enhances watch-to-watch continuity.

A *Three and Two* system employs three watch sections, but on any given day only two sections stand watch, while the third performs shipkeeping duties. The active sections use a rotating port and starboard pattern. The shipkeeping section, which does chores such as meal preparation, boat cleanup and routine maintenance, changes daily. If the section transition occurs at 0700 or 0800, the shipkeeping section enjoys a night of uninterrupted sleep before it returns to the watch schedule.

Whichever system you select, it will be necessary to customize the plan to balance crew skills, match personal wake-sleep patterns, or compensate for unusual situations. The primary objective is a system to maintain on-watch alertness, while a secondary goal is to have the off-watch(es) ready to respond if the duty section needs help. If the crew is large enough, it may be possible to have "floaters" not assigned to a particular watch but available when needed. This role is suitable for a designated cook or navigator, whose duties may conflict with regular watches. Above all, the system must remain flexible so it can be adapted to circumstances. If the weather changes, if someone is injured or gets ill, if a critical repair job requires the undivided attention of a particular crewmember, be prepared to modify the watch plan until conditions return to normal. Morale may benefit from rotating the watch schedule after five or six days to change the crew assigned to the less popular watches (midnight until dawn).

Crew responsibilities. Quite apart from watchstanding, crewmembers should be allocated responsibility for maintaining the boat and equipment. One might be designated as engineer and charged with giving daily attention to power, machinery and propulsion systems. The engineer's duties would include daily engine checks (oil, coolant, fuel separator, stuffing box), determining battery charge needs and inspecting battery condition (connections, specific gravity readings for wet cells), checking through-hull fittings, testing bilge pumps, and generally looking after the boat's mechanical systems. While all watchstanders are involved in navigation, one crewmember should be the primary navigator, responsible for logs, recording positions and DRs on charts, obtaining celestial and electronic position data, and recommending course alterations to the skipper. The navigator often oversees collection and assessment of weather forecasts and observations. While cooking duties may be shared by all, someone ought to be designated as galley manager, charged with overseeing menu changes, keeping track of provisions, and ensuring that snacks are available for the watch (to preclude their rummaging through provision lockers). Another functional assignment is that of the boatswain (bosun, for short), who gives special attention to the standing and running rigging, winches, tackles, sails, lifelines, topside stowage and lashings, and crew overboard gear.

Allocating responsibilities shares the workload, decreases the likelihood that care of important equipment will be overlooked, and allows each crewmember to develop expertise in some area of boat operation. It's great to have each crewmember be a "jack of all trades," but it's also nice if each can serve as a "master of one."

Leadership. The vital role of leadership, mentioned in our chapter on the skipper, bears repeating, since leadership is the lubricant that keeps the crew running smoothly. It's not a trait reserved exclusively for the skipper, who cannot be present in the cockpit 24 hours a day, but must be exercised by other crewmembers as well. Whenever a task requires more than one, someone must act as the leader to coordinate and direct the activity. Each member of the crew must be prepared to lead if called upon. Each must also be a good follower, ready to be a willing cooperator.

Children. The presence of children as part of the crew deserves special mention, since passages are frequently made by families that include youngsters. Perhaps the most important issue is the additional safety precautions required to protect children at sea. Strong netting strung between lifelines and deck is advisable to prevent them from falling under or between the lifelines. This also will keep toys from going overboard, possibly endangering the child who tries to pursue them. Children definitely need their own PFDs, of proper size and fit, and they should be accustomed to wearing them whenever they are topside. Inherently buoyant PFDs are preferable to inflatables for younger children, who may not have the presence of mind to operate an inflation mechanism in a crisis. Automatic inflation devices, while highly reliable, have a small but finite failure rate, and are of doubtful suitability for young crewmembers. Older children, especially those used to swimming, may find the inflatable type more comfortable. A youthful crew's transition from inherently buoyant to inflatable PFD can be a rite of passage, accompanying an increased role on the boat and greater watch standing responsibilities.

Consideration must be given to sleeping sites for children. They need less room than an adult, so a normal bunk is often too big to provide adequate security. Children need a small, well protected sleeping area, with high, strong lee cloths to keep them in place despite boat motion. It's usually advisable to provide a similarly well protected place for children to play, especially when the weather kicks up, making youthful movement in the cabin risky and perhaps precluding their presence topside.

As they grow older, children should be incorporated into daily activities, with defined duties consistent with their capabilities. They can share watch duties such as steering, checking sail trim and keeping a lookout, but young attention spans may be short, so supervision is necessary until they have proven their reliability. Recording log data, making boat checks, responding to radio calls and assisting in repair and maintenance activity (by passing tools or holding parts) are other activities that give the young a sense of usefulness and belonging to the crew.

Emergency plans must also give explicit consideration to children. There should be special plans for taking care of those too young to be of assistance, while those able to help should be assigned clear responsibilities and taught how to perform them. A regular, periodic review of emergency plans and practice of emergency procedures is always advisable, but with children it's even more important. Frequent practice sessions will greatly reduce the likelihood of panic in the child should an emergency occur.

When children are part of the crew, provisions for their education will be necessary. Making a long passage does not mean suspension of formal education, and it often creates opportunities to enrich that education well beyond shore-based bounds. With the growth of interest in home schooling, more resources are available today to help parents teach their children. Correspondence programs offer outstanding plans for keeping seagoing children up with those ashore. Programs from the Calvert School are well known for elementary school levels, while Brigham Young University offers a fine program at the high school level.

Fulfilling education obligations will demand a high level of commitment and discipline, with certain hours set aside each day for school. It will be difficult to resist the temptation to declare frequent days off because some other boat activity competes with school for the children's interest, but the duty to teach and to learn on a regular basis must be kept sacrosanct. At the same time, the onboard educational program should allow the teacher to take advantage of special opportunities. Practical applications of math and trig used in navigation can spice up a difficult subject. Visiting new ports provides first-hand observation of different cultures and opportunities to develop language skills. Encountering the rich marine life found on the beach or in tide pools can add interest to science studies. Exploiting these situations requires preparation well before the cruise begins, for space must be found for a reference library to support learning: texts on marine plants and animals, foreign language dictionaries and tapes, perhaps even a computer-based encyclopedia.

For reasons well beyond the scope of this book, as children reach the teenage years life usually becomes difficult. Their struggle to cope with the physical and emotional changes that come with maturing affect all around them. In a passagemaking environment, with its frequent disruption of friendships and periods of social isolation, the challenges for both teens and adults are multiplied. Living with teenagers can be a trial; cruising with them can be an ordeal. Adults must work extra hard to keep communication open, to give credence to the views of the youngsters, and to compromise on noncritical issues that allow the teen an outlet for exercising independence. Many cruising parents have found it easier to get willing participation if the teenager has been allowed a real role in planning the voyage, creating an interest in its success.

Pets. While it is something of a stretch to include them in a chapter about crew, a few observations about pets are in order. For many cruising folk, pets really are part of the crew, providers of emotional companionship and support equivalent to (and in some cases more reliable than) that offered by fellow humans. They can also form an integral part of the boat's security system. Pets' sense of hearing and smell are often much more acute than that of their owners, and they can detect changes in ambient levels before the human crew does. They can alert their owners to smoke, unusual noises or the presence of other people before changes are apparent to the rest of the crew. Cats, with their instinctive hunting skills, can provide protection from rodents. Dogs can be a deterrent to intrusion if their bark is loud enough or deep enough.

Like children, pets require special attention to safety and care afloat. Measures to prevent pet overboard must be developed, and plans for recovering a pet overboard merit careful thought and practice. There are PFDs for pets, often fitted with a handle or attachment point for a lifting device to assist in recovery. Pet sanitation and hygiene deserve attention. Whether trained to use artificial turf in the cockpit or the foredeck, or a litter box tucked away in a secure corner of the cabin, the pets' toilet needs must be accommodated. Since boats provide the warm, moist environment in which fleas thrive, flea prevention/control is essential for healthy pets and happy owners. And don't forget to talk with a veterinarian about items needed for pet medical care in case of illness or injury.

Just as the two-legged crew must have passports and the vessel must have documentation to enter a foreign port, pets must have veterinary certifications to prove they are rabies-free and properly inoculated. Nevertheless, many ports will place restrictions on pets, ranging from absolute prohibition in some places to mandatory (and expensive) quarantine ashore in others. Honor-based voluntary quarantine onboard seems to be a common form of low-level control. Always determine the admissibility of pets before selecting the destination. Otherwise, you may be forced to choose between surrendering a beloved friend and going back to sea, probably without adequate preparation, to find a more hospitable port. This information is available from government representatives (consuls, embassies, port authorities) and from fellow cruising sailors. High frequency radio nets can be an excellent source for this type of information.

If the first strategy for success in passagemaking is to select a seaworthy boat and outfit it sensibly, the second is to select the crew carefully and train it well. The number of crew should be:
- large enough to share the load but small enough to fit the boat comfortably
- compatible, cooperative, physically and emotionally fit for daily routines
- organized to run the boat in all conditions, on a continuous basis
- prepared to accommodate the special requirements of children and pets.

With a sound ship, a capable captain and a good crew, all the building blocks for a successful passage are present. It's time to turn attention to the ways in which those three components work together to get from the departure point to the destination safely, comfortably and with reasonable speed.

CHAPTER 8

NAVIGATION STRATEGY

A successful voyage begins with a sound plan. One key part of that plan is navigation: when to go, what route to take and how to track your position along the way.

Passage timing is usually determined by seasonal weather. In the western Atlantic, long passages are best planned for the fall period between the end of the hurricane season (late October) and the onset of winter storms (mid-late November) or the spring period when winter storms are waning yet the hurricane threat is low (late April through June). Other waters have seasonal "weather windows" that offer the best opportunities for a storm-free passage. Good sources for the best times and preferred routes for a passage are *World Cruising Routes* and *Ocean Passages for the World* (see REFERENCES at end of this chapter.)

Selecting the route. Sailing routes (rather than being the straight line a power-boat would choose) are modified to make best use of prevailing winds and to avoid extended windward work. Consider the routes frequented by boats cruising between the US east coast and the Caribbean. Southbound in the fall, they head offshore toward and past Bermuda (32° 23'N, 64° 36'W), using the prevailing westerlies to make easting. They continue to or beyond 65° West longitude, then take a more southerly heading, still edging eastward another degree or two. The goal is to get far enough east that when the trade winds fill in (26°-24° North), they will not force the boat to sail close-hauled, even if the trades are a bit south of their usual easterly direction. Coming northward in the spring, voyagers heading for the mid-Atlantic coast use the trades to gain westing as they travel northwestward, roughly parallel to the Bahamas. They then steer northward off the east coast when they reach the westerlies. Boats heading to New England often use Bermuda as a convenient way station. These boats reach across the trades on a northerly course to Bermuda, waiting there for favorable weather for the onward passage.

Major currents. Any route must take into account the major ocean currents. The Gulf Stream plays a dominant role in both routes noted above. Boats heading south from New England must plan their track and navigate with care to avoid contrary-flowing meanders of the Stream. They may depart from the "normal" track to get boosted by a favorable meander. Boats departing from mid-Atlantic ports have less chance of encountering meanders, since the Stream's flow is swift and fairly straight until after it has been deflected northeast by the Hatteras banks. For these boats, the objective is to get across the Stream as quickly as possible. To do so, they head for the area where the latest observations show it is relatively narrow. The presence of eddies (rotating pools of water spun off by the Gulf Stream) will also influence the planned route. Clockwise-rotating warm-core eddies lie north and west of the Stream, while counterclockwise-rotating cold eddies are south and east of it. Encountering the favorable side of an eddy can boost the boat's progress, while running into the wrong side can seriously impede it.

Major ocean currents such as the Gulf Stream are significant for more than their ability to increase or decrease the boat's speed over the ground. Because the temperature of the moving water often differs markedly from that of the adjacent waters (warmer in the Gulf Stream), they tend to spawn intense local weather phenomena. These range from thunderstorms and sudden wind shifts over warm water to persistent dense fog over cold currents. A key factor will be the interaction of ocean current and wind direction and the resulting effect on sea state. When the wind blows counter to the current, surface waves build much more quickly than they would on still water. They develop a characteristic "square" shape: the waves are high, steep and close together with wave faces seemingly approaching vertical. Sailing in such a sea places tremendous stress on boat and crew. Make every effort to avoid these conditions. This situation is a particular risk for boats heading from the Caribbean to the central US east coast. Having made westing with the trades, it is very tempting to plan to "ride the Stream" as it sweeps northward off the Florida, Georgia and Carolina coasts. As the boat approaches the Stream, it will be 7-8 days into its passage and its initial weather forecast will have grown stale. If an unanticipated frontal system moves off the coast and swings the wind around to the north or northeast, the Stream will quickly become very inhospitable. The only alternatives are to beat northward while staying east of the Stream (not pleasant if winds are stiff), heave to and wait for improving conditions, or to seek shelter in the northern Bahamas.

Ocean currents such as the Gulf Stream can influence the choice of departure point and destination. Consider the choice between heading for the Caribbean from the mouth of Chesapeake Bay or doing so from the Beaufort/Morehead City area of North Carolina. At first glance, the latter site appears attractive. Since it is south of the Hatteras Banks, whose reputation for foul weather and rough seas is well established, it would avoid any need to sail across the shoals on the passage south. A closer look at the chart reveals that from either point, the track goes almost directly offshore, on a heading just south of east. Departing from the Chesapeake does not require one to "cross" the banks. More important is what the Gulf Stream would do if conditions were to turn bad shortly after departure. A boat leaving from the Chesapeake would be swept away from Hatteras by the current. One sailing from North Carolina would be carried directly toward the waters it was seeking to avoid. Similar study of current effects can impact the choice of a destination. Following the northbound route discussed earlier, the track does cut across the Hatteras shoals. It may therefore prove prudent to go "inside" at Beaufort and follow the Intracoastal Waterway north to the Chesapeake.

Alternate destinations. Another element of any good voyage plan is the selection of alternate destinations. For some reason it may prove impossible or undesirable to continue to the intended destination. Other options should be identified before departure and the boat equipped to pursue them (charts, tide and current data, port information). Using the east coast situation again, when heading to the Caribbean it would be prudent to have charts and data for Bermuda as well as the Bahamas and major entry points along the east coast, such as Chesapeake Bay, Wilmington and Charleston. *Reed's Nautical Almanac* is a particularly helpful information source for such alternate destinations.

Electronic systems. There's no doubt that the trend in contemporary navigation is dominated by electronic systems. While LORAN has given navigators excellent service for decades, it suffers from significant shortcomings. On the average, its accuracy is perfectly adequate for general navigation, although it remains suspect in areas where TD lines cross at shallow angles. It is vulnerable to interference generated by atmospheric disturbances such as thunderstorms and, in American waters at least, budgetary constraints are making its future uncertain. For the passagemaker, LORAN's greatest drawback is its limited range and the lack of coverage of many cruising grounds such as the Caribbean.

The Global Positioning System (GPS) has become the navigation system of choice. With high accuracy, continuous worldwide availability and low susceptibility to interference, it gives access to instant position information. Despite the random errors inserted in the system by the Department of Defense when "selective availability" is in effect, GPS provides the passagemaker with an adequately accurate position in all but the rarest instances. In terms of absolute accuracy with reference to the equator and the Greenwich meridian, GPS is often more accurate than our charts. Those documents are often based on data collected long ago, when positions were far less certain. But good as it is, GPS still has an Achilles' heel: it requires a power supply to operate the receiver. Like all the electronic gear that crowds most navigation stations today, GPS units are also vulnerable to moisture and corrosion that can interrupt their internal circuitry, and they can receive fatal damage from physical impacts and from overwhelming power surges created by lightning strikes and near-misses.

Take backup GPS units! In view of all this, the prudent voyager carries more than one GPS receiver and provides a redundant power supply. With the price of portable units dropping well below the $150 level, it has become economically feasible to have two or three backup GPS units ready in case the primary receiver fails.

These portables, along with an abundant supply of batteries, can provide a high level of comfort for the navigator.

Radar. Other electronic systems are growing increasingly common in the nav station. Radar can be exceedingly useful – especially in low visibility – for avoiding other vessels and for navigating close to a coast. It takes training and experience to use radar effectively. The set must be tuned and the controls (range scale, gain, sea return, etc.) adjusted for best results. Watchstanders should take advantage of opportunities in good visibility to track approaching ships on radar. This allows them to become skilled at calculating closest point of approach, determining course and speed, and selecting the best action to avoid risk of collision. Using radar for coastal navigation in good weather will provide experience in interpreting radar images and correlating them with charted features, experience that will prove valuable when darkness, haze or rain precludes reliable visual navigation.

"Gee whiz!" – and "Oops!" It's becoming increasingly popular to "integrate" the electronic installation, especially when combined with a computer to provide a single display that presents positioning data from the GPS and/or LORAN, superimposed on an electronic chart, possibly augmented by radar images. It's a simple matter to link the autopilot to the GPS and allow the electronically derived positions to determine the course to the next waypoint. All this is "Gee whiz!" stuff, but when boats start operating without any human intervention it is also scary. Not long ago, a large cruise ship went aground because no one noticed that the GPS was not getting good signals. The electronic system, assuming the ship was continuing to make its old course and speed, allowed it to steam into shoal water. As alluded to in Chapter 3, more than one vessel has come to grief because the electronics guiding it from Waypoint A to Waypoint C were ignorant of the fact that the straight line between those points crossed shoals, dry land or stone breakwaters. While "integrated" systems may be able to reduce navigation to a matter of pushing a few buttons every now and then, the prudent voyager will always incorporate human judgment into the process, to make sure output from the magic black boxes makes sense.

Celestial – no plug to be pulled. No matter how reliable the electronics, it's wise to have manual navigation backups. Passagemakers are well advised to have celestial navigation as part of their bag of tricks. This means carrying a sextant and knowing how to use it. It also requires a reliable timepiece and the sight reduction tables needed to convert an observation to a line of position. The beauty of celestial navigation is that while Mother Nature may interfere by causing cloud cover, no government agency can pull the plug on the sun, moon, planets and stars. As long as two or more of them are visible above a clear horizon, the navigator can get a good position. The traditional navigator began the day by obtaining a fix from stars at morning twilight, then took a forenoon sun line and advanced it to cross a latitude line computed from a Local Apparent Noon sight to get a running fix at midday. An afternoon sun line produced yet another running fix, and stars at twilight yielded an evening fix. With all that practice, it was easy to maintain proficiency. Few passagemakers follow such an intensive routine today, but to maintain proficiency, the navigator should try to take, reduce and plot at least one celestial observation every day. Using calculators or computers to work out the sights certainly makes celestial navigation quicker and eliminates many simple arithmetic and tabular entry errors that creep into the manual process. These devices are, however, prone to failure for the same reason as other electronics, so occasionally solving an observation with pencil and paper is advisable.

Dead reckoning. If all else fails, the navigator can fall back on dead reckoning (DR): plotting the course steered and the distance traveled since the last fix. Supplemented by careful estimates of known errors such as current and leeway, a meticulous DR plot can still enable the navigator to find the destination. To maintain a DR plot, the navigator must know what course has actually been steered, when course has been changed, and either the distance the boat has traveled or the speed it has made through the water. The implications for the watch standers who keep the boat's logs are obvious. A good DR track requires a good log, with accurate periodic entries of course, speed and/or distance.

Other helps. Remember to make use of natural signs that point toward the destination. Shore birds have an established pattern of flying to sea from their island home in the morning and returning at nightfall, giving clues to the island's location. Several phenomena (unequal heating of land and sea, cooling of moist air thrust upward by an island's elevation) cause clouds to form and hover above islands. These relatively motionless clouds can be seen far sooner than the island itself. At night, the loom of city lights can be seen for a long distance at sea. Ship and aircraft traffic patterns also suggest island locations. Any cruise ship near Bermuda, for example, can be assumed to be headed toward or away from the island, as can any low flying airplane.

Merchant ships can provide navigational support if approached properly. When a ship will pass within a few miles, use your very best, professional radio technique to call on VHF channel 16. (*"This is the white sailing vessel* Exemplar *calling the southbound container ship at about 29°30' North, 65° West."*) Allow plenty of time for them to find an English-speaking officer to reply. When contact is established, engage in some general conversation (*"We are en route from Norfolk to Tortola, Captain, where are you bound?" "How far away were you able to pick me up on your radar?" "Do you have a current weather forecast for this area?"*) and then ask him to "confirm" your position. Don't forget to conclude by wishing him a pleasant voyage. Steve Black has dubbed this position finding technique "Chat Nav."

Charts and publications. While electronic charts are growing in popularity and their convenience is undeniable, having an adequate stock of paper charts and hard copies of navigational publications is still the choice of the prudent navigator. Though it's practically impossible to keep all charts up to date, you'll want to establish certain minimum standards. Charts should always be the current edition, and Notices to Mariners should be reviewed regularly for changes significant to your boat and plans. (A changed light characteristic is probably important enough to note on the chart; a shoal with 20' of water over it probably isn't.) Give special attention to charts that will be used for landfalls and to harbor charts where details can be crucial. Do carry adequate charts to make a safe landfall and entry into alternate ports in addition to those for your intended destination.

In addition to the materials mentioned in the nav station inspection (Chapter 4), the navigator's library should include a copy of COLREGS (required by law aboard any vessel over 12 meters in length), an emergency handbook, a weather guide, navigation texts, and general seamanship references such as those cited at the end of this chapter. If there is radar aboard, the *Radar Navigation Manual* is worth having, as are several pads of Maneuvering Boards (DMA Stock No. WOBZP5090) for radar plotting. Despite their small scale, Universal Plotting Sheets (formerly DMA Stock No. VPOSX001, now published privately by Celestaire) are handy for plotting celestial lines and running DR tracks. Periodic positions transferred from these sheets to a major ocean chart will provide the crew with a geographic orientation and a sense of progress being made.

How much navigating is enough? In the absence of a full-time navigator who can maintain a continuous plot, how much navigation does a GPS-equipped passagemaker really need to do? While in coastal waters at the start and end of a journey, navigation needs to be every bit as careful and continuous as for a coastal passage, with fix frequency driven by the proximity of dangers: perhaps every 10-15 minutes, perhaps hourly. A DR at 15-minute intervals should suffice between fixes. Settling into an offshore mode, the time between fixes and DR updates can be stretched out.

One favorite routine. A voyaging navigation routine I've used with success is based on taking and recording a GPS position at 6-hour intervals (00, 06, 12 and 18 hours on the 24-hour clock). These positions are plotted on the master chart for comparison with our planned track and our projected progress, and on a UPS sheet, where they are compared to the DR plot. The DR track on the UPS is updated by the watch at two-hour intervals based on course and distance data in the logbook. If current or other influences (for which we strive to identify a reason) cause the DR and GPS positions to diverge by more than about 10 miles, we will start a new DR once a day, generally from the 0600 position. If the two plots stay fairly close together, we continue the old DR. Celestial observations are worked out and plotted on the UPS to check their consistency with the DR and GPS – partly as a way of assessing the accuracy of our celestial efforts. On the GPS, we rarely use more than a few waypoints to define a planned track (point of departure, 1-2 midcourse points and an offshore aiming point well clear of hazards near the destination). We seldom find it necessary to stay right on the planned track or pass through a particular point, but we keep an eye on the GPS cross-track error to avoid getting too far from our intended path. The GPS readouts of speed over the ground and course made good are monitored for early indications that we're being set by currents. We use the autopilot most of the time offshore, but never link it directly to the GPS. As we approach the destination aiming point, we shift back into the coastal navigation mode, with more frequent fixes and DRs as we head directly for the destination.

A navigation strategy that contributes to a successful passage thus includes a carefully developed voyage plan, adequate outfitting with navigational equipment, charts and publications, cultivating navigation skills, and establishing a routine that exploits all available information to provide a continuous, reliable record of the boat's position and progress toward the destination.

REFERENCES:

Jimmy Cornell, *World Cruising Routes;* The Hydrographer of the Navy, *Ocean Passages for the World*

Tony Meisel, *Nautical Emergencies*

William P. Crawford, *Mariner's Weather*

David Burch, *Emergency Navigation*

Bruce Bauer, *The Sextant Handbook* (Revised edition)

Elbert Maloney, *Chapman's Seamanship and Small Boat Handling*

William G. Van Dorn, *Oceanography and Seamanship*

Adlard Coles, *Heavy Weather Sailing* (Revised edition)

Defense Mapping Agency Hydrographic/Topographic Center, *Radar Navigation Manual,* Publication 1310

CHAPTER 9

COMMUNICATIONS

Modern communications give today's voyager a huge advantage. While the passagemaking yacht is still very much on its own, it no longer need be isolated from the world. Radio links enable the voyager to get information, guidance and help from many sources, a number of which were unavailable a decade ago. Good use of communications can add measurably to the safety and comfort of the passage.

A few hardy souls still make long voyages without radio transmitters, but only the most determined traditionalist would go without a receiver to get weather forecasts. To seek such "independence from shore-based support" is foolhardy. No boat should set out on a long passage without basic communication equipment and the ability to use it effectively. This outfit should include both Very High Frequency (VHF) and Medium/High Frequency (MF/HF) radio transceivers (single units that alternate function between transmitter and receiver).

VHF: rules, channels, procedures. Like many commercial broadcast stations, marine VHF radios employ the frequency modulation (FM) mode of transmission to minimize noise, static and interference. They operate on a set of fixed frequencies or channels in the 156-163 MHz range. At these frequencies, radio transmissions travel nearly in a straight line, with little bending to conform to the curvature of the earth. As a result, the distance at which they can be received is determined by the height of the transmitting and receiving antennas (Figure 9.1). Shore stations such as those operated

Figure 9.1 - The "Radio Horizon"

Vessel A's signal will reach tower C, but will pass above the antenna on vessel B.

Radio Horizon (in nautical miles) = 1.22 $\sqrt{\text{antenna height in feet}}$

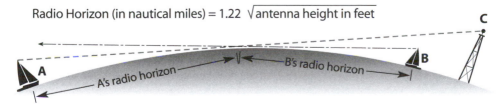

by the U.S. Coast Guard use antennas mounted on high coastal towers to produce signals receivable at distances of 50+ miles, but most VHF radio communication takes place at much shorter distances. Typically, ship-to-ship VHF radiotelephone traffic is limited to stations within about 15 miles of one another.

Neither Coast Guard nor Federal Communications Commission (FCC) rules require boats to be equipped with a VHF radio. A notable exception is that any vessel with an MF/HF radio installed for long-distance communications must have a VHF radio for use over shorter ranges. USCG safety regulations require all VHF-equipped vessels to maintain a watch on Channel 16, the distress frequency, whenever the radio is operating. A 1992 change to the Vessel Bridge-to-Bridge Radiotelephone Regulations also requires all power-driven vessels (this includes a sailboat under power) over 20 meters (65.5') to maintain a continuous watch on Channel 13, the Ship to Ship Navigation channel. A single radio, operating in a "dual watch" mode shifting between Channels 16 and 13, does not satisfy these requirements. If a boat is over 20 meters long, it is required to carry two separate VHF transceivers when operating in US waters.

As reflected in the accompanying tables, VHF radio channels have been assigned specific purposes by international agreement and domestic law (Figure 9.2). Some training is needed to ensure proper channel selection for any VHF communication. The operator must know which channels are authorized for the particular traffic to be sent or received. It is improper, for example, to use Channel 6 for non-safety communications, or Channel 67 to talk to a shore station. Note, too, that some internationally designated channels (such as 12, 22, and 24-28) operate in the duplex mode. In this format, the ship transmits on one frequency and receives on a different one. These channels are generally usable only for traffic with shore stations that can receive on the ship's transmitting frequency and transmit on the ship's receiving frequency. Other channels (such as 6, 13 and 16) operate in the simplex mode, using a single frequency for both transmitting and receiving.

Within the US, supplementary channels (designated by the suffix "A" after the channel number) operate in the simplex mode using the international channel's "ship transmit" frequency. (Thus the Coast Guard's working Channel 22A operates in the simplex mode on 157.100 MHz, the "ship transmit" side of International Channel 22.) Some radios include these US-only channels as separate channels on the selection menu. Others have a "US-International" switch to shift between the international (duplex) and US (simplex) versions of these channels.

Effective communication requires not only proper choice of channels, but also use of proper procedures, especially in coastal waters where high traffic levels keep frequencies full of signals. Make contact with another vessel on Channel 16 and promptly shift to a working channel (for most noncommercial craft, Channels 68, 69, 71 or 72). In some US coastal areas, the Coast Guard has prescribed Channel 9 for call-up, with Channel 16 reserved exclusively for emergency or distress. Once a boat is well offshore (100 miles or so), very little traffic will be encountered on the VHF radio. Although it is still correct to change to a working frequency, more liberal use of

Figure 9.2 - Designated VHF Radio Channels

UNITED STATES

Chan-nel	Frequency (MHz) Transmit	Receive	Traffic Type	Ship to Ship	Ship to Shore
WX 1		162.550	NOAA Weather	No	Rcv Only
WX 2		162.400	NOAA Weather	No	Rcv Only
WX 3		162.475	NOAA Weather	No	Rcv Only
WX 4		162.425	NOAA Weather	No	Rcv Only
WX 5		162.450	NOAA Weather	No	Rcv Only
WX 6		162.500	NOAA Weather	No	Rcv Only
WX 7		162.525	NOAA Weather	No	Rcv Only
WX 8		161.650	Canada Weather	No	Rcv Only
WX 9		161.775	Canada Weather	No	Rcv Only
WX 10		163.275	NOAA Weather	No	Rcv Only
01	156.050	156.050	Commercial, Port Operations, VTS	Yes	Yes
03	156.150	156.150	Commercial, Port Operations, VTS	Yes	Yes
05	156.250	156.250	Port Operations, VTS	Yes	Yes
06	156.300	156.300	Safety	Yes	No
07	156.350	156.350	Commercial	Yes	Yes
08	156.400	156.400	Commercial	Yes	No
09	156.450	156.450	Commercial & Noncommercial	Yes	Yes
10	156.500	156.500	Commercial	Yes	Yes
11	156.550	156.550	Commercial, VTS	Yes	Yes
12	156.600	156.600	Port Operations, VTS	Yes	Yes
13	156.650	156.650	Navigational (Low Power)	Yes	No
14	156.700	156.700	Port Operations	Yes	Yes
15	Rcv Only	156.750	Environmental		Rcv Only
16	156.800	156.800	Distress, Safety, Calling	Yes	Yes
17	156.850	156.850	State Controlled (Low Power)	Yes	Yes
18	156.900	156.900	Commercial	Yes	Yes
19	156.950	156.950	Commercial	Yes	Yes
20	157.00	157.00	Port Operations	Yes	Yes
21	157.050	157.050	U.S. Government Only	Yes	Yes
22	157.100	157.100	Coast Guard	Yes	Yes
23	157.150	157.150	U.S. Government Only	Yes	Yes

Chan-nel	Frequency (MHz) Transmit	Receive	Traffic Type	Ship to Ship	Ship to Shore
24	157.200	161.800	Public Correspondence (Marine Operator)	No	Yes
25	157.250	161.850	Public Correspondence (Marine Operator)	No	Yes
26	157.300	161.900	Public Correspondence (Marine Operator)	No	Yes
27	157.350	161.950	Public Correspondence (Marine Operator)	No	Yes
28	157.400	162.000	Public Correspondence (Marine Operator)	No	Yes
65	156.275	156.275	Port Operations	No	Yes
66	156.325	156.325	Port Operations	Yes	Yes
67	156.375	156.375	Commercial (Low Power)	Yes	No
68	156.425	156.425	Noncommercial	Yes	Yes
69	156.475	156.475	Noncommercial	Yes	Yes
70	156.525	156.525	Reserved for Digital Selective Calling Service		
71	156.575	156.575	Noncommercial	Yes	Yes
72	156.625	156.625	Noncommercial	Yes	No
73	156.675	156.675	Port Operations	Yes	Yes
74	156.725	156.725	Port Operations	Yes	Yes
77	156.875	156.875	Port Operations	Yes	No
78	156.925	156.925	Noncommercial	Yes	Yes
79	156.975	156.975	Commercial	Yes	Yes
80	157.025	157.025	Commercial	Yes	Yes
81	157.075	157.075	U.S. Government Only	Yes	Yes
82	157.125	157.125	U.S. Government Only	Yes	Yes
83	157.175	157.175	U.S. Government Only	Yes	Yes
84	157.225	161.825	Public Correspondence (Marine Operator)	No	Yes
85	157.275	161.875	Public Correspondence (Marine Operator)	No	Yes
86	157.325	161.925	Public Correspondence (Marine Operator)	No	Yes
87	157.375	161.975	Public Correspondence (Marine Operator)	No	Yes
88	157.425	157.425	Commercial	Yes	No

INTERNATIONAL

Chan-nel	Frequency (MHz) Transmit	Receive	Traffic Type	Ship to Ship	Ship to Shore
WX 1		162.550	NOAA Weather		Rcv Only
WX 2		162.400	NOAA Weather		Rcv Only
WX 3		162.475	NOAA Weather		Rcv Only
WX 4		162.425	NOAA Weather		Rcv Only
WX 5		162.450	NOAA Weather		Rcv Only

Channel	Frequency (MHz) Transmit	Receive	Traffic Type	Ship to Ship	Ship to Shore
WX 6		162.500	NOAA Weather		Rcv Only
WX 7		162.525	NOAA Weather		Rcv Only
WX 8		161.650	Canadian Weather		Rcv Only
WX 9		161.775	Canadian Weather		Rcv Only
WX 10		163.275	NOAA Weather		Rcv Only
01	156.050	160.650	Commercial, Port Operations, VTS	Yes	Yes
02	156.100	160.700	Port Operations	Yes	Yes
03	156.150	160.750	Commercial, Port Operations, VTS	Yes	Yes
04	156.200	160.800	Port Operations	Yes	Yes
05	156.250	160.850	Port Operations, VTS	Yes	Yes
06	156.300	156.300	Safety	Yes	No
07	156.350	160.950	Commercial	Yes	Yes
08	156.400	156.400	Commercial	Yes	Yes
09	156.450	156.450	Commercial & Noncommercial	Yes	Yes
10	156.500	156.500	Commercial	Yes	Yes
11	156.550	156.550	Commercial, VTS	Yes	Yes
12	156.600	156.600	Port Operations, VTS	Yes	Yes
13	156.650	156.650	Navigational (Low Power)	Yes	Yes
14	156.700	156.700	Port Operations, VTS	Yes	No
15	156.750	156.750	Environmental	Yes	Yes
16	156.800	156.800	Distress, Safety, Calling	Yes	Yes
17	156.850	156.850	State Control	Yes	Yes
18	156.900	161.500	Commercial, Public Correspondence	Yes	Yes
19	156.950	161.550	Commercial, Public Correspondence	Yes	Yes
20	157.000	161.600	Port Operations, Public Correspondence	No	Yes
21	157.050	161.650	Government, Public Correspondence	Yes	Yes
22	157.100	161.700	Government, Public Correspondence	Yes	Yes
23	157.150	161.750	Government, Public Correspondence	Yes	Yes
24	157.200	161.800	Public Correspondence	No	Yes
25	157.250	161.850	Public Correspondence	No	Yes
26	157.300	161.900	Public Correspondence	No	Yes
27	157.350	161.950	Public Correspondence	No	Yes
28	157.400	162.000	Public Correspondence	No	Yes

Chan- nel	Frequency (MHz) Transmit	Receive	Traffic Type	Ship to Ship	Ship to Shore
60	156.025	160.625	Public Correspondence		
61	156.075	160.675	Public Correspondence		
62	156.125	160.725	Public Correspondence		
63	156.175	160.775	Public Correspondence		
64	156.225	160.825	Public Correspondence		
65	156.275	160.875	Port Operations	Yes	Yes
66	156.325	160.925	Port Operations	Yes	Yes
67	156.375	156.375	Commercial	Yes	No
68	156.425	156.425	Noncommercial	Yes	Yes
69	156.475	156.475	Noncommercial	Yes	Yes
70		156.525	Reserved for Digital Selective Calling Serv.	Yes	No
71	156.575	156.575	Noncommercial	Yes	Yes
72	156.625	156.625	Noncommercial	Yes	No
73	156.675	156.675	Port Operations	Yes	Yes
74	156.725	156.725	Port Operations	Yes	Yes
77	156.875	156.875	Port Operations	Yes	No
78	156.925	161.525	Noncommercial	Yes	Yes
79	156.975	161.575	Commercial	Yes	Yes
80	157.025	161.625	Commercial	Yes	Yes
81	157.075	161.675	Government	Yes	Yes
82	157.125	161.725	Government	Yes	Yes
83	157.175	161.775	Government	Yes	Yes
84	157.225	161.825	Public Correspondence	No	Yes
85	157.275	161.875	Public Correspondence	No	Yes
86	157.325	161.925	Public Correspondence	No	Yes
87	157.375	161.975	Not Assigned	No	Yes
88	157.425	162.025	Not Assigned	No	Yes

Pending Approval for International Use:

75	156.775		Not Assigned		
76	156.825		Not Assigned		
AIS-1	161.975	161.975	Automatic Ship Identification/Surveillance System		
AIS-2	162.025	162.025	Automatic Ship Identification/Surveillance System		

Channel 16 for very brief conversations is common.

Every member of the crew should know how to operate the VHF radio and how to communicate correctly. As a minimum, they should know how to call another vessel, how to choose and shift to the proper channel, and how to end a transmission. Everyone should also know how to send emergency messages and understand the distinctly different purposes served by "Mayday," "Pan," and "Securite" transmissions.

Technically correct call-up:
"[Name or description of vessel being called, often repeated] this is [name of your vessel] [your vessel's call sign], over."
Examples:
"EXEMPLAR, EXEMPLAR, this is CORONA, WX9876, over."
"Southbound merchant ship off Sawyer's Point, this is the sailing vessel CORONA, WX9876, one half mile on your starboard beam, over."

Informal call, often used when vessels are nearby or know each other well:
"[Name of vessel being called, often repeated] this is [name of your vessel], over."
Example:
"EXEMPLAR, EXEMPLAR this is CORONA, over."
Ending a transmission:
"Over" means "I have completed my transmission and am awaiting a reply."
"Out" means "I have completed my transmission and no reply is expected" (conversation is finished).
Always end with either "Over" or "Out". Never use both.

Emergency message purposes and format:
A **Mayday** call is limited to situations in which there is grave and imminent danger to a ship or person and immediate assistance is required. Following is the proper format for Mayday calls on 2182 KHz or VHF Channel 16:
Transmit alarm signal for 30-60 seconds if so equipped
"Mayday... Mayday... Mayday,
This is: BOAT'S NAME (3 times)
Mayday
• NAME OF VESSEL and CALL SIGN
• POSITION OF VESSEL
• NUMBER OF CREW
• NATURE OF EMERGENCY AND ASSISTANCE REQUIRED
• FURTHER INFORMATION TO ASSIST RESCUERS
Over."

A **Pan-Pan** (Pahn-Pahn) signal is used for a very urgent message concerning the safety of the ship or some person aboard or in sight. It does not imply that the vessel itself is in immediate danger. Following is proper format for a Pan-Pan transmission on 2182 KHz or VHF Channel 16:

> *"Pan-Pan... Pan-Pan... Pan-Pan,*
> *All stations..."* (or name of station/vessel from which assistance is requested)
> *This is BOAT'S NAME (3 times) and CALL SIGN*
> • *STATEMENT OF THE URGENCY SITUATION and ASSISTANCE DESIRED,*
>   *POSITION AND DESCRIPTION OF VESSEL*
>   *This is BOAT'S NAME and CALL SIGN, over."*

A **Securite** (Say-curi-tay) signal warns of a safety, meteorological or navigation situation that could be a hazard to other vessels. Following is proper format for a Securite message on 2182 KHz or VHF Channel 16:

> *"Securite... Securite... Securite...,*
> *All stations,"* (OR SPECIFIC ADDRESSEE)
> *This is BOAT'S NAME and CALL SIGN.*
> • *LISTEN CHANNEL ##* (working channel or frequency on which safety message will be given)
> • *BOAT'S NAME and CALL SIGN*
>   *Out."*

On working frequency:

> *"Securite... Securite... Securite...,*
> *All stations,"* (OR SPECIFIC ADDRESSEE)
> *This is BOAT'S NAME and CALL SIGN.*
> • *DETAILS OF SAFETY MESSAGE / SITUATION / CONDITION*
> • *BOAT'S NAME and CALL SIGN*
>   *Out."*

VHF changes in the works. With implementation of the Global Maritime Distress and Safety System (GMDSS), VHF communication – especially among commercial vessels – will change significantly. That system includes the use of Digital Selective Calling (DSC) technology that will make the VHF more like the telephone system. Only the station called – identified by its Marine Mobile Service Identifier (MMSI) – will hear a transmission addressed to it. Other stations monitoring the frequency (Channel 70 is currently reserved for this) will not hear it. Their receivers, recognizing that the transmission is addressed to a different vessel (MMSI), will ignore it. This should reduce the noise level on the VHF radio, but it also creates problems for those who wish to call a station whose identity and/or DSC code/MMSI are unknown. Commercial vessels will carry equipment that can interrogate unidentified radar contacts to determine their MMSI, but this sophisticated and expensive equipment will not soon be feasible for most voyaging yachts. GMDSS implementation was scheduled for completion in 1999, at which time commercial vessels would no longer be required to monitor Channel 16, the VHF hailing and distress frequency. Now, however, plans call for commercial vessels to continue to keep a watch on Channel 16 at least until February 1, 2005.

Installed vs. portable VHF. A permanently installed VHF radio, with its antenna mounted at the masthead, will give a boat the greatest communication range. These radios typically send a signal with up to 25 watts of power. Portable transceivers offer the advantage of small size and operator mobility, but since they operate at lower power levels (1-5 watts) and have lower and less efficient antennas, they are limited to communication at shorter ranges. Portables are also great for use from a dinghy or life raft, but many are vulnerable to water damage and need to be kept in watertight enclosure bags whenever used in a wet environment.

Uses of VHF. At sea, the principal use of VHF radio is for ship-to-ship communication, but in coastal waters it also provides ship-to-shore capability, including access to telephone circuits through public coast stations. VHF is also useful in North American coastal waters for receiving the continuous weather forecasts broadcast by the National Oceanic and Atmospheric Administration (and its Canadian counterpart) on VHF channels designated by the "WX" prefix.

HF/Single sideband radio. To communicate at longer distances with shore stations or other boats, we must look to systems other than VHF radio. For many years, the most practical choice has been Medium/High Frequency (referred to as HF) radio. This equipment operates in the 2-30 MHz frequency range, and uses a transmission technique called single sideband (SSB) that maximizes useful transmitter output. HF communication ability is influenced by a number of factors, the two most important being the equipment installation and the operator's choice of frequency.

Key aspects of radio installation include the antenna system, the ground plane or counterpoise, and the cables and connections that link the components. Unless it has an effective antenna, whether an insulated segment of a backstay or a transom-mounted whip, and a properly functioning tuning device, the HF radio cannot send a clear and powerful signal. Without an adequate ground plane provided by a metal keel, an engine block and grounding plate, copper sheeting inside the hull, or some other arrangement, the transmitted signal will be weak. Finally, the performance of the antenna and ground plane can be greatly reduced by corrosion or improper size/design of the cables and conductors that connect parts of the system. Loose, corroded or dirty connections anywhere in the system can sap a radio's output. The SSB installation requires periodic maintenance, mainly of its wires and connections, to function at its best.

Selecting HF frequency. Choosing the proper frequency for HF communication is largely a matter of experience, though guidelines and charts in the reference books and a few rules of thumb will help. At the lower end of the HF band, radio signals tend to follow the curve of the earth, allowing communication between stations as little as 100 miles apart during daylight hours and as much as 2,500 miles apart during the hours around local midnight in the spring and summer months. (During fall and winter, the maximum distances can expand to as much as 4,000 miles during hours of darkness.) Higher on the HF band, the signals do not bend to follow the earth's surface, but "bounce" off various ionized layers in the atmosphere and return to earth farther away (Figure 9.3). Local time of day is a factor since it is the sun's rays passing through the earth's atmosphere that create the reflecting layers. Generally, higher frequencies travel greater distances, especially during the day when they are not absorbed by lower levels of the atmosphere and when the higher layers "bounce" them back to the surface. During good propagation, these distances typically vary from 500 miles just after local sunrise to 7,000 miles or more as the sun moves west of the station's position. Lower frequencies travel shorter dis-

Figure 9.3 - High Frequency Radio Wave Reflection

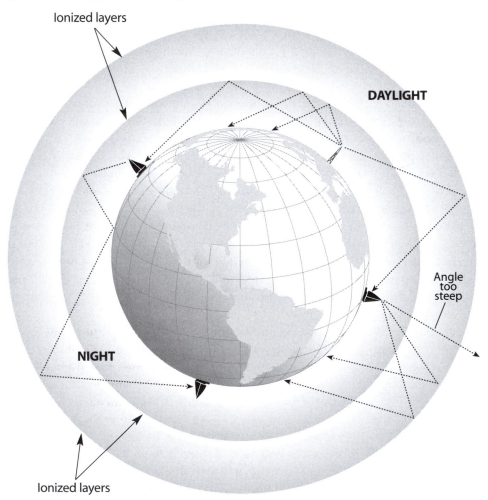

tances, doing better by night when they are reflected by upper ionic layers, than by day when they tend to be absorbed by lower layers.

Because transmitted signals follow a path similar to those being received, if you can hear signals from another station on a given frequency, that station can probably hear your signals on the same frequency. One way of estimating frequency propagation is to listen to a station such as NMN, the Coast Guard's Communication Area Master Station in Chesapeake, Virginia, during its weather broadcasts four times a day (see Chapter 11). The station transmits on 3-4 different frequencies. By changing from low to high and back again, you will hear the effects of frequency, propagation and distance. By comparing results for night broadcasts with those received during the day, you'll understand the role time of day plays. Another station to use as a propagation "beacon" is WWV, in Ft. Collins, Colorado. Operated by the National Bureau of Standards, this station gives continuous time ticks, announces the time every minute, and reports high seas weather at the top of each hour. It transmits on 2.5, 5.0, 10.0, 15.0, and 20.0 MHz. Knowing your approximate distance from the middle of Colorado will give a fair approximation of propagation conditions at each of these frequencies.

A handy guide in selecting an HF frequency is, "the higher the sun, the higher the frequency." During the night and early morning, lower frequencies – such as the four and six MHz bands – work well with both direct "ground wave" transmission and reflected "sky wave" signals. As the morning progresses, it will be necessary to use higher frequencies, such as 12 and 16 MHz to reach distant stations. In the afternoon, best results will be on the 16 and 22 MHz bands, especially to reach stations west of the transmitter, where the sun is generating strong ionic reflecting layers. As dusk approaches, the lower frequency bands will start to open again.

Like the VHF band, frequencies in the HF band have been allocated to radiotelephone communication by several government agencies. At the global level, the International Telecommunications Union (ITU) has assigned specific frequencies to numbered channels. At the national level, agencies such as the USA's FCC administer frequency usage within their jurisdiction. While some frequencies have been reserved for ship-to-ship use and others for ship-to-shore, still others have mixed usage. Some channels use the simplex mode, and others are duplex.

Making sense of those frequency numbers. Frequency designations can be confusing to those unfamiliar with HF operations. Sometimes operators will refer to the actual frequency involved, such as 4149.0 KHz. At other times, they'll use the ITU channel designation for that frequency (Channel 452). ITU channel numbers always start with the frequency band (2, 4, 6, 8, 12, 16 and 22) within which the channel lies. In each band, the channel whose number ends with 50 (e.g., 450 in the 4 MHz band) is designated a distress frequency. It is also used as a hailing frequency, just like Channel 16 on VHF. The next 2-4 numbered channels (e.g., 451, 452 and 453) are working channels for that frequency band, and are often referred to by citing the frequency band and adding A, B, C or D. Channel 451 is also known as 4 Alpha, 452 is 4

Bravo and 453 is 4 Charlie, while Channel 852 is 8 Bravo, and so on (Figure 9.4).

As an example of this varying designation system, consider Channel 650, at a frequency of 6215.0 KHz, known on the East Coast as the Sailor's Net. Every morning between about 0700 and 0900, sailors from New England to the Caribbean can be heard calling one another on this frequency. A typical exchange might sound like this:

"Exemplar, Exemplar, this is Corona WX9876, over."
"Corona this is Exemplar, Good morning Mike, let's try 6 Bravo, over."
"Exemplar this is Corona, Roger, Tim, shifting to 6227 [the frequency assigned to Channel 652], out."

Both boats would then establish contact on the new channel and conduct their conversation. If 6B was in use, they could wait until it was clear or they might come back to the calling channel (650) and try a different working channel. They might even move to a different frequency band (e.g., "Exemplar *this is* Corona, *6 Bravo is busy but 4 MHz sounds clear this morning. I'll call you on 451 [or 4146.0 KHz or 4 Alpha]"*).

To compound the channel designation/frequency confusion, the FCC has authorized use of a number of additional four and eight MHz frequencies for which there are no ITU channel designations. These frequencies supplement established channels and can only be identified by the actual transmit/receive frequency (e.g., 4030.0 KHz). These frequencies are shared with other uses such as data transmission and shore station traffic on a noninterference basis.

Learn the authorized frequencies – and resist the temptation to shift to unauthorized frequencies in an effort to escape heavy traffic loads. While the number of channels available on the popular six MHz band is very limited, the additional frequencies in the four and eight MHz bands offer practical alternatives. Far too many cruising sailors use improper frequencies without regard to the potentially harmful interference they may be causing. Continued abuse can result in severe penalties.

Despite their seeming irrationality, you'll grasp SSB channel and frequency designations quickly with experience. Using the HF radio frequently will build confidence until it soon becomes as natural as using a shore-based telephone.

Tying into the land phone system. For many years, an important component of the HF communication system was a network of commercial shore stations that enabled a vessel offshore to tie into the land phone system. They functioned very much like the VHF public correspondence channels available in coastal waters. Since commercial vessels now use satellite communciation systems instead of HF radio, the future of this system is uncertain at best. The network of stations once operated by AT&T have closed, and only Mobile Marine Radio still offers telephone links to cruising boats.

Mobile Marine Radio, in Mobile, Alabama, offers high seas, high frequency SSB radiotelephone service along with many other services, such as e-mail, to help voyagers stay in touch with shore contacts. The company operates station WLO, and with its field

Figure 9.4 - Authorized SSB Frequencies/designations
Exclusively allocated to Maritime Mobile Service

ITU	Freq.	Designation	Notes
450	4125		4 MHz Calling and Distress
451	4146	4A	
452	4149	4B	
650	6215		6 MHz Calling and Distress
651	6224	6A	
652	6227	6B	
653	6230	6C	
–	8291		Distress and Safety only
851	8294	8A	
852	8297	8B	
1250	12290		12 MHz Calling and Distress
1251	12353	12A	
1252	12356	12B	
1253	12359	12C	
1254	12362	12D	
1255	12365	12E	
1650	16420		16 MHz Calling and Distress
1651	16528	16A	
1652	16531	16B	
1653	16534	16C	
1654	16537	16D	
1655	16540	16E	
1656	16543	16F	
1657	16546	16G	
–	18825	18A	
–	18828	18B	
–	18831	18C	
–	18834	18D	
–	18837	18E	
–	18840	18F	
–	18843	18G	
2248	22159	22A	
2249	22162	22B	
2250	22165	22C	
2254	22168	22D	
2255	22171	22E	
–	22174	22F	
–	22177	22G	
–	25100	25A	
–	2S103	25B	
–	2S106	25C	
–	25109	25D	
–	25112	25E	
2505	25115	25F	
–	25118	25G	

Note that ITU channels 453 (4417 KHz/4C) and 654 (6516 KHz/6D), formerly approved for simplex ship to ship communications, are now allocated solely to coast stations and are no longer authorized for ship to ship use.

Additional (shared) frequencies (in KHz)

4 MHz band: 4000, 4003, 4006, 4009, 4012, 4015, 4018, 4021, 4024, 4027, 4030, 4033, 4036, 4039, 4042, 4045, 4048, 4051, 4054, 4057, 4060

8 MHz band: 8101, 8104, 8107, 8110, 8116, 8119, 8122, 8125, 8131, 8134, 8137, 8140, 8143, 8146, 8149, 8152, 8155, 8158, 8161, 8164, 8167, 8170, 8173, 8176, 8179, 8182, 8185, 8188, 8191

of antennas in the Mobile area it offers service to the Atlantic, Caribbean, Gulf of Mexico and eastern Pacific areas. The station operates in seven frequency bands (Figure 9.5) using the following procedures.

Figure 9.5 - WLO Marine Radio Operating Channels

405*	607	824*	1212*	1607	1807	2237*
				1641*		
419		830	1226			
						2503

* Primary working channels

To contact someone ashore, select a frequency band using time of day and distance from the station as factors. Listen for several minutes on one or more channels. If you hear communication between the shore station and ships, you have selected a good frequency band. If nothing is heard, try higher and lower bands, searching until you hear shore station transmissions. If you can hear nothing on any band, go back to your first choice and start the process over, calling the shore station on each channel in succession until contact is made.

Always listen for several minutes before transmitting to be sure the channel is not in use. If you hear the shore station transmitting (or the shore side of a telephone conversation), wait until the operator reports being clear with the previous station. These stations employ channels that operate in the duplex mode. The boat's receiver is tuned to the shore station's tramsmit frequency, so it receives only the signals transmitted from the shore station, not those (on a different frequency) transmitted from the other vessel. When the channel appears clear, call the shore station with an extended call:

"WLO, WLO, WLO, Whiskey Lima Oscar, this is the sailing vessel EXEMPLAR, EXEMPLAR, WK1234, Whiskey Kilo 1234, 400 miles north of the Virgin Islands, calling on channel 1212, Whiskey Lima Oscar, Whiskey Lima Oscar, this EXEMPLAR, over."

This long call gives the station operator, who is monitoring a number of frequencies and may be working with other vessels, adequate opportuntiy to hear your call and identify the channel you are using. Give the station a minute or so to respond before repeating the call – the operator may not be able to reply instantly. Try at least four or five times and give the shore station plenty of time to respond before shifting to another frequency or trying another band. Above all, be patient.

Once the shore station responds, be prepared to give the operator your approximate position (location relative to a geographic feature or latitude and longitude to the nearest degree) so he can adjust the antenna to get the best signals. Once clear contact is established, tell the operator you wish to place a high seas call. The operator will take the phone number you want to call, settle billing arrangements, then place the call. When your party answers, the system operates just like a telephone except that you are still limited by the duplex nature of the radio link: You can talk (on your transmit frequency) or you can hear (on the shore transmit frequency), but you cannot do both simultaneously. The conversation must proceed like a radio exchange, using "over" to indicate when you shift from talk to listen mode. When the conversation is complete and the party called hangs up the phone, the telephone operator will come on, ask if there are other calls and cite time and charges if requested. If you don't want to make any more calls, the operator will sign off with you and stand by to work another caller.

Calls from a party ashore. High seas radiotelephone service enables someone ashore to contact a voyaging boat as well. To reach a vessel via WLO, a person calls the station operator at 334-666-5110 (the area code changes from 334 to 251 on July 1, 2001) between 1230 and 0330 UTC (0730-2230 EST). The operator will ask the vessel's name and radio call sign, and may ask for its general location. The telephone operator places the vessel's name and call sign on the traffic list – a list of afloat stations with calls waiting – which is broadcast every hour. Vessels on the traffic list can call the station at any time and the connection to the calling party is completed.

If a voyager anticipates a need for someone ashore to contact the boat during a passage, it's best to set an agreed time for making the connection. For example, while en route to the Caribbean, we tell friends, family and associates that we will listen to the traffic list at 1300 and 0100 UTC each day (0800 and 2000 EST). If anyone needs to contact us, they should call WLO around 0730 or 1930 EST to put our boat's name on the traffic list. We can then contact WLO shortly after the traffic list is broadcast to respond to the call.

The cost of making calls via HF radio varies, and in some cases lower rates are available to those who have registered with the station and paid a subscription fee. WLO requires billing to a credit card, with advance arrangements to ensure security of billing details. For up-to-date information on WLO's current services, log on to www.wloradio.com.

Computer + modem + SSB = e-mail at sea. The combination of a computer and an SSB radio, linked by a modem, now offers passagemakers the ability to send and receive e-mail from the high seas. Such services are available commercially from firms such as WLO, PinOak Digital, Cruise Email and MarineNet. West Marine has sponsored a membership-based service called SailMail, and a worldwide network of amateur stations provides no-cost linkage between amateur operators and land-based e-mail networks.

HF shines for weather and medical advice. HF radio is particularly useful for getting weather info and for obtaining advice in a medical emergency. First, *weather*: Offshore and high seas weather forecasts are broadcast periodically over HF (see Chapter 11). This alone amply justifies installing an HF SSB radio receiver. Second, guidance in a *medical or other emergency*: This requires the ability to transmit as well as receive. At virtually any hour of the day, a vessel offshore can get emergency medical help from several sources. The Coast Guard and commercial High Seas stations can link a vessel to a doctor, and several medical services provide access to medical staff. NMN, the Coast Guard Communications Area Master Station, Atlantic, maintains a watch 24/7 on two duplex channels used for offshore weather forecasts. Technicians at NMN will route calls for assistance, including medical emergencies, to the appropriate Rescue Coordination Center (RCC). NMC, at Pt. Reyes, California and NMG in New Orleans (the Pacific coast and Caribbean counterparts to NMN) provide similar service on four duplex channels (Figure 9.6). Coast Guard groups along the US coastline normally maintain a watch on the shorter-range HF distress frequency (2182.0 KHz), but staffing limitations may not allow continuous coverage. Most RCC's have arrangements for consulting with a Coast Guard flight surgeon or local medical facility in a medical emergency. For details on medical guidance sources, see Chapter 27. If the risk of a medical emergency at sea is one of the things that generates fear in your mind, then a good SSB installation offers a proven strategy for easing that concern.

Figure 9.6 - USCG Distress and Safety Watch Keeping Schedules

ITU Channel	Schedule (UTC)		
	NMN (VA)	NMC (CA)	NMG (LA)
424	2300-1100	24 hours	24 hours
601	24 hours	24 hours	24 hours
816	24 hours	24 hours	24 hours
1205	1100-2300	24 hours	24 hours
1625	(On Request Only for all stations)		

Source: USCG web site

What about cell phones? Cellular telephone service generally does not extend far enough offshore to be useful to a passagemaker, and coverage is incomplete in many cruising areas. In some places, however, it can be exceedingly helpful. In the Gulf of Mexico, a cellular system serves offshore oil rigs, and dialing "911" in this system puts the caller in contact with the Coast Guard RCC in New Orleans. Cellular service is expanding rapidly, and cellular/satellite combinations may one day cover vastly larger areas, including high seas.

Satellite systems coming on strong. Relatively new to the cruising scene, but with enormous potential for expansion, are satellite-based communication systems. Technology is making the equipment more compact and less power-hungry, and competition is making yacht-sized units more affordable. When AT&T announced its intention to shut down its HF coast stations, it offered as a substitute (albeit at considerable equipment cost) discounted service through an Inmarsat satellite system. These and new "low earth orbit" systems promise instant voice and data communications between any two points on earth, regardless of location. Add an onboard computer and the options expand to include transmission and receipt of e-mail, receipt of real-time satellite imagery, weather forecasts, even links to online computer services and the Internet. Many of these services are already available through HF radio links, but future options will surely include an expanded array of choices, some of which seem beyond belief today.

For very short range: FRS. For communicating at much shorter distances, the recently authorized Family Radio Service (FRS) offers the passagemaker significant benefits. Operating in the 460 MHz (UHF) band and with power output of only ½ watt, these portable units reach out for a nominal range of one to two miles. They are intended for personal, noncommercial use and offer 14 channels, each of which can incorporate up to 39 selective squelch codes known as "talk groups." The result is like having 546 channels, which should keep interference to a very low level. These radios operate in the FM mode for clear, quiet communications. They can be very useful onboard (bow-cockpit, deck-masthead), for boat-to-boat chatting, and even ship-shore calls (a use that is not legal for most marine VHF-FM handheld radios). FRS transceivers require no licenses and can be used ashore as well.

What you should know about licenses. Government's role in communications is not limited to establishing channels and allocating the use of radio frequencies. In the US, the FCC also plays a very important role for cruising sailors: It issues licenses that give operators and stations the legal authority to transmit on specified radio frequencies. In anything but a bona fide emergency, transmitting without a license can lead to fines, confiscation of equipment, and even jail.

FCC-issued operator licenses give an individual permission to operate equipment that transmits on designated frequency bands. The FCC does not require or issue a license to operate a VHF or HF radio aboard a noncommercial vessel in US waters or on the high seas. It will, however, issue a license for these activities on request if an operator will be in foreign waters where a license is required by local laws. Operating on frequencies allocated to the amateur radio service does require an operator's license. We'll discuss amateur service and its role for voyagers shortly.

Far more important to the passagemaker is the station license the FCC issues to a vessel. This is the document that assigns a vessel its call sign and specifies the frequency bands in which equipment aboard that vessel can operate. Virtually all cruising boats must have a valid station license. Since the fee for obtaining a station license is not affected by the number of frequency bands, file a single application covering all frequencies you may wish to use, now or in the future. As a minimum, include VHF and HF radio, both 121.5/243.0 MHz and 406.025 MHz EPIRBs, and 9300 and 3100 MHz radars; also request assignment of a DSC identifier. Doing this all at one time precludes the need to go back later and pay another fee if you add a radar, for example, not included on the original license. Remember that the license only authorizes use of specified frequencies, it does not obligate the station to operate on all those frequencies.

An FCC ship's station license to operate on designated marine radio channels covers transmissions from afloat units only. This can extend to mobile support/service craft such as tenders, provided they are also afloat. Technically, you can call your boat from your dinghy (*"EXEMPLAR this is EXEMPLAR MOBILE, over"*) with a handheld VHF transceiver if it is afloat, but you can't lawfully make such a call from shore. (This is where FRS units are particularly useful.) To transmit on a marine frequency from shore requires a separate FCC shore station license, and they are difficult to obtain.

Figure 9.7 - Entities with which US amateurs may legally handle 3rd party messages (as of March 1999).

Prefix	Entity	Prefix	Entity
3DA	Swaziland	JY	Jordan
4X, 4Z	Israel	K,W,N,AA-AK	USA (includes
6Y	Jamaica		the Virgin Is. and
8R	Guyana		Puerto Rico)
9G	Ghana	LO-LW	Argentina
9L	Sierra Leone	OA-OC	Peru
9Y-9Z	Trinidad & Tobago	PP-PY	Brazil
C5	The Gambia	TG, TO	Guatemala
CA-CE	Chile	TI, TE	Costa Rica
CM, CO	Cuba	V2	Antigua & Barbuda
CP	Bolivia	V3	Belize
CV–CX	Uruguay	V4	St. Kitts & Nevis
D6	Comoros	V7	Marshall Is.
DU-DZ	Philippines	VA, VE, VO, VY	Canada
EL	Liberia	VK	Australia
HC–HD	Ecuador	VR6	Pitcairn Is.
HI-I	Haiti	XZ-XI	Mexico
HI	Dominican Republic	YN	Nicaragua
HJ-HK	Colombia	YS	El Salvador
HO-HP	Panama	YV-YY	Venezuela
HQ-HR	Honduras	ZP	Paraguay
J3	Grenada		
J6	St. Lucia		
J7	Dominica		
J8	St. Vincent		

Amateur ("ham") radio. There is a standing disagreement, sometimes emotionally charged, over the role of amateur ("ham") radio as a communication mode for passage-makers. The functions and objectives of the amateur service and the marine service are very different. Despite some overlap, the two cannot be viewed as interchangeable.

Amateur radio – though it does have valuable safety uses – is essentially a hobby. An operator's license is required to use the frequencies reserved for this service. Obtaining a license involves passing written exams on radio principles and theory and being able to receive Morse code. A code speed of 5 words per minute is needed to obtain a General Class license, the lowest level that gives access to the long distance, HF voice frequencies. Because it is a hobby, amateur radio cannot be used to conduct any sort of business transactions (such as ordering repair parts or making slip reservations). It is predominantly limited to friendly conversation. It is also generally constrained to traffic between the operators themselves, although the US has "Third Party" agreements with certain other countries. These agreements permit amateur operators to pass messages on behalf of third parties. For instance, a US station, WB2XXX, can receive a message for someone else in the US from a station in St. Lucia, J6YY. (Again, it cannot be a business or commercial transaction.) The accompanying table lists those states and entities with which the US currently has Third Party Agreements.

Despite these technical limitations, many amateur networks provide valuable services to passagemakers. They provide a way to file and monitor float plans (departure/route/arrival expectations, including measures for alerting authorities if a vessel fails to report as expected). Amateur operators often relay weather forecasts, and even link vessels offshore to telephone lines ashore (at no cost). Unlike the marine service, with its specific, fixed frequency/channel assignments, amateurs can operate anywhere within much wider frequency limits. Nets are usually managed by volunteer operators (often members of a club) at agreed times and frequencies (e.g., the east coast's Waterway Net, which works on 7268.0 KHz/lower sideband, starting at 0745 local daily). Amateurs are not limited to such nets, but can communicate on any open frequency within the authorized amateur band. This means that aside from established nets, in the absence of prior arrangement, one can never be certain of finding an amateur operator on any given frequency at any particular time. There is no amateur counterpart to the calling and distress frequencies designated in the maritime service, so in an emergency, there's less assurance of being able to reach someone on the amateur service than on marine.

Marine vs. ham: equipment, frequencies, overseas use. There are also major differences in equipment. To be operated in the marine service, a transceiver must be "type accepted" by the FCC for that purpose. The technical basis for this approval is well beyond our scope here, but the result is relevant. Compared to "amateur" equipment, it usually produces a radio that is simpler to operate, with fewer adjustments, fewer operating modes, higher frequency stability, and better capable of withstanding the marine environment (humid, salty air; impact and vibration). There's a flip side, of course.

While equipment for amateur service tends to be more complex and harder to learn, it also has more controls to cope with interference and adverse propagation conditions. Though the gap is narrowing, amateur equipment is often less expensive, which may offset vulnerability to sea conditions. Since all marine traffic uses the upper sideband mode, many marine service units operate only in that mode. Amateurs use lower sideband in the lower frequencies, so amateur equipment can operate in either mode.

Both marine and amateur service receivers generally cover all frequencies within a wide range (from 2 to 30 MHz is common), and most can receive shortwave broadcast frequencies as well as marine and amateur signals. On the transmit side, however, most marine units can operate only on frequencies in the designated marine bands, and amateur equipment can transmit only on the amateur frequencies. It is reportedly a simple task to disable the blocking circuits that prevent a modern amateur radio from transmitting on frequencies outside the amateur band, and many voyagers have modified amateur equipment to work on marine frequencies. Adapting a marine transmitter to amateur service is less common. If a unit has been type accepted for marine service and can transmit and receive on amateur frequencies, it is not in violation of any FCC rules if a licensed amateur operator uses it on the amateur frequencies. Technically, to use an amateur transceiver, type accepted only for use in amateur service, on the marine bands is a violation of those rules. There are, however, a few dual-purpose radios designed to operate on both services. They are essentially marine service transceivers that do not have circuits that prevent them from transmitting on amateur bands, and they seldom have the range of controls available on purely amateur equipment. Although these transceivers can be used lawfully for either amateur or marine service operations, it is another technical violation of FCC rules to use the same transceiver on both services.

A government's grant of authority, through a station or operator license, for communicating on the marine bands is generally recognized worldwide, on the high seas or in another country's territorial waters. To operate on the amateur bands from another country or its territorial waters, however, it is first necessary to obtain permission from the local government (often in the form of a "reciprocal license"). Failure to do so can result in stiff penalties. The strictness with which the content of amateur communications is regulated also varies somewhat from one country to another, and amateur operations require a greater awareness of these local differences than do operations on the marine band. Unless a cruising skipper is truly interested in the "hobby" aspects of amateur radio, a marine HF radio is probably a better choice for long distance communication.

In conclusion, modern communication systems can increase the safety and comfort of a passage. As a minimum, the voyager should be able to receive weather and other information transmitted by radio. Beyond that are the options to establish links to other boats and shore sites by marine or amateur radio, or even through satellite-based systems with a global reach. Being able to keep in touch can go a long way toward relieving anxiety during a passage, and getting regular weather forecasts will help in decisions leading to a better trip. It's reassuring to know that medical guidance is available if needed. Choose your communication equipment thoughtfully, install it carefully, and use it regularly. By becoming thoroughly familiar with its operation, you and your crew can enjoy its maximum contribution to the voyage.

REFERENCES:

Frederick Graves, *Mariners Guide to Single Sideband*

SGC, Inc., *Marine SSB Latest Fact Book*

Gordon West, *Marine Single Sideband Simplified*

Mobile Marine Radio, Inc. (Station WLO), 7700 Rinla Avenue, Mobile, AL 36619
    (334*)666-5110; Fax (334)666-833 *(251) as of July 1, 2001

CHAPTER 10

WATCHSTANDING

Establishing crew routines for operating the boat – standard ways of doing things that everyone must learn and follow – will go a long way toward avoiding confusion, conflict and overlooked actions or duties.

Standing watch is one area where establishing a standard procedure will pay strong dividends. Watches take some excessive lumps in casual conversation – "three or four hours of utter boredom, struggling to stay awake in the middle of the night when sensible people are asleep…." In fact, a watch involves sufficient duties to keep one or more watch standers quite busy.

By day or night, those on watch must never forget they are responsible for the safety of boat and crew. This creates external and internal responsibilities.

External responsibilities. Externally, the watch is charged with detecting and avoiding ships, debris, whales or anything else that could "go bump in the night". As lookouts, they must remain alert for distress signals from vessels or aircraft. Navigation is another central watch responsibility. The watch must know where the boat is and where it is going. If there are hazards en route, the watch must know when and where the boat may encounter them and what action the skipper wants to take to avoid them. If navigation aids are expected to become visible, the watch must know when and in what direction. They must also know the visual characteristics of any lighted aid, as well as what to do if it's not sighted as expected. The watch should update the DR plot periodically, showing the distance and direction the boat has traveled.

The watch also oversees communications. This can include listening for and answering calls on the VHF radio, initiating calls to passing ships, coming up on single sideband frequencies to monitor ship-to-shore traffic lists or copy weather broadcasts, or calling other boats on a preset schedule and frequency. Those standing watch also act as the onboard weather station, keeping an eye out for changes of wind direction and speed, sea conditions, barometric pressure and cloud composition and coverage. They must detect the threat or onset of adverse weather and take the initial actions to deal with it. They should be equally ready to take advantage of improvements in the weather.

Internal responsibilities. Changing sails and taking or shaking out a reef are part of the watch's internal responsibilities. If changes in sail trim are needed to reduce heeling, pounding or porpoising, the watch should take the necessary action.

Another internal responsibility is keeping the boat on course. This may involve manual steering, which can be demanding in rough conditions. Even when an autopilot or wind vane is in use, the watch must monitor the course those systems actually steer. If adjustments are needed, the watch standers must implement them. The watch also ensures the physical integrity of the boat. This means periodic inspections below to look for any conditions that could affect the seaworthiness of the boat. The watch must know if the engine is ready to start: Are the oil, transmission and coolant levels OK? Is the shaft locked? Is the transmission engaged? Is the battery switch set correctly? Each of these factors could make the difference between success and failure if an emergency requires instant engine use.

Handing over the watch. Establish routines for the watch to follow. At the change of watch, standard information should pass from the old watch to the new. It should include course, speed, log readings, intentions for the next few hours (perhaps from night orders written by the skipper), sails set and their trim status (are preventers rigged?), weather and visibility trends, steering patterns, radio, radar or visual contacts with other vessels, engine status, navigational position, status of any navigation aids in use, and any unusual experiences/conditions noted. A checklist helps make sure all points are covered, and a status board with current information noted in grease pencil will keep the new watch from forgetting details passed orally.

Systematic inspection. Each watch should inspect the boat systematically on a regular schedule. This might be as frequently as hourly, but at least once per watch, night and day. This inspection should include a look aloft to check sails, halyards, sheets, vangs, guys and other running rigging for fouling or chafe. Also check:

☐ deck lines and gear for proper stowage
☐ crew overboard equipment for readiness
☐ navigation lights status (on from sunset to sunrise or restricted visibility, otherwise off to conserve power)
☐ heads for status of overboard valves and any salt- or freshwater leaks
☐ bilge water (clearing any water with a manual pump and noting in the log the pump strokes required will make abnormal water accumulation quickly evident)
☐ galley for stove fuel valve status, freshwater leaks and ice box/refrigeration closure and temperature
☐ engine lube oil, transmission fluid and coolant water levels
☐ engine fuel valve and battery switch status
☐ shaft stuffing box for overheating or excess water leakage
☐ battery charge level and electrical system status for unnecessary loads and signs that charging is due.

The inspection should include touching, listening and smelling as well as looking. The benefits of these checkups have been confirmed repeatedly in our rally experience, where incipient electrical fires, bilge pump back-siphoning and potentially fatal fatigue damage to rigging has been detected early enough to avoid serious consequences.

Keeping that important log. Though it takes only a few minutes each hour, maintaining the boat's log may be one of the watch's most important duties. The information recorded can be crucial to safe navigation and can clarify developing weather changes. At a minimum, the watch must record hourly the course steered and distance traveled. This should be the average course actually steered during the previous hour, not the intended course or the heading when the big hand of the clock is straight up. Similarly, distance should be recorded in terms of a log reading on the hour if the boat has a distance recording log, or else the average speed maintained during the previous hour. Accurate average speed estimates demand frequent, conscientious instrument checks to avoid a natural bias toward noting higher speeds.

The watch should also record regularly the sea state (height and direction of swells and waves), wind condition (direction and speed), and weather (barometer readings and trends, cloud types and coverage, air and sea temperatures). While individual hourly entries provide a snapshot of prevailing conditions, as a body these readings provide a wealth of information about what is happening in the boat's tiny sector of the global sea-air interface. Barometric trends over six to ten hours, shifting swell directions, and progressive development of cloud cover provide a backdrop against which current weather conditions can be projected into the future. Recording this information and reviewing previous entries will help the watch prepare boat and crew for future conditions.

Log entries should also be made whenever a significant event occurs. To keep an accurate DR plot, speed and course changes and the time (and log reading) when they occur should be recorded. Sail changes, bilge pumping, engine operation (whether for battery charging or propulsion), radio contacts (there's a legal obligation to keep a log of radio transmissions), equipment failures, personal injuries and any deviations from normal routine should be logged. Record time of occurrence and sufficient detail to make the facts clear. The log constitutes a legal record of the boat's operation, and it needs to be kept conscientiously.

On sighting/detecting another vessel, the watch should record its initial compass bearing so subsequent observations will show whether the bearing is changing, and hence whether a risk of collision exists. If radar is available, the watch should turn it on and use range and bearing to calculate the vessel's closest point of approach (CPA), and determine when it will reach that point. Ascertaining course and speed will enable the watch to determine right of way under the COLREGS. If there is risk of collision, a good radar plot can reveal the most effective avoidance options. Regardless of what radar and visual observations suggest, the watch must maintain surveillance until the other vessel has clearly passed its CPA and is no longer a hazard. Many a vessel that first looked like it would pass safely has changed course or speed and come dangerously close to a sailboat, often without being noticed by a slack watch. Vessels approaching from or passing astern are particularly likely to surprise a watch lounging comfortably on the lee cockpit seat looking out intently, but only forward!

Steering by hand, rotating duties. It's not a bad idea to have the watch steer by hand for a part of each watch. This polishes steering skills and develops the crew's "feel" for the boat and the way it responds to wind and wave. It will pay great dividends if the autopilot/wind vane system should fail (pessimists might say "when", not "if") or sea/wind conditions make vane/pilot steering unsatisfactory. Hand steering will also tell the helmsman how well the sails are trimmed, essential to achieve best performance and to avoid overworking the autopilot or vane. Hand steering may even provide warning of steering problems (slack in the system, binding or roughness in the mechanism) which are otherwise concealed by the vane/pilot.

If more than one person is on watch, rotate duties regularly. This improves concentration and spreads the workload, giving each crew broader experience while reducing fatigue. For various watch schedules, see Figure 7.1 (page 77).

Developing sound procedures for standing watch is a valuable strategy for the passagemaker to improve the quality of any voyage. A watch aware of its responsibilities, both external and internal, and carrying out its duties according to an established routine, contributes greatly to the safety of boat and crew. The system assures that the many operating details are followed and that there's an alert hand in control of the boat at all times.

CHAPTER 11

UNDERSTANDING WEATHER

This chapter was inspired by Michael Carr, whose enthusiastic, lively and energetic presentations on weather have added greatly to Passagemaker Seminars.

The weather and its effects on the sea, the boat and crew influence every aspect of passagemaking. Our objectives here are to highlight the importance of a sound under-standing of weather, to sketch the characteristics of commonly encountered weather features, and to identify sources to which you can turn to get weather information.

Modern technology (satellite photography, complex computer modeling) has greatly increased the accuracy of weather predictions in recent years. An improved understanding of the dynamics of weather enables a voyager today to better exploit favorable weather and to avoid or cope with adverse conditions.

Learning sources – books, computer programs, seminars. You'll be well served by learning as much as possible about weather. This is not a simple task. Many books are superficial, focused on a single aspect such as wind or rain, or limited to conditions experienced in a specific geographic area (usually ashore). Others are so complex and filled with theory and technical details that few find them comprehensible. Our refer-enced works include titles that combine good conceptual treatment with useful guidelines for anticipating weather changes in a maritime environment. Even so, it takes a careful reading of several books to acquire a comfortable grasp of the subject.

One innovative method for learning about weather is the computer program mar-keted by David Burch at Starpath Navigation. Combining a wealth of information with a practical maritime focus, it is both learning tool and reference source, and makes learning about weather both easy and enjoyable.

Also excellent are the weather seminars conducted by *Ocean Navigator* magazine. These well organized sessions explain the fundamental processes involved in weather formation and development, cover a wide range of weather information available to the passagemaker and provide an opportunity to pursue weather concepts until they are clearly understood. It is one of the better opportunities for a prospective voyager to learn how to interpret and draw useful conclusions from data presented graphically by facsimile broadcasts and other sources.

Common weather features. Every passagemaker will encounter a number of common weather features, each of which carries reasonably predictable implications for wind and sea conditions. A high (short for high pressure system) consists of a mass of air at relatively high pressure. "Normal" sea level pressure is 1013 millibars – abbreviated "mb." A strong high might have a pressure up to 1030 mb. Within high pressure systems, winds tend to be light in strength and variable in direction, with clear skies and calm seas. Winds tend to flow outward from highs and spiral in a clockwise direction in the northern hemisphere. (All rotational directions cited here are for the northern hemisphere; south of the equator, rotational patterns are reversed.) Highs are marked on weather charts with a large capital "H," often with the barometric pressure noted adjacent to the "H." If a projected future position for the high is shown, it is marked with a circled "X".

By contrast, lows are areas of reduced barometric pressure, with a very deep low dropping as far as 960 mb. They characteristically include strong winds, poor visibility in heavy precipitation and rough seas. Winds spiral inward toward the center of a low, rotating counterclockwise as they do so. Lows are marked on weather charts with a heavy capital "L" and with the barometric pressure noted nearby. Future positions for lows are indicated with an "X" that is not circled.

Fronts are the boundaries between two masses of air having different temperatures and moisture content. In a warm front (Figure 11.1), warm moist air is displacing cooler air. It does so by riding up and over the cool air as it pushes it away. A warm front has a gradually sloped leading edge. The edge of the front at upper altitudes can be as much as 600 miles ahead of the edge at the earth's surface. The

Figure 11.1 - Warm Front Development

In a warm front, an approaching warm air mass rises up and over a cooler air mass. As the warm air rises and condenses, clouds and rain are formed.

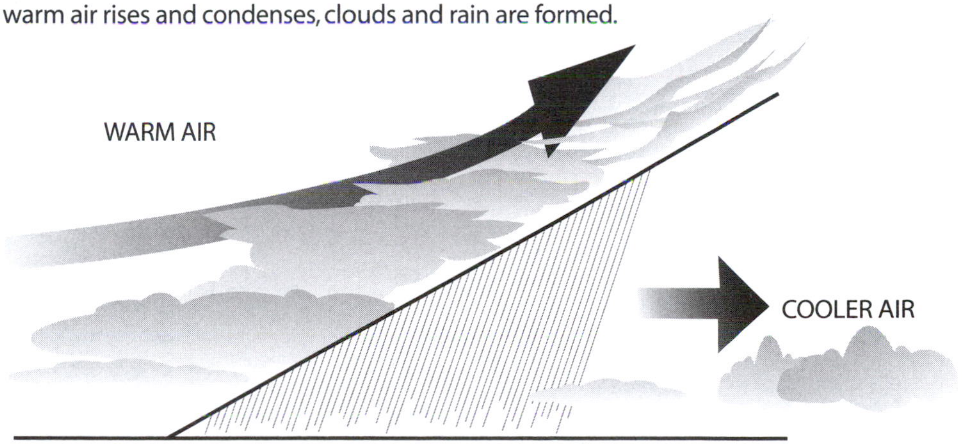

approach of a warm front is marked by a gradual increase in cloud cover. Starting with high, thin cirrus clouds they grow progressively thicker and lower, eventually becoming nimbostratus clouds producing steady rain. When a warm front passes, the surface wind will veer (shift clockwise), possibly suddenly but often more gradually. Depending on position along the front, the shift can range from south or southeast to about southwest. A warm front is shown on a weather chart as a heavy line with solid semicircular bumps on the leading side.

By contrast, in a cold front (Figure 11.2), relatively dense cold air is displacing lighter, warmer air by wedging under and lifting the warm air. The leading edge has a much steeper slope than does a warm front, with the upper-altitude edge trailing only 300 or so miles behind the surface edge. Lifting of the warm air creates a characteristic band of tall cumulus clouds accompanied by strong squalls, thunderstorms and heavy rains just ahead of the front itself. When the front passes, the surface winds veer sharply, generally from a southwesterly direction to a northwesterly one, with the northwesterly wind being quite brisk. On a weather chart, a cold front is shown as a heavy line with solid triangular bumps on the leading edge.

Lows normally develop along the boundary between air masses, and as they move there are usually two fronts extending out from the low. The leading or eastern one is a warm front, which generally moves more slowly than the cold front that trails the low. As a result, the cold front gradually overtakes the warm front to form an occluded front.

Figure 11.2 - Cold Front Development

In a cold front, a cooler air mass overtakes a warmer air mass, forcing the warm air up into cooler air above. As the warm air condenses, clouds and rain are formed. Changes caused by a cold front are more abrupt than those cause by warm fronts.

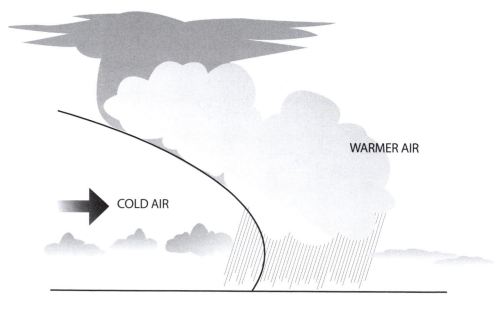

WARMER AIR

COLD AIR

Figure 11.3 - Development of a Depression

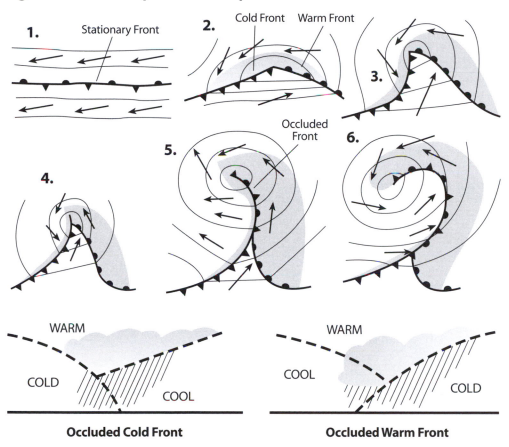

Occluded Cold Front   **Occluded Warm Front**

When this happens, the low tends to weaken and dissipate. Occluded fronts, shown on charts as lines with alternating semicircular and triangular bumps on the leading edge, are areas of confused winds and heavy rains.

Weather charts also contain isobars – lines linking points of identical barometric pressure. They're usually shown at intervals of 4 mb of barometric pressure and labeled with the last two digits of that pressure. The arrangement of these lines can reveal much about the winds and weather in their area. If the lines are widely spaced, it indicates little variation in atmospheric pressure across a large area of the earth's surface, and this low pressure differential will generate only relatively light winds. If, however, the isobars are packed closely together, it means a large pressure differential exists, and this will cause strong winds that will probably kick up significant seas, as well.

On surface weather charts, a trough (often written as "trof") is an elongated area of lower pressure around which the winds tend to blow in a counterclockwise direction, like a low. They are not closed systems, but have an open end across which the wind pattern does not flow. They appear on a chart as "U" shaped deviations in the isobars, with the lower pressures inside the U. Troughs are areas of stronger winds flowing inward, rough seas and frequent rain.

A ridge is the high pressure counterpart of a trough. It is an elongated area of relatively high pressure, marked by light air or calm along the central axis, and light, outwardly clockwise flowing winds at the edges. It appears on a weather chart as a "U" pattern in the isobars, with higher pressure inside the U.

When they are available, weather charts can provide a wealth of information about current and projected weather. Weather charts include surface analysis (based on actual observations), 24- to 48-hour prognosis (based on computer models and analysts' assessments), and wind strength and sea height forecasts.

Figure 11.4 - Isobars

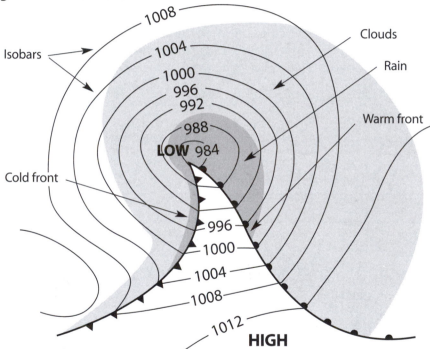

The 500mb chart and jet stream winds. Another chart of special value is called the 500mb chart. To appreciate its significance, one must understand how surface weather features relate to conditions in the upper atmosphere. Circling the earth, moving from west to east at an altitude of about 18,000 feet, are ribbons of air called "jet stream" winds. These winds, not being slowed by surface friction, can reach speeds in excess of 200 knots, although speeds between 50 and 150 knots are typical. Through their direction and speed, these jet stream winds act as steering currents for surface weather features and influence the development of surface highs, lows, troughs, ridges and fronts. Meteorologists use computer programs to analyze jet stream activity while developing surface analyses and predictions.

Jet stream data are presented on the 500mb chart (Figure 11.5). The lines on this chart are not the isobars found on surface charts. Instead, they mark the altitude (measured in meters and plotted at 60-meter intervals) at which the atmospheric pressure is 500mb (roughly one-half the "normal" surface pressure). This is the layer that forms the bottom of the jet stream. The jet stream wind flows parallel to these lines at speeds indicated by arrows on the chart (full feathers = 10 knots, half feathers = 5, solid triangular feathers = 50). Although jet stream flow is generally from west to east, the stream does meander – at times substantially. In a given area, the flow can be described as "zonal" or "meridional." Zonal flow is predominantly west to east without undulations, and since it does not tend to mix cold and warm air below it, it produces stable, settled weather. Meridional flow is north-south or south-north flow that is part of a meander or undulation. It mixes cold air from northern latitudes with warm air from the tropics and leads to unsettled, possibly stormy weather.

Remember that a 500mb chart is like a topographic chart. It portrays altitudes and contours, not the barometric pressure distribution that appears on surface charts. A feature marked as a Low is an area of low elevation for the 500mb level, not an area of low pressure. In fact, low elevation of the 500mb level suggests that the air below it (between the surface and 500mb level) is relatively dense and heavy. This is like a high pressure air mass on the surface, where air is sinking and warming. Similarly, a High area on the

Figure 11.5 - 500mb Chart

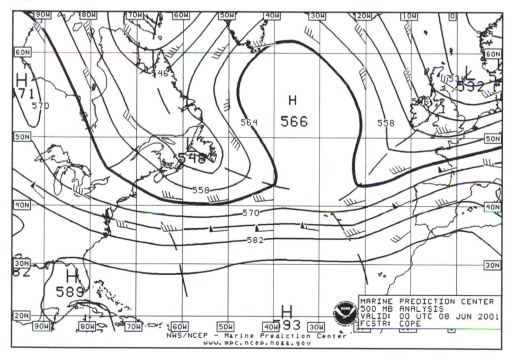

500mb chart denotes a region of less dense, lighter air below the 500mb level, like a surface low, where air is rising and cooling.

When the 500mb chart shows meridional flow, further clues about surface weather patterns and their likely development are available. Surface low pressure systems tend to form in areas beneath and to the east of upper level troughs – U shaped patterns that have winds flowing in the same counterclockwise direction as low pressure systems. Troughs sufficiently developed to influence surface lows are drawn on the 500mb chart with a bold dashed line. Surface highs tend to develop under 500mb ridges – inverted-U patterns that contain winds rotating clockwise, like a high pressure cell.

Two further bits of information can be derived from the 500mb chart. First, surface lows move across the earth's surface in roughly the same direction as and at a speed of ⅓ to ½ that of the wind on the 500mb chart directly above that surface feature. Second, the location of the 5640 meter contour, highlighted as a bold line on the 500mb chart, is a general indicator of storm track movement. It also shows the southernmost limit of sustained surface wind at or above Beaufort Force 7 (28-33 knots) in the winter and Force 6 (22-27 knots) in the summer.

A thorough understanding of 500mb charts and their implications for surface weather conditions will require patient effort. It takes close scrutiny of both 500mb and surface weather charts over an extended period. The effort will pay off, though, as the 500mb charts will help you anticipate changes in surface weather systems.

Pilot charts. For the voyager, attention to prevailing weather patterns comes into play early in the planning stage. It is a key factor in timing the trip. You'll find the Pilot Charts published by the Defense Mapping Agency Hydrographic/ Topographic Center in Washington, DC, invaluable. Drawing on data collected by ships over many years, each monthly chart includes so much information that considerable study is needed to absorb it all. A wind rose in the center of each five- degree square of latitude and longitude shows the winds that have prevailed in that area. Eight arrows show wind directions, and the length of each arrow shows the percentage of the total observations in which the wind has blown from that direction. The number of feathers on each arrow show the average wind force, as measured on the Beaufort scale. A number in the center of each rose gives the percentage of calm conditions. Another Pilot Chart feature is current data, with arrows showing the prevailing direction and adjacent numbers giving the average speed in knots. Other data include the reported frequency of wave heights of 12 feet or more, mean barometric pressure, mean sea surface and air temperatures, percentage of low visibility, ice limits, tropical and extratropical cyclone tracks, magnetic variation, and common ship routes.

NOTE: Pilot Charts are based largely on ship reports, and since ships tend to avoid areas of bad weather, the data are probably biased toward good weather conditions. High seas and gales are probably under-reported. Formerly published on a quarterly basis (three monthly charts in each), Pilot Charts are now published as an annual set.

Pre-departure daily review. Before the passage begins, a daily review of weather charts found in newspapers, on television, or through on-line computer services can give you a grasp of developing weather patterns: Where is the jet stream? Which way are the high and low pressure cells moving, and how quickly? Where are the frontal boundaries, and how are they moving? Watching the sequence of weather systems will often reveal the existence of periodic "weather windows" in which favorable conditions will prevail for a period of several days or more. By knowing the conditions that precede such a window, you can move quickly when a window opens.

Electronic info sources. Weather information sources accessible electronically are proliferating at an explosive rate. For example, when you enter the National Weather Service home page on the World Wide Web (http://www.nws.noaa.gov), you find marine forecasts as one of some 65 different weather products on the menu. Selecting that category gives a choice of over 30 specific forecasts/reports. They include surface charts that describe existing and anticipated conditions at sea level, and 500mb charts which portray jet stream location.

A couple of examples will show how the alert passagemaker can take advantage of weather patterns. On the mid-Atlantic coast, cold front passages are often preceded by a period of strong and persistent winds gradually veering from southeast to southwesterly. These winds flow with the Gulf Stream, so they allow the Stream's waters to smooth out considerably. The frontal passage is marked by an abrupt shift to northwesterly wind, strong and blustery at first, but easing off before veering gradually to the north and then northeast. Such winds tend to make the Gulf Stream rough and uncomfortable at best. A voyager headed offshore can pursue either of two strategies. The first is to depart as soon as the wind permits comfortable reaching on a southeasterly heading. The goal here is to use the south and southwest winds to get offshore quickly and transit a smooth Gulf Stream (about 100-150 miles from the mouth of Chesapeake Bay) before being overtaken by the cold front with its strong winds and possibly violent squalls. The second alternative is to get ready to go as the southwesterly blows, wait for the cold front to pass, and depart as soon as the wind eases off to a comfortable strength. The point is to use the favorable northwesterly to get to and across the Gulf Stream before the wind goes far enough north and east to raise the Stream's notoriously steep, choppy seas.

Boats working their way toward the Caribbean through the Bahamas frequently take advantage of a similar wind shift pattern. The arrival of a continental cold front that disrupts the pleasant Bahamian winter also causes the easterly trade winds to diminish, then veer to south before continuing all the way around the compass back to the east. Voyagers can exploit this "bad" weather pattern to make mileage to the south and east, directions that normally entail hard, wet upwind passages.

VHF and HF weather broadcasts. Among the uses for VHF and HF radio (Chapter 9) are weather forecasts. In North American coastal waters, continuous forecasts are available from NOAA stations broadcasting on dedicated VHF frequencies. (Although

10 frequencies are allocated to weather, only 3-4 are used.) These forecasts usually cover areas up to 20 miles offshore and may extend out to 50 miles, just enough for the first half day of an ocean passage. For waters further offshore, HF radio offers the best forecast information.

The focus here is on the services available to passagemakers along the US east and gulf coasts, the Caribbean and the western North Atlantic. Comparable sources exist in other areas, and conversation with local cruising sailors will usually disclose the best and most reliable.

Excellent offshore forecasts are prepared by the National Weather Service (Figure 11.6). Passagemakers can obtain them in a number of ways. They are broadcast by the US Coast Guard from radio stations at a number of locations. Various Ham radio nets repeat all or a portion of the forecast as part of their daily routine.

Coast Guard NMN and "Perfect Paul". The forecasts broadcast by the Coast Guard Communications Area Master Station, Atlantic, call sign NMN, will be used as an illustration. These broadcasts follow a pattern that makes it very easy to receive and record your desired information. Since the broadcast uses a computer generated voice (known as "Perfect Paul"), it's helpful to listen for several days before departure to "train" your ear. The computer has trouble pronouncing a few words, and if it fails to recognize a word (perhaps one that's been misspelled) or abbreviation, "Paul" may suddenly spew out a string of letters before resuming, without hesitation, the flow of words. If the written copy used "WSW" for west southwest and "fcst" for forecast, you might hear this: "light winds becoming double-you ess double-you late in the eff sea ess tee period before building to one five knots." Recently, a typo in the text (using a zero in place of an "o") led to a forecast of winds from the "north tee zero northeast." Using a small tape recorder to record each broadcast can be very helpful.

You may find useful, in your pre-departure phase, NMN's toll-free telephone line (1-800-742-8519), which enables you to talk with technicians who operate the station. They can provide current information on broadcast schedules, frequencies and content, and discuss technical aspects of the station's operations and the broadcast service.

Offshore forecasts cover prescribed areas along the east coast from the Gulf of Maine to the Caribbean, as well as the Gulf of Mexico, and include detailed forecasts for various subareas (Figure 11.7). High seas forecasts cover the entire North Atlantic north of 3° North and west of 35° West, the Caribbean and the Gulf of Mexico, and deal mainly with the location and movement of major storms, low pressure areas and regions with adverse sea conditions.

The typical NMN offshore broadcast begins with a forecast for the waters off the New England coast, stretching from the Hague Line (separating US and Canadian fishery areas) to Hudson Canyon (off New York City), and the offshore waters out to 60° West and as far south as 41° North. The next segment originates from the Weather Service office in Washington, DC, and it covers inshore waters from Hudson Canyon to 31° North and offshore waters out to 65° West and south to 31° North. The third part

Figure 11.6 – USCG Weather Broadcast Schedule (as of 4/01)

Station: NMN Chesapeake, VA

OFFSHORE FORECASTS		HIGH SEAS FORECASTS	
Time(UTC)	Frequencies	Time (UTC)	Frequencies
0330	A, B, C	0500	A, B, C
0930	A, B, C	1130	B, C, D
1600	B, C, D	1730	C, D, E
2200	B, C, D	2330	B, C, D

Station: NMG, New Orleans, LA

OFFSHORE FORECASTS		HIGH SEAS FORECASTS	
Time (UTC)	Frequencies	Time (UTC)	Frequencies
0330	F, G, H	0500	F, G, H
0930	F, G, H	1130	F, G, H
1600	F, G, H	1730	F, G, H
2200	F, G, H	2330	F, G, H

Station: NMC, Pt. Reyes, CA

Time (UTC)	Frequencies
0430	A, C, D
1030	A, C, D
1630	C, D, E
2230	C, D, E

Station: NRV, Guam

Time (UTC)	Frequency
0330	D
0930	B
1530	B
2130	D

Station: NOJ, Kodiak, AK

Time (UTC)	Frequency
0203	B
1645	B

Frequency List

A: 4426.0 KHz ("Ship Receive" side of ITU Channel 424)
B: 6501.0 KHz ("Ship Receive," Channel 601)
C: 8764.0 KHz ("Ship Receive," Channel 816)
D: 13089.0 KHz ("Ship Receive," Channel 1205)
E: 17314.0 KHz ("Ship Receive," Channel 1625)
F: 4316.0 KHz
G: 8502.0 KHz
H: 12788.0 KHz

comes from the Weather Service office in Miami, and it has two components. The first is for the Caribbean Sea, and the second is for the Southwest North Atlantic, the waters between 31° North and the Caribbean island chain and out as far as 65° West. The fourth segment, from the New Orleans office, covers the Gulf of Mexico.

A typical Washington office forecast will illustrate the regular pattern the forecasts follow, a pattern that makes it much easier to hear and record the specific information you are looking for. The forecast starts with a synopsis, a general description of the major atmospheric features driving the forecast (Example: "A low pressure area in the Ohio Valley will move to northern New England tonight and be off the Canadian Maritimes by Thursday night. A trailing cold front will reach coastal waters by

Figure 11.7 – Forecast Area Boundaries

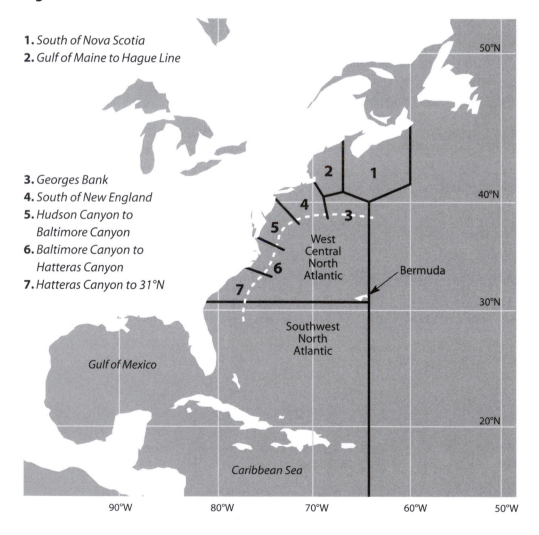

tomorrow morning and stall along 35° North before dissipating Thursday."). Next will come the forecast for the coastal waters, from 20 miles offshore out to the 1,000-fathom curve, starting with the area from Hudson Canyon to Baltimore Canyon (off the Delaware-Maryland-Virginia peninsula), then from Baltimore Canyon to Hatteras Canyon, and finally from Hatteras Canyon to 31° North. The next component covers the waters south and east of the 1,000-fathom curve, out to 65° West longitude.

Within each of these forecast areas, the data usually cover 24-36 hours in three phases: the next six hours ("this afternoon"), the subsequent 6-12 hours ("tonight") and the following 12 hours ("tomorrow"). For each time period, the forecast contains predicted wind direction and speed ("winds southeast, 20-25 knots, diminishing to 20 late in the period"), average sea height ("seas six feet"), and any conditions that could cause reduced visibility ("scattered showers reducing visibility below two miles" or "occasional thunderstorms, mainly in the southern portion"). After this detailed information for each coastal zone and the offshore area, the last element of the forecast is an outlook for major developments anticipated in the next 3-5 days ("the stalled front will drift northward as a warm front, while a high pressure ridge builds along 33° North").

Out of a broadcast that may last 20-25 minutes, most passagemakers will need to record just a few short pieces: the general situation, specific forecasts for their own and adjacent waters, and the prognosis. Since the data come in an orderly and predictable sequence, most listeners quickly develop the ability to copy all they need to know. For an even better comprehension of the ongoing weather scenario, many voyagers use a plastic-covered chartlet to record the data, sketching in frontal boundaries and noting wind directions and other details to provide a picture of current and anticipated weather.

Custom forecasters. Passagemakers can also obtain weather information from custom forecasters, who specialize in developing forecasts for specific purposes ranging from hot air ballooning to ocean racing and cruising. These commercial services have access to the data used by the National Weather Service, and often use additional information and computer programs to generate highly specific weather predictions. They can even recommend alterations of planned routes to take advantage of better weather or to avoid adverse conditions. These commercial sources can also provide data on Gulf Stream features and location, information that was provided by National Weather Service before October 1995, when budget constraints forced service reductions. These services are available on a fee-basis from sources included in our references.

Southbound II. For Atlantic cruising skippers, another well-known source is Herb Hilgenberg, whose forecasts are frequently a step ahead of those from the National Weather Service. Herb began his weather watching/forecasting hobby in Bermuda, collecting data and providing detailed (and accurate) forecasts to cruising boats along the East Coast, across the Atlantic, even in the southeast Pacific. Working on marine channels in the HF band, Herb used his boat's call, *Southbound II,* as he gathered reports on wind speed and direction, sea conditions, barometer readings and cloud cover from cruising boats and then gave each a detailed forecast. Herb relocated to Canada in 1995 and has resumed his weather forecasting from his new base. Although he still responds to SOUTHBOUND II, his official call is now "SOUTHBOUND II COASTAL," and his call sign is "VAX 498." He currently (2001) comes on the air on ITU channel 1253 (12359.0 KHz) at 2000 UTC (4:00 pm EDT) daily. At about 2100 UTC, he may shift to channel 851 (8294.0 KHz) to talk with boats unable to receive him on the higher frequency, primarily those north of 37° North. When that traffic is clear, he returns to channel 1253 and works additional contacts until 2300 UTC or later.

Boats start checking in with Herb around 1945 UTC. Unless you've been talking to him and he knows where you are, the initial check-in should include your general position and destination (*"Southbound II,* this is *Escapace* standing by, north of San Juan en route to Nassau.") When Herb first comes on the air, he will acknowledge the boats he has heard check in and those he has been tracking in his log. The number of boats trying to contact Herb usually far exceeds the number he can handle. Fortunately, patient listening will usually enable you to hear a forecast for a boat relatively close to your position, and this will suggest the conditions you can expect, as well. Herb works contacts by geographic areas, depending on the quality of radio transmissions, often starting with those in the eastern Atlantic and then moving to those approaching or departing Bermuda before talking to those in the Caribbean, Bahamas, Gulf of Mexico and eastern Pacific as radio propagation patterns change at dusk.

Virgin Islands radio and a Caribbean net. Regional weather sources and services exist in other areas of the world, and local cruising folk are the best guide to their reliability and schedules. The following discussion of resources available in the Caribbean will serve as an example of such sources. One is Virgin Islands Radio, station WAH, which broadcasts offshore and Caribbean forecasts on several VHF and HF channels at eight-hour intervals.

Another is David Jones, who uses the call sign "MISSTINE" for check-ins and operates a Caribbean SSB weather net each morning at 0830 on 8104 KHz. He works primarily with boats from the Virgin Islands and northern Leewards to those further south in the Windwards, but also serves some in the Bahamas. When there is an active hurricane in or approaching the Caribbean, this net is also active from 1815 until 1845 each evening. A typical morning session starts with a summary of the Caribbean weather situation, wind and sea forecasts for the next 24 to 48 hours, and a review of satellite imagery. Rising operating costs have forced David to shift the net to a subscription basis. For an annual fee, sponsoring vessels may check in with position and weather reports (wind, clouds, sea and barometer), and David responds with specific forecast data. David Jones has also written a superb reference book, the only work that focuses strictly on the weather patterns and phenomena that drive Caribbean weather.

(See References.) David also provides marine forecasts to radio station ZBVI (AM 780 KHz) for transmission at 0805, Monday-Friday, 0745 Saturday and 0945 Sunday, with weather updates every hour on the half hour, 0730-2130.

There are also continuous NOAA forecast services on VHF Weather channels that cover the US and British Virgin Islands, the Spanish Virgins and Puerto Rico.

Other types of weather information (facsimile weather charts and prognoses, satellite images) are also available on HF radio. Although the future of radio facsimile transmissions has been clouded by budgetary constraints, if no-cost-to-the-receiver public broadcasts are suspended, they will almost certainly be replaced by similar commercial products for which the user will pay a fee. As the communication revolution (see Chapter 9) unfolds, additional weather information is likely to become available to voyagers through an increasing number of channels. Any communication installation that provides access to the Internet permits a vast array of weather charts, analyses, forecasts and raw data to be downloaded from various Web sites.

No replacing your own observations! No matter how many ways you have to acquire processed and raw weather data from sources ashore, none should replace conscientious observations made from your own boat. If shore-based forecasts are in conflict or inconsistent with actual conditions, trust your own observations. A steadily falling barometer is a reliable indication of an approaching storm, and the more rapid the fall, the higher the storm winds and sea heights are likely to be. In assessing trends, remember that there is a daily cycle of barometric pressures, with highs at about 1000 and 2200 and lows at about 0400 and 1600 (local time). This daily variation is typically about 3 mb near the equator, decreasing with latitude to about 1 mb at 50°.

The approximate direction to the center of an approaching low can be determined (in the northern hemisphere) by standing with one's back to the wind and extending the left arm straight out to the side. The center of the low will be a bit (perhaps 10°) forward of this extended arm. If a series of observations indicates the low center will pass north of your position, you can anticipate the veering (clockwise) wind shifts that will come with a warm front passage followed by a cold front passage. If the center will pass south of you, the winds are likely to back steadily (counterclockwise) from southeast through north to northwest. If the low will pass directly over your position, you can expect a fairly steady wind direction, but increasing strength, succeeded by light air and chaotic seas as the center of the low passes, and a violent resumption of winds from the opposite direction as the western side of the system arrives.

Cloud coverage that starts with cirrus and gradually gets thicker and lower warns of an approaching warm front, which will likely be followed by a cold front. Long swells, especially from a direction other than that from which the current wind is coming, indicate a storm of significant strength in that direction. Abrupt changes of sea temperature can signal crossing of the Gulf Stream wall or entanglement in an eddy. These and many other known patterns can give invaluable clues about the wind and sea conditions that lie ahead, and create opportunities to prepare for those conditions before they arrive.

With respect to weather, then, your best strategy is to learn to understand weather patterns and the conditions that accompany various weather features well before departure, to keep in touch with developing weather conditions by regularly copying forecasts, and to make periodic observations of local weather and trends. The voyager can't control the weather, but a sound weather strategy can go a long way toward making the best of whatever nature provides.

REFERENCES/SOURCES:

Weather facsimile broadcast schedules (times and frequencies) can be obtained from NOAA's Port Meteorological Office in Houston, which maintains updated schedules for the three Coast Guard fax transmission sites (Boston, New Orleans and Pt. Reyes). Online at: *www.srh.noaa.gov/ftproot/hgx/html/marine/pmo.htm*. This site can be reached through *www.starpath.com* and links to useful marine weather sources.

Jenifer Clark's Gulfstream 301-952-0930; Fax 301-574-0289; e-mail: *gulfstrm@erols.com*

David Jones, *The Concise Guide to Caribbean Weather*. Every Caribbean cruising skipper should have a copy and study it carefully.

Steve and Linda Dashew, *Mariner's Weather Handbook*

David Burch, *Starpath Weather Trainer* (computer program)

Michael W. Carr, *Weather Predicting Simplified*

CHAPTER 12

PREPARING FOR HEAVY WEATHER

Heavy weather is certainly on the short list of anxiety producers for most prospective passagemakers. Luckily, this is an area where our comments on fear (Chapter 5) can be applied effectively to relieve the stress. Thorough preparation may not make heavy weather less uncomfortable, but it can go a long way toward making it less scary.

What is it? First let's define "heavy weather" and identify exactly what can or should induce concern. Sometimes bad weather is equated to reduced visibility ("raining so hard I couldn't see beyond the mast"). On an offshore passage, one is well removed from the hazards that litter the coastline. Modern navigation systems have all-weather capabilities, so accurate positions are available regardless of the visibility. Radar, radar detectors and radar reflectors can reduce the risk of collision. So reduced visibility seldom imposes a real threat to safety.

Heavy weather is more frequently described in terms of wind speed: "It was blowing 40 knots" or "the wind was shrieking through the rigging and a gust over 75 knots blew off the anemometer spinner!" But high winds alone are not really a cause for fear. Sailboats are designed to cope with strong winds. As we will see in Chapter 21, the first step in coping with increased wind is to reduce sail. Even before sail area is reduced, however, a sailboat's design produces a natural response to stronger wind: it heels away from it. In so doing, the amount of the sail exposed to the wind's force is effectively reduced (Figure 12.1). While excessive heel can create hazardous conditions if not corrected, wind-induced heel has a natural limit: As a boat's mast approaches horizontal, exposed sail area nears zero and the wind cannot push the boat any further over. Any offshore boat should have positive stability well beyond 90°, so even if knocked flat by a gust, it will return toward the normal mast-upright position when the wind abates. Wind can cause extreme discomfort, and an unexpected knockdown can lead to damage and injuries, but wind alone seldom poses a survival threat to a boat.

The wind, of course, acts not only on the boat but also on the water. The wind creates waves, and their size and shape depend on many factors: the strength of the wind, the length of time it has been blowing, and its fetch (the distance of open water across which it blows), water depth, sea current, and the interaction of multiple wave patterns. As they get tall and unstable, waves break, causing water to tumble down their leading face, sometimes as a foaming crest, sometimes in a pounding curl. It is the movement of the upper layers of the sea surface, the waves, that causes water to slam against a boat's hull, lifts it bodily and dumps it on its side, or sends tons of solid water cascading onto its decks. It is this moving water that can damage a boat, so the sea state is the part of "heavy weather" that merits closest attention and for which the passagemaker must be prepared.

As we will see shortly, much can be done to get the boat ready for deteriorating weather, but developing the crew's coping skills is at least equally important. Indeed, many a boat has survived conditions that defeated the crew. To feel a degree of comfort despite heavy weather, the crew needs confidence in their own ability to weather the storm as well as the boat's capacity to do so.

Building crew experience. Too many coastal cruising sailors set out on an ocean passage without adequate experience in strong winds and their accompanying rough seas. Whenever conditions are less than ideal, we (and the author acknowledges his membership in this band) tend to huddle in port instead of venturing out to accumulate experience coping with stormy winds and seas. Little surprise, then, that too many new passagemakers find themselves in mid-ocean with deteriorating weather, insufficient

Figure 12.1 - Heeling Reduces Effective Sail Area

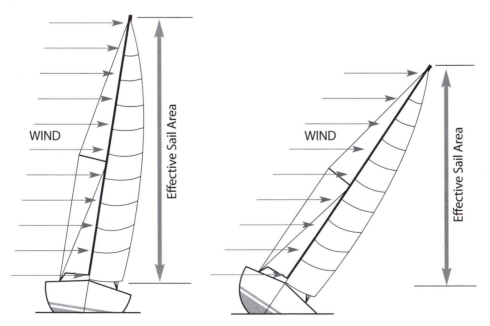

experience, and no place to hide. By contrast, in some places (parts of New Zealand and South Africa) sailors routinely experience winds well above 30 knots and don't find those winds or the choppy seas daunting. They have learned they can manage to sail in such conditions, safely and happily, if not always comfortably.

The lesson here is to gradually expand the crew's operating envelope. Thirty knots of wind and eight-foot seas are intimidating the first time, but having been survived once, they are less threatening the next time. After coming through a 35-knot/10' storm, the 30-knot/8' situation seems practically routine. Raising the operating threshold in small steps is far less traumatic than facing storm conditions for the first time 400 miles offshore, with a nasty low making a beeline for your position, and everyone nervous because they've never encountered more than 25 knots or four-foot seas.

Practice, practice. The need for experience extends to performing many tasks that will be discussed as heavy-weather tactics (see Chapter 21). The crew should practice securing the boat for rough seas, both by developing good stowage habits and by consciously conducting a drill to button the boat up, inside and out, as if it were going to encounter a storm. Taking a reef should be such a routine event, by night or day, on or off the wind, that it can be accomplished with no more fuss than tacking or gybing. Practice rigging storm sail in nice weather until it becomes easy. It may look peculiar to other boats, but it's far better than struggling with a recalcitrant storm jib for the first time when it's blowing 40 knots and the boat's vertical movement is quicker than its horizontal progress. The same applies to heaving to, deploying a drogue or setting a sea anchor. Learn what's involved and develop the essential teamwork when the weather is nice. The whole crew will collect the dividends when conditions deteriorate, because doing a familiar job in bad weather is much less demanding than having to figure out how to do the job itself in addition to struggling with weather-created complications.

Compared to readying the crew, preparing the boat is a simpler process, though demanding. Since the reliability of weather forecasts diminishes rapidly beyond four or five days, any passage of a week or more likely will include a brush with adverse weather. It's prudent to prepare well before the voyage begins. Heavy weather preparation can be considered in two parts – first, before the passage, and second, during the passage, when the prospect of heavy weather develops.

Crew assignments – pre-voyage. In the pre-voyage phase, readiness for heavy weather is best incorporated into the overall voyage preparation process. Many years of experience with the Navy's offshore sailing program have gone into the development of a checklist to help the crew prepare a boat for a passage. Assigning specific responsibilities to individual crew members not only avoids problems later but strengthens crew organization and helps familiarize crew with the boat's systems. Known as the BlueWater Checklist, this plan assigns duties as follows (repetition of items previously prescribed for the inspection process in Chapter 4 is intentional):

Actions for all crew members:
1. Identify the seasickness remedy found most effective for each individual, have an adequate supply, and know when and how much to take.
2. Mark safety harnesses and PFDs with crew's name and adjust to fit comfortably. Strength-test the harness and tether (hang from halyard, yank as hard as you can on each seam/fitting, have a harness-to-harness tug-o-war with a crewmate). Test the PFD in a swimming pool to see how much support it provides, how much effort is required to stay head-up, how much freeboard is available to keep waves from slopping up into the face and nose.
3. Inventory personal safety gear listed in Chapter 16.

Actions for the Skipper:
1. Bring all emergency assignments up to date, with crew assigned to duties by name, and post at a convenient location onboard. Give each crew member a copy of the assignment list.
2. Monitor crew members' preparations, especially for critical functions such as assembling abandon ship kit, crew overboard gear, and medical supplies.

Actions for the crew member designated Bosun:
1. Inspect all standing rigging from deck to masthead, ensuring that cotters are in place, taped as necessary, and that swages show no cracks or broken wire strands.
2. Inspect all running rigging end-for-end, whip all loose ends and install chafing gear or change leads to prevent chafe. Carefully examine areas under strain in heavy weather, such as reefing outhauls where they pass through cringles.
3. Bend on all storm sails, install sheets, determine proper sheeting location, and mark with permanent felt-tip pen. Mark "tack", "head," "clew" on storm sail corners. Prepare secure stowage plan for boom when storm trysail is set.
4. Mark reef tack and clew cringles on main and mizzen with reef numbers (1,2,3).
5. Inventory sail ties; carry triple the normal number to allow for loss, lashings, etc.)
6. Lay out safety lines on deck and in the cockpit. Check condition of fastenings (including strength of fittings). If wire, check swages for cracks or unlaying wire. If braided webbing, check condition (vulnerable to UV deterioration) and any stitching. Run tether hooks fore and aft to ensure free travel.
7. Inspect and inventory safety harnesses. Check for sprung clips, torn webbing, inoperative strobes. Issue one to each crew member.
8. Inspect and inventory PFDs. Check whistles, lights and reflecting tape. Be sure boat's name is on each one. Issue one to each crew member.
9. Inspect life raft for secure stowage. Verify inspection date and make sure painter/operating lanyard is secured to boat, preferably with a weak link or hydrostatic release mechanism. Be sure any in-port security devices (locks, wires) are removed before departure.
10. Inventory sail repair kit (see Chapter 23).

Actions for crew member designated Engineer:
1. Clean bilges, removing all debris and clearing limber holes.
2. Clean bilge pump strainers and test each bilge pump by pumping clean water.
3. Ensure batteries and other heavy equipment items are secured against rollover.
4. Ensure all batteries are fully charged (use a hydrometer to verify wet-cell condition); consult with skipper if any are doubtful or need replacement.
5. Inspect steering for correct cable tension, proper clamps, lubrication and freedom from binding. Remove or secure any loose gear near quadrant. Check and fill hydraulic steering reservoir and air charge.
6. Test emergency tiller and stow in readily accessible place.
7. Inventory engine spares (see Chapter 24).

Actions for crew member designated Navigator:
1. Test receipt of VHF and SSB weather information by copying at least two broadcasts. Make sure a complete list of weather frequencies is aboard.
2. Test weather fax, if installed, and carry sufficient paper for 1.5 times anticipated need. Test any radio-computer linkage for proper signal processing.
3. Test all navigation equipment and inventory supplies.
4. Verify ability to receive time signals on at least two frequencies.
5. Check barometer accuracy against standard barometer.
6. Verify accuracy of compass alignment and deviation table.
7. Inventory emergency gear: distress signals, EPIRB, survival mirror, radar reflector, space blankets, and abandon ship bag (see Chapter 16 for details)
8. Ensure sufficient spare batteries for 1.5 times anticipated needs for flashlight and portable electronic devices (tape recorder, GPS).

Actions for crew member designated Galley Manager:
1. Prepare menu for 30 hours of storm conditions.
2. Ensure Sea Swing-type stove is aboard with sufficient fuel.
3. Secure all stores for possible rollover.
4. Rig all berth lee cloths and check for strength of attachment.
5. Inventory and inspect immersion suits, if carried.
6. Inspect galley area for fire hazards.

Actions for crew member designated Damage Control Manager:
1. Fit all companionway washboards and hatch closure devices. Ensure covers for large windows are onboard and properly stored with plenty of fasteners.
2. Cycle all through-hull valves and lubricate as necessary. Check for wood plugs of correct size adjacent to each fitting. Ensure all hoses connected to through-hulls below the waterline are double clamped and clamps are sound and tight.
3. Check topsides watertightness by applying water with a high-pressure hose to hatches, ports, deck edge, windows and mast boot. Repair any leaks.

4. Locate covers for all dorade vents.

5. Inventory damage-control kit and toolbox (see Chapter 29).

If there are fewer than six people aboard, there will have to be some doubling up of assignments, because it's essential that each task be accomplished.

About lightning. In your pre-voyage preparation for lightning, you should know there are two diametrically opposed theories. One says to bond all metal hull fittings in order to give lightning charges a safe path for dispersal into the water. The other says to bond nothing, so the hull and rig offer a less efficient path for lightning to reach ground. Since most boats are fitted with extensive bonding systems to control electrolytic corrosion, the bonding approach is probably more suitable. There is little persuasive evidence of the effectiveness of mast-mounted lightning "protection" devices now on the market. Lightning seems to impact boats in highly unpredictable ways, and there is no guaranteed way to protect against lightning damage. Take consolation from the fact that sailboats at sea are rarely struck by lightning, despite being the highest objects for miles around and sailing through some extremely active electrical storms. More boats experience lightning damage in port, frequently in a marina with many boats nearby, of which only one or two may be struck.

Many measures have been suggested to avoid lightning damage. There is little evidence to confirm the effectiveness of efforts to enhance grounding of the rig (clamping battery jumper cables to the shrouds and letting them dangle in the water). Neither is there clear evidence that damage to electronics is reduced by disconnecting antenna leads, power supply lines and other electrical connections. A lightning charge passing through a boat's grounded conductors will induce electrical currents in totally disconnected equipment strong enough to permanently damage electrical and electronic components. It is prudent to remind the crew of hazards that accompany lightning strikes. Although well shielded by the "Farraday Cage" effect created by the rigging, the crew should avoid contact with shrouds, stays, lifelines and other grounded metallic equipment that could receive direct or induced electrical charges from a lightning strike.

Crew assignments – when heavy weather is expected. With the preparatory actions noted above completed, a boat can head offshore with the crew confident they're as ready as possible for adverse weather, should it develop. During the passage, when forecasts first suggest the prospect of heavy weather, preparation shifts into its second phase. Here again, Navy offshore sailing experience has produced a checklist of actions. As a general guideline, the steps on this Heavy Weather Checklist should be started on receiving information that winds above 30 knots can be expected within 24 hours:

Actions for the Skipper:

1. Adjust the watches to get as much expertise as possible on each watch; modify watch lengths and schedules.

2. Ensure crew members get maximum rest before weather deteriorates.

3. Closely monitor weather conditions and evaluate situation for need to alter route to reduce storm impact.

4. Brief crew on storm tactics and procedures to be followed when weather gets worse. Discuss sail changes, tacks, jibes, use of supplementary stays to strengthen rig, crew overboard considerations, response to possible flooding, dismasting or abandon ship.

5. Ensure crew takes seasickness medications at least four hours before onset of heavy weather.

Actions for crew member designated Bosun:

1. Inspect all running rigging; replace or end-for-end any frayed lines.
2. Inspect all standing rigging visible from deck.
3. Rig deck and cockpit safety lines if not already in place, check attachment points.
4. Set up inner forestays and running backstays.
5. Break out storm sails and place in secure but readily accessible storage point.
6. Break out extra sail ties and sheets.
7. Stow below any unused sails or other equipment topside that might be ripped from on-deck locations by seas.
8. Rig cockpit weather cloths.
9. Check crew overboard gear for security and readiness for use.
10. Check life raft security.
11. Be sure radar reflector is rigged and padded to prevent chafe.

Actions for crew member designated Engineer:

1. Get a full charge on batteries.
2. Top off liquid levels in engine and batteries.
3. Connect engine to tank with most fuel and check primary separator for good filter element.
4. Pump bilges completely, flushing if necessary, and remove any debris. Clean pump strainers.
5. Double-check engine space storage for security against knockdown/rollover.
6. Inspect steering gear for correct cable tension and remove any loose gear that could foul the system. Check and fill hydraulic reservoir and air charge.
7. Secure engine through-hull valves, including any closure in exhaust system to prevent water from flowing into manifold. Remove engine starter key and stow in navigation table with tag warning not to start engine until valves have been opened.

Actions for crew member designated Navigator:

1. Obtain most accurate possible position.
2. Establish DR track on large-scale plotting sheet.
3. Monitor weather information from all sources.

4. Record barometer reading every 30 minutes.

5. Get time check for navigational watch.

6. Put fresh batteries in all flashlights.

7. Inventory critical emergency gear (flares, EPIRB, abandon ship bag) and stow in ready location

8. Monitor VHF Channel 16; establish contact with any nearby vessels.

Actions for crew member designated Galley Manager:

1. Prepare and serve hot, substantial meal before storm arrives.

2. Prepare individually wrapped sandwiches for at least 12-hour period.

3. Secure regular stove before storm arrives; bleed off gas pressure and secure bottles.

4. Rig Sea Swing stove.

5. Break out snacks and hand food for watches (granola bars, peanut butter crackers, cheese crackers) and place in secure, convenient lockers.

6. Secure all stowage compartments, backing up latches with duct tape.

7. Check rigging of lee cloths, and inspect cabins for secure stowage of personal gear and any objects that could become missiles in a knockdown or heavy seaway.

8. Break out immersion suits if temperatures suggest advisability.

Actions for crew designated Damage Control Manager:

1. Check all hatch-securing devices. Install heavy-duty companionway boards and secure in place.

2. Remove cockpit drain grates.

3. Break out and install shutters for large windows.

4. Put damage control kit in cabin in a secure, ready position. Have two buckets ready as emergency bailers.

5. Remove Dorade hoods and install vent covers.

Items on this checklist, added to pre-departure preparation, will enable the crew to substantially enhance the readiness of the boat for severe weather. Crew confidence will be increased by the knowledge that the boat has been made as ready as possible.

The strategy for being ready for heavy weather leans heavily on the three P's that will recur frequently throughout this book: Planning to anticipate what can happen, Preparing to be ready to handle the adversities, and Practicing all the available tactics. Get the crew ready for heavy weather, get the boat ready for heavy weather, then do your best to enjoy the sailing in abundant winds!

REFERENCES:

Adlard Coles, *Heavy Weather Sailing* (Revised edition)
Tom Cunliffe, *Heavy Weather Cruising*
Gary Jobson, *Storm Sailing*
William Van Dorn, *Oceanography and Seamanship*

CHAPTER 13

PREVENTIVE MEASURES

The goal of preventive measures is to avoid problems. In many areas of boat operation, a passagemaker can reduce risk of casualties through active prevention. While these measures may consume time in a busy day, they're far less demanding than the mishaps they help to avert. Many have been mentioned in discussing boat inspection (Chapter 4), and are reviewed here to emphasize their preventive value on a continuing basis.

The electrical system. We begin with the electrical system, lifeblood of so many conveniences. Among the most common problems encountered during passages are electrical system failures. The most serious are those that interfere with battery charging. It is essential that the system be able to put back into the battery bank each day at least as many amp-hours as are used. Without the ability to generate sufficient electrical power, the voyager must first forego conveniences (autopilots, cabin lights), and soon face the loss of vital equipment - electronic navigation, communication, navigation lights.

Too often, a boat's engine-driven battery charging system is inoperative or working at a reduced capacity long before a voyage, but the skipper is unaware of it. The boat lives in a slip with shore power connected. Short trips don't put enough load on the electrical system to reveal the inadequacy of the charging system. To avoid this trap, simply stop using shore power for at least two weeks, well before departure, relying on the onboard system to recharge the batteries. If it fails to maintain a good charge or takes too long to do so, get a marine electrician to correct the situation. Causes commonly include blown diodes in the alternator, inadequate wiring and malfunctioning voltage regulators, all relatively easy to correct before departure but difficult to fix at sea.

The engine-driven system often gets forgotten when a separate electrical generator is installed. Generator problems (mechanical and electrical) are quite common during passages. Having the propulsion engine's generating system in good shape stands as an invaluable backup.

Unsatisfactory charging may also result from inadequate alternator capacity, compounded by insufficient battery capacity (see Chapter 3). *Address these issues well before departure.* The prudent skipper will verify that these systems have the capability of supplying the boat's electrical needs and are in top working order.

Another valuable preventive measure is the preparation of electrical wiring diagrams. Sometimes the builder will supply diagrams, but the quality and completeness varies drastically. These drawings will always lack information about any equipment added. Updating drawings to include new equipment, verifying accuracy of old diagrams and preparing new ones are time consuming jobs, easily deferred, but of enormous value when electrical problems arise. Note wire numbers and color coding to trace power supplies or find grounded/shorted circuits. A good wiring diagram and practice with a multimeter that measures voltage, resistance and amperage will ease troubleshooting.

Aside from catastrophic damage such as lightning-induced power surges or internal self-destruction of electronic components, most electrical problems can be traced to simple failures such as blown fuses and poor connections. While fuse failure can seldom be anticipated, a supply of spares and a meter to find the cause can expedite repairs. Bad connections can often be detected before they cause a problem, especially if the crew look for them as they go about daily routines. Crew should always keep an eye out for loose/corroded connections, signs of chafed insulation, exposed connections, wires lying in wet spots, and other conditions that can disrupt electrical circuits. Clean, tighten, tape and secure them before they cause trouble.

The rigging. The boat's rigging also benefits from preventive effort. Before departure, a comprehensive inspection is essential. During the passage, standing and running rigging should be inspected at least daily. On the standing rig, look for slack in the wires. Check turnbuckles and toggles for signs of stress. Be sure cotters are in place and taped. Look for signs of wire unlaying. Glance up the mast to be sure it is still in column. Use binoculars to check conditions aloft, where wind instrument and antenna fastenings can vibrate loose. On deck, check the safety jackline and its fastenings, as well as any equipment stowed topside.

Running rigging should get a similar examination, mainly for chafe. Lubricate blocks, fairleads and other moving parts to minimize friction. Look for wear on canvas work. Install padding to protect against chafe, or take a few stitches to help carry the load. Make sure tails of halyards and sheets are ready to run.

The engine and fuel system. Reliable engine performance depends heavily on good preventive maintenance, much of which should be accomplished before departure. In addition to periodic oil changes and replacement of oil, fuel and air filters, also service these items immediately before departure, since they're far easier to do in port than underway. This is also the time to check the engine alignment, for which you need the boat at rest. Tracing fuel, coolant, exhaust and electrical systems (see Chapter 4) allows you to correct conditions that could cause difficulty offshore, while increasing familiarity with the systems. If you commonly need to bleed the fuel system, find out how the air is getting into the system and stop it. If the system is tight and bleeding is rare, learn where the bleed points are, just in case.

Another task much easier to do at dockside than underway is replacing the raw water pump impeller. If the impeller hasn't been changed in over six months, install a new one before departing and save the old one as a spare. Make sure there are replacement pump gaskets in the spare parts kit.

If the boat is over 2-3 years old, especially if it has been in protected waters, cleaning the fuel tank before a first ocean passage can prevent major problems. Over time, a layer of dirt, water and debris accumulates on the bottom of the tank. Diesel fuel, with its vulnerability to biofouling, is especially likely to have sludge on the tank floor. Short coastal cruises don't disturb this sediment. When the boat goes offshore, the constant motion churns the contaminants and mixes them into the fuel. When the engine tries to use this fuel, the best that can happen is that the primary and secondary filters do their job and get clogged. This causes the engine to die for lack of fuel. The worst that can happen is that the junk will get past the filters and into the injection system, where it scores the injector pump and fouls injectors, also causing the engine to die – but now requiring an expensive repair job.

Clean the tank and fuel. If the tank has access plates, the job can be done manually by draining the fuel and mucking out the debris before refilling the tank. In the absence of large access openings, a nozzle can be inserted through a pipe opening and a jet of high-pressure fuel used to blast sediment loose so it can be picked up by a suction hose inserted through another pipe opening. Fuel and contaminants drawn out through the suction line are passed through one or more high volume filters to clean the fuel before it is pumped back to the nozzle for another cycle through the tank. In many places, this tank and fuel cleaning is offered commercially under the name of "fuel polishing".

Once a diesel tank is cleaned, adding the proper amount of a good biocide, such as Bio-Bor®, at each refueling will help control further fouling. Introducing a biocide to an older tank that has not been cleaned can be counterproductive. As the agent kills the organisms resident in the tank, it creates additional detritus suspended in the fuel, aggravating the contamination problem. The key is to get the whole system clean first, then take steps to keep it clean. Installation of a magnetic fuel treatment unit (De-Bug® and Algae-X®, for example) also seems to help maintain fuel quality.

A handy way to monitor the condition of the primary filter element is to install a vacuum gauge on the discharge side of the filter. When the engine is running, this gauge shows how hard the lift pump has to suck to draw fuel through the filter. As the filter element becomes clogged, the vacuum level rises, signifying the need for a filter change. Racor makes such a gauge for mounting atop the filter unit, color coded to reflect filter condition.

Another worthwhile pre-voyaging step is to protect the engine against a condition known as "hydro-lock" that can cause serious damage. This occurs when water flows back through the exhaust line into the engine manifold and cylinders. This water can come from the cooling system or from seawater at the exhaust outlet. To prevent raw cooling water from siphoning into the exhaust system after the engine is shut down, there should be an anti-siphon/vacuum-breaker valve at the high point in the hose that carries raw water from the manifold casing to the exhaust elbow where the water is

Figure 13.1 – Siphon Breaks Prevent Hydro-Lock

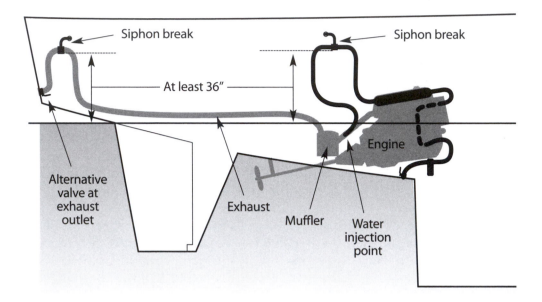

injected into the exhaust stream (Figure 13.1). To prevent seawater from siphoning through the exhaust line, the line should also be fitted with a vertical loop on its run from the muffler to its overboard discharge point; this loop should rise at least three feet above the waterline (even when heeled). It's even better if it, too, includes an anti-siphon fitting at the top of the loop. If such a loop is absent or the line cannot attain the needed height, an alternative is a valve at the overboard discharge point. This valve must be large enough that it doesn't impair the flow of exhaust gases and cooling water or increase back pressure on the exhaust system. Gate valves have a very poor record of performance at sea. Their stems snap, and turning the handwheel does not move the internal gate. The valve appears to work but in fact does not. A ball valve is a better choice, but insist on the highest quality because it must cope with a highly corrosive mix of exhaust and salt water.

If a valve is installed, establish positive measures for ensuring that it is opened before attempting to start the engine. One way is to hang the engine key on the valve handle when the engine is secured.

Also important to preventive engine maintenance is assembling adequate spare parts and supplies. Most engine manufacturers will provide a list of recommended spares; some make special suggestions for passages. In addition, useful spares and supplies might include a starter and starter solenoid, an alternator (perhaps the old low-capacity unit that came with the engine), a full set of belts for engine accessories as well as an emergency V-belt that can be cut to length, gasket material, water pump impellers, extra oil-absorbent pads to keep under the engine, engine oil for at least two oil changes, half a dozen oil filters, transmission fluid, 3-4 secondary fuel filter elements and a dozen primary fuel separator/filter elements. A manufacturer's engine service manual (much more comprehensive than the usual owner's manual) can be extremely helpful, especially if repairs must be done in a remote location. Also check that the toolbox contains a proper size wrench for every engine fitting – a Caribbean 1500 boat once had to divert to Bermuda and enter harbor under sail after hydro-lock disabled its engine, all for lack of the metric wrench needed to remove the injectors and drain the flooded cylinders.

Periodic replacement of the pencil zincs installed in heat exchangers in the engine cooling system can avoid an expensive repair. In the absence of these zincs, electrolytic corrosion will gradually eat away at the heat exchanger tubes and baffles and cause leaks. In the water cooling unit, the result will usually be a freshwater system contaminated with salt water. In the oil cooling unit, the result can range from catastrophic loss of lubricating oil to equally destructive contamination of the lubricating system with salt water. Check zincs regularly, as part of the regular oil change, and carry several spares.

The best preventive measures for the engine during a passage consist of daily fluid-level checks before starting the engine and a few minutes spent looking the engine over while it is running. Check for fuel, water and oil leaks. Look at the filter vacuum gauge, if installed. Watch the belts for sloppiness. Look at rotating units for unusual vibration. Feel hoses for mushiness/rigidity. Look for chafe or loose, vibrating wires and lines. Check the stuffing box for temperature (shouldn't be so hot you can't keep a hand on it) and water lubrication (slow drips, 6-10 seconds apart) when the shaft is turning. Be sure no loose gear can foul moving parts or contact hot engine surfaces.

The freshwater system. Just as many boat systems need reliable electricity, the crew needs a reliable supply of fresh water. Keeping the potable water system in top condition merits the skipper's attention. The system consists of the tanks, distribution lines and pumps.

There should be more than one water tank. This will prevent contamination of the entire system by a single mishap. The tanks must be strong. Fresh water weighs in at about 62.5 pounds per cubic foot, 8.35 pounds per gallon. Tanks must be fastened down well enough to prevent any movement in a seaway. They should be fitted with internal baffles to reduce sloshing of water when partially full, and they should have ample watertight access plates to allow cleaning, the first preventive measure to take before a voyage. Fill pipes must be tightly clamped at both tank and deck fitting, and the cap on the deck fitting should include an O-ring seal to prevent seawater leakage. (There should also be an O-ring to seal the fuel fill cap, which hopefully is located far from the water fill points and clearly labeled to avoid any confusion.)

A diagram of the water system is worth compiling. While you're at it, trace the suction line from each tank to the pump, looking for kinks, loose connections and potential chafe points (where lines pass through bulkheads, etc.). Trace vent lines, too. If the tank is overfilled, that's where the excess is likely to come out (perhaps in a hanging locker or above a bunk!). If the vent gets obstructed, the pump won't be able to draw water from the tank. Trace the lines from the pump to each outlet, following hot and cold water lines and checking each along the way. Draw it all out on a sketch, complete with valves, and you'll have a schematic that shows the entire crew how the system works and where key components are located.

Water pumps are generally reliable and durable. They live quietly, in a remote spot, and do their job on demand for years. Then they quit without warning. The moral: Carry a spare water pump and/or a pump rebuild kit. Pumps can fall victim to electrical or mechanical ills, and you need to be able to cope with either.

Because powered pumps can fail, every passagemaker's water system should include at least one manual pump. Manual pumps have an advantage beyond their independence from electrical failures. They deliver water in smaller quantities than pressurized systems, contributing to water conservation. Perhaps the greatest risk with pressure systems is that a leak will develop or a hose will pop loose, and the pressure pump will then cheerfully pump water out of the system until the tank runs dry. In the worst case scenario, the next step is for the pump to self destruct by overheating as it tries to pump air through the system. Many voyagers find it best to energize the pump and pressurize the system only while water is actually being used. Otherwise, the pump remains turned off at the switchboard.

If the pressure pump is left on, it's important that everyone be alert to it. If it's running, they should check to find out why. If it runs in short cycles at long intervals, it signifies a leak that is allowing a very gradual drop in pressure. Find it and fix it, because it will only get worse. Water leaks are rarely self-correcting.

Water treatment is another preventive measure. There should be bulk treatment of water in the tanks to prevent fouling or the breeding of organisms that could be harmful to crew. Two agents are commonly used: chlorine-based bleach, such as Clorox, or hydrogen peroxide. The bleach can be added at the rate of one teaspoon per 10 gallons of water. Hydrogen peroxide (use the 27% solution available for swimming pools) can be added at the rate of ½ to 1 ounce per 10 gallons. If tanks or water lines become foul from disuse, they can be treated by soaking for 12 hours with a very strong (50%) bleach solution, flushing with fresh water, then adding a small amount of baking soda to sweeten the water. (For more on treating small quantities of water, see Chapter 28).

Another water quality measure is a filtration unit downstream of the water distribution pump. These devices remove suspended solids and, if the filter elements include charcoal, they can also reduce bad odors and disagreeable flavors. Modern filtration units can produce remarkably pure drinking water.

A final freshwater precautionary measure is carrying an emergency supply, totally separate from the usual water system. It should include at least two gallons per crew member and can incorporate planned abandon-ship water. This water protects crew health against contamination of the primary water system as well as failures in the normal delivery system (pump, piping) or depletion of water tanks due to leakage, pump malfunction or excess usage.

Bilge pumps. Let's turn to another type of water – bilge water – and consider measures to make sure the disposal system works. The bilge drainage system normally consists of one or more pumps and their discharge lines. Some pumps may be electrically driven, often fitted with a float switch that causes the pump to activate automatically when bilge water rises to a preset level. At least one and preferably two of a boat's pumps should be manually operated and not reliant on the electrical system.

In evaluating adequacy of bilge pumping capacity, the passagemaker must take a number of factors into account. One is pump capacity. In real use, few pumps will move as much water as their rated capacity suggests. That capacity usually assumes the pump won't have to lift the water from a point below its intake opening or push the discharged water to a point higher than the pump housing. These conditions, especially the latter, virtually never exist. As a result, pump output is less, maybe far less, than its nominal rated output. Ratings also ignore resistance to water flow through intake or discharge hoses. Electrically driven pump capacity will also decline if its power supply is at less than fully charged battery voltage.

How much capacity is needed? That is highly subjective, but deserves thought. Consider how rapidly water can come in: a 6" hole four feet below the waterline will admit 870 gallons per minute. A broken 1 ½" through-hull can allow 31 gallons of water to enter every minute. Few pumps can handle that kind of flooding, so multiple pumps are clearly needed.

Automatic pumps are wonderfully convenient, but for a passagemaker they can be deceiving. By kicking on, unobserved, whenever the bilge level rises, they can conceal a developing leak. The problem becomes noticeable only when it overwhelms the pump or the pump clogs, overheats or loses power. This will happen sooner on a boat with shallow bilges than on one with a deep keel sump that can hold considerable water before the cabin sole gets wet.

Automatic systems are also prone to malfunctions of the automatic float switch. They can stick in the "off" position, failing to start the pump despite rising water. Or they can fail in the "on" position, causing the pump to run continuously until the battery dies or the pump overheats and seizes. Passagemakers are well advised to shun the automatic mode for bilge pumps. If the pump operates only under manual control, the crew remains aware of the amount of water it is pumping and the frequency with which pumping is needed.

For boats going offshore, it's standard to have at least two manual pumps to supplement any electrical pumps. One of those pumps should be operable from below, without having to open companionways or hatches to discharge water, and the other should be operable from the cockpit. The purpose is to permit pumping from either or both without exposing the interior to flooding from seawater on deck. Diaphragm pumps have demonstrated a high level of reliability. They can work despite debris in the water and are simple to maintain. The cabin pump should be as big as possible, and it will be far easier to operate if it is mounted so the operator can stand in a position that provides good bracing against sea motion and operate the pump with long swings of a vertical pump handle. The handle, regardless of size and installation, should be fitted with a lanyard to keep it from going astray. Each bilge pump should have its own overboard discharge. Plumbing pumps to a common discharge line or into a cockpit drain needlessly limits their output.

Before a voyage, test all pumps to assure they are working and to get a feel for their adequacy. Understanding just how laborious it will be to operate the installed pumps for an extended period (even days) may persuade you to increase capacity or modify the installation. One good test is to put a substantial quantity of fresh water in the bilge and see how long it takes to clear it with each pump, and how much work is involved. Electrical pumps should undergo the same test.

The spare parts bin should contain a rebuild kit for each bilge pump, manual or electric. The same applies for any sump pumps such as those that serve showers and refrigerator drains. Despite their usual longevity, pump components do wear out and being able to rebuild them at sea is good insurance.

Cockpit drainage system. Another drainage system that deserves assessment is that serving the cockpit. Having a boarding sea fill the cockpit is not uncommon in heavy weather. A 31 cubic foot cockpit (roughly 3.5' wide by 4' long and 2.5' deep) will hold a ton of seawater, which will have significant adverse effects on trim, stability and steering control until it drains out. Current ORC recommendations call for a minimum of 4 cockpit drains, each of ¾" diameter (after allowing for reduction of effective size due to gratings or screens). Test cockpit drainage by covering existing drains and filling the cockpit with water. Then open the drains and measure the time it takes to clear the water. Drainage in less than a minute is desirable. This exercise may also reveal the potential for previously unobserved hazards: immersion of non-watertight instruments, water leakage into the hull through lockers, binnacles or other concealed openings.

Preventing back flooding. A surprisingly common drainage problem offshore is back flooding, primarily through electric bilge pumps, occasionally through heads. (The same process produces hydro-lock of the engine.) If a boat is heeling far enough to immerse the pump discharge opening, a siphoning phenomenon can occur. The bilge pump, for example, may be activated by a benign rise in water level (perhaps sloshing due to boat movement triggers the float switch), and it begins to pump water out through the discharge line. When the pump stops, the weight of the water in the hose between the pump and the high point in the discharge line exceeds that between the high point and the exterior water level, so water starts siphoning backward through the line into the boat. It doesn't take a very great height difference to create back pressure that exceeds the pump's output pressure (remember, it was rated and designed to operate with zero output resistance), so water flows into the hull despite the pump's best effort to push it out. On other occasions, the pump has been observed to cycle on and off due to seaway movements, and in the periods when it is off, more water comes in than the pump can remove during its next "on" cycle, so the water level gradually rises.

Back flooding through the toilet occurs if a similar process is initiated when the head is pumped out and the protective through-hull is left open.

To prevent this from happening, fit overboard discharge lines with vacuum breakers at the top of the discharge loop. The purpose of this tiny valve is to let air enter the discharge line and disrupt the siphoning process. There are several designs, each of which causes the valve to close when there is positive pressure inside the discharge line. When the discharge stops and negative pressure develops in the line, it opens to allow air to enter the hose until the pressure difference is eliminated. It's a simple and elegant solution to a vexing problem, but it has one easily overlooked shortcoming: The tiny air passages are prone to clogging by dirt, sediment and other debris from the discharge line. When air can no longer pass through, the valve ceases to do its job, allowing back flooding to start.

This situation can be prevented by periodically removing the valve and cleaning the air passages. Though this measure is discussed with participants before every rally, it is not uncommon for one or more boats to ignore the guidance – because they've never had a problem with their vents – and experience back flooding during their passage.

If back flooding occurs through the head, the result will be obvious: seawater flooding out of the toilet bowl. If the bilge level is rising and the cause is unknown, a quick way to determine if back flooding is responsible is to tack the boat. The siphoning process depends on immersion of the external opening. Tacking the boat will often bring the opening above the waterline and end the siphon sequence. Stay on the new tack until the bilge is clear, clean the vacuum breaker, and return to the old tack. If this resolves the problem, further pumping on the old tack should not cause resumption of siphoning and back flooding.

Sea valves. Cruising boats have plumbing systems that remove other liquids and wastes besides bilge water. These include sink and shower drains, possibly incorporating a sump and pump arrangement, and marine toilets. One feature common to these and other drainage systems is the inclusion of through-hull valves or seacocks, each of which requires some maintenance to operate properly. Every sea valve should be disassembled, cleaned and lubricated during periodic haul-outs. Once the boat is afloat, the best way to keep valves working freely is to cycle each one regularly to prevent it from sticking in one position. Many are fitted with grease plugs to assist in lubrication. They should be given a shot of grease (a type designed for exposure to water) every month or so and at any sign of increasing resistance to operation. Through-hull valves should be either traditional plug-type seacocks or high quality ball valves. Gate valves are a poor choice for this important function.

The toilet system. Keeping the toilet system operating smoothly is exceedingly important, not just for crew health but for morale and quality of life, too. Train the crew in proper use. Keeping objects such as matches, safety pins, cigarette butts and all other foreign objects out of the toilet is essential. So is liberal use of flushing water to prevent build-up of waste inside the lines. Even properly used head systems tend to accumulate sedimentation and mineral crystallization in the lines, causing gradual reduction in water flow. These can be controlled to some extent by periodic treatment with cleaning agents such as vinegar, but in the long term, mechanical removal will be necessary. Since this entails removing the lines, flexing and pounding them to break loose the hard, rock-like sediments, it's best done during haul-out or an extended stay dockside. Preventively, it should be scheduled well before departure, since it's not a quick or pleasant job.

Check owner's manuals and manufacturers' guidance concerning the maintenance requirements for toilets and other components of the waste system, including MSD units (macerator/chlorinators, waste pumps, Y-valves, etc.) We've found that the manual pump on the toilet benefits from lubrication with mineral oil whenever it starts to feel tight. Just putting a tablespoon of oil in the empty bowl then pumping it out will restore easy, quiet operation.

Carry rebuild kits for toilets and other mechanical components of the waste system. Preventive measures can increase the time between major repairs, but eventually the less robust parts of these units (neoprene valves, O-rings, seals) have to be replaced.

Hose clamps. Hose clamps are found in various systems throughout the boat. Check frequently to be sure they are sound. When a repair job or inspection takes you into the bilge, around the engine, or into a seldom visited locker, take the opportunity to check hose clamps. A $5/16$" socket driver is better than a screwdriver for tightening most clamps.

The steering system. Few systems are more important than the steering system. Its failure can take all the joy out of an otherwise pleasant voyage. It deserves every measure to ensure that it will function reliably all the way to the destination and beyond. Since its operation entails constant movement of its components, the No. 1 enemy is friction and the wear it causes. The keys to avoiding friction are precise alignment and good lubrication of everything that moves.

As we discussed in Chapter 4, the steering system requires a close inspection to make sure all the components are aligned. Fairlead blocks must be securely fastened and located so the steering cables enter and exit without rubbing against the cheeks or sides of the groove in the sheave. At the rudder post, cables must lie in the same plane as the quadrant to eliminate any tendency to chafe or slip. Alignment of mechanical components in drag link, worm gear and rack and pinion steering systems is equally critical. In hydraulic systems, alignment of drive cylinders and tiller arm linkages is essential to prevent wear and binding. Whatever the system, accurate alignment will reduce wear, making the steering easier to operate as well as protecting against breakdown.

Lubrication also reduces friction, and oil or grease applied regularly to moving parts will keep the system running smoothly. Check these points for lubrication: bearings on steering wheel shaft, sprocket and link-chains inside the pedestal, every turning block/sheave that leads the cable to the quadrant, bearings, bushings and gear teeth on rack and pinion systems, and bearings at the rudder post. Linkages between tiller arms and hydraulic drives and autopilots also should be lubricated.

In cable systems, regular checks of the wire can prevent breakdowns. The cable should be tight enough to eliminate play, and there should be no slack that would let the cable slip out of its grooves in the fairleads or quadrant. It should not be so tight you can play a tune on it, because that will inflict excessive strain on the fairleads, pivots and linkages. Tension adjustment devices should be secured against accidental loosening: double nuts on eyebolts, cotter pins in turnbuckles. Cable end fittings should include thimbles in eyes to distribute stress, and if clamps are used there should be at least two, all fastened with the U-bolt bearing on the bitter end side of the loop, not the working side.

In all systems, check the mounting of any component fastened to the boat's structure. Fairleads, autopilot drives and hydraulic rams can undergo severe loading, and failure can occur quickly if fastenings are loose.

Just as important as preventive measures are plans for keeping the boat on course if the steering system fails. Several techniques for coping with a steering casualty will be discussed in Chapter 25, but the important point is to have given the matter consideration in advance. Whether the alternate steering system involves an emergency tiller and rudder, a vane or autopilot, sail trim, or objects dragged astern, thinking about it in advance will make it much easier to implement alternate steering if need arises.

Fire prevention. A final, vital area for preventive measures is fire prevention and preparedness. Thucydides reportedly wrote that "a collision at sea can spoil your whole day." A fire at sea can do even more damage, and just as quickly. Prevention is far easier than cure, and much preferable. An awareness of the hazards of fire must pervade daily life onboard. It influences stowage plans (all flammables topside, no combustibles near hot engine parts), mandates operating procedures (galley stove precautions, periodic boat inspections by watch standers), and guides daily repair/maintenance work (no jury-rig electrical connections, regular extinguisher checks). The key to fire prevention is crew training – making sure everyone is conscious of the potential for fires and establishing safe working practices that will minimize exposure to fire hazards.

Many old adages recognize the advantages of prevention over correction: A stitch in time saves nine; an ounce of prevention is worth a pound of cure. For a passagemaker, taking steps to prevent mishaps and malfunctions must become a way of life. From electrical systems to bilge pumps, from standing rig to water supply, there are many things a voyager should do long before the passage begins that will contribute significantly to its completion. Daily preventive measures will allow early detection and permit corrective action. By focusing on prevention, there'll be less need to struggle with correction. Pursuing steps to prevent casualties is thus a basic strategy for a successful passage.

CHAPTER 14

MEDICAL PREPAREDNESS

Because of the physical isolation and the self-sufficiency required, every passage-maker needs to be ready to cope with medical problems. Everyone hopes to complete the passage without incident. The vast majority will do so. Should someone become ill or injured, however, the adequacy of onboard supplies and knowledge will play a decisive role in that person's recovery.

The three medical kits. On the "supplies" side, the chief component is the boat's medical kit. Actually there should be at least two kits, perhaps three. One should be stocked for minor problems - scrapes, cuts, blisters, minor burns. The second should be reserved for more serious situations. The third is for abandoning ship. The first kit should be stowed where it is readily accessible to all. It should contain: Band-Aids, adhesive tape, antiseptic ointments, tweezers (for splinters), petroleum jelly and analgesics (aspirin or equivalents). It is intended for self-treatment, so each crew member should be free to draw from this stock as needed, advising the skipper if any supplies are growing low. Anything beyond the most minor or superficial injury should be reported to the skipper. He or she must be continuously aware of the crew's physical fitness and any potential for complications.

The second kit is the major medical kit, which contains supplies and medications for more serious conditions. It should be stowed where it's reasonably accessible yet well protected. Access should be limited to the skipper or a designated medical supervisor. This insures that all the contents will be there when needed.

Outfitting the major medical kit is a very subjective process. It should contain a good text on first aid or emergency medical care. (See References). Keep in mind that first aid literature gets outdated quickly. Understanding and management of some conditions, such as dehydration and diarrhea, improves every few years. The choice of antibiotics and other pharmaceutical products progresses just as rapidly. The boat's library should always contain one or two recent medical publications.

A good medical kit should include a wide array of standard first aid supplies. Figure 14.1 lists the contents of medical kits recommended by Dr. Dan Carlin. He is an emergency medicine specialist who founded WorldClinic at Lahey. Other medical kit contents are noted in Chapter 28, where Dr. Rob Amsler has provided specific guidance for treatment of medical problems that may be encountered during a passage.

The main medical kit should contain bandages of various sizes, gauze pads, alcohol wipes, adhesive tape, elastic support bandages, slings, safety pins, splinting material, nonprescription medications (antiseptics, analgesics, hydrocortisone cream, eyewash, ear drops, antacids, laxatives, antihistamines, cough and cold medicines, antifungal ointment, sunscreen, zinc oxide ointment, burn salves), eye patches, butterfly bandages, sterile and nonsterile latex gloves, thermometers, cotton and betadine swabs, isopropyl alcohol, hydrogen peroxide, tongue depressors and antiseptic soap solution. The kit should also contain prescription medications for issue only under close supervision: painkillers, antibiotics and allergy reaction medications. Emergency dental repair supplies should be part of the major medical kit.

In deciding how to stock the main medical kit beyond these basics, two factors come

---

Figure 14.1 – Medical Kit Checklist

☐ antibiotics
☐ analgesics: one narcotic, one nonnarcotic
☐ personal medications and emergency supply
☐ bandages, tape, dressings, antibiotic ointment (Neosporin)
☐ splinting material
☐ nitroglycerin; a metered dose spray bottle, long shelf life
☐ seasickness medications: two oral and at least one suppository type
☐ antacids and Metamucil
☐ a good medical reference book
☐ an allergic reaction kit with an adrenaline syringe
☐ an organized medical report form
☐ all meds blister packaged as individual doses w/anti-moisture additives

optional:
☐ urinalysis strips and interpretation chart
☐ Metamucil
☐ antacids
☐ eyewash
☐ antifungal cream
☐ iodine solution 2%
☐ surgical soap
☐ EMT shears

into play: the physical condition of the crew and the skills required for more sophisticated equipment. The kit must be tailored to the crew's needs. If crew members have known medical conditions, the kit must include the appropriate medications for treating them. It is also essential that someone other than the victim knows how and when to use these drugs. Crew medical skills can also influence the contents. It makes little sense to carry equipment such as hypodermic needles or normal saline solutions if no one is trained to use them. If, however, one or more crew members know how to suture a laceration, give an injection or administer an intravenous solution, the kit might usefully be expanded to include those supplies and corresponding medications. The kit can also include less technical equipment, such as a blood pressure cuff and stethoscope, to monitor vital signs.

Having a digital camera onboard can be useful in the event of an injury. Not only can it document the situation, but the images can be sent electronically to supporting medical authorities to improve their understanding of the case.

The third kit should be a separate medical kit for the abandon-ship ditch bag, and its contents are off-limits to all except in the genuine emergency for which it was assembled. In planning the abandon-ship medical bag, keep in mind that space aboard a life raft is extremely limited, so stick to basics and keep it small. Put contents in sealed containers or zipped plastic bags to protect against moisture. Include Band-Aids, antiseptic/antibiotic ointments (Bacitracin, Neosporin), analgesics, seasickness medications, sunscreen, petroleum jelly, hydrocortisone cream, and some broad-spectrum antibiotics. Supplement these with an emergency supply of any crew member's routine medications (e.g., hypertension or thyroid pills).

Shots. Ensure that all crew members have current routine immunizations for tetanus, polio, mumps, rubella and influenza. Tetanus boosters are valid for ten years. Be sure you are covered for the full duration of your voyaging plans. Unless cruising destinations include areas known to pose a risk of diseases such as yellow fever, cholera, typhoid fever or plague, additional immunization is probably not required. It's worth discussing this with a personal physician for specific guidance.

In preparing the medical kits, the help of a physician can be most beneficial. It's even better if the doctor is a sailor who appreciates the conditions under which a passage-maker will be working and the risks to which voyagers are exposed. The doctor can provide guidance not only about what to include but how and when to use it. He or she can write prescriptions and ensure that the skipper or designated medical supervisor is adequately informed about their use. (See Chapter 28 for specific recommendations.)

Crew medical histories. This brings us to the "knowledge" side of medical preparedness. This part of preparedness starts with assembling crew medical histories. Unless there's a trained health care professional in the crew who could make good use of detailed histories in assessing a situation, these can be brief. Any ongoing medical problems should be listed, along with prior or recent injuries/illnesses, since they could recur.

The history should include any known allergies or other special situations that would influence medical treatment. The name and phone number of a family physician familiar with the individual's medical background could prove valuable in an emergency. The history should list all medications being taken regularly. It's also prudent to include a copy of a current EKG (for use as a basis of comparison if heart problems occur) for all crew over 45, anyone with a family history of heart disease, smokers and those suffering from (treating) hypertension. Having such basic knowledge about the crew's medical condition may enable the skipper to anticipate possible medical requirements and to outfit the boat and train the crew accordingly. Figure 14.2 provides a sample medical history form. (Also see Chapter 28.)

Seasickness medications. Medical preparations should definitely address the most common medical problems encountered in passagemaking, the management of which is discussed in Chapters 27 and 28. Seasickness heads the list, followed by cuts, abrasions, burns, bruises, abdominal upsets, skin problems, fractures and ear infections. A few observations about being prepared for these common problems are in order. Although seasickness will be addressed in greater detail later, here it will suffice to note that motion-induced sickness is a very real challenge to almost every voyaging crew. A little preparation can greatly improve your ability to deal with it and minimize its impact.

There are many medications, both prescription and over the counter, for motion sickness. There are also folk remedies such as the consumption of ginger or wearing wrist bands that press on an accupressure point. Recently, an herbal oil rubbed behind the ear has appeared on the market. Individuals respond to these approaches differently. What works for one may be utterly ineffective for another. Many medications have side effects, such as drowsiness or dry mouth. Some people find the side effects as disagreeable as the sickness. The key point is that there is no single solution. Ideally, each crew member should try different treatments to find out which is most effective, and what dosage rate is appropriate. If you've never taken a specific medication, take it on land well before the voyage to determine how it affects you. If this is not possible, it is probably best to stick to a recognized product such as dimenhydrinate (Dramamine), meclizine (Bonine) or cinnarizine (Stugeron – unfortunately not available in the US). Now that dosage rate problems have been resolved, transdermal scopolamine patches are back on the market. They are a widely accepted and highly effective prescription medication, although they must be handled with great caution to avoid overdosing or misapplication.

Remain aware that yawning, drowsiness, cool sweats, headaches, unusual fatigue, and stomach uneasiness may be early symptoms of motion sickness. Being ready to take a medication of known effectiveness can go a long way toward reducing the adverse impact of "ocean motion" on the passagemaking crew.

Crew first aid training. Another part of medical preparedness is to ensure that crew members are familiar with standard first aid measures. Courses offered by the

Figure 14.2 – Medical Fact Sheet

MEDICAL HISTORY SUMMARY

Name: _____

Address: _____

Telephone: _____ FAX: _____ E-Mail: _____

Billing Info: MasterCard / Visa Number: _____ Exp. Date: _____

Vessel Name / Country of Registration / Home Port

_____

Emergency Point of Contact (name , address, telephone #):

_____

Private Physician: _____

Address: _____

Tel: _____ Fax: _____

Private Dentist: _____ Tel: _____

Medical Insurance: _____

Company: _____ State: _____

Policy Number: _____ Group Plan: _____

Name of Policy Holder: _____

Social Security Number of Policy Holder: _____

Medical History

Prior Hospitalizations: _____

_____

_____

Prior Surgeries: _____

_____

Active Medical Problems / Ongoing Medical Conditions:

_____

_____

Medications and Dosage Schedule: _____

_____

Inactive Medical Problems / Conditions in Remission: _____

_____

Allergies and Type of Allergic Reaction: _____

_____

Family History of Illness (parents or siblings with early or significant medical conditions):

_____

Smoker: ☐ No ☐ Yes _____ packs per day: Alcohol: ☐ No ☐ Yes quantity per day: _____

BLOOD TYPE: _____

American Red Cross are very reasonably priced, and although they focus on shoreside scenarios, the basic procedures are applicable afloat. The big difference, of course, is that a voyager cannot rely on an emergency responder network triggered by a 911 call, but must go well beyond the "protect the victim and call for help" phase to provide actual medical care. Having at least one crew member with advanced first aid training, or possibly even a course in emergency medical care, can be a significant asset during a passage. It can be a source of emotional reassurance for the whole crew, as well as a priceless advantage in an emergency.

Outside help. *Before you leave,* test a method for receiving assistance or guidance from shore sources in the event of a medical emergency beyond the capabilities of those on board. Know how to contact a source of medical guidance. As noted in Chapter 9, Coast Guard and High Seas radio stations can link a vessel at sea to a doctor ashore. The references include several commercial medical support companies. They have been established principally to provide service to commercial fleets that do not carry medical personnel, but they will usually try to assist other vessels in an emergency.

Several organizations exist to help members in locating suitable medical care when away from their home country. For a modest fee, MEDEX, for example, offers services ranging from finding sources of proper medical care to managing medical evacuations and coordinating emergency blood and vaccine transfers. The International Association for Medical Assistance to Travelers (IAMAT) is an organization supported by voluntary contributions. Membership is free. IAMAT provides references to medically qualified, English-speaking doctors at fixed fee rates in over 130 countries. Enrollment with such organizations can simplify getting needed medical support and care at your destination or ports along the way.

Avoiding injuries. A most important element of medical preparedness is injury avoidance: taking precautions in the routine operation of the boat to avert injuries. Examples include wearing shoes (especially watch standers) to prevent foot and toe injuries. Exercise extreme care in the galley when pouring hot liquids or handling sharp knives and by wearing a heavy apron or bib-top foul weather trousers when working at the stove in rough weather. Rig preventers to avoid surprise gybing of the boom. Make sure the boat is fitted with handholds and grab rails that permit a crew member to hold on in a seaway. Crew must remember that they are often working with lines under extreme tension, capable of inflicting serious injuries. Keep hands well back from winches when tailing a line. If a line starts to run away, never try to stop it with the hands. Don't straddle tensioned lines while working them. By remaining conscious of the potential for injury, the crew can avoid needless exposure. Avoiding an injury is far better than treating one.

A sound strategy for medical preparation has implications for boat outfitting, crew training and onboard operating routines. Because medical problems can have such serious consequences, conscientious attention to this preparedness is very important.

The vast majority of passages are completed with little more than an occasional minor injury, but in the exceptional case when a medical emergency arises, adequate preparatory effort can literally spell the difference between life and death.

REFERENCES:

Peter F. Eastman, MD, *Advanced First Aid Afloat*

Paul Gill, MD, *First Aid and Emergency Medicine Afloat: The Onboard Medical Handbook*

Department of Transport, Her Majesty's Stationery Office, *The Ship Captain's Medical Guide*

David Werner, *Where There Is No Doctor*

Murray Dickson, *Where There Is No Dentist*

SERVICES:

Medical Advisory Systems Inc., Owings Mills, MD (800) 368-2110

Maritime Health Services, Inc., Seattle, WA (206) 781-8770

Maritime Medical Access, Washington, DC (202) 994-3291

AEA/SOS, Philadelphia, PA (800) 523-8930

World Clinic at Lahey, Burlington, MA (800) 636-9186

ORGANIZATIONS:

MEDEX Assistance Corporation, 9515 Deereco Road, Timonium, MD 21093; (800) 537-2029; fax: (410) 453-6301; e-mail: medexasst@aol.com

International Association for Medical Assistance to Travelers, 417 Center Street, Lewiston, NY 14092 (716) 754-4883

CHAPTER 15

PROVISIONING, STOWAGE AND COOKING

Provisioning is a real challenge for passagemakers, with a need for self-sufficiency offset by the boat's limited storage capacity. Food planning, stowage and easy retrieval all may take organizational skills never before demanded by meals.

The importance of retrieval can be illustrated by a personal experience. As we prepared for our boat's first passage with the Caribbean 1500, my wife was suffering extreme pain from a back problem. She prepared a wonderful list of provisions based on detailed meal plans. We managed to get them purchased, and all but the refrigerated stores had been stowed several days before departure. The refrigerated items came aboard the night before we sailed, when last minute details were demanding attention. Helen was unable to lift these items or bend to put them in the refrigerator. A helpful friend offered to load and stow the fresh food, and he worked diligently to get it all aboard and tucked into the refrigerator. It seemed a real godsend at the time. Alas, he was not making the passage, and no one in the crew had a clue where he had put anything. A high level of frustration prevailed in the galley the first 3-4 days, because we had to search through all the refrigerated stores to find what we needed for a particular meal. The problem wasn't resolved until we had depleted the supplies enough to take everything out and restow it following a plan that everyone understood.

Provisioning starts here. Successful provisioning begins with a meal plan. Prepare menus that cover the entire passage plus a couple of days. (This allows for adverse weather or an unexpected diversion.) Include all three meals each day, plus snacks and light rations for the night watches. Aside from the first day or so, when light meals seem best suited to stomachs getting used to offshore, plan for one hearty meal each day. The constant motion, 24-hour routine and frequent activity tend to induce healthy appetites.

Much of the dining during a passage takes place in the cockpit, where gracious living is rarely the rule of the day. Strong wind can blow light items right off a dinner plate. Lumpy seas can make all but the stickiest food slide off a plate in the cockpit, the galley or the saloon. So be sure the galley gear includes a set of deep bowls in which meals can be served when conditions get rough. Also carry big mugs that will let the crew enjoy soup or beverages without spilling.

Keep the meals simple. Complicated recipes and multi-course meals that are delightful in a pleasant anchorage can be exhausting at sea. A hearty main dish, one side dish and a beverage will usually satisfy a hungry crew. An optional salad, bread or dessert can be added when conditions permit. One-pot meals are invaluable parts of the menu plan. Many voyagers find it helpful to prepare in advance (and freeze, if possible) several meals for the first few days while everyone adjusts to the onboard routine.

A 3-part list. Working from the menu, prepare a list of all the food and associated supplies (aluminum foil, plastic wrap). This forms the basic provisioning list, and it's useful to divide it into three categories: staples and supplies that can be purchased well in advance, often in bulk; items with shorter life span that should be purchased just before departure (bread and baked products, some refrigerated items such as butter and cheese); and finally the fresh items that should be purchased immediately before departure (eggs, fresh milk, fruit, vegetables).

Decide on food stowage early. Before making any purchases, decide how and where the food will be stowed. Stowage capacity may lead you to modify the menu plan. By making storage decisions well in advance, the actual loading and stowing will be immensely easier. It's neither hygienic nor appealing to have food stored in the same locker with a toolbox, chemically fragrant fuel filters and a jug of laundry detergent, so specific storage areas should be dedicated to food alone. Identify all these areas and then decide how to allocate the space available to the planned stores. This is definitely a matter of individual preference. Some prefer to store like products together (canned vegetables, canned fruit, pasta, beverages, bread and pastry products, etc), while others organize by the meal, putting all ingredients of a particular menu in one package. The latter simplifies the cook's chore, but the former makes it easier to adapt meal plans to changing conditions or unexpected bonanzas such as catching a nice wahoo.

Both the provision plan and the stowage plan must include plenty of high energy snacks, especially for the night watches. Fresh fruit is a healthy choice, and individual packages of cookies and crackers stay fresh and appetizing. Hard candies, trail mix and small candy bars are also popular. A supply of snacks should always be available, and the crew should feel free to help themselves. At the same time, the crew must understand that foraging through the provision lockers is not okay. It tends to confuse the stowage plan – and nothing will annoy a galley manager more than discovering that a prime ingredient of Thursday's dinner was eaten by a marauding crew member at 0400 on Tuesday.

Refrigerated stowage. Refrigerated stowage deserves special mention. It is usually limited in volume, often difficult to keep cold, and all too frequently unreliable. Use the refrigerated space only for items that really require refrigeration. Many things we customarily refrigerate in our homes (eggs, many hard vegetables, opened containers of jam, etc.), can survive quite well for a week or more without refrigeration. Use cool storage spaces to best advantage: eggs and many vegetables kept in a locker below the waterline and close to the hull will last a surprisingly long time.

Because the refrigeration system works hard to remove heat from the box, don't open the reefer more than necessary. Think about what you need for a meal before opening, and get all refrigerated items out at one time. At least one rally boat carried this to an extreme: The galley manager (dictator?) allowed only two daily refrigerator openings, one in the morning (breakfast and lunch items came out) and one in the afternoon (supper and overnight needs)! Crew had to think ahead or do without. That system preserved refrigeration, but paid too dearly in crew happiness.

A handy way to reduce refrigerator openings is to have a secondary storage site, such as an insulated chest, for cold drinks. Drinks can be chilled in the reefer overnight then moved to the cooler in the morning.

If the reefer fails. Refrigeration failure is an altogether too common experience during passages. This forces a sudden drastic change in the menu plan. The crew has to eat as much of the refrigerated food as possible before it goes bad. Meal planning is reduced to, "What is still good, and what will go bad next if we don't eat it?" After a day or so, Neptune's marine scavengers are eating better than the crew. The moral is that provisioning must take into account the possibility that refrigeration will fail. Have a substantial capability to feed from nonrefrigerated supplies. Prepackaged, freeze-dried, mountaineering meals are one option, but a wide variety of meals can be prepared from canned and dry ingredients. Pastas, dishes that use canned chicken, ham or beef, and packaged dry mixes all provide alternatives to refrigerated items, and should be included in the provisioning list in ample amounts. So should UHT (long life) milk and sugar-free instant drink mixes such as Tang® and Crystal Light®. Since these foods generally have an extended shelf life, they can always be kept for subsequent use.

What's available far from home? Keep in mind that many staples – white sugar, flour, rice, pasta, potatoes, onions, butter and mayonnaise products, coffee, tea, bread, eggs and boxed milk – are usually available in many cruising grounds. Although at somewhat higher prices, they can be replenished fairly easily. Specialty products – maple syrup, grits, your favorite brands of peanut butter or margarine, "designer" coffees and teas, nonprescription vitamins – may be difficult or impossible to find. They should be well stocked before departure.

Fishing for dinner. While it is nice to supplement the menu with fresh fish caught during the passage, don't depend on it. Some boats seem to catch as many fish as they can eat; others troll in vain for weeks on end. We've averaged about one fish catch per 10-12 day passage, and only once have we stopped fishing because we had all we could eat. Usual catches include dorado and wahoo, as well as an occasional spanish mackerel, albacore or tuna. We only fish when we're well offshore, not near reefs where there is a risk of ciguatera poisoning. Each catch typically yields 3-5 meals (baked, broiled, fried, or steamed and served as main course, chowder or salad).

We use a handline and 100-150 pound test line. There's no pretext of light tackle or rod-and-reel sportsmanship here – we're harvesting food. Using a stainless wire leader about 6' long, we keep the trailing red or blue/green "squid" lure well behind the boat (150' or more). Best results have been achieved with boat speeds of five knots or more, and if you can tow the lure past a patch of floating debris you have an excellent chance of catching one of the dorado that hang out in the shade the debris creates. A shock cord-clothespin rig to absorb the impact of the fish strike is important. So too are sturdy gloves, to prevent cuts from the line and wire as the fish is hauled back to the boat. Use a gaff to bring the fish aboard and put it down quickly by pouring a few ounces of rum (or other high-proof alcohol) in the gills on both sides. Covering the fish's eyes with a wet rag sometimes reduces the unavoidable flopping. Once the fish is dispatched, use a sharp, thin knife to trim a full-length fillet (gills to tail) on each side. Slice or pull the skin from the fillets and toss it overboard along with the carcass. Wash the fillets in fresh water and refrigerate until ready for cooking.

Coping with trash. Trash is an unavoidable by-product of provisioning. Since throwing plastics overboard is prohibited by law and dumping any other non-biodegradable material is at the very least undesirable, minimizing trash is another part of provisioning. Look for supplies that have less packaging material, and put boxed items into reusable canisters, disposing of the boxes ashore. Many nonperishable products wrapped in paper or plastic (paper towels, toilet paper, bar soap) can be unwrapped and placed in reusable zip bags. Sealable, reusable containers (e.g., Rubbermaid and Tupperware products) selected to fit the space available reduce trash and increase stowage efficiency. In tropical areas, be careful not to bring cardboard cartons, beer and soda cases, or even paper bags aboard. They often contain cockroach eggs that can bring unwanted "crew" aboard. Leave the paperboard products in the dinghy or cockpit and dispose of them ashore.

Trash management can affect the quality of life; no one wants to share the boat with a foul smell. We've found these measures work: All food scraps go overboard as quickly as possible. All packaging goes in the trash bin (lined with a plastic bag); if wet with food residue, it's first rinsed with seawater. Steel cans are rinsed, then top and bottom are removed and they're flattened to reduce volume. Aluminum drink cans are rinsed, crushed and stowed separately in hopes of finding a recycling bin at the destination. Plastic containers are rinsed and flattened. Bottles, carried only when unavoidable, are rinsed and stowed in the trash bin or a separate bag for recycling. With a crew of 4-5, on a passage between the US and Bermuda (5-6 days) we usually generate one full and one partial bag of trash; on a 12-14 day passage to the Caribbean, we seldom exceed two full bags, and we still avoid putting anything other than food scraps overboard.

Before departure, choose a spot to stow filled trash bags. Many voyagers use part of a cockpit locker, others keep it topside (under a dinghy, perhaps) – preferably where it's downwind of the cockpit on most points of sail. Extra heavy-duty trash bags, large enough to hold several full smaller bags, help keep the trash consolidated and are less likely to rip.

Galley hazards. The galley can be a hazardous area for many reasons. One is the risks associated with the galley stove fuel (see Chapter 3) and the consequent need to follow safety and operating instructions meticulously. In addition, the cook is dealing with hot objects, including fluids that can splash, in a constantly moving environment. Great care is necessary to avoid dangerous burns. When seas kick up, a fanny sling for support is necessary, as is a strong bar across the stove front to keep the cook from being tossed against the hot elements. The cook should always wear protection against burns, as well. The rougher the weather, the more complete the protection needs to be, ranging from a heavy apron to bib-top foul weather pants. Pouring hot liquids is always risky, as is removing heated dishes from an oven (which can become unstable with its door open, causing hot pots atop the stove to tumble). The cook is also handling sharp knives, pointed galley tools, and so forth. Cooking demands a very high degree of safety awareness, and developing this awareness must be part of the crew training program.

With galley-related matters playing such an important role in the success of a voyage – ranging from the food supply to personal safety of those doing the cooking – it's a good idea to designate one crew member as galley manager. The galley manager's job is to oversee all galley-related matters discussed above, including development of the menu and shopping list, stowage plan, and safe preparation of the meals. This does not mean the galley manager should be the full-time cook and galley slave. Those duties should be shared by the entire crew, with meal preparation responsibility rotated like watch assignments. The galley manager ought to know enough about cooking and meal preparation to assist and educate those crew members who lack galley skills, and he or she should maintain oversight of details such as menu variations, adequacy of snack supplies and galley cleanliness. Since meal preparation is often a hot and physically demanding chore, there's a sound basis for the rule that says the cook never cleans up. The cook is more likely to focus on producing a good meal if not distracted by the extent of the post-meal cleanup.

Stowage for safety and access. While provisioning is an important part of the boat's overall stowage plan, there are many other important stowage considerations throughout the boat. First is the need for security: Stowed gear must stay stowed, even in the event of a knockdown or rollover. This means all lockers must have positive latching closures. For saloon cabinets, sliding external barrel bolts offer the best security. The traditional latches that use spring loaded catches inside the door (requiring one to insert a finger through a hole, grope around for the latch, release it and try to extract the finger without losing control of the door or breaking the finger) are highly vulnerable to accidental opening. All it takes is a heavy object inside the cabinet that can slide, strike the lever and release the latch.

Deck plates and locker lids under bunks are also potentially self-opening storage closures unless they are equipped with positive means of closure. These areas can produce especially hazardous possibilities if there is a knockdown, and heavy gear normally stowed deep in the boat starts to go adrift. Take special precautions to secure heavy objects such as batteries, stove, toolboxes, sewing machines, scuba tanks, and anchors. Each must be fastened down so they could go through even a 360° roll without coming loose. Bookcases and open storage bins also warrant special attention.

In addition to being secure, stowage must be rational. Keep compatible things together. Assign individual stowage of personal gear. Put food together, preferably near the galley. Put tools, spare/repair parts and maintenance supplies in dedicated lockers, stowed so the most frequently used items are the most accessible. All flammables should get topside stowage. Safety and emergency equipment such as fire extinguishers and perhaps a few basic tools should be stowed in several locations to ensure availability in case damage or an accident precludes access to some part of the boat. Medical kits and abandon-ship bags must be secure yet quickly accessible. Since the large amount of material stowed for a long cruise can affect the boat's center of gravity, and hence its stability, make every effort to store heavy items as low as possible. The stowage plan deserves careful thought before the first supplies come aboard.

The case for neatness. Good plan or bad, nothing will detract from safe and smooth cruising more rapidly than a failure to keep things stowed. Clutter aboard a boat can be contagious. What starts with one object left on a countertop quickly turns into a jumble of clothing, harnesses, personal gear and equipment. The prudent voyager will establish two rules and enforce them relentlessly:

• *A place for everything, and everything in its place.*
• *Don't put it down, put it back.*

Keeping the boat stowed means being able to find whatever is needed because it is where it belongs. It means not having to sort through loose gear to get access to a through-hull or the box with the spare cotter pins. It means keeping life orderly as well as the boat, and it enhances the quality of life onboard.

Successful provisioning, meal preparation and stowage start with a well thought-out meal plan and a carefully considered allocation of limited storage space throughout the boat. Next requirements are sound operating procedures, attentive management and group responsibility for sharing the work burden and keeping the boat neat. Here again, the key will be the crew's training and each member's readiness to give the group's welfare precedence over personal ease.

CHAPTER 16

SAFETY AND EMERGENCIES

One hallmark of a successful voyage is safety. A well-conceived strategy to complete a passage without injury takes high precedence in preparations. This strategy will include preventive measures, as well as effective response if an emergency occurs.

Simply having all the requisite safety equipment aboard cannot ensure a safe voyage. Sailing with a safety-oriented mind-set and observing the principles of prudent seamanship are equally important. Also, knowing how and when to use safety equipment is crucial. *While it is easiest to focus on the equipment, what really counts when something goes wrong is the crew's training in established safety routines.*

Safety equipment can be conveniently divided into personal gear and boat gear. The former is normally used by a single specific crew member and often is provided by the individual. The latter is for common usage and is part of the boat's outfit.

PFDs – what the ratings mean. The personal safety equipment list starts with personal flotation devices (PFDs), formerly known by their less bureaucratic title of life vests. Coast Guard regulations require that a boat carry at least one Coast Guard approved wearable PFD for each person onboard. These devices must be stowed where they are accessible and ready to use (not sealed in the plastic wrappers in which they were purchased). The Coast Guard has established five types of PFDs. Type I PFDs, also referred to as Offshore Life Jackets, provide the greatest protection. They supply at least 22 pounds of buoyancy located in a manner that will turn most unconscious wearers face up in the water. Type II, or Near Shore Buoyant Vests, have only 15.5 pounds of buoyancy and are less able to keep wearers face up. Type III PFDs, or Flotation Aids, were designed to be more comfortable and create less interference with movement and activity than Types I or II. They also provide at least 15.5 pounds of buoyancy, but its distribution is such that most wearers will have to exert active efforts to stay face up. Also assigned to the Type III category are water sports vests (with multiple closure devices to withstand high-speed water impact), float coats and one-piece flotation suits, and inflatable vests (except those with an integral harness). Type IV PFDs are throwable devices, such as seat cushions and life rings. Providing 16.5 to 20 pounds of buoyancy, they do not meet the "wearability" test in the "one per person" requirement, but boats over 16' must carry at least one throwable device in addition to the wearable PFDs. Type V PFDs include Hybrid Devices, specialized white-water vests and inflatable vests with a built-in safety harness. Hybrid Devices have at least 7.5 pounds of inherent buoyancy that can be increased to 22 pounds by an inflation device. They're not very common, primarily because they cannot be counted toward the "one per person" requirement unless they're actually being worn. White-water vests are approved only for white-water rafting and are not applicable to voyaging boats. Like the Hybrid Device, an inflatable vest with an integral harness must be worn to count toward the minimum quantity required.

Choosing offshore PFDs. Choosing PFDs for a passage involves weighing important trade-offs. Type I PFDs, with their higher buoyancy, are clearly the best choice for a survival situation, where a person faces an extended period in the water. The problem is that they are bulky and uncomfortable. They make it difficult to grind winches, fit into narrow spaces and move about the boat. Because they impede the crew's ability to work, they're impractical in anything short of a general emergency. When it becomes a question of leaving a sinking boat, though, they are far better than the other Coast Guard approved models.

Type II PFDs generally have only one redeeming characteristic: They are the lowest priced approved PFDs. Inferior to Type I in terms of flotation, they are almost as uncomfortable and offer little advantage. Inherently buoyant Type III devices provide just as much buoyancy as Type II models and are far more comfortable and wearable. Relocating the buoyancy material for comfort and easier movement has, however, impeded the device's ability to keep the wearer's face up, making them unsuitable for use in rough water. For routine use, Type III PFDs offer a compromise between protection and ease of wear, so they are the type most commonly found aboard sailboats. Unfortunately, the dictates of "style" have sometimes overridden common sense in designing Type III PFDs. They come in many colors and designs, some of which make the wearer difficult to see against blue water and white wave tops. Any PFD aboard an offshore boat should be a bright, conspicuous color, preferably international orange or yellow, the colors most easily detected against an ocean background.

Inflatable PFDs. After many years of research, testing and negotiation with manufacturers, the Coast Guard has finally approved some inflatable PFDs. Those devices offer buoyancy equal to or greater than Type I PFDs, yet are more comfortable. When inflated, many of these devices provide 35 pounds of buoyancy. A number of European studies have shown this to be the minimum necessary to keep a wearer's face and mouth high enough to minimize breathing difficulties from frequent wave immersions.

Inflatable PFDs come in two general forms: shawl style units worn on the upper torso and devices worn on a belt at the waist. Shawl types have the advantage of being worn in the ready-to-use position. They simply need inflation, normally by pulling a toggle or rip cord. This punctures a small cylinder of compressed carbon dioxide

(CO_2) that fills the inflation chamber and provides the desired buoyancy. They will keep the wearer afloat, face up. Units worn in belt packs require some donning effort, either before or after inflation, to gain the desired buoyancy. Some are vests that must be unfolded and pulled over the head before inflation. Others are horseshoe rings that are inflated, then strapped around the torso beneath the arms.

Some inflatable devices, primarily the shawl style units, can be fitted with automatic inflating devices. They use either a bobbin which crumbles when it gets wet, or a paper cone which collapses when wet, to release a compressed spring and puncture the CO_2 cylinder to inflate the device. Automatic inflation mechanisms are not 100% reliable – a recent test produced a failure rate of over 15%. As a result, Coast Guard approval currently extends only to manually operated models, not those fitted with automatic inflation mechanisms. All inflatables, including those with automatic devices, can be inflated manually by pulling a cord or lever that causes a pin to puncture the cylinder. All inflatables also have oral inflation fittings to permit initial inflation if the CO_2 system fails and to restore an inflated unit that has lost some of its charge.

Inflatable units are best used in situations when the wearer does not anticipate spending a long period in the water. Rather than the survival situation when a crew must abandon a boat, they are more appropriate to the crew overboard scenario, where a person is suddenly in the water and must stay afloat until the boat can return and make a rescue. The additional buoyancy of an inflatable device can keep the victim afloat while conserving energy. Since virtually all inflated devices are bright yellow, they also increase the wearer's visibility.

Maintaining PFDs and using them. All PFDs require a degree of maintenance. Inherently buoyant types must be inspected to make sure fabric and stitching are sound, fasteners operate properly, and the buoyant material has not disintegrated or become waterlogged. Inflatable devices require similar inspection. They also need further checks to ensure the bladder is leak-free, the operating mechanism works smoothly, and the CO_2 cylinder is corrosion-free, charged, and properly seated in its socket. Since all PFDs are intended to be used in the water, it's not a bad idea to try them out in that environment. Experiencing firsthand the degree of support and comfort provided by a specific PFD, whether USCG approved or not, can be enlightening. It may well lead to a decision to change the type of PFD carried.

For actual use, the key questions regarding PFDs of any kind are where they are kept and when they are worn. Stowage must be in a place that permits quick, unobstructed access. A cockpit locker is a good choice, provided care is taken to ensure that the PFDs do not migrate to the bottom of the locker, buried beneath other gear. Or you might assign a specific PFD to each crew member and have it stowed near their bunk.

Voluntary PFD wear should be encouraged at any time, but there should also be clear understanding about when wearing becomes mandatory. Linking PFD wear to taking a second/deeper reef or setting the trysail eliminates any ambiguity. You might well consider a policy adopted by the Cruising Rally Association for offshore passages. Every crew member is required to wear some form of flotation device whenever outside the protection of the cabin during a passage. This requirement has proved quite tolerable, with most crew choosing some minimally intrusive inflatable device. After a few days, wearing it becomes perfectly normal and, in fact, one begins to feel vulnerable without it.

Harnesses and tethers. Second on the list of personal safety equipment is the safety harness and tether. They could easily be considered more important than PFDs, since their proper use can prevent a mishap, whereas the principal value of a PFD does not come into play until after something has gone wrong. The function of a harness and tether are to keep a person attached to the boat – to prevent crew-overboard situations. They should be worn whenever a condition exists that increases the risk of going overboard or impedes the boat's ability to recover a victim: darkness, high seas, proximity of shoals. It's a sound practice to wear harnesses regularly to become accustomed to working the boat and moving around while remaining tethered. Learning to operate effectively while staying hooked to the boat is an essential element of crew training.

Harnesses and tethers come in a significant range of styles and prices. Stay away from the bargain-basement specials and homemade substitutes. Good harnesses save lives. Get the best you can afford, treat them with care and look on them as modestly priced life insurance. Technical standards for design and construction of safety harnesses are found in Appendix I to the Offshore Racing Council's Special Regulations. Good harnesses are made of wide webbing arranged to keep the tether connection point at about armpit level. (Lower connection points concentrate strain on the lower back rather than the torso and rib cage, and increase the probability that a towed victim will be submerged). Several manufacturers market models designed to give women greater comfort by arranging the body straps to reduce crushing at the bustline.

Tethers should be no more than six feet (two meters) long and have releasable fastening devices at both ends. Strong materials (braided webbing, top quality hardware) and brawny stitching are essential. The fastening at the harness end should enable the wearer to detach the tether while it is under substantial strain. This fastening is necessary to allow the wearer to disconnect the tether if being dragged under the water by a sinking boat or one moving at significant speed. In such cases, water resistance can prevent the wearer from reaching the fastening at the far end of the tether. The latter fastening should be self closing, not subject to accidental opening, and operable with one hand. Tethers that provide dual connection arrangements (either two legs, one long and one short, or an intermediate hook on a single long leg) provide the wearer with extra options. Using the short tether keeps the wearer closer to the attachment point and provides greater security while using both hands to work the boat. Having two connection points allows the wearer to clip on to a new fastening before detaching from the old one, assuring continuous attachment to the boat. Innovative tethers include models with internal bungee cord to reduce the amount of slack tether when not under strain, and versions with shock absorbing sections to reduce the effect of sudden loading.

As with PFDs, every boat should have clearly defined practices for wearing harnesses and using tethers. It's common to require safety harnesses from sunset to sunrise, when darkness increases the risk of losing anyone who goes overboard. This policy also gives every crew member regular opportunity to get accustomed to working the boat while remaining attached by harness. Harness wear should also be linked to sea state or weather, when a specified wind speed is reached or when sail reduction reaches a chosen threshold (e.g., working jib and reefed main). Even when properly tethered, a person who loses his or her balance or is struck by a boarding wave will be able to fall as much as six feet from the attachment point. Crew should favor the windward side of the boat when it is heeled. Then if they fall, they will fall across the deck or cabin top to the limit of the tether, rather than over the side where they will be dragged through the water.

Regular use of harnesses and tethers is the best way to preclude crew overboard situations. An overboard incident not only puts the victim at risk, but also creates serious hazards for the boat and other crew members as they maneuver for the recovery. *There is simply no substitute for wearing a harness consistently throughout a passage.* The question of proper places to attach the tether will be addressed shortly.

Crew apparel. Crew apparel also forms a part of personal safety equipment. A crew member who is cold and/or wet is more likely to make mistakes, and errors lead to injuries. Having and wearing proper foul weather gear has direct implications for safety. So does appropriate clothing, with plenty of warm clothes (jackets, sweaters, thermal underwear, gloves) in cold conditions and adequate sun protection (hat, light long sleeved shirts, light trousers, sunscreen) in hot spots. Hats are important protection from both sun and cold. Wearing good shoes can improve traction on deck as well as avoid toe and foot injuries. Quality sunglasses will protect eyes from the damaging effects of UV radiation as well as glare that can produce headaches and fatigue. Carrying a good knife, preferably fitted with a spike or a shackle key, or a multipurpose tool like a Leatherman 7, can pay dividends in a situation that requires quick action to cut or disconnect a line under stress. At night, a small personal flashlight, preferably with a red lens to preserve night vision, is vital for safe movement about the boat. And somewhere in the crew member's clothing should be a pocket to hold a few mini-flare distress signals or a tethered strobe light that could help the boat to locate them in a crew overboard situation.

Attachment points for harness tethers. The boat equipment list is extensive, but it links to personal equipment in several places. Chief among these is adequate attachment points for safety harness tethers. These should include fixed points at the most common crew operating stations plus a system that allows a crew member to remain attached to the boat while moving from point to point on deck. The fixed points should consist of sturdy padeyes, through-bolted to hull or deck structures with strong fastenings and substantial backing plates to distribute the load imposed by a falling crew member.

There should be one or more attachment points in the cockpit for watch standing crew, including the helmsman, who must be able to steer without having the tether get in the way. Selected fastening points at the mast, near the bow pulpit and other common top-side work stations are also desirable. The most important single point is one that can be reached by a crew member from the safety of the cabin. He or she should be able to attach to this point before starting up the companionway, and remain connected until seated in the cockpit, providing security while making the potentially risky transition between cabin and cockpit. This point offers similar assurance to those going below, who can remain attached until safely within the cabin.

Jacklines. The system that allows crew members to remain clipped on while moving about topside usually takes the form of one or more jacklines rigged from strong points near the bow to strong points near the stern. They must allow a crew member to clip on to the line while in the cockpit, then move all the way to the bow or to the stern without having to unclip. Careful planning may be needed to prevent interference with running rigging such as sheets and vangs. While some boats may be able to rig a single jackline along or near the boat's centerline, most opt for a pair of lines, one on each side, with the crew using the one to windward when the boat is heeled.

The choice of jackline material is generally limited to two. One is stainless steel wire rope or cable, sometimes with a plastic coating such as that used on lifelines. Wire rope offers the advantages of being unaffected by sunlight and extremely strong, and because it has very little stretch it is effective in minimizing the distance an attached crew member can move or fall. The principal disadvantage of wire is its tendency to roll under foot when stepped on, which can be very hazardous. This risk can be reduced if the cable can be pulled very tight, so it lies against the sides of the cabin house, rather than on the flat of the deck. The other usual jackline material is flat or tubular braided webbing such as that used for mountain climbing. While this material has greater stretch, it lies flat under foot and does not pose a hazard to those walking on deck. Many of these braids are vulnerable to UV deterioration, so choice of a UV-protected material is important when the lines will be rigged on deck for extended periods. Use only braid designed for high load applications (in excess of 4,000 pounds). Do not be misled by flat woven strapping that has a breaking strength of only a few hundred pounds.

Whatever the jackline material, be sure the end fastenings are sufficiently strong. The effectiveness of a strong jackline can be eliminated by weak stitching, low strength shackles or under-strength attachment points. Using sturdy shackles to connect the lines to mooring cleats is often a simple solution.

Other than strong padeyes and carefully installed jacklines, there are few safe places to attach tethers. Standing rigging might be okay, but running rigging is not. Lifelines or stanchions are definitely unacceptable attachment points. They are not designed to absorb the impact of a falling crew member. Make sure the crew knows where – and where not – to clip a tether.

Overboard retrieval equipment. While harnesses and jacklines are intended to keep crew onboard, the boat must also be equipped to retrieve a crew overboard. The ORC Regulations offer excellent guidance. They specify that a boat must have within reach of the helmsman and ready for instant use a lifebuoy equipped with a drogue and a self-igniting light. There must be an additional lifebuoy, also within reach and ready for use, that is equipped with a whistle, drogue, self-igniting light and a pole and flag that will fly at least 6 feet above the water. US SAILING modifications specify that the buoys must be within easy reach of the helmsman, and prescribe a Lifesling® in lieu of the first lifebuoy for all but short daytime inshore races. Yet another alternative is Survival Technology Group's Man Overboard Module® (MOM), which provides an inflatable life ring and an inflatable pylon in lieu of the traditional pole and flag. Since Navy offshore sailing experience has demonstrated that it is difficult, perhaps impossible, to deploy a traditional man overboard pole and its associated gear quickly enough to be effective, the MOM is a very attractive option. It can be deployed in a few seconds by pulling a single release pin, placing the pylon and life ring within a very short distance of the victim.

Whatever equipment you choose, you need to provide for getting flotation to the victim immediately. You will also need a plan for responding to a crew overboard situation, one that is written down, understood by everyone onboard, and practiced until it can be implemented swiftly. This plan should: specify the alarm to be sounded in the event of a crew overboard (e.g., a police whistle hung at the helm), define the immediate maneuvers to be initiated by the helmsman, assign responsibility for activating the man-overboard function of electronic navigation systems, appoint a lookout to keep the victim constantly in sight, and address sail handling, preparing recovery equipment and assembling first aid supplies.

Practice, practice. Step-by-step techniques for crew overboard retrievals will be addressed in Chapter 20, but for your safety strategy, practicing those techniques is paramount. Crew overboard recovery trials by the Seattle Sailing Foundation and California's Modern Sailing Academy leave no doubt that the prospects of success improve substantially if a crew has had practice. Mistakes – ranging from ineffective maneuvers to fouled recovery lines – are common on first attempts at a crew overboard drill, but the number drops sharply after just a few practice sessions.

Practice drills must be realistic. Passing a floating seat cushion at two knots and snagging it with a boat hook is not adequate preparation for a real recovery, when the boat must be stopped and 200 pounds of wet, scared, tired, and possibly injured crew hauled from the water to the deck. It will even pay to practice just the recovery process without performing boat maneuvers. On a quiet day at anchor, put someone in the dinghy alongside and devise methods for getting this "victim" on deck without his/her assistance. Try it again in rougher conditions to get a better appreciation of how much more difficult a real recovery could be if you were at sea in bad weather.

For recovery maneuvers, find out how your boat responds to differing sea and wind conditions, and learn if there are situations when you will have to use the engine. Experience has shown that engine use often leads to major problems (fouled props, endangered victims) and is best avoided. There are, however, some cases where a given boat simply will not perform the requisite maneuvers in certain wind/sea conditions, unless under power.

Consider the complications that could arise if the overboard crew needs medical attention. An injured crew may need help to be recovered, and any crew who has gone overboard should be treated for shock and given a mandatory rest period of at least six hours before returning to normal duties.

Be wary of recovery schemes that sound simple, but have proven ineffective. Chief among these is the line towed astern to be grabbed by a crew overboard. Unless the boat is moving very slowly, the line is fresh and clean, very long and fitted with grips/knots, and the crew is uninjured, quick-witted, agile and fit, this system just doesn't work. A floating line rigged to disengage an autopilot or steering vane may be worthwhile, but there are also electronic systems that can perform the same function.

A good heaving line. A good heaving line can be useful in many situations, including crew overboard. The traditional lines, with a weighted monkey fist or quoit and a coiled line, take some skill to use. And if they're not properly prepared each time, the result is a tangled mess that falls far short. Much more reliable are heaving lines that use a sock or bag with the line stuffed loosely inside so it will pay out when the bag is thrown. They can be thrown with fair accuracy and distance, even into the wind, with minimal experience. Survival Technology Group markets one that includes an automatically-inflating life ring in the thrown bag to provide flotation as well as establishing the essential physical contact. When maneuvering to recover a person overboard, a good heaving line, kept ready and accessible, can convert a near-miss into a successful rescue.

Fire extinguishers. The boat's fire fighting system is composed of fire extinguishers and educated crew members. Just as wearing harnesses and tethers doesn't invalidate the need for overboard recovery preparations, even with meticulous fire prevention measures (Chapter 13) you still need to be able to fight a fire. A discussion of fires and fire fighting agents and techniques is included in Chapter 29. From a safety equipment standpoint, it's essential that the boat carries the proper type and quantity of fire extinguishers, that they are ready to use, and that each crew member knows how to use them.

The Coast Guard has established minimum requirements for fire extinguishers aboard boats (Figure 16.1), but common sense suggests a larger number. For example, there should be at least one extinguisher in each cabin, plus one accessible from the cockpit. These should be multipurpose extinguishers that can be used against all types of fire. Reserving extinguishers with a clean agent such as Halon or CO_2 for the galley and electronics/electrical panel in the nav station is a good idea, and an automatic system in the engine space is highly desirable. Another good galley option is a chemically-treated fire extinguishing blanket that can be thrown over a stove-top fire.

Figure 16.1 - USCG Fire Extinguisher Requirements

Boat Length	Minimum Extinguisher Requirement
Up to 26'	1 B-I
Over 26', to 40'	2 B-I or 1 B-II
Over 40', to 65'	3 B-I or 1 B-II and 1 B-I

Class B-I extinguishers

Type	Recommended Volume of Extinguishing Agent
CO_2	at least 4 pounds of agent
Dry chemical	at least 2 pounds of agent

Class B-II extinguishers

Type	Recommended Volume of Extinguishing Agent
CO_2	at least 15 pounds of agent
Dry chemical	at least 10 pounds of agent

To be reliable, fire extinguishers require maintenance. They should be inspected periodically to ensure that internal gas pressures have not fallen, that seals and safety pins are in place, and that the operating mechanism is clean and free of corrosion or rust. CO_2 and Halon units can be weighed to verify the amount of gas, while dry chemical units should be dismounted, inverted, rapped sharply with a wood or rubber mallet to loosen the powder inside and shaken vigorously to make sure the powder has not become caked or solidified. If there is any doubt about the condition of an extinguisher, take it to a servicing agency for inspection or replace it.

Each crew member must know where fire extinguishers are located and how to use them. Few sailors have personal experience in using a fire extinguisher, so it's not a bad idea to run a drill from time to time. One successful plan involves periodically replacing the oldest fire extinguisher onboard with a new unit and using the old one to put out a fire set in a controlled environment ashore (e.g., a camp fire or a small amount of gasoline floated atop water in a large pan). Procedures for fighting a fire are addressed in Chapter 29, and making certain the crew is thoroughly familiar with proper use of the boat's fire fighting equipment is an important component of your overall safety strategy.

A safety strategy must also take into account the ultimate disaster situation, when lives are at stake and the issue is survival. In this situation, distress signals, an emergency radio beacon, an abandon ship kit and a life raft constitute the principal resources to help sustain the crew until rescue arrives.

Visual distress signals. Coast Guard regulations require each boat to carry visual distress signals suitable for day and for night use. While some acceptable signals, such as an orange distress flag, are limited to daytime use and others, such as an electric SOS signal lamp, are only for night use, most skippers choose to carry pyrotechnic distress signals, many of which are effective both day and night. Distress signals can be divided into two functional categories: alerting signals and locating signals. The former group is designed primarily to draw attention to the existence of a distress situation. It includes meteors and parachute flares. The latter type are intended to assist rescuers in finding the site of an emergency. They include handheld and floating flares and smoke signals that burn for several minutes and disclose the location of the distressed boat or victims. While some signals, such as handheld flares, are effective in both roles, a boat's signal kit should be checked to make sure it includes signals that will perform alerting and locating functions by day and by night.

Coast Guard regulations also specify that each boat must carry a minimum of three day and three night signals (or three combination day/night signals), but voyagers are wise to carry a substantially larger number. The history of distress situations is replete with reports of victims who expended all their distress signals long before their rescue, and who were subsequently passed by many potential rescuers who were unaware of their plight. One of the rules set forth by Michael Greenwald in his book, *Survivor,* is "Signals are like blessings: You can never have too many." The longer your planned passage, the truer this guidance becomes.

Pyrotechnic signals are designed to comply with one of two sets of performance standards. One set was prepared by the US Coast Guard, while the other has been established pursuant to an international agreement known as the SOLAS (Safety of Life At Sea) convention. (SOLAS agreements on maritime safety measures are generated through the UN's International Maritime Organization and adopted by national legislative bodies as law.) There is a substantial difference between the performance levels required by the two standards, with SOLAS-grade signals generally being far brighter and more effective than their Coast Guard counterparts. Since SOLAS standards exceed Coast Guard requirements, SOLAS grade signals satisfy the regulatory requirement for boats to carry "Coast Guard approved" distress signals.

All pyrotechnic signals have a fixed shelf life. Coast Guard grade signals are marked with an expiration date 42 months after manufacture while SOLAS signals expire at 36 months, so both provide about three years of useful life. Experience has shown that at the expiration date, the reliability of Coast Guard grade signals is seriously diminished. Well over 50% may fail to function. By contrast, SOLAS signals have demonstrated very high reliability, functioning with only slightly diminished intensity or color as much as eight years subsequent to the expiration date. Organizations such as US SAILING and the Cruising Rally Association recognize this and accept SOLAS grade signals up to five years old for meeting their requirements. (Boats must still carry the minimum number of in-date signals to comply with legal requirements.) Retaining out-of-date signals – particularly SOLAS grade signals – as backup distress devices is a good practice.

Figure 16.2 - Standard Signal Brightness: USCG vs. SOLAS

Signal	USCG standard	SOLAS standard
Handheld flare	500 candela 120 seconds	15,000 candela 60 seconds
Smoke signal	**handheld** 50 seconds	**floating** 180 seconds
Meteor flares	250-400' altitude 10,000-35,000 candela 6-8 seconds	(Meteors not included in SOLAS grade signals)
Parachute flares	1,000' altitude 10,000 candela 25 seconds	1,000' altitude 30,000 candela 40 seconds

The effectiveness of a distress signal is a function of its distinctiveness (making the victim stand out against a background), its intensity (the brighter the better), its duration (longer is better), and its altitude (higher is better, because it increases the area from which it is visible). Color is the chief contributor to distinctiveness, with orange flags and smoke, and red meteors and flares being typical examples. Both SOLAS and Coast Guard signals use color. Except for the duration of handheld flares, on virtually all the other attributes, SOLAS grade signals surpass their Coast Guard grade equivalents by a large margin, as reflected in Figure 16.2.

Other factors contribute to SOLAS signals' advantages. The output of the smoke signal is denser and does not dissipate as rapidly in a breeze, the handheld flares do not drip hazardous hot, molten slag when they burn, and the aerial devices are hand launched and do not require mechanical devices such as pistols. Without doubt, the vastly greater intensity of the SOLAS signals is their chief asset. Anyone who has seen a demo at a Safety at Sea Seminar can attest to the impressive difference that makes SOLAS signals well worth their higher price.

Whichever distress signals you select, the crew must be trained in their use. Everyone aboard should know where the signals are stowed and exactly how to use them. Different manufacturers employ slightly different methods for igniting flares and launching parachute rockets, and the crew should be intimately familiar with those aboard. During a life raft test on Chesapeake Bay, our Viking raft was outfitted with European-made SOLAS grade signals. Each carried instructions, but they were printed in many languages in fine print. It would have been extremely difficult to find and read the proper section in a real emergency. Doing so at night would have been next to impossible. Moral: The time for everyone to learn how the distress signals operate is on a quiet afternoon dockside, before the voyage begins.

EPIRBs. Thanks to one very specialized distress signal, the Emergency Position Indicating Radio Beacon (EPIRB), the whole concept of sea survival has changed in the past 20 years. For centuries, the only option open to those forced to abandon their ship at sea was to board a lifeboat or raft and navigate it to a friendly destination, because no one else knew where they were or what had befallen them. Today, thanks to EPIRBs and the position-finding capabilities of the satellite system that receives their signals, the entire situation has changed. A mariner in distress can now notify a worldwide system, the system can determine where he is, and his objective is to stay there and await help.

EPIRBs are radio transmitters that send a distinctive signal on designated distress frequencies. When first introduced, they used aircraft distress frequencies so the signals could be received by aircraft, later supplemented by reception capability built into certain weather satellites. Around 1990, a new system was introduced that operates on its own dedicated frequency and includes significant improvements over the earlier system. Since the older system is still in operation, a review and comparison is worthwhile.

EPIRBs designated Class A and Class B transmit their signals on 121.5 MHz and 243.0 MHz, the commercial and military aircraft distress frequencies. Class A units must be installed so they will float free if a vessel sinks, and they turn on automatically when afloat. Class B units must be turned on manually. These EPIRBs have saved many lives, but the system is subject to serious shortcomings. There is a high false alarm rate – up to 95% of the signals detected do not come from true emergencies. (For example, aircraft emergency locator transponders operate on the same frequencies, and a hard landing by a plane can set off the transponder. Also there is no simple way to determine if a unit has been turned on accidentally or if it is a real distress situation.) There is no way to identify the source of the emergency signal, which would help in assessing its validity. Because the signal's frequency tolerance is relatively wide, the accuracy of the position obtained by satellite measurement is rough. It results in a search circle some 12-20 miles across. Another difficulty is that the satellites, on detecting an EPIRB signal, can only relay it immediately for reception by an earth-based tracking station. If there is no land station within range of the satellite at the time – a situation largely limited to more remote parts of the southern hemisphere – the relayed signal is simply lost.

The new system was developed to cope with these limitations. These EPIRBs operate on a higher, dedicated radio frequency, 406.025 MHz (their generic designation is "406" models). This frees the system from interference or confusion from signals generated by other systems. The detection system is wholly satellite based. Officially, the EPIRBs are described as Category I (float free, automatic initiation) and Category II (manually activated) devices, and further defined as Class 1 (for very cold regions, operates down to -40°C/-40°F) or Class 2 (operates down to -20°C/-4°F). Each EPIRB unit has embedded in its distress signal a unique identifier code. Assuming the unit is properly registered when purchased, this identifier enables national authorities (in the US it's NOAA) to call the contact points listed on the registration form to confirm a possible genuine distress situation. This telephone verification will serve as the confirmation of an emergency that the Coast Guard requires before launching a rescue mission. Registration data also enable search and rescue authorities to determine exactly what they are looking for (e.g., a dark green 58' ketch named *Neptune's Trident*). When the satellites in the 406 system detect a signal, they store all the data in memory until they can download it to a land station, so signals don't get lost. Because the frequency tolerances for 406 MHz signals are much tighter than for earlier EPIRBs, position-finding is significantly improved, cutting the search radius down to about two miles. The net result is a reduction of false alarms – signals subsequently determined not to require rescue – from 95% to about 5%.

These advantages of the 406 MHz EPIRB make it the system of choice for any passage-maker. Though the units cost more than their older 121.5/243.0 MHz counterparts, they are certainly worth it. They give speedy access to help if a life threatening situation develops, and they enable rescuers to respond more quickly with better information. In fact, 406 MHz EPIRBs have removed much of the "search" phase from search and rescue and made possible swift rescues, even from remote locations.

A new item on the EPIRB market combines EPIRB and GPS features. In addition to its unique identifying signal, these units transmit their exact position, as determined by internal circuitry or downloaded from a separate GPS unit. Besides providing rescuers with precise location data, these units enable geostationary satellites to join the search and rescue system. These satellites can detect a standard EPIRB's signal and instantly relay it to a ground station, but because they do not move relative to the transmitting beacon, they cannot determine its location. By providing the necessary positioning data, these units can get an emergency signal to a shore station in as little as five minutes, and cut the total time delay in response to an EPIRB alarm by as much as an hour.

The EPIRB should be stowed where it will always be instantly available, since catastrophes can strike with astonishing speed. It very definitely should accompany the crew if it becomes necessary to abandon the boat, so many voyagers keep their EPIRB in the abandon ship bag. Others choose to stow the less expensive manually activated models in or adjacent to the cockpit. The automatic, float-free models (required on commercial vessels) must be stowed topside where they can launch themselves if the vessel sinks.

EPIRBs have built-in test circuitry, usually employing a small light that flashes when the unit operates. On older Class A and B EPIRBs, the test circuits sometimes gave false indications, flashing the light even though the unit was not in fact transmitting. The 406 MHz models have a highly reliable self-test system: If the light flashes, it's working. Both types can also be tested with a portable FM radio. With the radio tuned to the central part of the FM dial, put the EPIRB antenna near the radio's antenna. When the EPIRB is turned on, the FM radio will produce a series of short, rising pitch tones. On a 121.5/243.0 MHz unit, that is the sound of the primary distress signal. On a 406 MHz unit, it is a low-powered 121.5 MHz signal the beacon generates to allow search aircraft to home in on the signal source with direction-finding receivers.

Testing an EPIRB of any kind is permitted only during the first five minutes of any hour, and then only for the few seconds necessary to verify that it is operating. They should never be turned on for longer periods or at other times. Doing so could trigger a search and rescue effort.

Using the EPIRB. In a MAYDAY situation, when life is endangered, the proper way to use the EPIRB is to turn it on (following the instructions, which may call for the unit to be floating in water for better signal generation) and leave it on. The batteries will power the unit for at least 48 hours (probably more in temperate or tropical waters). Attempting to conserve battery life by turning the unit on and off will only confuse, frustrate and delay search operations.

The abandon ship bag. The third part of the boat's safety outfit for disaster situations is the abandon ship bag. This is the collection of vital equipment and supplies that will be needed to sustain life in the raft until rescuers arrive. The quantity of stores packed in most rafts is exceedingly spartan, and they must be supplemented by items rescued from the abandoned craft. The starting point for assembling any abandon ship kit is a review of supplies packed in the raft. To preclude untimely surprises, this review must go beyond reading the manufacturer's list and include a visual sighting of those contents. (This can be accomplished during the raft's annual inspection or by visiting a large dealer or service agency.) Too many survivors have felt let down when they discover that the "fishing kit" consists of a small polyethylene bag containing a couple of loosely coiled lengths of monofilament and several small fishhooks, or that the "repair kit" consists of glue-on patches whose instructions tell you to start with a clean, dry surface, which is virtually impossible aboard a raft.

The abandon ship kit should be packed in one or perhaps two watertight containers, each with sufficient inherent buoyancy to float when loaded. This buoyancy is needed to minimize the possibility of losing the bag in transfer from boat to raft. It will also allow the bag to be stowed outside the raft in fair weather if crowding becomes a problem inside the raft.

While the contents of any abandon ship bag must be customized to each passage-making boat and crew, there are several high-priority items. *In addition to the EPIRB, the most important is a reverse osmosis watermaker.* We can get along quite well over a surprisingly long period without food, but without water, our life expectancy is measured in a small number of days, especially when we're exposed to adverse weather. Packaged water, whether in jugs, cans or plastic bags, is vulnerable to loss or contamination, and at best provides only a finite supply. Small, hand-operated units such as the Survivor 06® can generate sufficient pure water to keep two or three people well hydrated. For larger crews, the Survivor 35® can produce much more water with only a little greater effort. With an adequate water supply, even long-term survivors can stay remarkably healthy. After 66 days on the high seas in a coastal life raft with minimal food but a good water maker, Bill and Simone Butler looked so healthy when they were rescued that many doubted their claims about how long they'd been adrift.

A second high-priority abandon ship item is a portable VHF radio, with fully charged battery and perhaps a charged spare, and a watertight bag in which to keep the radio. At least one manufacturer (ICOM) now markets a handheld radio powered by lithium batteries with a shelf life of five years. Other models can operate on easily-replaced AA batteries. The ability to communicate with search aircraft and prospective rescue vessels can be invaluable. And a handheld GPS unit that will enable you to report a very accurate position will accelerate rescue. One pair of Rally veterans, transiting back to New England independently, experienced sudden uncontrollable flooding from unknown causes. The couple had to take to their raft, and the husband, a former Air National Guard pilot, coordinated their rescue by talking with Coast Guard aircraft on a handheld VHF radio and providing precise location data from his portable GPS unit.

Although most rafts will include a minimal number of distress signals (usually 3), the abandon ship bag should include as many more as space permits. If time allows, it is worth taking all the unexpired signals from the abandoned vessel, as well as any back-up over-age SOLAS signals.

Devices such as a radar reflector or a Search and Rescue Transponder (SART) could also greatly enhance the ability of passing vessels to detect a raft and effect rescue. A raft's fabric will reflect so little radar energy that it will seldom show on a ship's radar screen. A reflector will create a much larger image. A SART is a device that actually transmits a coded signal whenever it detects a ship's radar beam trained in its direction. This appears on the ship's radar screen as a series of dashes extending from the position of the SART-carrying raft to the center of the ship's radar scope. The result is a combination of an accurate position on the raft and a confirmation that a distress situation exists and rescue is desired.

If any crew members require glasses for reading or for distant vision (as a lookout, for example), the abandon ship bag is an excellent place to stow a spare pair. Similarly, if any crew members must take regular medication (hypertension pills, insulin, thyroid tablets), keep a supply adequate for at least a week (more if voyaging in remote waters) in the abandon ship bag.

The abandon ship bag should include a dedicated medical kit with first aid supplies (bandages, antiseptic ointments, zinc oxide, sunscreen, hydrocortisone ointment, seasickness medications, etc.), but the boat's first aid and medical kits should also be high on the priority list of items to grab if abandoning ship.

Looking beyond the abandon ship situation to life following rescue, it is worth protecting vital personal documents such as wallets and passports. Since they are seldom of use during a passage, it causes little inconvenience to collect them from all crew members and stow them in the abandon ship kit for the duration of the voyage.

Other items worth tucking into the abandon ship kit would include extra flashlights and spare batteries, high carbohydrate foods, light line for lashings and lanyards, trash bags and sealable polyethylene bags, a drinking cup, logbook/notebook with pencils or pens, multi-tool pocket knife, and thermal blankets. The size of the abandon ship bag(s) and the extent of the kit's contents must be limited by consideration of space and weight. There will be little spare room in the raft, so stowing the abandon ship gear will prove challenging. Keeping the bags light enough to handle easily will facilitate their retrieval and transfer to the raft and contribute to their buoyancy should they end up in the water.

The life raft. The final component of the disaster outfit is the life raft itself. Taking to the raft is strictly a last-ditch measure, a step that should be taken only when there is definite evidence that the boat is no longer safe (e.g., fire out of control) or on the verge of sinking (decks awash and losing buoyancy). Always observe the maxim that you don't enter the life raft until you have to step UP to get there (or, as Michael Greenwald put it in *Survivor,* "Never abandon the ship until the ship abandons you"). The procedure for abandoning ship will be treated in Chapter 20, but some considerations regarding rafts are part of the safety strategy and deserve mention here.

A raft's capacity is usually expressed in terms of the number of occupants it was designed to carry (four, six or eight person rafts). For rafts approved by the US Coast Guard or constructed to SOLAS standards, one "person" equals four square feet of floor space in the raft. Other rafts may use even smaller allocations. (One manufacturer cited a "yacht" standard that turned out to be only 3.5 square feet/person.) Note that there is no consideration of volume or headroom, so the space beneath a low canopy-supporting arch tube counts just as much as unobstructed space in determining capacity. Virtually everyone who has spent more than a few minutes in a raft loaded to its nominal capacity has concluded that life in such crowded conditions would be extremely difficult. Taking into account the space needed for survival supplies and the equipment salvaged along with the abandon ship kit, there is a convincing case for carrying a raft whose rated capacity is larger than crew size. Since the designer anticipated that the raft would contain the rated number of occupants in calculating its stability, it would be a mistake to go too far with excess capacity. Generally, one step up (a six-person raft for a crew of four, an eight-person raft for crew of six) is a good compromise.

Life rafts come in a wide array of shapes and styles, and no single choice is perfectly suitable for every boat and crew. Selecting a raft will involve compromises, just as in the boat that carries the raft. Examine as many rafts as possible (preferably fully inflated at boat shows or at service stations) and compare their features. The choice will ultimately be based on personal preferences, but a number of characteristics should be weighed in the process.

Rafts are generally divided into coastal and ocean types. The biggest difference is usually the number of buoyancy tubes – the large peripheral tubes that keep the raft afloat. Coastal rafts usually have only one tube. It often has an internal sleeve arrangement to prevent total deflation from a single puncture. Ocean rafts usually have two independent tubes, each of which can provide minimally adequate buoyancy for a raft loaded to its rated capacity. *Ocean rafts* often have automatically-inflating arch tubes that support a protective canopy to shield the crew from sun, rain, wind and sea, while coastal rafts may have none or such tubes may require separate manual inflation.

Coastal rafts have saved many lives on the high seas, but a passagemaker is well advised to select a raft intended for ocean service.

Canopy designs range from simple unsupported nylon fabric covers to cave-like enclosures that resemble an igloo to provide maximum protection. Some have provisions for opening one or more sides for ventilation and to facilitate access. In a warm-weather environment, such an arrangement offers significant advantages. Most canopies are orange to improve visibility, an important feature since black buoyancy tubes and raft bottoms are very difficult for a searcher to spot. Canopies may also contain rainwater collection systems and viewing ports to make it easier to keep a lookout.

Rafts need a ballast system to provide stability and reduce the likelihood of raft (and occupants) being rolled by seas. Systems range from massive hemispheric bags to doughnut shaped rings under the floor or smaller individual ballast bags that work with a sea anchor to provide stability. All have been tested, and claims of superiority have not been resolved definitively. Regardless of type, *a good ballast system is essential* to a raft suitable for high sea use.

An optional feature for most rafts is an *inflatable interior floor*. It provides a number of advantages. It increases the rigidity of interior accommodations and provides a substantial insulating layer to reduce thermal losses. For voyages anywhere other than the tropics, this is extremely important, since hypothermia can be a deadly hazard for survivors.

Arrangements for boarding rafts also vary widely. Some rafts have only braided fabric "cargo net" style ladders that are difficult to use. They swing under the raft rather than providing a base for pushing the body upward into the raft. Others have inflatable "boarding ramps" that make it easier to get out of the water and into the raft.

Beyond a standard list of basic raft supplies (a few distress signals, bailer, air pump, patching kit, paddles, sea anchor, flashlight and seasickness pills), outfitting a life raft can vary widely. Standard or optional kits may include food and water, signaling mirror, first aid kit, and other life-sustaining supplies. Occasionally, it is possible to add a few small items to the raft's outfit when it is being serviced (e.g., tiny "mini-B" EPIRB, special Search and Rescue VHF radio with long shelf life lithium battery), but rafts are packed so tightly and so carefully (to ensure proper opening and inflation) that there's very little room for extra gear. Knowing and seeing exactly what is packed in the raft is the first step in deciding what must be included in the abandon ship bag.

Stowing the raft. Life rafts come in hard fiberglass boxes suitable for mounting topside or in soft valise packs that must be stowed out of the weather and protected from damage. Because of the difficulty of getting a raft up through a companionway in a crisis, the ORC Regulations limit the weight of valise-packed rafts stowed belowdecks to 88 pounds. As a result, a valise can seldom be used for anything larger than a six-person raft. Cabin or cockpit locker stowage of a valise-packed raft certainly provides maximum weather protection. But if a raft is well secured and shielded from inadvertent damage (where it cannot be stepped or sat on, kicked, or buried beneath other gear), it will also be difficult to unstow and get topside quickly. The ORC Regulations call for the raft to be stowed so it can be moved to the lifelines within 15 seconds.

Rafts in hard containers are usually stowed topside, and choosing the location is difficult. The best arrangement is a dedicated cockpit locker specifically designed for the raft, but boats incorporating this feature are rare. The alternatives generally consist of deck-mounted cradles on the foredeck, amidships or aft. Occasionally, a raft is mounted in a cradle attached to the stern pulpit, overhanging the transom, but a raft stowed that way is highly vulnerable. Even though the canisters are designed to be watertight, leakage through the seals or around the operating lanyard opening is not uncommon. Therefore a foredeck location, where the raft is exposed to the full force of any boarding seas, increases the risk of seawater damaging the raft and its operating mechanism. A foredeck location also increases the hazards faced by a crew member who must launch the raft or make a routine check of its security in rough weather. A raft stowed on the foredeck or cabin top is also vulnerable to damage in a dismasting.

For the best compromise of ready access with protection from the elements, stowage amidships or aft (especially for a boat with a center cockpit) seems to be a good choice. It's relatively easy to monitor raft security, it's an easier area in which to work when launching, and access is quick and unobstructed. On the other hand, a midships location often obstructs visibility from the cockpit. Avoid placing the raft where it will be a tempting bench seat or a step stool for reaching boom or mast fittings. The containers are not as rigid as they may appear. Cyclic loading of the canister will quickly open the seals and permit water leakage.

Whatever location you choose, the raft should be stowed so it is ready for immediate use. Locks and pendants used to prevent pilferage in port must be removed before the boat gets underway. The operating lanyard, which doubles as the raft's painter, should be securely fastened to the boat's structure. This is necessary to prevent loss of the raft when it is launched and inflated. In conjunction with a hydrostatic release on the raft lashings, use a specially designed weak link to connect the operating lanyard to the boat. This will allow a sinking boat to trigger inflation of a deck-mounted raft after it has floated free of the boat.

There are two schools of thought on mounting the raft's cradle. The more conventional says to mount it in the most secure manner possible, with sturdy through bolts and ample backing plates to distribute the stress over a large area. This approach gives priority to keeping the raft aboard. The alternative espoused by experienced voyager Larry Pardey is to use only screws to hold the raft cradle, making the connection in a sense a sacrificial weak point. Assuming that severe boarding seas would be strong enough to tear any cradle loose, he considers a screwed-down cradle less risky than a through-bolted one, since the latter would likely cause the cradle to take large chunks of the deck along with it. This approach gives priority to maintaining the boat's integrity, even at the cost of losing the raft. The choice depends on your personal preference.

Rafts need annual inspection. Regardless of capacity, model, container type, outfit and stowage arrangements, life rafts require annual inspections to insure that raft and contents are ready for use. Consider the cost of raft inspection and servicing a modestly priced life insurance premium; it's not worth skipping inspections to save a few dollars. Servicing should be done only by an agency approved in writing by the raft manufacturer to perform annual inspections. The service agency will inflate the raft (using a warmed dry air/nitrogen mix rather than the super-cold CO_2 that comes out of the installed inflation bottle) and check it for leaks. They will inspect the raft seams, fittings and fastenings, weigh the CO_2 bottle to verify its full charge, and make sure the inflation mechanism operates properly. They will inventory and inspect all the supplies packed with the raft and replace any that are malfunctioning or outdated. Most reputable service agencies will allow an owner to see a raft while it is inflated for service and to inspect the supplies that accompany the raft. If a service shop refuses to grant access, choose another agency, if possible. It's also wise to insist on getting back any replaced items, to insure against needless replacement.

Rent a raft? Many first-time voyagers, uncertain of their long-term plans, are reluctant to make the major financial commitment entailed in buying a life raft. They ask about the alternative of renting a life raft until they are sure they will be doing sufficient passagemaking to justify buying one. This is certainly a prudent approach, and one that is quite feasible to implement. There are, however, two points that should be investigated before committing to a rental.

The first concerns the raft itself. Deal only with an agency that performs more than a cursory inspection of each raft between rentals. It need not be a full annual inspection, but it must be thorough enough to verify the integrity of the raft, its operating mechanism and its supplies. Don't hesitate to ask about the specific checks that are performed to make sure you are getting a reliable raft. (The ultimate horror story recounts how a rental agency that did not check rafts between rentals finally opened a raft container to perform the annual service on the raft, only to find the raft missing – replaced with rocks wrapped in rags! Most distressing: they did not know when the raft had been stolen or how many times the unit had been rented after that.) For an insight into the rental agency's ethics, ask what is done with rafts considered no longer suitable for rental. If the reply is something on the order of, "We sell them at a deep discount to people looking for bargain rafts," you'd be well advised to look elsewhere for your rental raft.

The second point concerns return of the raft at the end of the voyage. If the passage is a round trip, such as a cruise to Bermuda and back, returning the raft is seldom a problem. If, however, a raft is rented for the offshore portion of an extended trip – to the Caribbean for the winter, for example – getting the raft back can prove challenging. A packed life raft contains a cylinder of compressed CO_2 gas and a number of pyrotechnic distress signals, neither of which may be carried aboard commercial airliners. Most airlines will refuse to carry a raft as checked baggage or as unaccompanied cargo. Other carriers, such as UPS, FedEx or DHL, may also have restrictive rules. Be sure to resolve these details well before committing to any rental arrangement.

The safety strategy for a successful passage embraces both personal safety equipment such as PFDs, harnesses and tethers, and boat equipment such as jacklines, crew overboard rigs, distress signals, fire extinguishers, EPIRBs and life rafts. Having the equipment is only one part of the complete strategy. Training the crew to use the equipment properly is equally important, and these topics will get further attention in Chapter 20. Sailing and passagemaking are supposed to be fun, and full enjoyment depends on completing the passage safely. A safety strategy focuses on preventing casualties and reinforces those measures with readiness to respond if mishaps occur despite the preventive efforts.

REFERENCES:

US SAILING, *Special Regulations Governing Offshore Racing and/or Safety Recommendations for Cruising Sailboats* (adaptations of the Offshore Racing Council Special Regulations)

Michael Greenwald, *Survivor*

CHAPTER 17

PERSONAL AFFAIRS

There always remain some shore-based responsibilities that need tending. For a short trip that permits the skipper and crew to return to their life ashore after a few weeks, most matters can be dealt with in advance or delayed. The longer the trip, the more important it becomes to establish effective ways to handle property management, mail and financial affairs. Many long-term cruising folk sell their houses and cars, resign from organizations and cut most ties to affairs ashore. Even then, a few obligations will remain. An effective strategy for administering these details will contribute to the enjoyment of passagemaking. It's no fun to chase mail from port to port or to be stuck somewhere waiting for money to arrive.

About burning bridges. Different cruising sailors have found quite different ways to deal with their ongoing personal affairs. We sometimes find Rally participants who have "sold everything", even when they have spent little or no time living aboard a boat or otherwise verifying their tolerance for the peculiarities of cruising life. Lured by the "romance of the sea," a significant proportion of these people decide within a few months that the realities of the cruising life are not their cup of tea, after all. Dreams can be shattered, relationships stressed, planned circumnavigations or long-term voyages abandoned, and a disillusioned return to life ashore soon follows. Unless a prospective cruising sailor has substantial experience in living afloat, the bridge-burning approach carries many underestimated risks.

Other voyagers, not wanting to completely abandon their "roots" ashore, have rented their homes or found a friend or relative to live there and serve as caretaker. Some, including my wife and me, are still searching for an effective and comfortable solution.

On the face of it, the simplest strategy is to have someone ashore take over the job. Often a relative (parents or children) or a friend will be willing to serve as an agent for the voyaging sailor. Many others rely on commercial management services. Because it's easy to underestimate the job and responsibilities involved, it is essential to have a clear, preferably written, understanding of exactly what the personal affairs manager is expected to do. This is especially important when the responsibilities are accepted by a friend or relative. A few examples will clarify the difficulties.

Property management. Passagemakers who own property ashore must arrange for its care and maintenance. If they own a home, someone must take care of keeping the grass cut, performing urgent repairs (a frozen pipe or a broken window), and checking the property regularly. Renting the home is one way to handle these issues, but someone must still oversee the situation, respond to renters' bona fide needs and ensure that the renters are doing what's expected. Rental also entails complications such as storage of furnishings and modifications of insurance coverage.

Cars. Cars need similar attention. If they're to be ready for use when the voyager returns, they must be securely and conveniently parked, and someone should operate them periodically. This may entail extended insurance coverage. Keeping state inspection current may also require vehicle operation.

Mail. Perhaps the most common personal matter requiring management is the handling of mail. It would appear that the easiest solution is to have everything forwarded to a friend or a commercial service which can then send it to the cruising sailor at his/her current location. This approach can get expensive very quickly. Even though we made a strenuous effort to reduce the amount of mail we received (by canceling more than a hundred catalogs and all nonessential subscriptions), during our first winter cruising in the Caribbean, the average cost of getting a batch of mail forwarded was over $50. And it was slow. It took a week for a shipment to reach us in the islands from a forwarding service in Florida (despite using expensive "overnight" delivery services such as FedEx and DHL). Add the week it took mail to get to Florida and the time it took us to identify a reliable delivery address in the islands, and we found that most of our mail was a month or more old when it reached us. We rarely received anything as new as two weeks old. Bills commonly arrived weeks after they were due, and the postage charges were often inflated by the inclusion of advertising and correspondence that could have waited for our return. The administrative nuisance of changing addresses (discussed below) was considerable.

Clearly a better mail strategy includes retaining a trustworthy agent who can collect it all, screen it and forward only the important pieces. Screening would include removing obviously unwanted material (weekly advertising flyers) and setting aside that which may be of long-term interest but is not important enough to forward (journals, investment reports). The agent would have authority to act on items needing timely response (utility, tax and other bills). Material forwarded may then be limited to items of current interest and those whose value would diminish if not received reasonably soon (letters from friends, bank and credit card statements). This would be supplemented by a list of pieces set aside awaiting instructions (forward, hold it, or dispose of it) and a report of actions taken (bills paid). This is no simple task. It entails the exercise of good judgment and requires an intimate understanding of your priorities and interests. Trustworthiness is crucial, because this agent will have access to details of your life, finances and relationships seldom exposed to outsiders.

Many commercial mail forwarding services will perform these duties (screening mail, paying bills). Recognizing the responsibilities involved, they charge fees that are not unwarranted, but which can add up quickly. The passagemaker who chooses this solution should provide the service with explicit instructions so a realistic estimate can be developed of how much it will cost to get the services desired. The goal is to avoid surprises that eat up the cruising fund faster than anticipated.

Friends and relatives will offer to take care of mail or look after property on a purely voluntary basis, but they seldom realize how big a job that can become, or how much time and responsibility it entails. They may approach the matter casually and then perform haphazardly, to the detriment of the distant sailor. This might be tolerable for a short voyage, but if your passage involves an absence of months, it's preferable to create a business relationship in which agreed-on duties are performed at set intervals for a specified fee. This clarifies the extent and the details of the job, sets guidelines for doing it, and provides the cruising sailor with some leverage (refusal to pay) in the event of nonperformance.

Though the price will often be higher, contracting with an established forwarding service will usually produce reliable results. Many of these firms advertise in sailing magazines, and some have been in business for many years, enjoying good reputations among long-term cruising folk. If a voyage will last only six months or so, the principal drawback will be the administrative headache of changing your mailing address. First you must notify all correspondents to route mail to the forwarding company. Then you must notify everyone when you return to your original address. When we used such a service, the US Postal Service was willing to forward first class mail to the service we used, but only for a limited time. The forwarding term for other items such as magazines was even shorter. When we returned home, Postal Service forwarding was not available because we were only one set of names out of hundreds using the forwarding service. As a result, we had to notify each sender of our new, post-cruise address. Because a few pieces of mail continued to go to the forwarding service address for some time, we had to continue to pay for that service for several months after our return.

Bill paying. Unless you use an agent, timely payment of bills can be a problem. The delays involved with mail delivery are beyond control. If fixed amounts are involved, automatic payment through a bank or credit union may be possible. We established a credit balance with several utilities to cover the accounts for the delays encountered by monthly statements. Other utilities found it impossible to cope with credit balances and insisted on refunding the excess. Using debit cards, which automatically draw from a bank account each time the card is used, can ease the problem by eliminating monthly bills. So can a credit card issued through a bank or credit union that automatically pays the monthly balance from your savings or checking account. In the Caribbean, we found the latter very helpful in reducing both the need for cash and the challenge of paying the bill on time.

Money. Access to money is another challenge you'll want to resolve before you go. Opportunities for using personal checks, either for merchandise or as a source of cash, are extremely limited away from home. Even cashing certified checks and bank drafts may involve considerable delays. Many cruising people use credit card cash advances as a convenient way to obtain cash at a low cost. With the growth of international credit card systems and links to banking associations, widely recognized credit cards such as VISA and MasterCard can be used to draw cash from automated teller machines in many parts of the world. Increasingly common ATM service fees have boosted the price of this alternative considerably. An approach that has sustained us through several winter cruises has been to carry a substantial reserve of traveler's checks that can be cashed as needed for expenses that can't be charged to an automatically-paid credit card. We've also carried a couple of no-fee, high limit "gold" type credit cards reserved for emergencies. There are many different, often ingenious ways to provide a continuing supply of funds. The important point is to think about it well before departure and to develop an arrangement that will allow you to feel comfortable as you cruise. Many get by on remarkably small budgets, while others seem to spend just as much as they always did ashore. Wherever you fit on the income-expense spectrum, passagemaking and cruising will be far more enjoyable if your personal affairs strategy includes a smoothly-functioning financial mechanism.

Contact in emergency. You'll probably need to make arrangements to be contacted in an emergency. Systems for communicating through telephone and high seas radio services were mentioned in Chapter 9. Emergency messages can often be relayed through amateur radio operators and their maritime mobile nets. If a cruising skipper's general location is known, a short message ("We have an emergency message for the yacht *Phoenix* cruising in the USVI. The captain should contact his brother, Fred") can be passed to a local Ham operator, who can relay it to other boats, hoping someone will be able to deliver it to *Phoenix.* As the age of instant, global, satellite-based communications becomes a reality, emergency contact promises to become as simple as making a telephone call or sending an e-mail message. Boats at sea will be as easy to reach as a next-door neighbor or Aunt Suzi in Sheboygan. The number of boats able to send and receive e-mail from afloat locations is rapidly increasing. At least one service already offers satellite-based cellular-like phone service that extends off the US east coast to Bermuda and across the Caribbean from Trinidad to the Panama Canal. Competition is likely to drive downward both the equipment and service costs.

Insurance. On a different note is the question of insurance coverage for the cruising boat. Its cost can be prohibitive, and at times it can be difficult to obtain the desired level and type of coverage. Maintaining liability coverage (claims by others for damages for which you are allegedly responsible) is very important. Without it, you could find yourself confined in a foreign port (even a jail) until the claims are resolved. You could even have your boat and its contents seized by a foreign government or its court system to settle a claim.

Property damage insurance covering the boat itself, as well as equipment and possessions aboard, is the more expensive component of most insurance policies, and one that many passagemakers opt not to carry. They have chosen to accept the risk of damage to or loss of the boat. Frequently, they will invest the money saved on insurance premiums to better equip the boat to undertake the passage. They buy stronger, redundant ground tackle systems and enhance damage control capability such as positive flotation and watertight bulkheads, or they get better navigation and communication equipment. If the boat is collateral for a loan, however, the lender will often require the owner to maintain insurance coverage sufficient to pay off the loan balance in the event the boat is lost.

Whatever your choices, *insurance arrangements cannot be left to the last minute.* Getting the right coverage can mean shopping through one or more brokers or agents. A quote for coverage can often be obtained very quickly, but completing the requirements for finalizing coverage could require a comprehensive survey (including haul-out to determine condition of the underwater hull). The whole process can consume weeks and add to the cost of voyage preparation.

Developing the right personal affairs strategy will take time. Initial arrangements probably won't work out as well as expected, making modifications necessary. Giving these issues plenty of thought and exploring alternatives well before departure will be worth the effort. Certainly one appeal of passagemaking is the opportunity to escape from demands of the workaday world, but a few ties always persist. As one circumnavigator summarized it, "The fewer strings attached, the better." Nevertheless, thorough planning for the remaining obligations will add substantially to the pleasure of getting away.

CHAPTER 18

SAIL SELECTION
AND CARE

Selecting sails that will drive the boat reliably over wide-ranging conditions, caring for them and being equipped to repair them are important to your voyaging strategy. Your goal of a safe, comfortable and reasonably swift passage calls for sails that are the right size, shaped efficiently, well balanced, and protected from wear.

A day sailor can get by with a main and a working jib. The coastal cruising sailor soon learns that a larger headsail earns its keep when wind is light, and so adds a genoa and perhaps a spinnaker to the inventory. For passagemaking, there's more chance of encountering stronger winds, so adding storm sails and setting up effective methods for reducing sail area will be necessary.

How much reaching/running/beating? We found very useful Beth Leonard's analysis of wind conditions during a three-year circumnavigation. Overall, they had the apparent wind on the quarter and aft ⅔ of the time. It was on the beam 15% of the time, and forward of 70° only 20%. Considering only their time in the tropics, the figures were slanted even more: 75% aft, 10% abeam and 10% forward. In higher latitudes (above 25° North and below 25° South), the spread was more equal: 45% aft, 17% abeam and 35% forward. They spent as much time in true winds over 22 knots as in true winds under 10 knots. Because so often the wind was aft of the beam, the apparent wind was under 10 knots a good ⅓ of the time. Winds exceeded 28 knots only 5% of the time, and they encountered winds stronger than 45 knots only once. This suggests that for tropical cruising, a passagemaker's suit of sails should be optimized for off-wind sailing and relatively light apparent wind. Cruising at higher latitudes (and getting to and from the tropics) requires sails that can handle a greater spectrum of wind speeds and directions.

Few participants in rallies such as the Caribbean 1500 actually extend their passage into a circumnavigation. Most go south to the tropics and stay in an area such as the Caribbean for 6-8 months, sailing back and forth among islands. This frequently involves going against the prevailing trades. Many report using large headsails (150% genoas, big spinnakers) only briefly on their passage north and south, and not at all during their island cruising where 20-knot trade winds prevail.

The number of sails any boat carries is limited by available storage. Thanks to modern roller furling and reefing systems, new fabrics and construction techniques, a passagemaker's sails today are usable over a wide range of conditions. So fewer sails are needed for voyaging now than 25-30 years ago.

Important choices. When adding or replacing sails, many choices must be made: fabric, weight, cut, etc. Each choice affects the sail's durability, performance and cost. Durability can be viewed as the sail's ultimate life (how long before it disintegrates) or its performance life (how long before its shape deteriorates to substantial inefficiency). Passagemakers' sails are exposed to sustained use, damaging ultraviolet rays, and stowage in unfriendly environments. A sail's ultimate life becomes a priority in these circumstances, and so has often led to choices that favor durability over shape retention. Many voyagers still tend to select long-lasting heavy polyester fabrics. Despite the higher cost, a growing number are turning to sails that use cruising grade high-tech film/fabric sandwich construction which results in superior shape-holding.

The modern composites. Composite sails incorporating technologically advanced materials such as Mylar, Vectran and Spectra are appearing aboard an increasing number of cruising boats. Constructed in several layers, these sails use a film of polyester (Mylar) to carry a grid or scrim of high-strength fibers that bear the sail's load. These layers are protected from chafe, ultraviolet degradation and other damaging influences by outer layers of polyester taffeta. Such laminated construction makes possible high strength at light weights, sophisticated shape control and advanced techniques as with tri-radial jibs, but also carries a significantly higher initial cost. If you decide to go with composites, make certain they are specifically designed for the cruising environment. These sails are increasingly well up to the tough job of passagemaking, despite their greater tendency to mildew because of their layered construction. The most common sail fabric probably is still the polyester fiber known as Dacron. Simple crosscut Dacron has proven its durability over the years, and its popularity is still high. Regardless of fabric or construction, sail strength is the principal objective, and this generally correlates to the weight and weave characteristics of the cloth. Sails are designed to work well over a range of wind speeds, and the fabric should always be selected to provide strength at the upper end of that range. The designed wind range for each sail should be known to watch standers so they can avoid damage by leaving a sail up over its limit. Most sailmakers can suggest wind ranges for older sails whose designed limits may be unknown.

Clew height is another significant aspect of an offshore headsail. The deck-sweeping, low clew genoas that maximize speed on racing boats are poorly suited to passagemaking. They can hang up on lifelines or catch waves in the foot of the sail. The greatest advantage of a higher clew is that less change in jib lead is needed as the sail is eased. This makes it better for reaching, the point of sail favored by cruising voyagers. A higher clew also reduces the load on the clew itself.

Needed: versatility, easy handling. A sail's performance also includes the capacity to hold its shape, as well as the range of wind speeds and directions over which it will work effectively. A further point is the ease with which a sail can be handled: setting, reefing, dousing and stowing, whether with a roller furling system or a bag on deck. Cruising sailors need sails built to serve acceptably across a broad range of conditions. The shorthanded crews on most cruising boats also place a premium on ease of handling.

Sail construction checklist. Regardless of fabric, a sail for use in a cruising environment will benefit from several construction details. These sails should have wider seams than normal, secured with glue as well as a triple row of stitching. They need sturdy reinforcing patches at batten ends and extra layers of cloth in both the batten pockets and large corner patches. Corner rings should be secured with strong webbing, even if pressed-in rings are used. Double tapes along all edges will boost sail endurance, and a leech cord that runs up the leech and down the luff of a high-clewed jib will keep it within easy reach for adjustment. Extra reinforcement where the sail rubs against shrouds and spreaders is essential.

The cost of a sail can vary dramatically depending on fabric, construction and features. Keeping the cost under control frequently forces compromises with durability and performance. A frank discussion with a sailmaker about durability and performance objectives, cost constraints, and a realistic assessment of the way the sail will be used is essential if the sailmaker is to deliver a product that will best serve your needs. Sails are far too important to a passagemaker's safety to cut corners or settle for lower quality to save a few dollars.

Shape is key. The key to a sail's performance is the shape of the foil it creates, and the ability to adjust that shape to suit the prevailing wind strength. Techniques and controls available to adjust sail shape to match wind conditions will be discussed with sail trim in Chapter 22, but the ideal sail is one that can be made flatter, while keeping the maximum draft well forward, as the breeze increases. Trim controls minimize the increase in depth and the tendency for the depth to move aft as the wind builds. It is vital to start with sails that are flat enough initially and strong enough to resist stretch as the wind load increases, because passagemaking sails must perform through a wide range of wind speeds (especially with roller systems and partial furling). Heeling and lee/weather helm can be controlled only with sails that are flat enough for the conditions. It is usually better to err on the heavy air (flat) side, because sails that are too full are much more of a problem than ones that are too flat.

Headsail size. A headsail's size is described in terms of a measurement known as its LP. This is the distance from the clew to the luff, measured perpendicular to the luff – hence "LP," for Luff Perpendicular (Figure 18.1). It is expressed as a percentage of the distance from the forward face of the mast to the stem where the headstay connects (the dimension known to sailmakers as "J"). If the J distance is 10', then a sail that measures 10' from clew to luff is referred to as a 100% headsail. If another sail for the same boat measured 12'6" from clew to luff, it would be a 125% headsail. If the length of the luff is the same for both sails (both are full-hoist sails reaching all the way to the top of the forestay, with no pendants at top or bottom), the latter sail's area will be 25% greater. Headsails with an LP greater than 100% overlap the mast and are usually referred to as genoas, while those with LPs of about 100% are known as working jibs. Storm jibs will have even smaller LP dimensions, and probably much shorter luff lengths as well to reduce sail area still further.

Figure 18.1 - LP Measurement

Headsail A
LP = 10
J = 10
Headsail = 100%
Area = 30 x 10 ÷ 2 =150 sq.ft.

Headsail B
LP = 12.5
J = 10
Headsail = 125%
Area = 30 x 12.5 ÷ 2 = 187.5 sq.ft.

Area of Headsail B is 25% greater than Headsail A.

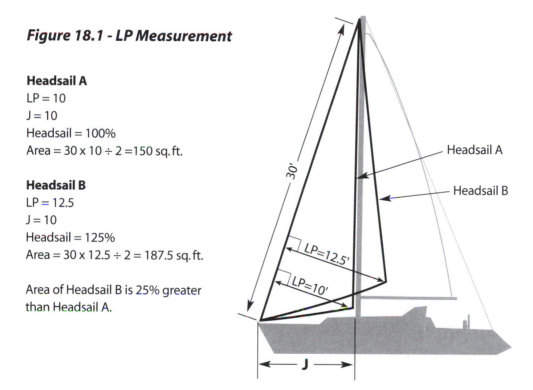

Roller furling headsails. The vast majority of passagemaking boats today are outfitted with roller furling systems for their headsails. In their modern form, these systems are highly reliable and provide much more flexibility than did hanked-on sails. The chief advantages of roller furling systems are that they allow the sail to be stowed on its stay, ready for quick and easy deployment, and they can – within limits – be reduced in size by partially furling them. Setting a big genoa by trimming a sheet and easing a control line is a wonderful advantage compared to the labor involved in hauling a large genoa to the foredeck, unbagging it without losing either the sail or the bag overboard, hanking it on, attaching and leading the sheets, then hoisting it with the halyard. Similarly, reducing sail area a bit when the breeze picks up entails only easing the sheet and hauling the control line to roll up some of the sail. One person on watch can do the job, instead of having to call for help to take down one sail and replace it with a smaller one.

While racers usually carry genoas of 150% or larger as their largest headsail, most offshore sailors settle for something in the 130% area. They may be giving up a bit of power in very light airs, but they have a sail that is suited for a wider range of wind speeds and is less likely to need to be furled or changed. How big a genoa to choose depends on three things. First is the size of the foretriangle (J dimension – a large J means a bigger sail for the same percentage of overlap); second is the size of the foretri-angle relative to the mainsail (the larger the main, the smaller the headsail needed); and third is how light and easily driven the boat is. Generally, it is best to choose the smallest genoa that will drive the boat adequately in more than seven knots of wind. Smaller sails are more versatile and much easier to handle during maneuvers (tacking). For large headsails to be effective in light air, they need to be made of relatively light materials that often are not strong enough to be used in windier condition. Moderately sized genoas, such as a 130%, are built of heavier cloth and can handle a higher range of wind speeds. From a mechanical standpoint, because of the amount of fabric and the shape of the sails, smaller sails tend to roll up more smoothly and evenly than larger ones, and main-tain their shape better when partially furled.

It is tempting to think that because a roller furling system permits infinite adjust-ments to the amount of sail area exposed, such a system will make it possible to carry just one large headsail and reduce its area as appropriate to the wind strength. Unfortunately, quite apart from sailcloth weight and strength, a headsail roller furling system can only function effectively as a reefing system for about 25-30% of the sail's size. A 150% jib can be reduced to about 115%, a 130% to about 100%. This is especially true sailing to windward, when sail shape becomes crucial. Going beyond these limits results in a sail that is less and less efficiently shaped for reasons discussed below.

A few words about roller furling jib construction: Whatever their design, fabric and construction, jibs must be fitted with ultraviolet-resistant cover fabric along the foot and leech. When rolled up, none of the sailcloth should be exposed to the damaging effects of sunlight, which can destroy fabric strength in months. It is best to have reinforcing patches along the foot and leech at several "reefed down" positions to handle the extra strains these corners will bear (corner stress is $\frac{2}{3}$ greater than that along the edges). Fitting the central portion of the luff with foam padding will help preserve luff tension and reduce midsection draft when the sail is reefed.

Remember that a sail's ability to drive the boat depends on its curved shape. Consider what happens when a sail is rolled up around its furling extrusion on the head-stay. The first part to get wrapped up is the part to which the sailmaker devoted great effort to achieve the rounded entry that contributes substantially to the sail's lift. As more sail is rolled up, less of the sail's designed shape remains. Its efficiency plummets.

Rolling the sail has other effects, as well. The chief control for positioning the max-imum draft in a sail is halyard tension, which stretches the luff of the sail. When the sail is partially rolled up, the luff edge is effectively moved aft into the body of the sail, but the halyard can pull only on the original luff, now buried inside the rolled fabric on the foil. The result is a loss of tension along the leading edge of the sail. This allows the sail to assume an increasingly baggy shape, with horizontal wrinkles developing along the leading edge (reminiscent of the scalloped luff that signifies insufficient luff tension on a hanked-on sail). This shape is exactly the opposite of that desired for stronger winds, when a flatter sail is needed to provide drive and lift without excessive heeling force. The baggy rolled-up sail generates more heeling and less forward drive.

A partially rolled-up sail also changes the stress distribution in the foil and stay system on which it is mounted. With the sail fully set, the sail's load is distributed all along the stay. The highest concentrations are at the head and tack, where swivels and toggles are installed to handle side loading. As the sail is rolled, the upper edge of the leech and the leading end of the foot move toward the center of the foil. This concentrates the sail's loading forces in the central parts of the foil. Headstay sag will probably increase as concentrated sheet- and sail-induced lateral loading place stress on less well reinforced sections of the foil system.

As the sail is rolled, its clew moves forward, rising as it does so. To maintain proper trim, keeping the tightness of leech and foot properly balanced, the sheet's fairlead location must change. The turning block must normally be moved forward as the sail is rolled.

When reducing sail area, the balance of the sail plan must be maintained. It would be best to move the center of the sail plan downward (reducing its tendency to heel the boat) and to keep it close to the center of the boat. Partially rolling a headsail works contrary to this objective. It keeps sail area forward. Moving the driving force of the jib forward by partially furling it also accentuates the pitching moment it induces. The effect is not unlike that of moving a rider on a seesaw further from the pivot point: a given weight produces much larger movements.

Perhaps the biggest drawback to roller-furled headsails is the problem of changing them. When the wind has picked up enough to require a smaller headsail, but the installed sail has been "reefed" as much as possible by partially rolling it up, the skipper faces a dilemma. The best solution would be to change the headsail. To do that, though, the sail that is currently set must first be fully unrolled, for it cannot be doused while rolled around the headstay foil. The sail that already has too much area exposed must be increased in size still further before it can be exchanged for something smaller. This poses hazards for boat and crew. The boat will be temporarily overcanvassed and difficult to keep upright. The crew must cling to a violently moving foredeck while capturing a flogging sail as it comes out of the luff foil, relead the sheets, then control a replacement sail until it can be fed into the foil, raised with the halyard and trimmed with its sheet.

Dual headstays? To avoid this nightmare, many passagemakers employ a dual headstay system. If foredeck space permits, two roller-furling headstays can be installed, one carrying a genoa (perhaps 130%), the other a working jib (85-100%). When there's too much wind for the 130, it is rolled up on its stay and the working jib is unrolled from the other stay. Space constraints and headstay sag considerations usually require these dual headstays to be placed in line, fore and aft, along the centerline. This, of course, complicates tacking with the sail set on the forward stay. Because there is little space between the stays through which the body of the sail must pass, it may be necessary to roll the sail, tack, then reset it on the other side.

Other cruising skippers have opted for a pseudo-cutter rig. They carry a moderate genoa on their stem-mounted roller furling rig with plans to reef it down to about 100% as winds increase, and then roll it up entirely. It is supplanted by a smaller stay-sail set on a separate forestay well aft of the headstay. This reduces the sail area substantially and keeps the center of effort of the whole sail plan close to the center of the boat. The inner forestay is often rigged so it can be disconnected and stowed adjacent to the mast, clearing the foretriangle for easier tacking of full-size headsails. The disadvantage of this plan is that the staysail is usually too small to be of much use unless there's a lot of wind. It can serve as a storm jib, but not as a working jib. Retro-fitted removable inner forestays are typically set well forward (compared to a true cutter arrangement) to increase sail area and simplify the structural challenges. With the stay connected closer to the stem at the bottom and nearer the masthead at the top, the need for running backstays to balance its load and preclude excessive bending of the mast can be reduced.

Any roller furling rig used offshore should be able to be pinned or locked to prevent inadvertent unrolling of a furled sail. When it's blowing 40 knots and the boat is booming along under deeply reefed sails, one of the last things a skipper wants is a failure of a roller furling control line that lets the full 135% genoa roll out. If the unrolled sail's sheets are trimmed, the boat will be greatly overpowered and knocked down. If they are left slack, the sail will flog itself to destruction and tie the most exquisite knots in the slack sheets, while trying simultaneously to shake the mast out of the boat. Not a pretty picture. There should be sufficient wraps of control line on the roller furling drum to allow the sail to be rolled up all the way (even when rolled very snugly, as happens when rolling it in high winds) and then make a couple of extra turns to wrap a few feet of sheet around the rolled-up sail. This plus inserting a pin in the roller furler's drum to lock it in position can prevent the ugly scenario above.

Back to smaller jibs, larger mains. Over the years, yacht designers have changed the relative size of the jib and the mainsail, largely in response to racing rules. Many older designs drew their principal driving power from the mainsail, with the jib functioning as a balancing auxiliary. Then the trend shifted to large overlapping genoa jibs as the major power source, with an undersized high-aspect ratio main relegated to a secondary role as a steering sail. More recently, designs are returning to smaller jibs and larger mains, especially among cruising boats. This reflects, in part, a recognition of the fact that a small or undersized crew can handle such a sail plan more easily. With the role of mainsails on the rise, their design and construction have received increased attention.

The mainsail. The traditional mainsail was built with a moderate amount of roach – the excess sail area that extends beyond a straight line drawn from the head to the clew. To keep this extra fabric extended and smoothly matched to the rest of the sail's foil shape, stiffening battens are inserted into pockets perpendicular to the leech. While effective at their designed function, these battens also introduce a few problems. They and their pockets tend to experience chafe, and the fabric undergoes severe wear at the inner end of the battens, where it is flexed repeatedly by each movement of the stiff batten. These partial battens also have a habit of flipping out of their pockets when the sail flogs (even for a short, unavoidable period, such as when tacking), especially in a high wind. Once the batten is gone, the roach fabric begins to flutter and flap, causing extensive damage and degrading the designed shape.

The fully battened main. Many cruising skippers have avoided the batten problem by having their mains cut with a hollow or negative roach to preclude the need for battens. They do so at the cost of sail area, structural strength, and ability to control sail shape. Overall horsepower to drive the boat may be reduced by as much as 25%. Recently, full-length battens have become a more popular method for controlling sail shape, allowing maximum roach and sail area and also avoiding the batten-end-flex problem. Full battens run all the way from the mast to the leech of the sail, keeping the sail stretched out to full size and preserving its designed shape. They eliminate flogging, even when tacking, so they reduce wear and extend sail life. They also allow the roach to be extended until the sail just clears the backstay when tacking. Full battens run parallel to the boom, rather than perpendicular to the leech, to allow them to lay flat along the boom when the sail is reefed or furled.

Along with these significant advantages, full battens introduce a couple of new problems. The first is the need for specialized hardware at the mast end of each batten. The battens are installed under compression to keep the desired curvature in the sail's shape. This means they push against the mast, with sufficient force to cause traditional sail slides to jam and obstruct efforts to raise or lower the sail. Several lines of hardware have been developed to cope with this problem by including bearings and swivels, and no full batten sail should be installed without some system to handle the compression force. The cost of options can vary widely, but this factor can significantly increase the price of shifting from a traditional to a fully battened main.

Because they maintain their shape so well, fully battened mains can be more difficult to trim properly. The revealing signs of luffing at the leading edge do not appear as readily, so it's not as easy to tell when the sail is out far enough. Telltales along the leech will help, but there seems to be a natural tendency to overtrim a fully battened sail, reducing its efficiency. Keeping it properly trimmed requires greater vigilance.

Most fully battened mainsails are accompanied by a *lazy jack system* for controlling the loose sail when it is lowered. Because the long horizontal battens make it somewhat easier to keep the sail in place, lazy jacks (a cradle of light lines) effectively prevent the loose sail from flopping all over the deck as it is lowered. Unless they can be slacked off and pulled all the way forward, however, these same lazy jacks can create headaches when the sail is raised. The outboard ends of the upper battens will foul in the jacks unless the boat is headed directly into the wind when hoisting the sail (or shaking out a deep reef). Lazy jacks can also cause chafe on the lee side of a fully battened sail if not slacked off sufficiently when the sail is set. If any sail is allowed to rub against lazy jacks, holes can be worn in the sail. Full length battens provide hard spots at which that chafe will be concentrated. This is yet another reason for rigging lazy jacks so they can be slacked, pulled forward and kept stowed at the mast except when needed.

A significant number of new boats are fitted with radically swept-back spreaders. This feature can reduce loading on the backstay or allow the backstay to be eliminated, which permits use of a very large roach to increase sail area. Here full length battens can chafe against spreaders and upper shrouds when the sail is properly eased on a broad reach or run. Specific chafe protection is needed to address this problem. Improper sail trim can lead to bent or broken battens where they lie against the rig, and the sail will press against the shrouds with sufficient force to prevent its being raised, lowered or reefed. A boom vang is essential to minimize this pressure and keep sail battens from wrapping around spreaders and shrouds.

Reefing the main. The mainsail reefing arrangement is key to your sail design. For offshore cruising, a mainsail should have at least two substantial reef points, perhaps three if the fully reefed main will be used for storm sailing. Often sailmakers will specify a first reef that is relatively small (less than 10% of luff length), the principal function of which is to flatten the sail to get better shape for rising wind speeds. This may be useful for coastal cruisers, but offshore the objective is to decrease sail area rather than adjust shape. In a passagemaking main, the first reef ought to achieve a significant reduction, at least 10-15% of luff length. The second reef, at about 30% of luff length, should achieve another substantial reduction of area while a third reef, if you go that route, should bring the main down to storm sail size by reducing the luff to about 60% of its original length.

The choice of triple-reefed main rather than storm trysail is subject to debate. While the deeply reefed sail may have the correct area, prolonged use while deeply reefed is tough on the sail. Also, carrying aloft the extra weight of the reinforcing patches, tack fittings and outhaul pendant for a seldom-used third reef may detract from performance in more frequent lighter airs and induce extra wear. In short, it may be false economy to substitute a third reef for a storm trysail.

The mainsail reefing system deserves careful consideration, because keeping a passage comfortable will require its frequent use. Taking or shaking out a reef should be as routine as altering course or tacking. The watch should be able to do it without having to call for help. The alternatives range from traditional reefing to roller furling, the latter on either mast or boom.

Traditional reefing systems involve lowering the main until a new set of cringles can be used for the tack and clew. You change sail area by a predetermined amount, based on where the sailmaker placed the cringles. The new tack is secured at the mast and after the halyard is retensioned, the new clew is drawn tight with a pendant. There are provisions for bundling up and tying the loose bunt of now-unused fabric along the boom. The simplest systems use a hook at the mast and an outhaul pendant led forward along the boom. The disadvantage is that someone must go forward to the mast to set or shake out a reef. If the tack is hauled down tight with a pendant rather than secured on a hook, that pendant plus the outhaul pendant and the halyard can be led to the cockpit, enabling reefing changes to be made without someone going forward. The system can be simplified further, using a single line to control both tack and outhaul. This reduces the reefing process to slacking the halyard while simultaneously hauling on the reefing pendant. Once the tack and clew are snug against the mast and boom, the halyard is retensioned and the job is done. For short term reefs, the loose sail is simply left hanging at the boom. Shaking out a reef is even easier: Slack the reefing pendant and haul on the halyard. It can all be done by one person from the cockpit in less than a minute. The only disadvantage to single-line systems (or any system that leads the lines aft) is the higher friction loads that will be encountered in the reefing pendant. These make it necessary to use a winch to do the hauling. This in turn requires an observant winch operator, for if the sail gets fouled, the winch can easily rip it.

Traditional systems work well with either partially or fully battened mains, and they impose no special restrictions on the cut or design of the sail. They also involve the fewest moving parts and so are least vulnerable to mechanical failure. Their principal disadvantage is that they limit reefing to fixed increments. By contrast, with roller furling you can change sail area in variable amounts, but you also need additional mechanical gear and special sail design.

Roller furling mains. Roller furling mainsail systems use a rotating luff extrusion like those used for headsails. The sail can be adjusted to any point between fully set and completely furled. Changing sail size becomes a quick and easy job, accomplished from the cockpit with a couple of lines. All this convenience and flexibility comes at a price, of course. Being mechanical, the roller furling system requires maintenance, and the added weight aloft has an adverse impact on stability, albeit minor. Improved designs and better engineering have greatly reduced the jamming that was common with early roller furlers. Jamming today is usually traceable to operator error. Keeping insufficient tension on the control lines can easily lead to loose rolling and surplus folds of fabric that jam in the mast opening.

Roller furling mainsails produce their greatest challenge to the sailmaker. To roll smoothly without developing bags or wrinkles, these sails must be cut quite flat compared to the rounded form of traditional sails. This is most noticeable at the luff, where excess fabric could jam the sail as it rolls. Like the roller furling jib, once the rolling starts, there's no way to adjust the tension of the sail's leading edge. By shaping the sail flat, the sailmaker minimizes this problem. To minimize chafe, individual panels must be laid out to avoid seam overlaps that would create bulges as the sail rolls. The luff of a roller furling main must be shortened to leave room for the upper swivel near the top of the mast, and its clew must be cut relatively high to prevent having excess fabric pile up at the lower end of the extrusion as the sail rolls. Despite innovative efforts to design battens that will not obstruct the rolling, most roller furling mains are battenless, cut with a straight or hollow leech. Many also have a hollow luff to compensate for sag of the furling extrusion in or behind the mast. These adjustments result in a loss of sail area, often ranging from 10% to 20% relative to a traditional sail for the same spar dimensions.

While the flatter shape and reduced sail area may impair performance somewhat, especially in light air, roller furling mains offer important compensating advantages. Because it's so much easier to adjust sail area, cruising crews (typically short-handed) are much more likely to keep sail area matched to changing wind conditions. They'll be less likely to endure being overpowered until it's clear the wind will remain strong enough to justify a labor-intensive reef, and less prone to delay shaking out a reef. When the wind is strong enough for the boat to approach hull speed, sail plan compromises probably have little impact on performance.

Boom furled mains. Boom-oriented roller furling systems are less common than those mounted in or behind the mast, and they have strengths and weaknesses. Because they can operate with battens set parallel to the boom, they permit the sail to have greater area, with roach and a fair amount of fullness along the luff. While some designs allow infinitely adjustable reefing, others limit reefs to the location of the battens (usually full-length type). Proper reefing and furling (smooth rolling of the sail without bunching at tack or clew) depends on having the boom set at precisely the correct angle to the mast whenever rolling takes place. Where mast roller furling systems compromise luff tension, boom versions compromise foot tension.

Because the full luff of the sail must ride in a groove or slot, raising a boom-furled main means overcoming a greater friction load than unrolling a sail furled in or behind the mast. This friction will increase wear along the luff tape and boltrope, and it causes greater reefing/furling loads than slab or mast-oriented systems. So it may be necessary to head into the wind or luff the main to reduce luff loading before rolling or unrolling. Perhaps the most reassuring aspect of boom furling is its fail-safe nature. If the furling system jams or fails for any reason, the sail can still be dropped conventionally. If a mast furling system jams, the partially furled sail can be neither rolled nor lowered.

In assessing any sail management system, you'll want to consider maintenance and repair. Access to parts can be crucial in determining maintainability, and the ocean environment can play havoc with all but the most robustly built components. A system supported by a widespread service network can be highly beneficial. If riggers are unfamiliar with a system or if parts must be imported from a distance, a minor casualty can become time consuming. *You'll seldom go wrong keeping systems as simple as possible.*

Split rigs. Many passagemaking boats are cutters or ketches, with a few yawls and schooners. While these rigs may be inherently less efficient than a sloop when going to windward, they offer attractive advantages for voyaging. Cutters, with their double headsail system, provide a powerful sail plan for reaching and the flexibility of an effective staysail for heavy weather. Rigs with two masts provide more versatility, with greater variations possible, including the jib and mizzen combination that's simple to set and easy to handle in freshening breezes. Split rigs also keep the size of each sail smaller, making sails easier to handle with a small crew. Off the wind, these rigs can carry a large area, with special sails such as mizzen staysails. Though the individual masts are shorter than on a comparable sloop, which tends to reduce heeling, this effect is largely offset by the additional spar and rigging. Finally, having two masts provides a measure of redundancy that will allow a boat to carry a fair amount of sail should one mast fail.

Because they have so many sail plan variations available, there's a steeper learning curve for the crew. Knowing when to shift from the jib to the staysail – or when to add the staysail with the genoa already set – is a skill that must be developed. Deciding when to douse the mizzen while shifting from close reach to beat, or when to drop the main and keep the mizzen set, will vary from boat to boat. They can be determined only by experimenting over a wide range of wind and sea conditions. Skipper and crew must be willing to try different combinations and see how the boat responds.

Spinnakers. For broad reaching and running, most voyaging boats carry one or more spinnakers. Those with a racing background may prefer a conventional spinnaker, with its pole and additional rigging, while others – especially the shorthanded crews – will choose the newer asymmetrical spinnakers that are simpler to handle. Modern asymmetricals offer many advantages. They can be designed to be very close-winded, which makes them more versatile than the classic cruising spinnaker geared to broad reaching and running. With smaller genoas, they offer a good alternative for light air performance through many wind angles and velocities. Many sizes and shapes are possible, so you'll want to specify whether the sail is to be optimized for reaching or running. Often, a sail capable of close reaching is more useful to the passagemaker. A reaching oriented asymmetrical can still broad reach and run quite effectively, while a larger, deeper sail designed for off-wind sailing cannot reach well at all. Also, the smaller reaching asymmetrical is easier to handle. There's no question these sails earn their keep, especially when winds are light.

Adding a "sock" in which to stow the sail makes setting and dousing much simpler than the old method of manhandling hundreds of square feet of uncontrolled light nylon. The key to using a spinnaker successfully on passages is to know when to set it and, more importantly, when to take it down. It's usually worth setting the spinnaker when the genoa starts to collapse from lack of wind. It's safest to take it down when wind speed approaches the speed for which the sail was designed or with the onset of any condition that would make handling the large and potentially overpowering sail more hazardous (darkness, signs of a squall, etc.). Prudence is the secret to good cruising under the spinnaker.

Storm sails. Shifting to the other end of the wind spectrum, the well-outfitted passagemaker will carry storm sails suited to the season and cruising region. If there's a reasonable prospect of strong winds, both a storm jib and a storm trysail should be in the boat's inventory. A storm jib or staysail should be small; the *ORC Special Regulations* (as a guide) call for storm jib area to be no more than 5% of the height of the foretriangle squared, while its luff length should be no greater than 65% of the foretriangle height. It is cut very flat, of fabric durable enough to take high winds and flogging. It should have pendants at top and bottom (fitted with hanks or luff tapes to keep them close to the headstay) to permit hoisting the halyard to its normal height. If it is set with a boltrope or luff tape in a groove in the headstay extrusion, it should have grommets and stops or some other method for keeping it attached to the headstay. The sail should be fitted with strong sheets run through solidly mounted fairleads. Since visibility is likely to be reduced in any situation requiring the use of storm sails, many sailmakers choose bright orange fabric for maximum conspicuousness.

The storm trysail should be equally strong, built with boltroping on all three sides. Since the storm trysail won't be set until the wind is in the 40-knot range, it's wise to have a separate mast track so you don't have to detach any mainsail luff to feed the trysail into the normal track/groove. This auxiliary track should run all the way to the deck so the trysail can be hanked onto the bottom of the track while stowed in its bag, below the boom where it won't interfere with normal sail use. Another common arrangement consists of a stowage track low on the mast that connects to the normal mainsail track with a switch positioned so it is above the head of the furled main. The goal is an arrangement that precludes hanking on a loose trysail in storm conditions.

Like the storm jib, the trysail should be fitted with pendants at head and tack that will allow it to be set above the stacked and furled main while hoisting the halyard to its normal height. The *ORC Special Regulations* limit the maximum size of a storm trysail to 17.5% of the mainsail luff length multiplied by mainsail foot length. It should be sheeted directly to turning blocks on deck and not fastened to the boom. Fairlead locations and sheeting arrangements should be established by setting the sail at the dock and recording the rigging plan. This plan should include a method for securing the main boom by stowing it in a gallows if one is installed, or lowering it to the deck and lashing it in place. It must also insure that the main topping lift and any lazy jacks used to control the main as it is dropped can be unrigged or stowed in a way that will prevent interference with setting or tacking the trysail.

Your sails deserve TLC. Since the sails drive your boat, keeping them in good condition is essential. Watch standers must be alert to sail trim and course control to minimize damage by flogging when tacking or rolling/unrolling a headsail. Use the leech line to stop flutter. Chafe is the leading hazard, so you'll want to make every effort to avoid it. This requires regular inspections to remove/cover any rough/sharp surfaces against which a sail can rub. The parts of the headsail that strike the spreaders when tacking should be fitted with sacrificial patches to take the wear. Lazy jacks must be slacked off sufficiently to prevent them from rubbing against the sail when set. When off the wind, the watch must be alert to a sail rubbing against the shrouds (full battens are particularly vulnerable) and use vang tension to reduce sail movements caused by rising and falling of the boom. A daily inspection of battens and batten pockets can stop chafe at those commonly afflicted spots.

Are sail slides the weakest link? A surprisingly common sail casualty among Rally boats is broken sail slides, especially if choppy sea conditions or near calms cause sails to fill and collapse repeatedly. If the resulting cyclic loading on the slides causes one to break, its load is passed to adjacent slides, which break under the extra stress, and so on until a whole section of sail is suddenly loose from its spar. Plastic slides can be weakened by long UV exposure; watch for cracks and crazing. Spot-welded steel slides are highly vulnerable to breakage under repeated sharp loading and unloading. Be sure to replace any suspicious slides before the passage, and carry sufficient spares.

This brings us to the final element of a successful sail strategy: Be prepared to repair a sail damaged during the voyage. You'll find specific repair techniques in Chapter 23. In addition, sail care planning calls for carrying an adequate sail repair kit and being familiar with some basic sewing and patching skills. Sail repair during a passage aims to make a temporary fix that will hold until you reach port.

Your successful strategy for sails begins with having a proper inventory. Sails must work efficiently in all the wind and sea conditions that can be expected during the passage. They must be rigged to permit easy adjustment and change by the crew. Mechanical systems (furlers, etc.) must be wholly reliable. The crew should be alert to protect sails against damage caused by chafe or poor trimming. Should damage occur, you'll need materials to make temporary repairs. Sails may be the most important system on a passagemaking boat, and so deserve the best care you can give them.

Some questions to ask yourself...
- How long do you plan to own the boat?
- How long do you expect your sails to last?
- What is your crew/sailing ability?
- How concerned are you about sail shape? Are you a fiddler who loves to max speed/performance, or are sails just triangles somewhere above the bimini?
- How important is ease of handling – hoisting, lowering, flaking, trimming?
- Where will your passage be taking you, and how much will you be sailing once you get there?
- Finally, how much do you have to spend?

The answers will help focus your search for the appropriate level of technology. After all, you can get to the train station in a Ford Escort, or you can go by Mercedes Benz.

– Provided by David Flynn, Quantum Sail Design Group, Annapolis, MD

CHAPTER 19

DINGHIES

Though the dinghy truly comes into its own after a passage, choosing and stowing it are definitely up-front considerations. It will be your local transportation, cargo hauler, work platform, secondary anchor carrier, and shallow-water exploration vehicle. It must be tough enough to withstand beaching and encounters with barnacle encrusted piers, yet easy to handle in a wind and sea. It must be large enough to carry the crew and accommodate a load of supplies, scuba/snorkeling gear or baggage, yet capable of being stowed onboard without obstructing normal sailing activities. The right dinghy is a key piece of your cruising equipment.

Rigid dinghies – pros & cons. There are two basic choices: rigid hull or inflatable. The #1 advantage of a rigid hull dinghy is its suitability for handling under oars as well as power. A well designed solid dinghy tracks straight and drives smoothly in all directions. It should be fitted with tanks or sufficient flotation to give it positive buoyancy, even when swamped. A rigid dinghy can usually absorb the abrasion inherent in beaching or riding against a rough wall. Even significant damage to it can be repaired on board or on a convenient beach with some epoxy resin and fiberglass cloth. When a chop kicks up, the higher freeboard of a lightly loaded rigid dinghy will protect the occupants and cargo from spray, especially when driven into wind and sea. Heavily laden, a rigid dinghy's freeboard can be dangerously low, making it vulnerable to swamping. Because easy handling under oars requires a relatively long and narrow hull, rigid dinghies must be boarded and loaded with care to prevent heeling, capsize or inefficient trim.

Driven by an outboard motor, most rigid dinghies perform well, although their displacement hull seldom permits the high speed operation typical of planing hulls. They can generate substantial wake at the upper end of their speed capability, especially if heavily loaded.

The main disadvantage of a rigid dinghy is the problem of stowing it during passages. Coastal cruising options, such as towing it or hanging it from davits, are not feasible. Dinks towed astern are easily lost. Constant surging and slewing cause cyclic loading and chafe that weaken the towing painter until it quietly parts, usually in the middle of the night – and it is daybreak before anyone notices that the faithful dinghy is no longer following in the boat's wake. Rough seas or high winds can flip or swamp a towed dinghy, turning it into a large drogue, and in such conditions righting or dewatering it is a hazardous and difficult operation. Large following seas can turn a towed dinghy into an unguided missile. It can hit the stern of the mother ship and damage both boats.

Stowed on davits, any type of dinghy is vulnerable to big seas. An ocean wave can easily snap the davits and carry away the dink, possibly leaving large holes in the deck or transom. In a seaway, the weight of the dinghy, cantilevered at the ends of the davits, exerts high loads on both the davits and their supporting structure. Should the dink be filled with water by a boarding sea or a tropical downpour, the loads are multiplied. Carrying the dinghy on davits during an ocean passage is clearly not a great tactic for a successful voyage.

The remaining option for a rigid dinghy is to stow it on deck. The challenge is to find a large enough area and a location where the dink does not interfere with sailing or seriously impede the crew's movements. Usual choices are the foredeck and the cabin top. On the foredeck, the dinghy may obstruct fair leading of sheets, block access to forward hatches, foul low-cut genoas, and leave little room for crew to get to the foredeck or to handle sails there. More importantly, a foredeck-mounted dinghy is exposed to the full impact of any boarding seas. These can damage the dinghy, loosen its lashings, or tear loose both the dinghy and the rails or deck fittings to which it has been secured. On the plus side, a hard dinghy stowed upside down on the foredeck can serve as a spray shield over the forward hatch, allowing it to be opened in conditions when it would normally have to be dogged tight.

On the cabin top, a rigid dinghy offers less obstruction to fore and aft passage on deck but can make it more difficult to reef the main or perform any other action that requires crew to mount the cabin. The dinghy stowed here is less vulnerable to waves, but it does obscure vision forward from the cockpit. Here, too, an inverted dinghy may function as a spray shield for a cabin-top hatch. Despite the difficulties, if there's room on the cabin top, that's usually the better place to stow a rigid dinghy.

Two- or three-piece rigid dinghies which can be disassembled and nested will be easier to stow, but they're still large enough to require topside mounting.

Inflatables – pros & cons. Many passagemakers turn to inflatable dinghies partly as a solution to the stowage problem. Though the ease of stowing varies widely among inflatables, all can be deflated, rolled into a relatively small package and stowed more easily than a full size dinghy. Stowage in the cabin or a cockpit locker is preferable to protect the dinghy and minimize the gear exposed to sea and wind. If there's no room below, apply the considerations for topside stowage of a rigid dinghy to the smaller, folded inflatable.

In addition to their stowability, inflatable dinghies have a number of advantages. Being very beamy, they are extremely stable and accept off-center loading without heeling or threatening to flip easily. They have a very shallow draft, seldom more than a few inches, so they can get to places that deeper draft rigid dinks can't reach. Inflatables, with their large buoyancy tubes, have enormous load-carrying capacity, enabling a relatively small dinghy to carry a number of passengers and lots of cargo.

They are also much softer for a swimsuited snorkeler scrambling back aboard.

Inflatables are not without their shortcomings. The most obvious is their vulnerability to puncture of the buoyancy tubes. They are made of surprisingly tough material, but there's always the chance that a sharp rock, protruding pier spike or broken bottle can suddenly put an inflatable out of commission. Damage to fabric floors is equally easy to inflict, although the results are less catastrophic. If an inflatable is damaged, making a durable repair is somewhat more difficult than patching a hard dinghy. Most repairs depend on glued patches, and achieving a good bond requires a clean, dry surface and keeping the surfaces pressed tightly together until the glue sets – conditions not easily achieved aboard or on the beach.

While inflatables perform very well under power, they are seldom easy to row. They have high windage and their flat bottoms provide little directional stability or resistance to leeway. Most are outfitted with oars far too short for effective rowing, and the flexible dinghy body precludes solid mounting for oarlocks. They're especially difficult to handle in wind. You don't want to depend on oars as the primary propulsion for an inflatable .

While inflatables have comparatively low freeboard, it does not decrease dramatically as loading increases. Combined with their enormous buoyancy, this minimizes the danger of swamping. An inflatable's hull lacks bow flare that would deflect spray and splash, so passengers and cargo may well get wet in even a slight chop. This drawback increases at higher speeds, and speed is one of an inflatable's assets. With its very shallow draft and light weight, an inflatable fitted with floorboards to keep the bottom flat can plane quickly, even with a small motor. In smooth water, a lightly loaded inflatable can zip around swiftly, creating only a minimal wake. Increasing the load substantially reduces planing ability with a given engine and greatly increases the wake created at sub-planing speeds. As conditions change from smooth to choppy, operating at planing speeds becomes less and less feasible, partly due to increased spray, but also because the boat pounds across wave tops with increasing force.

Hybrid hulls. The hybrid rigid (RIB) or hard bottom inflatable (usually a shallow fiberglass hull fitted with buoyancy tubes) seeks to achieve the good performance and capacity characteristics of the inflatable while preserving some of the durability and dry ride features of a rigid hull. They score high on performance, but they lose the inflatable's advantage of easy stowage. Even with tubes deflated, these are as difficult to stow as their noninflatable counterparts. For all but the smallest models, performing to their potential requires a powerful (heavy) motor. They are also relatively expensive and suffer from a high theft rate. While RIBs are great around the harbor, they are not ideal for offshore passagemaking.

The outboard motor. In selecting the motor, you'll be considering its power and its weight. If the dinghy is a planing hull, the outboard should be able to get it planing with a normal load (two people and their gear). If it's a rigid dinghy or soft-bottomed inflatable that won't plane, power beyond that needed to drive it to windward in a sloppy sea is wasted. Since power and weight generally increase together, it's best to avoid excess power because the extra weight makes the motor more difficult to handle. A heavier motor is harder to install and remove, and extra weight increases topside stowage risks.

In daily use around the harbor, the outboard can be left mounted on the dinghy, but for an ocean passage it must be stowed aboard the boat. The usual choices are a stern pulpit bracket, in the cabin or in a cockpit locker. A rail mounting leaves it exposed to weather and increases windage. If not fastened with absolute security, it can become a serious hazard if it gets loose in a seaway.

Stowing an outboard below keeps it safe but takes precious space. Even when the fuel tank is drained (necessary to prevent dangerous gasoline fumes from settling inside the hull), the outboard will exude an oily aroma that crew may find objectionable, possibly nauseating. Cockpit locker stowage can be a better choice, if the locker is adequately ventilated and separated from living areas.

Outboard fuel. The outboard's gasoline fuel supply, with or without its oil additive, must be kept topside to avoid the hazard of flammable vapors inside the hull. Stow it in a well ventilated locker to protect it from the sun's heating effect (which increases vapor generation) and to minimize exposure to rain and seawater, which can enter the container through vents to contaminate the fuel. To avoid the hazard of gasoline stowage, several experienced Rally participants simply use up or give away all their dinghy fuel before a long passage, and replace it with fresh fuel on arrival. With gasoline readily available in most popular cruising grounds, this has much to recommend it. The downside is the inconvenience of not having dinghy power when you may need it to clear customs and handle other arrival details.

Anti-theft measures. Before your passage, devise ways to keep the dinghy secure while in daily use at the destination. Dinghies and outboards are expensive and exceedingly useful, so they're frequently the target of thieves. In most cases, the target will be the dinghy that's easiest to steal. Anything that makes theft difficult will reduce the dinghy's attractiveness.

Never leave the dinghy unattended, at either a landing or the boat, secured only with a piece of line. Use a cable, preferably a long one that can be run through the handle of the outboard, under the dinghy thwarts, through the fuel tank handle and all the way to the dock or boat, where it is looped and locked to a solid fitting. At night, it pays to get the dinghy out of the water. Hoist it on davits or rig a bridle and haul it up with a halyard. Take the motor off and lock it to its storage rack. New dinghies and motors are especially vulnerable, so covers and misleading paint work can help make new gear look less desirable. A little ingenuity can go a long way.

In summary, your pre-passage decisions will include selecting the right dinghy and outboard motor, devising safe stowage for dinghy, outboard and its fuel during the passage, and taking steps to ensure their security at your destination. Once there, a dinghy is invaluable. Carrying the right one is essential, and doing it in a manner that least interferes with the boat's operation offshore is the key to success.

CHAPTER 20

COPING WITH ADVERSITY

So far we've discussed ways the skipper and crew can prepare for an offshore passage. These strategies for a successful voyage focus on ways to avoid adversity. Even the most thorough preparations cannot, however, guarantee an incident-free journey.

This and subsequent chapters will outline steps a passagemaker can take to cope with adversity should it occur despite careful preparation. When things do go wrong, you will have many tactics at your disposal to help reduce risks and control the impact of adversity. Whereas strategies for success are anticipatory, these tactics are responses to real situations. They are guides to action.

Because these actions respond to existing or impending conditions, practice will enhance their effectiveness. *Timeliness often makes the difference* between success and failure. *Practice is the best way* to assure that the response to a threatening situation is both swift and appropriate. This practice takes many forms. It ranges from full-scale simulation (crew overboard drills) to simply thinking about and discussing ways to respond to a situation such as a rigging failure or a sudden inflow of water.

If the primary objective in planning and preparing for a passage is to prevent hazards, then the secondary goal is to be ready to cope with any adversity. In a sense, the *objective is to prevent surprises*. Whatever may happen, it should not be totally unanticipated (unexpected, perhaps, but not unconsidered). Whenever Mother Nature or undetected material faults disrupt a passage, the preparation process will have been successful if any adversities that develop have been contemplated and ways to deal with them identified. This often becomes a matter of "thinking about the unthinkable" –which will pay off if and when the bad stuff starts to fly.

Being organized will be an enormous help to the crew's reaction to difficulty or danger. Thinking about an adversity, analyzing the steps needed and assigning responsibilities will facilitate appropriate coping actions. The crew will then know what must be done, when to do it and who is charged with doing it.

Crew overboard recovery . One event for which every crew must be organized is a crew member overboard. *Every recovery includes four phases: sounding an alert/alarm, maneuvering the boat, effecting the recovery, and treating the victim.*

Sounding the alarm. Anyone observing someone going overboard must sound the alarm, because responding to this is an "All Hands" situation. Shouting "Crew Overboard" and/or employing an agreed danger signal (long blasts with a police whistle kept at the helm for emergency) are good responses.

At the same time, get flotation in the water as close to the victim as possible. Life jackets or floating seat cushions kept in the cockpit can be tossed quickly. A Man Overboard Module® can be deployed in a few seconds by simply pulling a pin. Pulling the Lifesling® from its bag and dropping it in the water also takes little time. Launching a traditional man overboard pole and horseshoe ring may take somewhat longer. This step has two purposes. It provides flotation to help the victim stay afloat until the boat can return, and it establishes visible references to help get the boat back to the victim's position.

The person seeing the victim go overboard should act as lookout, keeping the victim in sight as long as possible. Pointing to the victim's location with an outstretched arm helps relocate a victim who periodically disappears between wave crests. It also helps the helmsman determine the course needed.

Make sure someone activates the Man Overboard feature incorporated in most GPS units. This can provide invaluable help in finding a victim lost from sight in darkness, seas, fog or rain.

Maneuvering the boat. Simultaneously with sounding the alarm, the helmsman plays the central role in the recovery by initiating the maneuvering phase. There are several successful maneuvering plans. The helmsman must choose the one best suited to the situation and implement it without hesitation. It's crucial for the helmsman to communicate this choice so the crew will be prepared to carry it out.

A recovery tactic with a demonstrated record of success is known as the Quick Stop. As with all the maneuvers, it keeps the boat as close to the victim as possible while positioning it to permit recovery. To start the Quick Stop, the helmsman turns the boat into and through the wind, as if tacking. If reaching or close-hauled, the jib sheet is not released, but kept secure on the new windward side. This puts the jib aback, acting as a brake to stop the boat's forward progress (away from the victim) and increasing the speed with which the bow turns as the boat begins to circle.

Once the boat has gone through the wind and turned about 180°, it is steadied up briefly, until the victim is slightly abaft the beam. During this time, the jib can be furled or dropped and the main hauled in to prepare for a jibe. This is also the time to prepare recovery equipment such as heaving lines, boarding ladder and hoisting tackles, or to get a swimmer ready to enter the water to help an injured victim.

The next step is to jibe the boat and approach the victim on a close reach, playing the mainsail as necessary to control speed. It can provide sufficient drive to approach the victim, yet at a slow enough speed that the boat can be stopped alongside and the victim brought aboard.

If the boat is off the wind with a spinnaker set, the Quick Stop employs the same maneuver. The boat rounds up into the wind while the spinnaker pole is eased forward to the headstay. When the spinnaker collapses as the boat comes head to wind, its halyard is cast free to drop the sail on deck, or the spinnaker sock is deployed to douse the sail. The boat then tacks to approach the victim on a close reach under main alone.

A second tactic, especially suitable for small crews, employs the Lifesling® recovery device. The Lifesling® is pulled from its storage bag and dropped into the water as soon as the victim goes overboard. It is allowed to stream out astern on its painter as the helmsman starts a Quick Stop maneuver. After the jibe, however, the helmsman does not steer to return to the victim. Instead, the helmsman steers the boat in a series of circles around the victim until the victim connects with the painter being towed astern. At this point, the boat is brought head to wind and all sails are dropped. The victim, meanwhile, works his or her way along the painter to the Lifesling's horse collar flotation, puts the collar around the body below the arms and secures the fastener at the chest to keep it in place. With the boat stopped to avoid dragging the victim through the water, the victim can be hauled back to the boat like a large fish. The painter is secured to a cleat to hold the victim close to the boat and as far out of the water as possible while rigging is set up to hoist him or her back aboard.

A third maneuver, known as the Fast Return, was developed to avoid the hazardous jibe that is part of the Quick Stop. It is reminiscent of the old "Figure 8" technique, but keeps the boat much closer to the victim. In the Fast Return, the helmsman tacks the boat after counting off six seconds from the time the victim goes overboard. If sailing upwind (beating or close reaching), during that six seconds the helmsman slowly turns the boat away from the wind. If off the wind (beam or broad reaching, running), the helmsman slowly turns the boat toward the wind during that six-second period. During the tack, at the instant the boat is head to wind (the boom crosses the boat's centerline), the helmsman observes the victim's position. If the victim is abeam or abaft the beam, the jib is held aback for a few seconds. This makes the boat turn rapidly until it is headed somewhat to leeward of the victim, a position from which the victim can be approached on a close reach. If the victim is forward of the beam, it is not necessary to back the jib to get to such a position. In either case, the final approach on a close reach allows boat speed to be controlled with sail trim.

One complication with the Fast Return is that it can get the boat back to the victim so quickly the crew doesn't have time to prepare for the actual retrieval by rigging recovery lines, etc. Focusing on this during practice sessions will enhance crew readiness.

Regardless of the maneuvering pattern, the approach to the victim is a critical element in the recovery. Normally you approach so the boat is upwind of the victim. Since wind and sea are usually from the same general direction, this creates a lee to provide the victim some protection. And since the boat will drift downwind faster than the victim, the boat will be blown toward him or her, not away. It is also far easier to make physical contact with a victim to leeward than one to windward. Stopping the boat is also critical to avoid dragging the victim or slipping past him or her and having to go around again. To avoid the danger of a victim being struck by a pitching boat's bow or its stern overhang, the boat must be stopped with the victim amidship.

During the maneuver phase, the skipper must also give thought to a search plan in case the victim is not found on the initial pass through the site of the loss. This is especially true if the crew overboard was not seen immediately, and the boat's distance from the victim is uncertain. The many alternatives include an expanding square pattern centered on the best estimate of the victim's position or crosswind sweeps that start to windward of that location and work gradually to leeward, the direction the victim probably will have drifted.

Search plans

Sector Search. An excellent choice if the area to be searched is small and the boat has sufficient power to motor on upwind headings (Figure 20.1).

Six sector search:

1) From the pole (or last known position of victim), proceed upwind for distance equal to radius of search pattern.
2) Turn either right or left 120° and travel distance equal to radius of search.

Figure 20.1 - 6 Sector Search Pattern

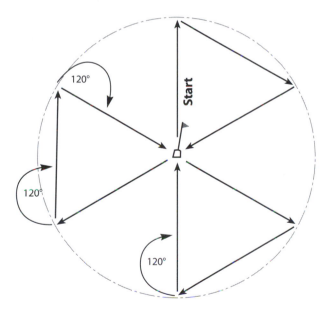

3) Turn in the same direction 120° and travel distance equal to diameter of search pattern, adjusting as necessary to pass close aboard pole at midpoint of leg.
4) Turn 120° in the same direction and travel distance equal to radius of search.
5) Continue to alternate long (diameter) and short (radius) legs to complete pattern, always making turns in the same direction.

Expanding Square Search. A simple pattern to execute, but it requires continuous position plotting to stay on the track. If oriented with one corner to windward, it can be done under sail if the boat can make a track 45° off wind. Orienting one corner toward sun will minimize glare for lookouts.

Procedure:
1) Select desired spacing for search runs (e.g., 200 yards). This becomes the unit for measuring all legs.
2) Starting from victim's last known/suspected position, go one unit (200 yards) in direction search will be oriented.

Figure 20.2 - Expanding Square Search

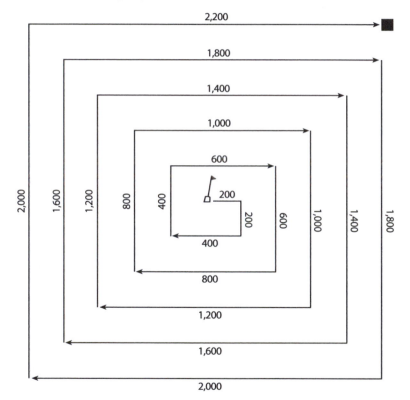

3) Turn 90° (in either direction, depending on conditions)
4) Run one unit (200 yards), then turn another 90° in the same direction.
5) Run two units (400 yards) on the new course, then turn 90°in the same direction.
6) Run two units (400 yards) on this leg and turn 90° again.
7) Increase the next two legs to three units (600 yards).
8) Continue the process, turning in the same direction at the end of each leg and extending the length of the legs by one unit after every other leg.

Figure 20.3 - Parallel Search

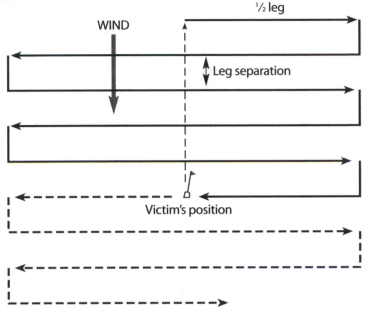

Parallel Search. A sailboat will find it easiest to conduct a parallel search with legs that are beam reaches, starting upwind or upcurrent of the victim's last known position. Sighting of the victim would be enhanced if the legs ran upwind and downwind so lookouts are looking parallel to the wave crests rather than across them.

Procedure:
1) Decide length of legs (perhaps ½ mile) and leg separation (e.g., 100 yards).
2) Start ½ leg upwind/upcurrent of victim's last known/suspected position and sail ½ leg across the wind/current.
3) Jibe, run downwind/current by the leg separation distance (100 yards)
4) Turn and make a crosswind pass in the opposite direction from the first leg, going the full length of a leg.
5) Jibe, go downwind by the separation distance and start the third leg in the same direction as the first.
6) Continue until at least ½ leg downwind/current of last known/suspected position.

Risks of engine use. Note that none of these recovery techniques include use of the engine. Turning on the engine adds risks to an already dangerous situation. The rotating propeller is a serious threat to the victim during final approach. More important, given all the activity and controlled chaos during a crew overboard situation, there's an excellent chance that one or more lines will be hanging overboard (sheet or halyard tails, spinnaker vangs and guys), just waiting to entangle the spinning prop. If that happens, the recovery becomes much more difficult and the crew's attention is distracted by this new problem. It's far better to learn to make recoveries under sail alone, and to save the engine for the rare instance in which maneuvering under sail is not possible (very light air or restricted maneuvering room). If the engine is used, check carefully for lines before starting it and again before putting the propeller in gear.

Recovering the victim. The third phase is the recovery itself: getting the victim back aboard. It starts by making physical contact, such as getting a heaving line to the victim. (The Lifesling® provides physical contact early on.) If the victim is injured, it may be necessary to provide assistance. An unconscious or badly injured victim will always need someone to enter the water (well secured with a tether and equipped with abundant flotation) to help. Getting the victim back aboard can be far more challenging than many sailors think. A cold, wet, probably frightened sailor may not have the strength to climb a ladder. A pitching, rolling boat may turn a rigid boarding ladder into a guillotine-like hazard to a victim, rather than an easy path to safe boarding. Thinking about this in advance and devising a rig to assist a victim back aboard will prove invaluable when there's a real person in the water.

Treating the victim. The final phase of recovery is seldom given much thought during practice sessions: treatment of the victim. He or she is probably in some degree of shock, may be hypothermic, and perhaps injured. No overboard victim should be allowed to resume duties without having had several hours to recuperate. Provide warm, dry clothes and a few hours in the bunk, plus treatment of any injuries, before allowing an overboard victim back into the watch keeping routine.

Making practice realistic. Fortunately, every phase of responding to a crew overboard can be practiced. The maneuvers, the approach, and the techniques for getting a victim back aboard can be done under good conditions and bad. The more frequent –and more realistic – the drills, the greater the likelihood that an actual emergency will be handled smoothly. Realism is essential. Passing a floating seat cushion at two knots and snagging it with a long boat hook does not equate to a successful crew overboard recovery – because you can't get a real person back aboard that way. The boat must come to a stop, to windward of the "victim" and close enough to establish physical contact.

Methods for getting a cold, heavy crew member, too weak to be much help, from the water to the deck can be practiced at anchor or alongside a dock by lifting a crew member out of a dinghy. Resolving the challenges involved during practice sessions will contribute to success in a real emergency. Seeing the difficulties may even motivate the crew to make extra efforts to avoid an overboard situation.

Having a crew overboard plan prepared, with duties identified and assigned, will increase the crew's readiness to respond properly. It may not be best to assign specific tasks to individuals by name – who will do the jobs assigned to the victim? Assign responsibilities to helmsman, watch captain, next person on watch, first person topside. This plan should be posted where everyone can review it frequently.

Sample crew overboard plan. Since we never know who will be the victim and who will be left on board to perform recovery functions, all crew must be ready to perform any duty as directed by the person in charge.

FIRST ACTIONS

Helmsman/Watch Stander:

Immediately and without waiting for orders, head the boat up into and through the wind, without releasing the jib sheets, to stop the boat's movement away from the victim. Simultaneously, sound the alarm.

Notify other crew members of the planned recovery method and boat maneuvers.

Helmsman:

Sound Alarm

Throw flotation to victim/launch Lifesling® or MOM® (but not both)

Start recovery maneuvers

Other Crew As Available:

First person to nav station: Record position on GPS by pressing "MOB" key

Lookout: Keep pointing to victim in water to help helmsman return to victim

Sail handler: Furl genoa/drop staysail after completion of Quick Stop; work mainsheet as boat bears off, jibes and approaches victim

Crew: Get heaving line from lazarette, prepare to throw to victim when within range

Drop main when directed if Lifesling® recovery is used

Rig Lifesling® recovery tackle to main halyard

Put on harness and PFD, attach long tether and prepare to enter water to assist a disabled victim

Rig rope slings/portable ladder to help victim out of water

Prepare towels and dry clothes for victim

Abandoning ship. Another situation for which the crew must be organized is abandoning ship. Should it ever appear likely that the boat will sink, a good abandon ship plan can make the difference between an orderly departure that salvages as much life-sustaining material as possible and a frenzy in which valuable gear is needlessly lost with the boat.

Preparing to abandon. Abandon ship plans should include two phases: preparing to abandon and actually departing. The *first phase* is implemented when it begins to appear likely that the boat will be lost. This consists of gathering vital supplies in preparation for departure and transmitting a distress message to alert potential rescuers. As discussed in Chapter 16, equipment to be gathered includes pyrotechnic distress signals, freshwater and watermakers, the EPIRB, handheld electronics, the medical kit and the abandon ship bag(s). Many lists for abandon ship bags have been suggested, but you should customize yours to fit individual needs. First verify what is packed with the raft, then select the "ditch kit" items to supplement that. Remember that space in the raft is very limited, so take only life sustaining supplies and the most important personal items (wallets, passports, spare eyeglasses, medications taken regularly). *Final preparation* includes updating the navigational plot, assembling the data for a MAYDAY message, and preparing the raft for deployment. While a MAYDAY message may be premature at this stage, use VHF radio to alert any nearby vessels of the situation and to advise them that you may need rescue or assistance. All these duties should be assigned to specific crew members who can carry them out with minimum guidance.

Before we move on to departing a sinking vessel, let's consider a situation somewhat short of "imminent sinking". What if conditions are grim, you foresee a possible abandon ship situation, initiate a MAYDAY or radio call, perhaps activate the EPIRB, and as a result a rescue vessel appears? Your boat is still afloat, but the other ship promises so much more safety and comfort that there is an irresistible urge to seek shelter there. Here are a few things worth thinking about before making that choice.

From a distance, that merchant ship steaming over the horizon looks steady and stable as a rock, moving little under the influence of the wind and seas that are making your boat so uncomfortable. As she draws closer, though, it becomes clear that she, too, rolls and pitches. Waves wash along her steel sides like surf along a seawall. You realize that taking a small boat alongside a large ship in heavy seas is like mooring it to a steel seawall in a hurricane. It's not a matter to be taken lightly.

No matter how cautious the approach, there's little doubt the larger vessel will eventually crash against the smaller one, perhaps with sufficient violence to sink it or throw its occupants into the sea. In those conditions, small boat fenders are utterly ineffectual and larger ship fenders become lethal weapons. The difficulties are compounded by a large ship's loss of steerage at speeds under 7-8 knots. Once they have begun to stop for a rescue attempt, most large ships can do little more than drift in response to wind and sea. They simply cannot maneuver to avoid hitting a small boat close alongside.

By all means, *communicate with the ship by radio* so both of you know what the other is doing. Make sure the ship stays to windward to flatten breaking wave crests and create some lee for the stricken small boat. Before approaching, remember that you are giving up your command and your control of the situation, and both you and your rescuers are being placed at risk.

To transfer from a damaged sailboat (or even a life raft) to safety on the deck of a ship presents serious challenges. Survivors may have to climb a cold, slippery steel ladder (or a swinging, elusive rope one) up the ship's side. With 30' waves and a ship rolling as little as 10-15 degrees, every few seconds a small boat can rise and fall 55 feet or more relative to the ship's deck. Timing of the move from boat to ship is crucial. Survivors must choose their moment, then grasp the ladder and climb swiftly to avoid being washed away by the next wave or struck by their boat when the next wave lifts it. If the ordeal preceding the rescue has left the crew too weak to climb, if timing is off by a fraction of a second, or if hulls strike and knock survivors off balance, the result can be injury or death instead of rescue. Perhaps the worst possibility is that someone might fall between the two vessels. Hopefully, the rescuers can drop lines that the survivors can secure to their harnesses so the rescuers can help hoist survivors or at least prevent them from falling.

It might be better to keep the damaged sailboat away from a ship to avoid collision. Increasing the separation may put the two vessels on different parts of the wave pattern, exaggerating the difference in height and the relative movement of the hulls. Even with rescue lines secured to the survivors, getting them up to the rescuer's deck is hazardous. Survivors can be snatched from the deck violently, possibly being pulled through tangled rigging or shredded sails, when a sea drops out from under their boat. Or a sea may rise under the ship and cause it to roll, dropping the survivors into the water or dragging them across their boat and into the sea. One crew member of a boat that was being abandoned was dropped into the sea despite diligent efforts to haul her aboard the rescue ship with lines. Fortunately, she was recovered uninjured. Efforts to evacuate injured crew from another boat were abandoned after the boat drifted under the overhanging stern of the ship and the sole uninjured crew member was unable to secure lines to enable the rescue ship to haul it to a safer position. Survivors should don survival suits or bulky Type I PFDs for buoyancy and wear layers of clothes for padding to minimize risk of injury during the rescue. Survivors might be able to transfer to the ship in a life raft or inflatable dinghy if the rescue vessel can hoist it with the survivors onboard. If this is attempted, everyone should be securely harnessed to keep them in the raft or dinghy.

If the distressed boat is within reach of a rescue helicopter, the outlook is somewhat brighter, but the process of getting off the boat is still hazardous. Modern helicopters such as the Coast Guard's H-60 Jayhawk can maintain a hover that at least partially compensates for the vertical distance between wave peaks and troughs. This reduces but does not eliminate the danger of survivors being snatched violently out of a trough or dragged through the water of a crest.

The rotors of a hovering helicopter generate a downwash that can pack winds at or above gale force. Loose or broken gear strewn on deck can be blown about and endanger both the survivors and the helicopter. Damage to a rotor blade or flying debris sucked into an engine can bring a helicopter down – right on top of the people it's trying to rescue. The wind and engine noise combine to make communication among the crew and with the helicopter nearly impossible. This creates opportunities for misunderstandings and accidents. As with a ship rescue, *communicate with the helicopter* as early and as long as possible to gain clear understanding of what will happen. Talk to your crew before the helicopter arrives to create a plan and assign responsibilities. US Coast Guard rescue helicopter crews include a rescue specialist who often drops down to the distressed boat to help with the rescue.

If you have a clear deck area from which a helo can lift survivors, a direct rescue may be possible. Here, the first danger the boat crew must avoid is the static electrical charge carried by the hoisting gear when it is first lowered. In part because of their composite construction, modern helicopters build up a strong static charge as they fly. Before anyone touches the hoisting cable or basket, allow the hoisting gear to touch the sea or a grounded metallic structure aboard the boat. This will safely bleed off the charge. Failure to do so will not have fatal results for a healthy person, but the jolt can be strong enough to knock down and temporarily disorient the victim. The helo crew will normally take care of grounding the lifting rig by dipping it in the sea before allowing it to be pulled aboard the disabled sailboat. In an adrenaline-charged moment, however, an eager crew member may pull the messenger line in fast and hard enough to bring the basket or cable onboard before it has been grounded.

If there is no clear deck space or masts and rigging preclude getting the helicopter close enough for a direct rescue, the survivors may have to accept the risks and board a raft or dinghy and move away from the stricken boat. They can be lifted from that platform to the helicopter. In a worst case scenario, it has sometimes been necessary for survivors to enter the water, wearing PFDs or survival suits, of course, and move clear of the distressed boat. The helo can then lift the floating/swimming survivors out of the water.

Rescue by another boat of similar size may be the least threatening way to get off a sinking boat. Such a rescue craft is probably more maneuverable than a big ship, the two boats will have smaller differences in their motion as they respond to the seas, and boarding a smaller boat is easier than scaling the side of a rolling merchant ship. To avoid a collision between the two boats, the best plan is to pass a line from the rescue boat to the one in distress. With plenty of slack in the line, secure it to the life raft or dinghy. When all crew have boarded the raft or dinghy, the line can be used to pull the survivors to the rescue vessel. Alternatively, use a long messenger line to pull a rescue line across. Tie that line to the harness and PFD of a survivor. Once this survivor enters the water, he or she can be pulled to and aboard the rescue craft. Use the messenger to haul the rescue line back for another survivor, and repeat the process for each person.

Before deciding to leave the boat in favor of a rescuing vessel, carefully assess the risks involved in accomplishing the transfer. They may make staying aboard the distressed boat the safest option.

Time to abandon ship. When it becomes clear the boat is within minutes of sinking, however, and there is no longer any prospect of keeping it afloat, it is time to abandon the ship. Resist the temptation to leave prematurely! The life raft provides poorer protection from sea and weather conditions than the big boat, it has fewer resources available to keep the crew alive, and it is a far smaller target for rescuers to find. Remember the rules: "Don't abandon the ship until the ship abandons you" and "Don't get into the life raft until you have to step UP to get there."

Depending on the raft's size, weight and storage, assign one or two crew the job of launching it. They must first verify that the raft's tether/operating lanyard is attached to the boat. Only then should they launch the raft over the lee side and pull the operating lanyard until the raft inflates. One person should then board the raft. (He or she may first have to right the raft in the event it inflates inverted.) All the collected gear is then passed to the person in the raft, who should lash each item in place to avoid loss. If it has not been done earlier, this is the time to activate the EPIRB and to send the MAYDAY message to inform the world that you have taken to the raft, your position, and any vital information such as injured crew members or other special circumstances that will affect rescue planning. Continue sending the MAYDAY message as long as possible or until it is acknowledged.

Once in the raft, be prepared to cut the painter connecting it to the boat, but do not do so until the boat actually sinks. Many a badly damaged boat has floated for days, decks awash and seemingly on the verge of slipping below the surface for good. As long as it stays on the surface, the derelict reduces the raft's drift and presents opportunities for subsequent salvage efforts that can yield additional useful equipment or supplies.

Life rafts are crowded, wet and uncomfortable. Their motion is an efficient generator of seasickness. Every activity is complicated by the absence of solid surfaces for support: everything one touches yields and flexes. Even if it is well equipped, a raft alone won't necessarily save lives. It does, however, provide a protected shelter in which the skipper and crew can make the decisions that will save their lives. A 406 MHz EPIRB will bring help, between four and 24 hours in popular cruising areas and in waters frequented by commercial vessels and aircraft. But even without immediate rescue, sailors have endured months in rafts, sustained by a hand-operated water maker or collecting rain while carefully rationing their water supplies and harvesting food and liquids from the marine farm that soon grows on the underwater surfaces of a raft. Keeping a positive attitude and maintaining a cooperative organization with strong leadership by the skipper is what saves lives.

Sample abandon ship plan

Preparation Phase

PERSON	TASKS
Hal	In charge; direct the actions; collect distress signals, water supplies
Ken	Update navigational plot; prepare MAYDAY messages; send alerting message; gather EPIRB, GPS and handheld VHF for transfer to raft
Bob	Prepare raft for launching, assemble abandon ship bags and additional equipment (see *Priorities for equipment and supplies* on next page)
Walt	Assist with raft and collecting

Execution Phase

PERSON	TASKS
Hal	In charge, coordinate activity
Ken	Send final MAYDAY messages; get VHF, EPIRB, GPS and logbook into raft; help load equipment and supplies
Bob	Launch raft; board raft to receive and lash gear securely in raft
Walt	Tend raft painter, help loading gear

Priorities for equipment and supplies

1. 406 MHz EPIRB
2. Distress signals, watermaker and abandon ship ditch bags in starboard cockpit locker
3. VHF radios, GPS
4. Sleeping bags (2)
5. Sun/cold/weather protection (clothes, jackets, hats, towels, rain gear)
6. Medical kit
7. Radar reflector (aluminum foil as substitute)
8. Light line for lashings
9. Trash bags, zip-close bags
10. Boat hook
11. Canned food and can opener

Sending someone aloft. Another challenging situation (less traumatic than crew overboard or abandon ship) that will benefit from advance planning is sending someone aloft at sea. This need can occur as a result of a lost/parted halyard, an instrument or antenna that comes loose from its masthead fastenings, a jammed sail or a broken spreader.

The best way to send a person aloft is in a mountain climber's harness, a device the wearer cannot fall out of, even if inverted. A snugly fitted soft boatswain's chair is a second option. Whoever goes aloft should be wearing a Type I PFD (for maximum padding to protect against being slammed into the mast) and a standard safety harness. A harness with a short tether can keep the worker close to the mast when the boat rolls, making it easier to use two hands for the job. Attached to the harness or lifting chair with a short lanyard should be a soft bag containing everything likely to be needed during the trip aloft. It should include a light line long enough to reach the deck, one that can be used to hoist any other items that may be needed.

The chair/harness should be hoisted with a reliable halyard. The worker's safety harness must be attached to a second halyard strong enough to accept the full load if the primary halyard fails or must be slacked off for some reason. Both halyards should be attached with a screw pin shackle or carefully tied bowline. Do not rely on a snap shackle except when there is no alternative, and then be sure the snap part is securely moused closed with tape or marline. Attaching a tag line to the bottom of the chair/harness will enable a person on deck to help keep the worker from swinging around too much as the boat rolls and pitches.

Before going aloft, discuss the planned work to be sure everyone understands what is to be done. Establish hand signals for the worker to use in lieu of voice communication, which will be difficult even under benign conditions. Signals for hauling up, hauling slowly, stopping, making fast, and slacking off will suffice. Using a set of 49 MHz headset-style walkie-talkie radios or the portable FRS units (in Chapter 9) will make it much easier to get reports from aloft, give guidance and respond to requests from the worker.

When the worker is rigged and ready to go aloft, take all the slack out of the halyards. Then have the worker bounce up and down a few times, putting a substantial load on the lifting rigs to be sure they are secure. Hoisting aloft should be done slowly. If possible, have one person standing away from the mast who can watch both the worker and the hoisters and serve as a safety observer. When the worker gets to the work position, cleat the halyards off securely and get people away from the mast so they are clear of anything that drops from aloft. When lowering the worker, do so smoothly, avoiding jolts. Coordinating the easing off of the lifting and safety halyards takes attentive line handling on deck.

Unless it's flat calm, it is best to have sail(s) set when sending a person aloft. While it complicates the rigging a bit and may make it more difficult for the worker to get access to certain areas, it also has a steadying effect that significantly diminishes the motion experienced aloft.

A passagemaker can encounter many other forms of adversity, as well. Devising tactics for coping with those situations is helpful in handling unwanted events when they occur. Weather is the factor over which the voyager has the least control, and the duration of passagemaking exposes the boat and crew to increased likelihood of encountering foul weather. Tactics for coping with heavy weather are next on our adversity-management agenda.

CHAPTER 21

COPING WITH
HEAVY WEATHER

Keeping an alert watch, carefully monitoring local weather conditions (especially the barometer) and regularly copying and analyzing forecasts will normally prevent heavy weather from coming as a surprise. For all but the most localized conditions, the crew should have sufficient warning to follow the preparatory steps discussed in Chapter 12. Generally speaking, the longer the heavy weather conditions are likely to prevail, the greater the advance notice available and the greater the opportunity to get ready. Large low pressure systems that may churn up the sea for days can usually be tracked as they march across the ocean, giving many hours to prepare for them.

By contrast, thunderstorms or severe squall lines may appear on short notice and allow only minutes to get ready. They're normally over quickly, not prevailing long enough to build the mountainous seas that are the principal hazard in a major storm, but they can do severe damage to a boat caught unaware. Knockdowns resulting in crew injury and rig/equipment damage can occur with astonishing suddenness.

To reduce sail quickly. If the wind builds gradually, use appropriate sail trim tactics (Chapters 18 & 22) first. Strong winds do not reduce the need for proper trim. In fact, good trim techniques are an integral part of coping with stronger winds, as you will be modifying sail shape to suit increased winds.

Aside from trim adjustments, *the basic tactic for coping with heavy weather, regardless of duration, is to reduce sail.* On short notice, the crew must be both able and willing to respond swiftly. When the black squall line or the heavy roll of clouds marking an oncoming front approach, there should be no hesitation about reducing sail immediately. Rolling up the jib and reefing the main should take only a few minutes. It's best to maintain sufficient mainsail area to keep steeragway, but sometimes the warning is so short there's no time for an orderly sail area reduction. In this case, simply roll the jib, douse the main and lash it quickly to the boom. The boat should ride safely through the worst of the squall.

Reducing sail methodically. When time is not so crucial, you can reduce sail area methodically. There's no universally correct answer to the question of which sail

Figure 21.1 - Sail Reduction Sequence for Typical Cruising Boats

Beaufort Force	Wind Speed (knots)	Sea State	Wind On or Forward of Beam		
			Sloop	Cutter	Ketch
0 calm	<1	Mirrorlike	Motor		
1 Light Air	1-3	Scale-like ripples	Full main, drifter	Full main, largest headsail	Full main, big headsail, mizzen
2 Light Breeze	4-6	Small wavelets, glassy crests	Full main, #1 genoa	Full main, largest headsail	Full main, big headsail, mizzen
3 Gentle Breeze	7-10	large wavelets, scattered whitecaps	Full main, #1 genoa	Full main, largest headsail	Full main, big headsail, mizzen
4 Moderate Breeze	11-16	Small waves (1-4 ') numerous whitecaps	Full main, #2 genoa	Full main, staysail, yankee jib	Full main, working jib, mizzen
5 Fresh Breeze	17-21	Moderate waves (4-8'), many white-caps, some spray	Single reefed main, working jib	Single reefed main, staysail, yankee jib	Single reefed main, working jib
6 Strong Breeze	22-27	Large waves (8-12'). long whitecaps, more spray	Double reefed main, reefed working jib	Double reefed main, staysail	Double reefed main, working jib
7 Moderate Gale	28-33	Waves 12-18', white foam from breaking waves blows in streaks	Triple reefed main, storm jib	Triple reefed main, staysail	Double reefed main, storm jib
8 Fresh Gale	34-40	Waves 12-18' widely spaced, blowing foam forms marked streaks	Storm trysail, storm jib	Triple reefed main, storm jib	Triple reefed main, storm jib
9 Strong Gale	41-47	Steep 20' waves, seas roll, spray cuts visibility	Heave to	Trysail, storm jib	Trysail, storm jib
10 Storm	48-55	20-30' waves with overhanging crests, dense white foam streaks, poor visibility	Heave to or deploy sea anchor	Heave to	Heave to

to reef first. The choice depends on the sail plan, point of sail and sea state. If a boat uses a large genoa as its primary driving sail, reducing the headsail area may be best. If the main is relatively large, it may be a better choice for first reefing.

Maintaining balance in the sail plan is always a factor. The sail reduction sequence must preserve balance and avoid strong weather or lee helm that will fight the helmsman. Minimize heeling by moving the sail plan's center of effort downward. Keep

Figure 21.1 *continued*
Sail Reduction Sequence for Typical Cruising Boats

Beaufort Force	Wind Speed (knots)	Sea State	Wind Abaft Beam		
			Sloop	Cutter	Ketch
0 calm	<1	Mirrorlike	Motoring		
1 Light Air	1-3	Scale-like ripples	Main, drifter/ spinnaker	Main, largest jib / spinnaker	Main, mizzen, largest jib / spinnaker
2 Light Breeze	4-6	Small wavelets, glassy crests	Main, drifter/ spinnaker	Main, largest jib / spinnaker	Main, mizzen, largest jib / spinnaker
3 Gentle Breeze	7-10	large wavelets, scattered whitecaps	Main, #1 genoa	Main, largest jib	Main, mizzen, largest jib / spinnaker
4 Moderate Breeze	11-16	Small waves (1-4 ') numerous whitecaps	Main, #2 jib	Main, working jib, staysail	Main, #2 jib, reefed mizzen
5 Fresh Breeze	17-21	Moderate waves (4-8'), many whitecaps, some spray	Single reefed main, #2 jib	Single reefed main, staysail, working jib	Single reefed main, #2 jib, reefed mizzen
6 Strong Breeze	22-27	Large waves (8-12'). long whitecaps, more spray	Double reefed main, #2 jib	Double reefed main, staysail, working jib	Single reefed main, #2 jib, double reefed or no mizzen
7 Moderate Gale	28-33	Waves 12-18', white foam from breaking waves blows in streaks	Triple reefed main, working jib	Triple reefed main, staysail	Triple reefed main, storm jib
8 Fresh Gale	34-40	Waves 12-18' widely spaced, blowing foam forms marked streaks	Storm trysail, storm jib	Triple reefed main, storm jib	Triple reefed main, storm jib
9 Strong Gale	41-47	Steep 20' waves, seas roll, spray cuts visibility	Storm jib or bare poles	Storm jib or bare poles	Storm jib
10 Storm	48-55	20-30' waves with overhanging crests, dense white foam streaks, poor visibility	Bare poles	Bare poles	Bare poles

it near the center of the boat, above the hull's center of lateral resistance, to reduce helm effect. The "jib and jigger" used on ketch and yawl rigs – sailing under jib and mizzen with the main struck – violates this principle but yields a balanced sail plan especially suitable for off-wind sailing. While this can be a good option for settled conditions with brisk winds and flat seas, it's not recommended for seriously deteriorating weather. In rough water, split rigs will usually balance better and pitch less under a reefed main and small headsail, with little or no mizzen.

If the wind is aft, most boats respond better if the sail plan favors the jib. Steering is easier if the wind is pulling the boat with a headsail rather than pushing it with the main. The reverse is also true. When close reaching or beating, reducing the jib while retaining more area in the main will keep the boat headed up, and "feathering" into the wind during gusts will be easier.

When to reef? Just as there is no universal rule for which sail to reef first, there's no single criterion for deciding when to reef. The boat's behavior should tell you. When close reaching or beating, *excessive heeling* is a key sign that it's time to reef. Most boats are designed to sail best at a heeling angle of 15° or less. Persistent strong heeling, especially enough to immerse the lee rail, is a clear sign that the boat is carrying too much sail. Heeling causes weather helm, which forces the helmsman to carry more rudder. The increased rudder creates drag that slows the boat. It's not uncommon to find that a boat actually gains speed from reducing sail area: It rides more upright, experiences less heel-induced weather helm and needs less rudder to stay on course.

Off the wind, a boat with too much sail will be difficult to steer, yawing heavily and requiring large rudder changes to keep on course as it surfs down waves. Its tendency to round up and broach can be controlled only with vigorous applications of the rudder. There's a lot of truth in the old saying that the time to take a reef is when you first start to wonder if a reef would be appropriate. When the boat's response to wind and sea start to make the skipper's stomach nervous, it's usually time to reduce sail and regain control of the situation.

For some reason, sailors tend to procrastinate when it comes to taking or shaking out a reef. They delay taking a reef until it becomes obvious that they need to do so, perhaps because they hope the increased wind strength will prove temporary (seldom the case). They are also curiously reluctant to shake out a reef as the wind diminishes. The occasional strong puffs that were ignored when the wind was building now justify keeping the sail reefed even though average wind speeds have diminished significantly. Sometimes the move may be delayed simply to put off what is viewed as a difficult task.

Reducing and restoring sail area should be so routine aboard a passagemaking boat that the watch can do it without help. Getting to this point simply takes crew training in an orderly sequence of tasks.

"Reefing" a roller furling jib. Changing headsail area with a roller furling jib is the simplest task. Ease the working sheet to reduce the load on the sail, but stop short of letting the sail flog. Heading up may help. Provided the main is well vanged to preclude an accidental jibe, bearing off to put the jib in the lee of the main can reduce the load on the jib. With the load reduced, haul in on the roller furling control line to roll up the desired amount of headsail. In a well designed system, it should not be

necessary to use a winch on the control line. With the sail unloaded but not flogging, you should be able to roll it in without mechanical assistance. Using a winch is a good way to part the control line, jam the system or do other permanent damage to the rig. If it's necessary to use a winch, inspect the system to identify the source of excess resistance. Roll up the desired amount of sail, preferably to an area reinforced at foot and leech to take the strains imposed as those areas become the tack and head. Before trimming the reefed jib, move the fairlead forward for even loading of the foot and leech. Then return the boat to its original course and trim the sail.

Removing a rolled reef is even easier: Simply reposition the fairlead, then ease out the control line and gently let the sail unroll, trimming with the sheet.

Reefing a roller furling main. Reefing and unreefing a roller furling main are done the same way, working with a roller furler control line and a clew outhaul pendant. Keeping a drag load on the outhaul line will help achieve a smooth roll-up of the mainsail. (Many mainsail systems are designed to include the use of a winch, so our comments about winches for headsail rolling may not apply here.)

Reefing a traditional main. Reefing a traditional main is a bit more complex, but organized properly it can be a routine event. First, make sure all lines are ready, especially that the halyard is ready to run. Then ease the vang, permitting the boom to rise. Next set the topping lift to support the boom while the sail is lowered. Easing the mainsheet will reduce the load on the sail before hauling it down. Ease the halyard and pull the luff of the sail down until the new tack cringle is at the boom, where you'll lash it or secure it to a hook. (This is easier if the halyard has been marked to show how far it needs to be let off.) Tension the halyard to take the horizontal wrinkles out of the luff. Next haul on the clew outhaul pendant until the new clew cringle is snug against the boom and the foot of the sail is tight (further easing of the vang and sheet may be needed to get the clew to the boom). Ease the topping lift and reset the vang. Before trimming the sheet to fill the sail, it's a good practice to provide a back-up to the outhaul pendant by lashing the reefed clew cringle to the boom with a piece of line or a spare sail tie. This guards against major sail damage in the event the outhaul pendant chafes and parts. Also examine the loose cloth along the foot (the bunt of the sail) to find any areas where the sail may chafe against itself, the boom or adjacent lines. Finally, trim the sail.

Though not necessary, many skippers prefer to keep the bunt neatly stowed by setting the lazy jacks or by rolling the loose fabric and securing it with a lanyard or reef points. When possible, reef points should pass between the foot of the sail and the boom to minimize contact between the sail and the spar and reduce the opportunity for chafing. Reef points are not designed to carry the load of the sail and should not be tied tight enough to pull downward along the foot of the sail. To reduce the risk of leaving a reef point tied when shaking out a reef – an error certain to cause a rip in the sail – reef points should be cut from a colored line that makes them clearly visible against the sail itself.

After each sail reduction, review the boat's readiness for the next reduction. Make sure outhaul pendants are led, fairleads properly positioned, lines and tails overhauled and ready for use. If the next step involves a sail change (to a storm jib, staysail or trysail), this is the time to make sure sheets are ready and review the sail change process with the crew.

Shaking out a conventional or "slab" reef merely reverses the reefing sequence. Make the halyard and clew outhaul tails ready, then ease the sheet to reduce the load on the sail. Set the topping lift. Ensure that all reef points have been cast off. Remove any clew lashings, then ease the clew outhaul reefing pendant. With the clew fully slacked, ease the halyard sufficiently to disconnect the tack cringle, then hoist the sail with the halyard. Tension it to remove wrinkles, and secure it. Then ease the topping lift, reset the vang and trim the sail.

With halyards and pendants led to the cockpit, setting and shaking out a reef can be accomplished without sending a crew member forward, a big safety advantage. Many modern designs also have reefing systems that use a single line to control both tack and clew. They greatly simplify the process, enabling a single crew member to work both the halyard and the reefing line from one winch in the cockpit. Taking and shaking out a reef becomes a matter of hauling on one line while slacking another.

The mizzen. The mizzen is normally handled the same way the main is, but since it's a much smaller sail, loads are lighter and the procedure is less demanding. Because it's located well aft of the center of lateral resistance, the mizzen can create strong weather helm as the wind increases. It may be the first sail reefed or doused when a split rig is working to weather in a blow.

Hand steering techniques. As the wind builds, so do the seas. Loads on the steering system will increase, and it may become necessary to steer by hand rather than rely on an autopilot or vane. Even if the self steering system has sufficient power to control the boat in storm conditions, a live helmsman has two advantages self steering systems lack. The first is anticipating the waves. The autopilot or vane can only react after the boat has started to veer off course, but a helmsman quickly develops a feel for the boat's response to waves and can act to prevent yawing before it starts. If a quartering sea, for example, pushes the stern to starboard and causes the bow to slew to port, the self steering system doesn't apply right rudder until the bow has started to swing left, by which time a lot of rudder is needed to stop the movement. The human helmsman, sensing the lift of a wave on the port quarter, can begin applying right rudder before the head starts to swing left. This keeps the boat closer to course and may require less rudder angle, hence less speed-reducing drag.

The second reason for hand steering in high seas is that steering a straight course may not be best for those conditions. When working to windward, it is exceedingly rough on gear and crew if the boat drives off the top of a wave with sufficient speed to cause it to crash into the succeeding trough. The impact produces a bone-shaking jolt and slows the boat so much that steerage is impaired. The boat can't regain speed before the next wave hits and stops it completely or pushes the bow off to leeward.

Figure 21.2 - Steering in Waves

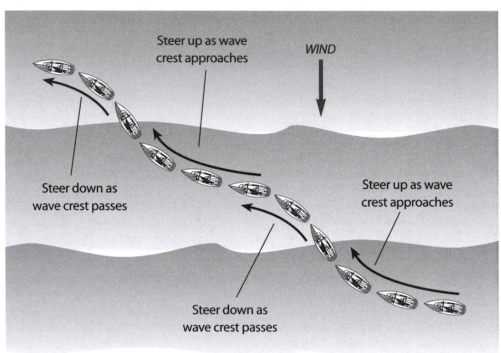

This sequence leaves the boat vulnerable to a knockdown. Careful steering can control both the speed and the boat's attitude toward the waves, giving an easier ride and maintaining a better average course. The most effective tactic is usually to head the boat up slightly as the crest of a wave approaches, slowing the boat's speed a bit. As the crest passes, bear away sharply and sail down the back of the wave somewhat further off the wind. This regains boat speed and provides momentum to carry through the heading-up process as the next wave approaches. When the seas are really large, this technique also adapts the boat to the differing wind speed between the crests and the troughs. On the crests, where wind force is greatest, the boat is pinched up to reduce exposed sail area. In the troughs, where the wind is weaker, the boat is reaching off with more sail area exposed.

This tactic can be applied by all boats when the seas are large and have a long period, allowing time to alter the heading between waves. Lighter, fin keel/spade rudder designs (most vulnerable to the high speed launch and sudden slamming stop described above) are sufficiently maneuverable to allow them to use this tactic in shorter, choppier seas as well. Heavier boats, less responsive to the helm, may best reduce the pounding hazard by falling off to a course that takes the seas at a more comfortable angle and using the increased driving power to keep the boat moving across the crests. In either case, the key is to keep the boat moving, because without a steady flow of water past the rudder, control of the boat is lost. When that happens, the boat is likely to end up in the trough, beam to the seas and exposed to a knockdown.

Reaching in high seas. When reaching in high seas, the greatest risk is getting knocked down by a sea that catches the boat on the beam. Rather than steer a fixed course, the helmsman must constantly adapt the heading to the waves. When beam or close reaching, head up and take particularly threatening seas broad on the bow, bearing off quickly once the crest has passed. Avoiding beam seas when broad reaching can be more tricky, since it means bearing off to keep the wave on the quarter. This exposes the boat to the risk of a yaw that could lead to an accidental jibe. It can also cause sudden

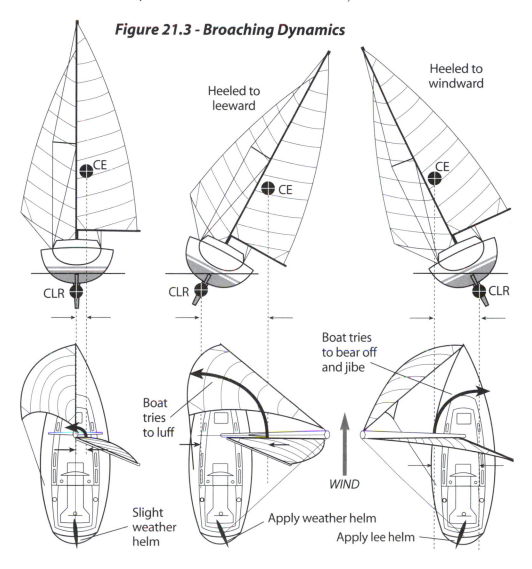

Figure 21.3 - Broaching Dynamics

surfing acceleration that may drive the boat into the back of the next swell. When that occurs, the boat slows or stops, and the apparent wind load on the sails and rig suddenly increases markedly. Steerage is reduced, and the risk of rig damage rises.

Running before heavy seas. Running before heavy seas brings the constant danger of jibing and broaching, and so is best done with only headsails set to reduce potential for a damaging accidental jibe. The greatest danger is caused by the boat's tendency to roll heavily when directly before the wind and sea. This causes the sails' center of effort (CE) to cross back and forth above the hull's center of lateral resistance (CLR), creating weather helm when heeled to leeward (the side the main boom would be on if the main were set) and lee helm when heeled to weather. The helmsman must be constantly alert to prevent loss of control, rounding up and knockdowns. The rule is to steer the boat into the roll: When the boat heels to port, lateral displacement of the center of effort will create a tendency to turn to the right, so left rudder is needed to counter it. Heeling to starboard calls for right rudder.

Broad reaching is generally easier to handle than running, if only because the forces working on the boat are more consistent and do not shift from side to side as they do when running. The risks associated with the higher speeds that can be produced on these points of sail will be addressed shortly.

Active and passive tactics. In their broadest sense, the tactics open to a passage-making boat in storm conditions can be divided into two categories: active and passive. Active tactics involve continuous crew effort to keep the boat going in a chosen direction; passive ones rely more on the boat's ability to take care of itself in a seaway.

The appropriateness of any tactic in a given situation depends on many factors, including the boat's location, its design and the condition of its crew. Location is mainly a question of the sea room available. When well offshore, a boat can head in the direction that produces the safest, most comfortable conditions. That may or may not be possible when shoals or shorelines are close. Running off to ride with the wind and sea, or heaving to while waiting for the storm to pass are not safe options off a lee shore. Navigational constraints are not limited to those created by a shoreline. A tactic that would carry a boat into a major ocean current such as the Gulf Stream when the wind is opposed to the current would be a poor choice.

If a boat's location would permit it to seek shelter in a harbor, the decision to do so must be weighed very carefully. It's essential to be sure the boat will arrive at the entrance while conditions there are still safe. It would be counterproductive to run for cover, only to find an impassable entrance and perhaps a lee shore.

The boat's design will influence your options, as well, because hull shape, displacement and stability affect the way a boat responds to wind and sea. In the most general terms, the more a boat resembles a heavy, traditional, full-keel "Colin Archer" design, the better suited it will be for passive tactics, and the more difficult for active tactics. A design resembling a dinghy, with light displacement, flat, shallow hull and fin keel with separate rudder will respond better to active tactics and less so to passive ones. The typical modern cruising design (if there is such a thing), with moderate displacement and draft, cut away forefoot and separate skeg-mounted rudder, will have a wide array of options, capable of using either active or passive tactics.

Crew condition can be a decisive factor, because active tactics place a heavy load on the crew, demanding physical endurance and mental alertness. A crew that is tired, short-handed, impaired by sickness is ill-equipped to handle the challenges of active storm sailing. In such a situation, a crew may be forced to pursue passive tactics for heavy weather if they don't have sufficient stamina for active ones.

Figure 21.4 - Avoiding the Storm Center (Northern Hemisphere)

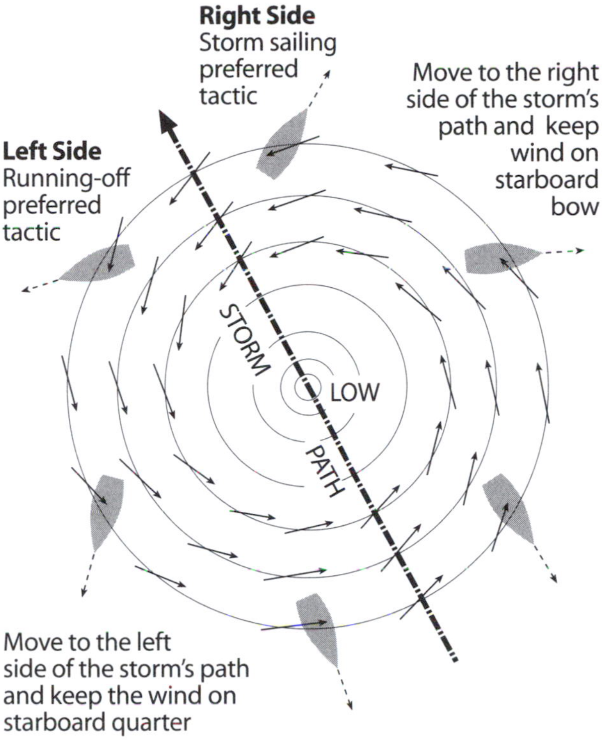

Right Side
Storm sailing preferred tactic

Move to the right side of the storm's path and keep wind on starboard bow

Left Side
Running-off preferred tactic

STORM

LOW

PATH

Move to the left side of the storm's path and keep the wind on starboard quarter

What, then, are these active and passive tactics between which the passagemaker must choose when storm winds and seas are making up? Under the "active" heading come storm sailing – pressing on to make the best possible progress toward the objective (usually upwind, of course) – and running off – going with the forces of nature rather than trying to oppose them. "Passive" tactics include heaving to, lying to a sea anchor and lying ahull.

Storm sailing to windward. Storm sailing to windward is tough on boat and crew. Even under greatly reduced sail, stresses on the rig will be high, and the boat's motion will tend to be violent, placing high loads on hull fittings and structures and making it hazardous for crew to move about performing their duties. Avoiding broaches, coping with aberrant seas and keeping the boat moving will demand intense concentration on the part of the helmsman. Frequent shifts of helm duty will be necessary to control fatigue and maintain alertness. If a boat's design is such that crew weight is an important factor in maintaining stability, active sailing under minimum sail area may be the boat's most effective heavy weather tactic. Such designs often prove difficult to control when passive tactics are attempted. Storm sailing has the major advantage that you're continuing to make progress in the right direction. A skillful hand at the helm, using the steering techniques described earlier, can do much to minimize the discomfort of crashing into high seas. If sea room is scarce, a lee shore may leave no alternatives to pursuing this tactic, so it's a skill that must be part of every passagemaker's bag of tricks.

The goal of storm sailing is to get the boat farther away from the highest winds and most dangerous seas near the storm's center. In the northern hemisphere, this is usually best accomplished by moving to the right side of the storm's path, then keeping the wind on the starboard bow. This moves the boat away from the storm.

Running off. The second "active" tactic, running off, can be adopted only if there's sufficient sea room to leeward to allow the boat to continue generally downwind until wind and seas abate. Like storm sailing, it's highly demanding of the crew, because active steering is essential to avoid broaches and jibes. When running off under the smallest scrap of jib – or even under bare poles, relying on the windage of hull and rig to propel the boat – an alert hand is needed on the helm to keep the boat under control. The principal advantage of running off is that it reduces apparent wind and avoids the risks to boat and crew associated with beating into head seas. These benefits come at a price. Running off frequently entails going a significant distance in the wrong direction, a distance that will have to be sailed again before reaching the destination. Because the boat is moving with the wind and sea, the relative speed of the storm system itself may be reduced and the boat may spend a longer period of time in storm conditions. If a low pressure system is the source of the heavy weather, running off can lead a boat toward the center of the system, where winds are strongest and seas most chaotic. Other things being equal, it is usually better in the northern hemisphere to move to the left side of the storm's path, then run off with the wind on the starboard quarter to reduce the likelihood of sailing into the storm's center.

If the main is used while running off, a stout preventer must be rigged to preclude an accidental jibe. Since the seas will be coming from astern, it is also prudent to keep the companionway closed and all the hatch boards in place to prevent a boarding sea from flooding into the cabin. Keep cockpit drains open to speed clearance of water if a wave fills the cockpit.

Perhaps the greatest danger in running off is excessive speed. As the boat reaches and passes its planing speed, directional control becomes crucial. The risk of broaching and suffering a knockdown rises as the boat becomes more difficult to control. Although the conditions necessary to produce it are seldom experienced in the temperate latitudes favored by most passagemakers, the ultimate running off disaster is a pitchpole. This occurs when a boat gets going so fast down the face of one wave that when it buries its bow into the back of the next wave, the bow stops while the stern keeps moving - upward and forward, over the bow, producing an end-over-end roll that almost invariably leads to dismasting and extensive hull and deck damage. Pitchpoling occurs only with mountainous seas and sustained screaming winds that are rarely experienced outside the high southern latitudes. Elsewhere, burying the bow at planing speed will usually lead to a quick broach and knockdown – hardly an insignificant hazard, but far less dangerous than true pitchpoling.

Slowing the boat – warps and drogues.

Fortunately, the best way to avoid these risks is simply to reduce the boat's speed, and effective preparation for slowing the boat down should be an integral part of any decision to run off. When sail area has been reduced to its minimum and the boat is still going too fast, the best way to cut speed is to drag things behind the boat. At its simplest, a drag device can consist of nothing more than a long length of line. Its drag load can be increased considerably if it includes a series of knots that will increase resistance to water flow. By deploying it as a bight of line with both ends secured to the boat's quarters, you can increase its drag. Many passagemakers have jury-rigged effective devices made of lines, fenders, car tires, and even lashed-together pieces of boat equipment streamed astern to slow the boat. Drogues marketed specifically to control boat speed include small parachute-like devices, rigid devices that increase resistance as their speed through the water increases, and basket-like devices constructed of heavy webbed material, all of which have been used very effectively. Though our firsthand experience with it is still limited, a system consisting of a series of small conical drogues connected by a central line has become popular. The purpose of all these devices is simply to slow the boat down to a speed that yields good steering control and a comfortable motion. They are always deployed from the stern and are designed to allow the boat to continue to make headway at a speed seldom exceeding 3-4 knots. They should never be confused with sea anchors, discussed later, which are much larger, have a different objective, and are deployed from the bow.

Reducing boat speed by means of warps or drogues often allows use of the self-

Figure 21.5 - Drogue Types

To slow a boat that is surfing too fast, trail anchor rodes or a dedicated device such as a Galerider from behind the boat.

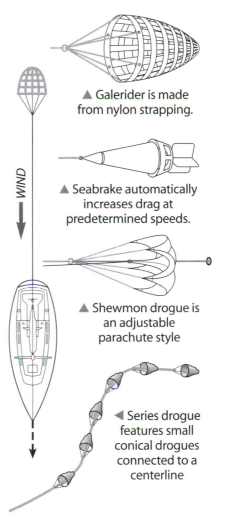

▲ Galerider is made from nylon strapping.

▲ Seabrake automatically increases drag at predetermined speeds.

▲ Shewmon drogue is an adjustable parachute style

◄ Series drogue features small conical drogues connected to a centerline

WIND

Figure 21.6 - Heaving To Under Reduced Sail

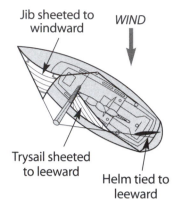

Jib sheeted to windward

WIND

Trysail sheeted to leeward

Helm tied to leeward

Figure 21.7 - Heaving To Under Triple-Reefed Mainsail

Triple-reefed mainsail sheeted to leeward

WIND

Helm centered

steering system. With sufficient boat speed for good steerage without the constant risk of broaching and with plenty of wind to allow use of a vane, the boat is considerably better able to take care of itself. This can allow the crew to get much-needed rest.

Heaving to. In contrast to active tactics, which require crew participation, passive tactics allow the boat to take care of itself with minimal crew intervention. The most basic of these is heaving to, a technique that is very useful in a number of situations. You can heave to when beating to weather is no longer possible or desirable but you don't want to give up significant ground to leeward. It provides a way to stop offshore and delay entry to a harbor until daylight arrives or weather improves. It can also be used whenever you need to dampen the boat's motion and make it ride more easily for a while, to prepare a meal, make a repair, take a round of star sights, or simply get some rest. It will also make the boat a more stable platform for taking a reef.

A boat can be hove to by the helmsman acting alone. With the sails appropriate for the wind strength set and sheeted in hard, simply turn the boat into and through the wind as if to tack, but do not cast off the jib sheet. Allow the jib to back, acting as a brake to stop forward progress. Once headway is lost, set and lock the helm in a position that will turn the boat into the wind whenever it gains headway. With patient adjustment of jib and mainsheet tension and rudder angle, most boats can be brought to lie with the wind 45-60° off the bow, drifting slowly across the wind and leaving a turbulent "wake" to windward that smooths approaching seas. If the boat's head falls off too far, the main begins to draw and the boat gains headway. Then the rudder steers it up into the wind again. The main loses its drive and the backed headsail kills the headway before the bow passes through the wind and tacks the boat.

The proper combination of sails and rudder position for heaving to will vary from boat to boat, depending on hull shapes and sail plans. Wind strength will also affect the combination that works best in a given situation. In the 1998 Caribbean 1500 rally, several boats that had been hove to successfully in winds under 25 knots

Figure 21.8 - Heaving To

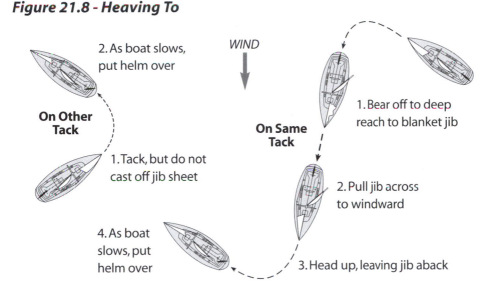

2. As boat slows, put helm over

WIND

1. Bear off to deep reach to blanket jib

On Other Tack

On Same Tack

1. Tack, but do not cast off jib sheet

2. Pull jib across to windward

4. As boat slows, put helm over

3. Head up, leaving jib aback

found that in stronger winds and rougher seas, different techniques were required. Some found their boat rode better with no headsail; others required more main to balance even a small backed staysail. Different rudder angles were needed to keep boats pointed high enough to avoid beam winds/seas. So *heaving to must be practiced in various conditions* to learn the best combinations. Boats whose design leans toward the traditional end of the spectrum (heavy displacement, full keel) will usually heave to readily under many sail configurations. More maneuverable boats with light, shallow hulls and fin keels may find it more challenging to determine the right combination. With a bit of experimentation, virtually all boats can heave to effectively, with the wind broad on the bow, making minimal headway, and riding comfortably over the sea crests like a resting gull.

A boat that is hove to tends to make a knot or so of progress across the wind, and this should be taken into account in deciding the tack on which to heave to. It is also better to heave to on the tack that puts the prevailing waves forward of the beam, rather than lying parallel to the seas. If the situation makes it best to heave to on the same tack on which the boat is currently sailing, the helmsman has two alternatives. The first is to complete a normal tack, then bring the boat back through the wind to lie hove to on the original tack. A second is to bear off until the main blankets the jib, haul the jib to windward, then round up again to lie hove to with the jib aback. The latter is riskier, since it creates an opportunity for an accidental jibe and may involve a few moments of hard heeling as the boat rounds up into the hove-to position.

When conditions have eased, the crew is rested, or the job is done, getting underway is simply a matter of centering the rudder and easing the sheet to allow the jib to cross to the leeward side. Once you have regained headway, the course can be set as you bring the boat back to the original tack and heading if desired.

Because it requires a certain amount of sea room, heaving to is seldom done while coastal cruising. Thus, new passagemakers will need to experience the usefulness of heaving to. It can be done quickly – "parking" the boat temporarily for any reason. The ease with which most boats ride hove to will substantially reduce the fatigue that accompanies heavy weather. Heaving to can significantly improve the quality of life during a passage. *It's an important technique for any passagemaker to master.*

Riding to a sea anchor. A second passive tactic is to deploy a sea anchor. A sea anchor is a parachute-type device streamed from the bow in order to keep the boat headed into the wind (and presumably the seas). It must be large enough that its drag very nearly stops the boat from moving through the water. Much of the adverse lore concerning sea

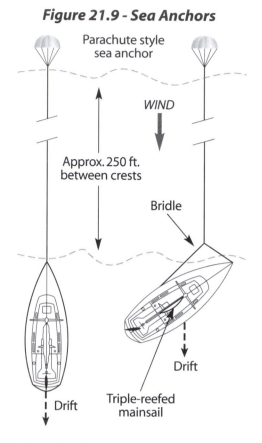

Figure 21.9 - Sea Anchors

Parachute style sea anchor

WIND

Approx. 250 ft. between crests

Bridle

Drift

Drift

Triple-reefed mainsail

anchors involves anchors too small to hold the boat in place. Typical cruising boats will need anchors 12' or more in diameter. Rigging and deploying a sea anchor can be tricky. If you carry one, you should practice several times in moderate conditions before attempting to use it in heavy air. A number of Rally boats have used sea anchors with great success, including several who used them to ride through the outer edge of Tropical Storm Mitch in 1998. Aside from chafe damage noted below, failures in sea anchor use during Rallies have been attributed in every case to inadequate preparation and lack of practice.

If conditions permit, it is safest to deploy most sea anchors using the technique known as a standing set. With minimum sail set, bring the boat nearly head to wind. Douse remaining sail and deploy the float and its line, followed by the sea anchor itself. Always deploy it from the bow or windward side. Pay out the rode as the boat drifts back from the anchor, snubbing it briefly to get the parachute canopy to open and fill with water. Continue to pay out the remainder of the rode, gradually snubbing the line to take up the strain as the rode approaches full length. Then secure the end and apply heavy chafing gear to any point where the rode may contact a sharp or rough surface.

When it's time to use the sea anchor, it is often unsafe to spend much time on the foredeck. Learning to deploy the sea anchor from the cockpit using the flying set technique is a somewhat risky but sometimes unavoidable alternative. With the boat reaching off at minimum speed (bare poles, and possibly a drogue to keep speed down) and the wind broad on the quarter, lead the bitter end of the rode from the cockpit forward, outboard of all rigging on the leeward side. (This can actually be done well before time to deploy the sea anchor.) Bring it in through the mooring fairleads and secure it to the bow cleats or samson post. When all is ready, put the sea anchor into the water from the cockpit (on the leeward side), trip line and float first. If the sea anchor has been neatly packed in a deployment bag, the entire anchor can be dumped in. Otherwise pay out the crown and body, then the bails, shackle and rode carefully as the boat moves away from the sea anchor body. Safety demands that this be done at absolutely slow speed. When about ¾ of the rode has been deployed, turn the boat 90° to leeward, jibing the boat and bringing the wind onto the same quarter as the sea anchor. Keeping speed at a minimum, hold the rudder amidships until all but a few coils of the rode have been deployed. As the sea anchor and rode begin to take up the strain, use the rudder to help the boat come head to wind. Apply generous chafing gear on the rode. Because the shock loads involved can be enormous, the slower the boat's movement during the flying set, the better.

Once riding to the sea anchor, make any final adjustment of the rode length and ensure that the rode is very well protected from chafe damage. Half the Rally boats that set sea anchors to ride out Tropical Storm Mitch lost them (after the storm had passed) because the rode chafed through, even though it had been carefully cased in chafing gear. One boat that did not lose its sea anchor controlled chafe by periodically easing the rode out a few inches.

Manufacturers differ on the type of rode that should be used with a sea anchor. Some recommend a laid nylon line for its stretchy, shock-absorbing qualities, rigged with a swivel to eliminate this line's tendency to twist when stressed. Others lack confidence in swivels in an ocean environment, and favor use of a braided rode that won't create a twisting torque on the anchor. They agree, however, that *the rode should be a long one.* One manufacturer (Shewmon) recommends a nylon rode at least 20 times the maximum wave height, or a dacron rode twice as long. Another (Para-Tech) recommends only a nylon rode at least ten times the boat's length. Both specify that *rode length must be adjusted* to keep the boat and the sea anchor "in phase" as they ride the seas. Both should be on a crest or in a trough at the same time to reduce cyclic shock loading that would occur in the rode if they lay at different points in the waves. It may be helpful to rig a length of chain in the rode, especially if rode length is limited. This provides greater catenary and reduces the possibility that the parachute could broach to the sea's surface, collapse, become tangled and lose its effectiveness. If the chain is rigged as the final segment of the rode, the risk of chafe damage to the rode might be reduced, but a substantial chain stopper will be needed to take the anchor loads (and it will be vulnerable to chafe).

Because it will generate very heavy loads, the sea anchor should be secured to the strongest possible points in the bow. Catamarans ride best if the rode connects to a bridle (length = 1.5 to 2.5 times the boat's beam) secured to the hulls. Once again, the rode must have plenty of chafing gear to protect it as it is stretched and relaxed by sea motion.

Sea anchors can be deployed with a trip line secured to the discharge orifice in the center of the canopy to facilitate recovery. Pulling on this line collapses the parachute and makes it much easier to get the rig back aboard. Trip lines that lead all the way back to the boat have a nasty habit of getting fouled in the rode, possibly leading to premature collapse of the canopy and loss of anchor effectiveness. A better solution may be a short trip line that ends at a buoy which can be retrieved as the boat recovers the main rode. The trip line should be about 20% of rode length to insure it will not prevent the parachute from reaching its proper operating depth.

Recovering a sea anchor can be slow and difficult, even when the weather has calmed down. Doing so sooner is nearly impossible. Taking the rode to a windlass will help. If there is no trip line to collapse the canopy, it will be necessary to recover the rode until the shackle is on deck and the parachute shroud lines are within reach. Pulling on several adjacent shrouds will slowly dump the parachute's water content, allowing it to be lifted clear.

Yawing by a boat riding to a sea anchor can be reduced with a riding sail deployed at the stern. While a small triangular sail attached to the backstay or a deeply reefed mizzen will be helpful, they will tend to flog somewhat whenever the boat is head to wind. A small triangular sail (up to 50 square feet) that can be deployed flat to the wind (raised with a halyard and sheeted to both quarter cleats) will maintain a steadier strain on the rode and help keep the bow pointed directly toward the sea anchor.

Larry Pardey has devised a technique for using a spring line in conjunction with a sea anchor to make the boat ride at an angle to the rode. This method would seem to be especially useful when seas and winds are coming from different directions. The purpose is to eliminate yawing and permit slow downwind drift so the turbulent water created by the boat's leeway reduces the likelihood of waves breaking on the boat. The loads generated by the rode and the spring line in such a configuration are considerably higher than those created by the usual bow-on deployment, so the stress on lines and fittings will increase accordingly. If the sea anchor were undersized and having difficulty keeping the boat head to wind, this technique would probably aggravate the situation.

Since a boat riding to a sea anchor will have some tendency to move astern as the sea anchor drags slowly through the water, the rudder should be placed amidships and held there securely. If it is loose or at an angle, there is a danger that it could be forced into the stops or jammed if the boat suddenly moves astern rapidly as a result of wave action or momentary slacking of the rode.

A deployed sea anchor functions as a very effective plankton net, and when recovered will be cluttered with sea life and tiny organisms. To control the aroma that will arise when these critters die, keep the sea anchor wet until it can be thoroughly rinsed with fresh water (usually not until arrival in port). An unused ice chest makes an excellent container. A freshwater rinsing is also needed to remove salt that will otherwise gradually reduce fabric and line strength through the abrasive effect of thousands of tiny salt crystals.

Lying ahull. The final passive tactic, lying ahull, is usually considered the last recourse for an exhausted crew or a damaged boat. It consists of dousing all sail, securing the helm amidships, dogging all the hatches and leaving the boat to take care of itself – to drift without guidance. The attitude a drifting boat assumes to the wind and sea depends on underwater hull shape and the size and distribution of topside and rig area, but most boats will lie more or less beam to the wind and sea. While traditional designs, with heavy displacement and full keel, seem to tolerate lying ahull better than lighter, fin keel designs, all tend to lie in a relatively vulnerable position. With seas on the beam, the risk of knockdown and capsize is maximized. The crew will often find it necessary to lash themselves into their bunks to cope with the boat's violent motion. It is almost always safer and easier on both boat and crew to use tactics that leave the boat less at the mercy of the sea, but when fatigue, damage or injury preclude other tactics, lying ahull may be the only option. It is certainly better than abandoning the boat with the false impression that a life raft is a safer place.

The case against engine use. Note that we've made no reference to the alternative frequently considered first by the coastal cruising sailor: using the engine, with or without sails. Motoring is the perfect tactic for no-wind situations, and motor sailing may provide better steerage going to weather in light to moderate conditions. Using the engine is seldom a good choice well offshore when the weather really turns bad. When winds approach storm strength, few sailboat auxiliary engines have sufficient power to oppose those winds, so the engine's contribution is marginal. It's extremely tough on the engine to operate when the boat is moving violently, with sharp heeling and exaggerated pitching. The load on the engine, transmission and shaft changes radically as the prop is alternately at the surface and deeply immersed. Many engines lose lubricating oil suction when heeled beyond 15-20° for more than a few seconds. The boat's movement in the seaway is also going to stir up every bit of sediment and debris in the fuel tank, which greatly increases the likelihood that fuel filters will clog quickly, perhaps resulting in loss of power at a critical instant. Changing fuel filters in storm conditions seldom appears on a sailor's list of favorite activities.

Perhaps the most important argument against using the engine to cope with heavy weather is the danger of fouling the prop. With sails shortened and boarding seas washing the decks and the cockpit, there is constant opportunity for halyard tails, sheets and other lines to get washed over the side. Once in the water, these lines quickly seek out the spinning propeller and wrap it in a strangling embrace. Not only is the boat then deprived of the power it was using to maintain control, it may also be limited in its ability to sail if the line involved is a sheet or a halyard. Using the engine can lead to a situation in which all the adversities of heavy weather alone are compounded by additional problems when they are least easily handled.

In summary, the tactics for coping with heavy weather start with the ability to reduce sail quickly and efficiently. This may allow the boat to continue making progress to windward using storm sailing techniques. Or, the skipper can run off to effectively reduce the strength of wind and sea, using a drogue if needed to keep boat speed down without losing control. The passive tactic of heaving to can enable the boat to weather a blow in relative comfort. It's like parking and waiting for better conditions. Deploying a sea anchor can also produce more comfortable, less stressful conditions aboard, allowing the crew to get rested and ready to resume the passage. Lying ahull, letting Mother Nature have her way with boat and crew, is a last resort, but one that a well designed and sturdily built boat should survive, possibly experiencing less damage than does the crew inside. Using the engine is seldom a good idea, often leading to further problems.

The well-prepared passagemaker, having practiced techniques such as reefing and shifting to storm sails and heaving to, will find that a storm at sea is not a source of great fear. It may be undesirable, uncomfortable and unpleasant, but there are established ways to cope with bad weather. Sensible use of these tactics can keep heavy weather from becoming a life-threatening event.

References:
Adlard Coles, *Heavy Weather Sailing* (4th edition, revised by Peter Bruce)
Tom Cunliffe, *Heavy Weather Cruising*
Gary Jobson, *Storm Sailing*
Larry & Lin Pardey, *Storm Tactics Handbook*
Victor Shane, *Drag Device Data Base*

CHAPTER 22

SAIL TRIM

The crew of a racing sailboat is vitally interested in perfect sail trim for maximum speed. Passagemakers may be less fanatic about trim and its impact on speed, but we need to understand how trim can affect the ease with which the boat rides the seas. For a cruising sailor, proper sail trim is largely a question of balance and boat motion.

The fundamentals of sail trim are taught in every basic sailing course: Ease the sheet until the sail begins to luff at its leading edge, then trim it in just enough to stop the luffing. Trimming the sail too far reduces its efficiency, creates drag and turbulence on the lee side of the sail and increases the sail's heeling effect. An overtrimmed headsail will cause lee helm, while an overtrimmed main or mizzen will induce weather helm. Insufficient trim reduces the sail's driving power and can cause damage if it leads to flutter, flapping or flogging. The impact of undertrimmed sails on steering is the opposite of that produced by overtrim.

Those aptly named telltales. The best device for checking sail trim is still a good set of telltales attached to each sail. Telltales made of yarn, light fabric strips or even old audio recording tape reveal the direction of airflow along the sail's surface. On a jib, telltales should be placed on both sides of the sail about six inches back from the luff, with one set about six feet above the tack, one about six feet below the head, and 1-3 more spaced evenly in between. On roller furling headsails, add a second set of telltales just aft of the part of the sail that forms the luff when at the maximum effective reefing position. They are for use when sail area has been reduced and the normal telltales have disappeared into the rolled up sail. Mainsail and mizzen telltales attach to the leech of the sail, usually one at the end of each batten.

A headsail is trimmed properly when the telltales on both sides of the sail are streaming smoothly aft. If telltales on the inner (windward) side of the sail are lying smooth while those on the outer (leeward) side are lifting and fluttering, the sail is overtrimmed. Ease the sheet. If the opposite occurs (outers are steady while inners lift), trim in on the sheet to correct an undertrimmed condition. Headsail telltales can also be used as a steering aid to keep the boat and the sails at their most efficient angle to the wind. Head up when the outer telltales lift, bear off when the inner ones do.

Main and mizzen telltales should stream straight aft, as well, reflecting smooth airflow off the sail's trailing edge. If they hang down or curl to windward, the sail is undertrimmed and the sheet should be hauled in until the telltales lift. If they curl to leeward, the sail is overtrimmed and the sheet should be eased.

Sail trim for the cruising sailor is particularly important in relation to steering. Most passagemakers use a wind vane or autopilot to steer the boat virtually all the time. Those systems will only do their best work if the boat's sail plan is balanced. This means that both sail area and sail trim are adjusted so the boat will head in the desired direction with only minimal corrections from the rudder. Wind vane systems are usually capable of making only relatively small changes in rudder angle. If excess sail area or an over-trimmed main creates strong weather helm, the vane will not be able to cope with it and the boat will keep rounding up and luffing. With its ability to apply larger rudder angles, an autopilot will often tolerate a wider range of sail imbalances, but at the cost of high power consumption and decreased autopilot life.

Balancing the sail plan. Sail balance is a key to efficient steering. Every sail has a center of effort, the single point at which its driving force appears to be located. It is at the geometric center of the sail, found at the intersection of lines drawn from each corner to the midpoint of the opposite side. A similar combined center of effort for several sails (e.g., main and jib) can be calculated graphically. The relationship between this point and the boat's center of lateral resistance – the geometric center of the immersed hull and the point at which the boat's lateral resistance appears to be located – is critical to the boat's balance and directional stability. If the center of effort is aft of the center of lateral resistance, or if marked heeling puts the center of effort far outboard to leeward of the hull, the boat develops weather helm, a tendency to turn into the wind. If the center of effort is forward of the center of lateral resistance, the boat tends to turn away from the wind, an undesirable and potentially dangerous condition known as lee helm. If the center of effort is directly above the center of lateral resistance, the result is neutral helm.

Most boats handle best with a slight weather helm to give the helmsman a feel for the balance of the sails. Another plus is that a puff of wind will increase the heel and the weather helm. This tends to head the boat up toward the wind, which reduces the heeling and restores balance.

Perfect balance and perfect sail trim (as reflected by the telltales) sometimes cannot be achieved simultaneously. Particularly on off-wind headings, it may be necessary to under- or overtrim a sail to keep the boat heading in a given direction. In such a case, the racing sailor would probably go for efficient sail trim and its speed advantage, relying on the helmsman to use rudder to keep the boat on course. The passagemaker will likely accept some sail inefficiency to achieve good sail balance so the self-steering system can keep the boat on course easily.

The principles involved in balancing the sail plan are few and simple. Excess sail area causes heeling, which causes weather helm. Good balance often requires taking a reef. With appropriate sail area set, trimming in on the jib tends to make the bow fall off, while easing the jib sheet will allow it to head up. By contrast, trimming in on the main will cause the boat to head up and easing it will allow the bow to bear off. The mizzen works the same way the main does, but with greater effectiveness – since its location farther aft gives it a longer lever arm with which to affect the boat's heading. One of the passagemaking watch stander's most important duties is to check sail trim and balance, making sure the boat is going where it wants to go. The steering system should not be fighting a strong tendency to bear off or head up.

Using halyard tension and outhaul. To get best performance from the sails, the passagemaker learns how to use the controls available to adjust sail shape. Halyard tension alters the location of the draft. Tightening the halyard flattens the forward part of the sail and resists the tendency for the draft to move aft as the wind loading increases. Easing it lets draft shift forward, the best shape for light airs. On the mainsail, the outhaul can change the amount of draft in the lower section of the sail. Greater outhaul tension flattens the sail to reduce drag and heeling force in strong winds. Easing the outhaul increases the draft to obtain more power in light air.

Making the most of "twist". The blend of drive, lift and drag forces generated by a sail can also be influenced by "twist". This is the difference in the angle of trim, relative to the boat's centerline, in the upper and lower parts of the sail. On boom-mounted sails, such as the main and mizzen, twist is adjusted by changing the inward and downward forces exerted on the boom by the sheet and the traveler. In light air and flat water, most sails are cut to give their best performance with relatively little twist – the upper and lower portions of the sail are set at the same angle to the boat's centerline.

As wind speed builds and the seas get sloppy, performance will improve if a sail has somewhat more twist, that is, the upper portion of the sail is set at a wider angle to the centerline than the lower part. In this configuration, the upper part of the sail generates less drive (and less heeling force) while the lower part provides sufficient power to propel the boat. Main and mizzen twist are increased by first easing the sheet. This allows the boom to move upward as well as outboard. Next, the traveler is moved to windward to bring the boom back to its original angle to the centerline. The net result is a raising of the boom, which allows the upper part of the sail to sag off to leeward.

As with the main, headsail draft location can be adjusted with halyard tension. The degree of twist is established by the sheet lead position. For light to moderate air and fairly flat water, the normal goal is to have no twist, with roughly equal tension on the foot and the leech of the sail. This can be checked by gently steering up to windward while watching the telltales. If the sheet lead is set properly, all the telltales will break at the same time as the sail starts to luff. If the upper telltales break before the lower ones, the leech may be too loose and the sail twisted in the upper sections. Correct this by adjusting the sheet fairlead forward. This applies more downward strain on the leech and reduces aft stress on the foot. It lets the foot of the sail billow out, increasing fullness for reaching and light air sailing. If the lower telltales break first, shift the lead aft. This flattens the foot and lower panels and increases twist, producing a better shape for stronger winds and lumpier seas.

In conditions other than moderate air and flat water, altering twist can improve the boat's ride. A boat is very uncomfortable when it "porpoises," an annoying condition that is common when moderate seas are accompanied by relatively light winds. The bow drives down hard and the boat seems to stop as it plunges into a sea. Then it bounces back up and drives down hard again. At the masthead, this motion is significant enough to cause radical changes in the apparent wind direction experienced by the upper parts of the sail (look for rapid cyclical shifts of the wind indicator). When the bow drives down, the masthead accelerates forward and apparent wind shifts forward. As the bow rises, the masthead moves aft and the apparent wind also swings aft. With a sail trimmed to have little or no twist, the head of the sail continues to generate driving force as the boat pitches down, and this aggravates the pitching moment. Reduced drive on the upward pitch allows the mast to move aft more rapidly – yet another aggravating effect.

This porpoising can often be reduced simply by introducing twist in the sails. Alter trim to allow the upper part of the sail to be at a wider angle to the boat's centerline than the lower sections. Move the jib fairlead aft and ease the mainsheet while pulling the traveler to weather. Now as the boat pitches downward and the apparent wind shifts forward, the upper part of the sail will actually luff, losing the driving force that contributed to the downward pitch. As the mast rocks back and the apparent wind swings aft, the upper part of the sail, being at a broader angle to the centerline, will act as a brake, further reducing the boat's ability to sustain the rhythmic pitching movement. This tactic can be used very effectively to increase the comfort of the ride. By eliminating the slowdowns that occur every time the boat buries its bow, you may well see your average speed rise after twist is increased.

Trimming with the traveler. Passagemakers should become adept at using the traveler as a trimming device. As the boom comes closer to the boat's centerline, the mainsheet's effect is increasingly downward rather than lateral. It affects sail shape (primarily twist and flatness) more than angle to the boat's centerline. The traveler, by contrast, provides a way to change the sail's angle without affecting its shape. When close hauled or close reaching in high winds, you want a relatively flat sail shape. Such a shape produces good forward drive with a minimum of sideways heeling force. In a gust, the normal response is to ease the sheet to reduce heeling. Unfortunately, this allows the boom to rise as well as move outboard. The sail assumes a fuller shape that results in further heeling, so the sail must be eased still more to successfully limit the heeling. Instead of easing the sheet, let the traveler down to leeward, changing the sail's angle to the boat without losing the desirable flattened shape. The driving force remains, and the boat has power to move through the water and over the seas.

The trim adjustments that accompany roller reefing of sails have been addressed in Chapter 18. Passagemakers tend to rely heavily on roller furling systems to reduce the workload while enjoying a flexible sail plan. Getting the most from those systems requires an awareness of their limitations and their need for trim adjustments as sail area is changed.

These sail trim techniques are yet another tool to help the cruising sailor achieve a safe and comfortable passage. They enable you to find trade-offs that balance easy riding, light steering loads and rapid transits. When weather or sea state pushes your comfort level into the unpleasant range, an adjustment to sail trim, a slight change of course or a combination of the two will almost always produce a marked improvement. Don't be reluctant to experiment until you find the best compromise.

CHAPTER 23

SAIL REPAIR

Here we'll address ways a passagemaker can make damaged sails usable. Sometimes, durable repairs can be accomplished at sea. In other cases, repairs will yield only a temporary solution, just good enough until permanent repairs can be made by a sailmaker ashore. To effect repairs offshore, the voyager must carry a well-equipped sail repair kit. Here is a suggested checklist.

Figure 23.1 - Sail Repair Kit
☐ Adhesive-backed Dacron sail repair tape, 3" x 30'
☐ Adhesive-backed rip-stop nylon sail repair tape, 30'
☐ Adhesive-backed Dacron sail fabric, 2' x 2'
☐ Sailcloth, 7 or 8 oz., 2' x 2'
☐ Rip-stop spinnaker cloth, 2' x 2'
☐ Flat nylon braided webbing, 1" x 30'
☐ Waxed sail thread, roll
☐ Sailmaker's palm (right- or left-handed, as appropriate)
☐ Assorted sailmaker's needles
☐ Appropriate size sail slides or slugs (dozen or more)
☐ Sail slide shackles (if used)
☐ Pliers
☐ Sharp, sturdy scissors or knife
☐ Stainless steel rings, 2" (3)
☐ Double-faced tape, ½" wide (to keep patches in place until stitched)
☐ Spare batten (as long as longest batten)
☐ Telltale material
☐ Soft leather for serious chafe protection
☐ Small, tightly sealed container of alcohol or acetone for cleaning and drying sail repair sites

Replacing sail slides. The most common damage experienced offshore by Rally participants has been not to the sail fabric, but to the slides that attach the sail to mast and boom. Broken slides are not repairable; they need to be replaced. The sail repair kit must contain plenty of slides of the proper sizes. Those along the foot may well differ from those on the luff, and mizzens generally use smaller slides. Make sure the spares will actually fit in the spars. If the sail links to the slides with shackles, the kit should include sufficient spares.

Sailmakers use a number of techniques to connect the sail to the slides, but aside from shackles, the simplest method for replacing slides at sea is to use braided webbing. Reeve a short length of webbing through the slide and the sail, making several passes if possible, and secure it with stitches through the webbing between the sail and slide. A simple stitch will suffice. Using a sailmaker's needle and sewing palm, drive the needle through the center of the webbing. Pull the twine through but leave a tail of several inches at the end. Bring the twine around one edge of the webbing and go back through the same center hole. Pull tight, then repeat the process around the other side of the webbing. Continue until there are at least 2-3 runs of twine around each side. Then haul the whole thing tight again and tie off the two ends as tightly and as close to the webbing as possible. If there is no hole in the sail through which to run the webbing or if the grommet has been ripped out, sewing a doubled "U" of webbing to the sail may create an adequate attachment point for the slide.

The key to effective slide replacement is to make sure the replacement slide is the same distance away from the sail edge as the original. If the replacement is closer to the sail, it will carry more than its share of the load. This can cause it to break quickly or to jam and hang up in the slot. If it is too far away, it will not bear its share of the load and adjacent slides will be overloaded, leading to breakage.

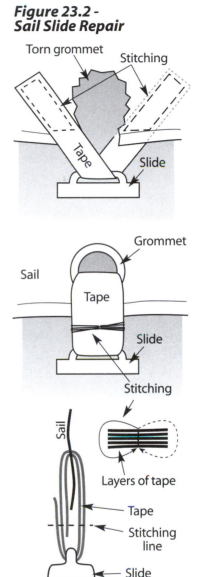

Figure 23.2 – Sail Slide Repair

Repairing seams, small holes and rips. Another common sail problem is seam failure, caused by chafe damage to the stitching. Damage to the sail fabric itself (chafed holes or rips created by snagging on a sharp object) is also frequent. In either case, the best temporary solution is the adhesive-backed fabric known to sailmakers as "sticky back." It comes in sheets and rolls of various widths and weights. Most sail repairs needed during a voyage can be accomplished with this cloth. If the sail fabric is dry and clean, this material sticks very tightly. Backed up by a few stitches with a needle and sail twine, such patches are remarkably strong and will last through most conditions.

If the sail is sopping wet, dry it as much as possible before applying the sticky-back. Paper towels are effective at removing the surface moisture. Modern sail fabrics absorb little water internally, but alcohol or acetone can help remove remaining dampness. If it is salt-encrusted, rinse off as much salt as possible, then dry the surface before applying adhesive-backed fabric. The fabric comes in a number of cloth weights, and the patching material used should match the sails. The standard weight is about eight ounces, which can be used on most sails for temporary fixes.

To apply this material, lay the damaged part of the sail on the flattest surface available. Make the edges meet as closely as possible to the way they met before the damage occurred. Cut a piece of adhesive-backed fabric large enough to overlap the damaged area by several inches on all sides. Round the corners of the patch to eliminate the tendency of square or pointed corners to come loose. Orient the patching material so its threads run in the same direction as those in the sail. Remove the protective backing paper and carefully smooth the patching fabric onto the sail. Rub it briskly and press it against a hard surface to achieve full contact of the sticky side. The heat generated by the friction of rubbing seems to improve adhesion. After applying the patch to one side, turn the sail over and apply a second layer on the opposite side, rubbing briskly again to get good contact. If there's any doubt the adhesive fabric will hold under the stress of sailing, reinforce the glue bond by using the needle and palm to sew around the edges with a simple running stitch.

Larger repairs. While small holes (up to about 6") can be covered by adhesive-backed fabric, larger areas should be fitted with patches. They can be attached with sail repair tape and/or stitching with a needle and palm. The patch should be large enough that its edges can be fastened to good, strong sailcloth, not fabric that has been weakened by flogging. To carry the sail loads without distortion, it is essential to align the thread pattern of the patch material with that of the sail. Orienting the patch on a diagonal to the weave of the sail will produce bias stress and result in unwanted stretch of the patch. Positioning larger patches and getting them properly aligned in your cramped and moving environment can be a major challenge. It may help to use narrow double-faced tape to hold the patch in place temporarily while it is being fitted and to keep it from shifting positions while the more permanent taping or sewing is completed. Large patches should always be sewn, in addition to any taping.

Use duct tape – and weep! Except as a last resort (when anything is better than nothing), avoid using duct tape to repair sails. This ubiquitous repair material does an extraordinary job in many places. It does not belong on sails, though. It doesn't hold as well as sail repair tape, and it breaks down under exposure to sunlight and weather. The silvery backing will peel off, but the adhesive material and the fabric scrim that supports it will remain. This gummy residue gradually turns hard as cement. It's very difficult to remove and will make any sailmaker cuss when it's time to do a permanent repair. It will foul sewing machine needles, cause thread to seize and generally make the repair work tougher (and, most likely, more expensive).

Eyes and grommets. The failure of an eye or grommet is not unheard of, though uncommon. The most vulnerable seem to be clew rings in headsails and reefing out-haul eyes in mainsails. They are under sustained severe stress in normal use, so their occasional failure is not surprising. Loss of the head or tack cringle is less common, but can be handled in the same way. In every case, the simplest at-sea repair consists of replacing the lost eye with one made of braided webbing.

The key to success here is to use a number of pieces of webbing, each of which distributes the corner strain to a large area of sail fabric. In replacing a clew eye, for example, sew one half of a strip along one side of the leech, extending at least a foot above the damaged area, then fold it over on a diagonal and sew the second half along the foot, applying it to the opposite side of the sail. A second strap should be sewn on a bit further from the edge, angled to meet the first strap at the corner, and applied to the opposite sides of the sail from the first strap. Add a third and possibly a fourth strap, fanning out from the corner into the body of the sail. Fit the straps carefully to ensure that they will share the load and transfer it to healthy sections of sail fabric. Use zigzag stitches to avoid creating a perfo-rated weak line in the fabric. While webbing alone will do an adequate job, if the repair kit includes stainless steel rings of the proper size, the webbing can be threaded through a ring at the corner. A series of stitches through the webbing close to the ring will keep the ring from slipping around and loosening its connection to the sail.

Figure 23.3 - Corner Webbing

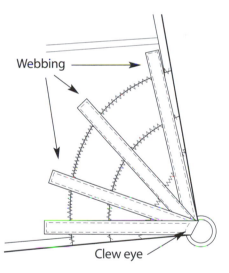

Webbing

Clew eye

Batten pocket repair. Within the body of the sail, the most likely area for damage is at the inner end of traditional battens. The batten pockets can be damaged by chafing against shrouds or torn loose by flogging. Sometimes the end of the batten will poke through the sail itself. Adhesive-backed fabric usually does the best job of repairing such damage. Better yet, it can be used preventively. At the first sign of wear, apply adhesive fabric to serve as a sacrificial layer while protecting the sail fabric.

Keep those telltales flying! A minor though important repair is the replacement of telltales. Since many of the boat's sail trim adjustments (and hence its sailing efficiency) will be governed by these little yarns or tapes, keeping a good set in place can contribute to the swiftness and comfort of your passage. Traditional telltales were made of yarns (originally rope yarns, but later wool or spun synthetic fibers) that were sewn through the sail. Thanks to the tenacity of adhesive-backed fabrics, today they're often fastened with small pieces of tape that avoid punching a hole through the sailcloth. The yarns themselves have been largely replaced by narrow strips of very light rip-stop nylon fabric, and an effective substitute is magnetic audio recording tape. Replacing lost or tattered telltales by securing a new yarn or tape with a 1" x 1" piece of sticky-back is easy and effective.

While minor sail damage is common on a long passage, prompt attention will usually keep it from turning into a major problem. By ensuring that the sail repair kit is properly stocked, most voyagers will be able to handle their en-route sail repairs. Items such as the sailmaker's palm, needles and twine will be useful for repairs to all the fabrics aboard the boat, including dodger and bimini, cushions and weather cloths. Working on these projects will develop sewing skills that will pay off if it becomes necessary to work on the boat's main propulsion system – the sails. Provided the essential materials are aboard, coping with sail damage is certainly within every voyager's ability. These at-sea repairs may not be pretty, but if they keep the sail together until the boat reaches its destination, they will have achieved their goal.

REFERENCE:
Emiliano Merino, *The Sailmaker's Apprentice*

CHAPTER 24

TROUBLESHOOTING
YOUR ENGINE

Although it's only an auxiliary in terms of propelling the boat, the engine in a passagemaking boat performs many vital functions. Often it's the main source of energy for recharging the batteries that power the boat's electrically dependent systems. On many boats it drives the refrigeration system, and some engines also power hydraulic systems. The good health of the engine is a matter of great interest.

For reasons of safety, reliability and simplicity, virtually all cruising boats today use diesel auxiliary engines. Unlike the gasoline engines in older boats, their fuel does not generate explosive vapors at normal atmospheric temperatures. They don't require the electrical ignition system (with its coil, points and high voltage wiring) that's often a trouble source for gasoline engines. Modern diesels are built ruggedly and will operate happily for many years with proper care. If it gets an adequate supply of fuel and air, is well lubricated, and its cooling system carries away the excess heat of combustion, a diesel engine will usually run well enough to do its job. While our discussion here relates directly to diesels, many problems we'll address can occur in gasoline engines, as well.

Efficient troubleshooting. Efficient troubleshooting of a malfunctioning engine requires a systematic analysis of the problem. Your diesel engine manual probably includes a troubleshooting section for your particular model. A "service manual" (as opposed to the more common "owner's manual") will provide the best guidance for identifying and correcting the problems. First, you'll want to identify the system causing the problem, then the difficulty within that system. If the engine won't turn over with sufficient speed to start, the electrical starting system is a likely culprit. If it turns over well but won't start, the fuel system is your prrimary suspect. If it starts but won't continue to run or come up to speed, inadequate fuel and/or air supply are indicated. If the engine overheats, one of the coolant systems (raw water or fresh water) is not doing its job. Focusing on one system at a time will simplify your detective work.

Starting problems. Starting problems are not uncommon, though they usually crop up at dockside. Check the simplest things first: Are all the switches and breakers in the proper position? Is the transmission in neutral? Many engines have internal switches to prevent starting in gear. Often, the transmission is engaged while sailing to keep the propeller shaft from rolling. Trying to start the engine without taking the transmission out of gear will produce the same symptoms as a dead battery.

Check all the wiring, from the battery to the starter, following both positive and negative leads. Look for broken wires and loose or heavily corroded connections that could be interrupting the flow of power. Unusual stiffness or swelling of cables (especially near the terminals) is often a sign of corrosion inside the insulating jacket, and this can greatly increase the cable's resistance to electrical current flow. Use a meter to check for continuity of the circuit from the starter switch to the solenoid on the starter. A bad starter switch or a stuck solenoid can sometimes be bypassed by shorting the solenoid contacts with a wrench or screwdriver. This will throw sparks and the arcing electricity may damage the shorting tool, but it will often cause the starter to engage and turn the engine over.

Sometimes a piece of debris can cause either the solenoid or the starter motor itself to stick in position. A sharp rap with a hammer or mallet may be all it takes to free it up.

If the starter turns the engine over but not fast enough to enable it to start, the battery charge is probably low. If possible, parallel all the batteries available to boost the amperage output and improve starting power. Another "if all else fails" trick is to connect the batteries in series. This produces a higher voltage output that may be sufficient to get the engine turning over despite the low amperage. If all the batteries are low, try heating the air intake manifold to make it easier for the pistons to raise the cylinder temperature to the ignition point. (With due regard for the fire hazard involved, some cruising skippers have successfully used a propane torch for this purpose.)

Reducing cylinder compression may help the starter turn the engine faster. If the engine is equipped with a decompression linkage, relieve engine compression until the starter has the engine spinning at a rapid rate, then restore compression to permit the engine to start. In the absence of a decompression mechanism, loosening several injectors or glow plugs may reduce compression enough to raise the starter speed until firing can start in the non-decompressed cylinders. Restore compression to the other cylinders to keep the engine running. Another way to reduce compression is to cover the engine's air intake with the palm of your hand until the starter gets the engine turning over rapidly. Once the engine is spinning, pull your hand away and the engine may have enough momentum to achieve sufficient compression to start firing.

Hydro-lock. Another starting problem that is surprisingly common during an ocean passage is a condition known as hydro-lock. It sometimes occurs when following seas have been slapping up against the boat's transom, driving seawater up the exhaust lines. It can also result from cooling water siphoning after a vacuum breaker fitting has become clogged or from excessive cranking of a hard-to-start engine, producing a muffler full of seawater. In the absence of a valve to close off the line or a functioning vacuum breaker loop in the exhaust hose, seawater can be forced all the way through the muffler and into the engine's exhaust manifold. From there, the seawater passes through open exhaust valves and fills one or more of the engine's cylinders. When this has happened, an attempt to start the engine will result in the engine turning over part of a revolution, then stopping cold when the piston in the first water-laden cylinder starts its upward movement. Since the water is incompressible, the piston cannot move and the engine cannot run. Further attempts to start the engine will produce heavy current drains through the starter as it tries vainly to turn the engine, and damage to the starter, the pistons and other internal parts can follow.

Once identified, hydro-lock is relatively easy to correct. You must remove the water from the cylinder(s) involved. This can be done by carefully removing the injectors, inserting a straw or piece of tubing into the cylinder and using it to suck any water out. On some engines, this can be done by removing the glow plugs rather than injectors. Once the water has been found and removed, turn the engine over by hand to verify that it is no longer seized up. Spray a water-displacing lubricant such as WD-40 into each cylinder. Secure the engine fuel supply with the shutdown mechanism or by pushing the fuel shutoff linkage on the engine to the closed position. (Don't close the cutoff valve in the fuel line ahead of the fuel filter unit. That can cause the engine to draw air into the fuel lines through imperfectly sealed fittings or connections.) Place rags or containers around the removed injectors to collect any fuel discharge, then briefly spin the engine with the starter. Any remaining water and excess WD-40 will be blown out the injector openings, so have absorbent material ready to catch it. Repeat the process until there are no signs of water in the discharge. Since it's likely that traces of water leaked past the pistons and contaminated the lubricating oil in the sump, the next step is to change the engine oil and oil filter. Then put a tablespoon of oil into each cylinder through the injector opening and turn the engine over for a few seconds with the starter to spread this oil around the upper surfaces of the cylinder.

Replace the injectors, restore the fuel supply, and start the engine. Run it for just a few minutes, then shut it down and draw a sample of oil out of the sump. If it looks normal, the engine can be run safely, but the oil condition should be checked frequently and changed again at the first opportunity – within the next few days. If at any time the oil shows signs of cocoa-brown frothiness, it contains water, and the oil and filter should be changed again before running the engine any longer.

If an engine turns over freely and reaches normal starting speed but fails to start, the first thing to check is the fuel supply. Again, check the obvious first: Has the tank run dry? Is there a closed manual or electrical valve in the supply system? Did someone leave the fuel shutoff in the "stop" position last time the engine was secured? Is air leaking into the system at a loose connection, most likely one at the filter drain or access cap?

Checking the fuel system. A contaminated or dirty fuel system is a common source of engine trouble, especially for older boats that have not been exposed to the turbulent motion of ocean sailing. Diesel fuel has a natural affinity for water, and will actually absorb some out of the atmosphere. Moisture will also condense on the inside of partially empty fuel tanks when damp ocean air is chilled by contact with the cooler metal of the tank. Missing O-rings or gaskets around deck fuel-fill caps can allow rainwater or seawater to get into the tank. It's not uncommon to find traces of water in diesel fuel as it is delivered from a shoreside source, and occasionally fuel dock supplies have been the source of major water contamination. The water content in the diesel tank rarely becomes so large that the engine actually draws in a slug of water instead of fuel. (The water situation should become evident much earlier, when traces of water accumulate in the bottom of the fuel filter-separator unit. Getting solid water into the fuel line will cause the engine to stop running immediately, and water can cause significant damage to fuel injectors.) Nevertheless, the water works in a more insidious way by sustaining bacteria and microbes that are normally present in diesel fuel. As mentioned in Chapter 13, when the bacteria breed, multiply and die, they produce silt-like muddy deposits that settle to the bottom of the fuel tank. Even if the level of this biofouling is low, over a period of years, a substantial accumulation of sediment builds in virtually every diesel tank.

So long as the sediment remains on the bottom of the tank, it creates few difficulties. The engine pulls clean fuel from above the sediment (the engine's fuel pickup tube normally draws from a point an inch or so above the tank's bottom) and the engine runs well. Coastal cruising seldom exposes the boat to the sustained motion necessary to stir the sediment up and put it into solution throughout the fuel tank. Ocean passages, however, almost always include extended periods of sea motion sufficient to churn up the fuel in the tank and mix the sediment with the fuel. That is the reason for the pre-voyage fuel and tank cleaning discussed in Chapter 13.

Fuel contamination usually announces its presence through clogged fuel filters, and regular periodic checks of the Racor® or other pre-engine separator should disclose the problem before it becomes acute. Periodic changing of both the separator and final fuel filter elements, as recommended by engine and filter manufacturers, should reduce the chance that fuel contamination will prevent the engine from starting. Rapid clogging of filter elements can, however, cause an operating engine to become sluggish, lose power and finally stall from fuel starvation. Installing a vacuum gauge on the discharge side of the fuel separator will provide early indications of filter clogging. Be wary, too, of using a separator filter that is too fine to allow adequate fuel flow. Some new diesels have a much higher fuel flow rate than older models, and filters capable of removing impurities as small as one or two microns may not allow sufficient fuel to pass through for proper operation. Coarser (10 or 20 micron) filters may be necessary to get full engine capability.

When changing fuel filter elements, reduce the risk of introducing air into the fuel system by flooding the new filter and its container with fresh, clean diesel fuel before reinstalling the filter unit on the engine. Unfortunately, some filters are positioned so this is difficult or impossible. Keep a quart or two of clean diesel fuel (clearly labeled) on board for this purpose.

Another insidious fuel system problem that can impair engine operation is an obstruction in the fuel tank vent line. Spider webs, corrosion of protective screening at the vent's topside end fitting and accumulations of airborne debris can get trapped in the vent line, preventing air from entering the tank as fuel is drawn out. When this happens, it becomes more and more difficult for the engine lift pump to suck fuel from the tank, and eventually the engine dies from fuel starvation. In severe cases, this can create a difference between internal and external pressures sufficient to collapse the tank.

Symptoms of a clogged vent line include inward-warping of the tank top, and the sharp sucking in of air when the fuel fill cap is loosened or the fuel line is opened between the filter and the tank. After checking to make sure the problem is not at the vent outlet, clearing an obstruction usually entails disconnecting the line from the tank to push any obstruction back out to the opening. Sometimes compressed air will do the trick; other times a snake may be needed.

Fuel lines and pickup tubes. Other faults that have produced engine failure due to fuel starvation include pinched fuel lines and fouled pickup tubes inside the fuel tank. The latter situation can be particularly baffling because it will occur on a chronic basis and seemingly cure itself each time. Some fuel systems include a screen across the bottom of the tube through which the engine draws its fuel from the tank.

Debris can get sucked up against the screen, blocking fuel flow and causing the engine to stall. When the engine stops, the suction at the pickup tube ceases and the debris falls to the bottom of the tank. A few minutes after stalling, the engine will restart and run normally – until debris builds up and clogs the screen again, at which point the sequence is repeated. The simplest solution to this problem (aside from keeping the tank clean of debris) is to take the

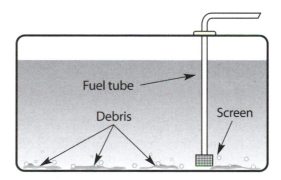

Figure 24.1 - Fuel Tube Filter

pickup tube out of the tank and remove the screen. The fuel filtration system will protect the engine, and chronic blockages will be prevented.

Leaks in the fuel system also can prevent engine operation. The problem is air leaking into the system more often than fuel leaking out. The latter is a hazard that can't be ignored, but aside from wasting fuel, it generally does not prevent engine operation. Getting air into the fuel system, on the other hand, will definitely cause the engine to fail. Bubbles of air mixed in with the fuel will prevent proper operation of the fuel pump and injectors, and without them, a diesel engine will not run. Finding air leaks can be frustratingly difficult, but a systematic approach works best. Start at the fuel tank and inspect every fitting and connection, looking for any looseness or signs of leakage. Work all the way through the system to the injectors at each cylinder. The problem is often found between the separator and the injection pump. Here it may be necessary to open connections and inspect mating surfaces for cracks, scratches, foreign objects or other conditions that could prevent an airtight seal, then tightly reconnect them.

The fuel lift pump. Failure of the fuel lift pump, which is usually driven by a cam inside the engine block, also can prevent engine operation. The lift pump draws fuel from the tank through the separator and delivers it under pressure to the injector pump via the final fuel filter. Some installations use an electric pump for this purpose, and loose or corroded electrical connections can disable the pump and the engine. More than one skipper has installed an electrical pump (often on a jury-rig basis) to replace a failed mechanical pump.

Not an empty tank? Although it seems ludicrous, an empty fuel tank situation can sneak up on you, especially if the system includes more than one tank and can direct return fuel to a tank other than the one from which fuel is being drawn. (Return fuel is fuel in excess of the engine's operating needs. It is run through the injector pump and injector bodies to help cool them and then returned to the tank.) Return fuel may be greater in quantity than the fuel being used to run the engine. If it is directed to a different tank, the level in the tank supplying the engine can drop with surprising speed.

Bleeding the engine. Whenever the engine has failed because air has gotten into the fuel system, it will be necessary to bleed that air out before the engine will run. Check the manufacturer's instruction book or consult with a good diesel mechanic to find out exactly how to bleed your engine. Methods, bleed points and sequences vary widely from one engine builder to another and even among different models from the same manufacturer. The usual approach is to start at the final filter and loosen a screw or bolt, then crank the engine over until the fuel leaking from the screw or bolt is clear: no foam or air bubbles. Tighten this fitting and move on, normally to the injection pump, where you follow a similar procedure: Loosen, crank until clear fuel flows, then tighten. The final step is generally to perform the same actions with one or more injectors. This procedure involves a lot of cranking and can draw the starting battery down severely. Actuating a decompression device, if there is one, to reduce the starter's load will be very helpful. Cranking can also fill the muffler with water and create risk of hydro-lock, so it's prudent to close the engine coolant seacock while bleeding. (Don't forget to open it as soon as the engine starts to fire.) Bleeding involves a lot of dribbling or spraying fuel, so have plenty of rags and cleanup gear ready before you start. An increasing number of small diesels are designed to be self-bleeding, which makes this entire procedure much simpler, though it may take a lot of cranking before the engine starts.

It is not a good sign when the bleed points on an engine are very easy to spot because all the paint is worn off and they are clean and easy to move. There's an excellent chance the fuel system has a persistent air leak that has required frequent bleeding. Find the source of the trouble and fix the leak, rather than having to bleed the engine every time it refuses to start.

If a diesel gets clean, air-free fuel and the starter spins the crankshaft rapidly enough to develop cylinder pressures and temperatures high enough to cause combustion, it will start and run provided it also gets an adequate supply of air to support the combustion. Problems such as leaking intake or exhaust valves, bad piston rings, improper injector timing or faulty injector spray patterns can also prevent proper combustion conditions. Aside from replacing bad injectors with spares, most of those conditions are beyond the scope of onboard repairs.

Air to the cylinders. Another vital engine system is that which supplies air to the cylinders for fuel combustion. It usually consists of an opening into the engine's intake manifold, protected with a screen or basket housing an air filter. If dirt, debris or foreign material (e.g., hair shed by an onboard pet) obstructs the opening or clogs the filter, the engine will lose power, be difficult to start and respond sluggishly to changed throttle settings. Cleaning or changing the filter and assuring a good air supply is usually a simple procedure and one that should be performed periodically.

The turbo-boost system. Engines that use turbo-assist to increase their power have yet another complex mechanical system that can create engine problems. A turbo-boost system uses engine exhaust gases to drive a turbine which, in turn, compresses the incoming air before it flows into the cylinders. The compressed air contains more oxygen than the atmospheric-pressure air drawn into a normally aspirated engine, so it can produce higher cylinder pressures, burn fuel more efficiently and deliver greater power to each piston as it is driven downward. Because turbo units run at very high speeds and are very finely balanced, they are susceptible to damage as a result of inadequate lubrication, advanced corrosion and the presence of foreign objects in the air supply. Fortunately, if a turbo unit fails, it only impairs the ability to attain maximum speed and power; it usually does not prevent engine operation at lower speeds.

Smelling salts for the engine. As a true "last resort" for an engine that will not start despite indications of a good fuel supply, adequate intake air and strong batteries driving the starter, many skippers carry a pressurized can of "diesel starting fluid." This is simply a can of compressed ether or other highly flammable gas which will ignite in the cylinder much more readily than pure diesel fuel. A vintage spray can of WD-40, which used propane as the propellant agent, can also fill this role. Using such fluids improperly risks permanent damage to the engine. If too much of the flammable gas gets into the cylinder, it can easily create combustion pressures and temperatures well above those for which the engine was designed. If there is no alternative, use a "starting fluid" by spraying the "fluid" onto a rag and holding the rag close to the engine's air intake while cranking the starter. Do not spray the fluid directly into the intake.

While it is running, every internal combustion engine generates a tremendous amount of heat. To keep it running, excess heat must be removed continuously. Otherwise, the engine will overheat, parts will expand and seize, and the engine will come to a sudden and perhaps permanent stop. Two systems help keep an engine at its designed operating temperature. One is the lubricating system, which removes heat while it performs its primary function of reducing friction between the hundreds of moving parts inside the engine. The second is a water cooling system that uses the sea-water surrounding the boat as a sink into which excess engine heat can be dumped.

The lubricating system. Let's consider the lubricating system first, since its role in the cooling process is secondary to its lubricating function. This system uses a pump to draw oil from a reservoir in the bottom of the engine, known as the sump, and push it through a series of passageways, holes and pipes to every point in the engine where moving surfaces meet. The objective is to maintain a thin film of oil between the metal surfaces to reduce friction (and the heat it creates) and minimize wear on the metallic parts. As it flows through the engine and back to the sump, the oil carries with it soot and chemical by-products of the combustion process that takes place in the cylinders, tiny bits of metal worn off various parts, and other waste products generated within the engine. During its cycles through the engine, the oil passes through a filter. This removes most of the solid impurities and keeps the oil clean enough to perform its lubricating function. As it flows through the engine, the oil also removes some of the heat generated by combustion and friction. Some engines include an oil cooler that allows the oil to pass some of its heat to the water in the cooler.

Failure of the lubricating system is rare, but potentially catastrophic, for an engine will not run long without lubrication. When it fails for lack of lubrication, the engine is often not fit for repair. That is why almost all engines have some form of alarm system to warn of inadequate oil pressure. Lubricating system failure can result from an oil pump that stops working (rare, and not easily repaired at sea), or an inadequate supply of oil. Regular checks of lubricant levels (in the engine oil sump, the transmission casing and – if you have one – the V-drive housing) are essential to reliable engine operation. All lubricating oil gradually breaks down under the heat of combustion, and both the oil and its filter have a limit to the contaminants they can hold and still perform their functions. Therefore, regular changes of both the fluids and the filters is key to preventing lubricating system failures. Prevention is definitely the name of the game. If the alarm goes off indicating a lack of lubricant, the only course of action is to shut the engine down instantly, then determine the cause and correct it before starting the engine again.

The water cooling system. A few engines use raw seawater to cool the engine directly. Most use a freshwater system to cool the engine and a raw water system to cool the freshwater. Rising engine operating temperatures usually suggest a problem in the raw water system, since it is much more vulnerable to fouling and obstruction.

To troubleshoot the raw water system, trace the system looking for leaks or obstructions. Verify that the through-hull fitting is clear by opening and cleaning the seawater strainer, then opening the through-hull valve. Water should flow out of the strainer in good quantity. Follow the raw water line to the engine, checking all connections along the way for tightness. Verify free flow of water through any coolers it passes through on the way to the engine, where it normally leads to a raw water circulating pump.

Test the pump by disconnecting a hose on the output side of the pump and turning the engine over briefly. The pump should produce a strong stream of water with sufficient pressure to push the water through the rest of the system and into the exhaust line. Weak output or low pressure indicates a malfunctioning pump.

Raw water pump problems are usually caused by failure of the drive system or the impeller that moves the water through the pump. Some pumps are driven by internal gearing, and failures can include a broken driveshaft or a loose connection between the driveshaft and the impeller itself. Other pumps are belt driven, and a broken or loose belt can prevent proper pumping action. (Carry an emergency V-belt – the type that can be cut to fit any length – as a general spare.) Other possible problems include worn bearings that impair pump rotation and leaking seals that bleed off the pump's output pressure. Suspect the latter if water is flowing out of the drain hole found in most pump bodies.

Bad seals can also let air into the system, which can allow the water to drain out when the engine is not running. This leads to an air-bound raw water pump. A symptom of this problem is difficulty getting good raw water flow when the engine is started after being shut down for several hours.

Impeller failure. By far the most common raw water pump problem is failure of the impeller, with damaged or missing blades the usual culprit. Replacing the impeller generally is not difficult, although access to the pump may prove challenging. Extra impellers should be a part of every boat's spares kit, and installing a new one before a major passage is a good preventive strategy. It's a job much easier to accomplish in harbor than at sea. If a damaged impeller is missing blades, be sure to find the torn off pieces. They often wind up in a right angle bend in the output hose or in the heat exchanger or other narrow passages downstream of the pump, where they can obstruct water flow. When checking the raw water pump, also examine the pump cover plate for wear. This plate forms the seal at the edge of the impeller blades. A worn cover plate may sometimes – though not always – prevent the impeller blades from developing normal output pressure and volume.

If the pump has a good, strong output, check each downstream component and fitting, looking for obstructions or leaks. Blocked passages in heat exchangers, blown hoses or hose connections, and obstructions at the injection point, where the raw water is dumped into the exhaust system, are common causes of cooling water problems. Use a 5/16" socket driver, which does a much better job than a screwdriver, when tightening suspect hose clamps. Following such a step-by-step method for tracing the raw cooling water system will usually turn up the problem.

A leak in muffler or exhaust can be serious. One raw water problem that has serious repercussions but is not accompanied by overheating of the engine is a leak in the muffler or exhaust system. Instead of passing overboard through the exhaust system, cooling water and exhaust gases are dumped inside the hull. Here, the water flows to the bilges, producing flooding, and the deadly exhaust gas invades the accommodations, placing the lives of the crew at risk. Immediate investigation and corrective action is called for if there's a marked reduction in cooling water at the exhaust outlet while engine operating temperature stays within normal limits.

Raw water is usually salty and corrosive and has a marked tendency to develop scale and mineral buildup on hot surfaces. Rather than circulate this through the narrow cooling passages inside the engine block, most engine builders choose a closed freshwater system to cool the engine. This freshwater is cooled in turn by raw water in a heat exchanger. A failure in the freshwater cooling system will usually be indicated by a sudden rise in engine temperature despite normal raw water discharge at the exhaust fitting.

Freshwater cooling system casualties are frequently caused by a ruptured hose or leaky fitting that has allowed the level of coolant in the engine to drop. Failure of the freshwater coolant circulating pump is another possibility. The latter pump is normally a belt driven accessory located on the front of the engine. A broken belt, worn bearings or failed seals are common types of freshwater pump failure. Other than replacing a belt, correction generally entails replacement or rebuild of the pump.

Another common freshwater system problem is a sticking thermostat, the device that regulates the amount of freshwater circulated through the engine heat exchanger. If it sticks in the closed position, very little water is allowed to pass through the heat exchanger to be cooled by the raw water system. The rest of the water simply recirculates within the engine block, getting hotter and hotter until the engine overheats. The leading symptom of this condition is a heat exchanger that's quite cool while the engine block is very hot. After the engine block has been allowed to cool, the thermostat can be removed, cleaned and tested. In an emergency, the engine can be operated for short periods without a thermostat, though it may operate at less than the optimum temperature. Also, since overheating can permanently alter the thermostatic valve's response to temperature changes, it is prudent to change the thermostat after overheating has occurred.

A more insidious freshwater system failure occurs when the heat exchanger develops a leak, often as a result of electrolytic corrosion between dissimilar metals in the exchanger body. This usually results in raw water contamination of the freshwater cooling system. This introduces all the raw water cooling system disadvantages the builder sought to avoid. Heat exchanger leaks don't create an emergency, but should be corrected at the first opportunity by replacing the heat exchanger body or the tube bundle inside the body. One symptom of heat exchanger leakage is a buildup of salt deposits around the freshwater fill cap. It can also be detected by draining the raw water cooling system: If the freshwater level in the engine also drops, it is strong evidence that the exchanger is leaking.

The diesel engine's reliable health can have a significant impact on the safety and comfort of the crew and on the seaworthiness of the boat. A combination of attentive preventive measures and careful, logically pursued troubleshooting will keep the diesel purring happily and performing its role in daily operations.

REFERENCE:
Nigel Calder, *Boatowner's Mechanical and Electrical Manual*
Nigel Calder, *Marine Diesel Engines: Maintenance, Troubleshooting and Repair*

CHAPTER 25

TROUBLESHOOTING YOUR STEERING

The steering system plays a vital role on a passage: It keeps the boat on the course chosen by the helmsman (hopefully, the same direction selected by the navigator!). When steering control is lost, the boat is more or less at the mercy of wind and sea.

A loss of the usual method of steering the boat – an autopilot or wind vane – does not affect the steering system itself but is still a significant casualty. Failure of autopilot or wind vane is right up there with sail damage as the most frequently encountered casualties during Rallies. Minor mechanical problems such as broken drive belts or chafed control lines can often be repaired by the crew, but electronic failures and major component breakage usually cannot. This means the crew must resort to hand steering for the remainder of the passage, even if that is a thousand miles. The negative impact on morale, fatigue levels and watch effectiveness is enormous. While an autopilot or vane casualty does not pose an immediate threat to boat or crew safety by itself, it is seriously unpleasant and can lead to flawed decisions that do place boat and crew at risk.

Steering systems range from the simple tiller attached to the top of the rudder post to wheel systems that use rigid mechanical linkages, cables and chains or hydraulic systems to translate rotation of the wheel into lateral motion of the rudder. Steering system problems can be broken into two categories: loss of control of rudder movement, and loss of the rudder itself.

Pinpointing loss of rudder control. Loss of rudder control can occur for a number of reasons. The tiller or its connection to the rudder post can break. Loose gear can go adrift under the cockpit sole and jam the quadrant atop the rudder post, preventing or restricting its movement. Stray objects may jam the steering cable of a wheel system. The cable itself can break, the conduit through which the cable passes can get pinched or damaged, the turning sheaves leading the cable from wheel to quadrant can jam, seize or come loose. The quadrant can jam against one of the end stops that limit its swing. In hydraulic systems, pumps, hoses or cylinders can develop leaks or become airbound. Occasionally the problem will develop inside the rudder itself, such as when the internal web framing or welding breaks and the rudder body no longer moves with the rudder post.

First steps. Whatever the problem, start with a careful inspection of the system. (Being familiar with the system – knowing how it looked when it was operating properly – will pay big dividends here. Remember the inspection described in Chapter 4.) If loose gear is the problem, restow it securely and your steering should be restored.

Normally, the first step is to retrieve the emergency tiller from its easily accessible stowage and install it on the rudder post. This should get you roughly back on course until you can find and fix the problem. Few emergency tillers provide adequate leverage for effective steering over an extended period. Rigging a pair of relieving tackles, one to each side of the tiller, will help.

Finding the problem and fixing it . If the steering system has seized up, and the rudder cannot be moved with the emergency tiller, you'll need to disconnect the jammed control system from the rudder. This may be as simple as removing a pin from a steering linkage or as complicated as disconnecting turnbuckles or eyebolts fastening cables to the quadrant. Here again, familiarity with the system will be a great advantage.

With hydraulic systems, tightening fittings to stop leaks, increasing the fluid level in the reservoir and pressurizing the system will often restore steering control. More complex actions, such as rebuilding pump units or replacing seals in hydraulic rams, are beyond the scope of onboard repairs, and jury rigs will have to supplant the hydraulics.

If an autopilot is rigged so it drives its own independent tiller arm on the rudder post (rather than using the cables or quadrant from the manual system), it offers an alternative steering method. Wind vanes that operate directly on the rudder, rather than through the normal steering system, can also serve as a backup.

With typical wheel/cable steering systems, it's not uncommon for the cables to stretch under the strains imposed by ocean passages. This is especially true if the cables are new or the system has not been exposed to the heavy loads created by ocean sailing. The stretch can create sufficient slack to allow the cables to drop out of the grooves cut in the outer edge of the quadrant casting. If this is the case, correction involves loosening the cables still further, repositioning them properly into the grooves, and then taking the slack out with the installed turnbuckles or eyebolts. This sounds fairly easy but can be exceptionally challenging when the boat is in constant motion. Also, the rudder itself is seldom still. In a seaway, it will want to swing from side to side. If the control system that normally constrains its movements is ineffective or disengaged during repairs, the challenge is compounded. Steering casualties seldom occur in calm water and light air. They are typically produced by the heavy stresses generated by high winds and boisterous seas.

If a sheave leading the cable between the wheel and the quadrant has broken or pulled loose, you may be able to replace it with a jury rig. Similarly, a broken cable can sometimes be repaired with cable clamps or other jury rigs. If the chain that rides over the sprocket on the steering wheel shaft breaks, you may be able to remove the broken link and reconnect the loose ends. Only the crew's ingenuity and the supply of spare parts will limit the solutions to such mechanical failures.

In some cases, the only way to control the rudder may be to fasten lines to it directly and use winches to haul it to one side or the other. Island Packet and a few other builders actually put a hole in the top of the rudder for this purpose. In an emergency, it may be possible to drill a hole while at sea, or lock a C-clamp or sturdy gripping-type pliers in place well aft on the top edge of the rudder blade. Lines connected to them could then be used to control rudder position. Such a system might be the only alternative for a tiller-steered boat that has no internal access to the rudder post and no quadrant to which steering lines could be connected.

If it's rudder bearing failure, heads up! Another steering system casualty is related to rudder bearing failure. This often creates serious leakage and may lead to the ominous threat of rudder loss. Boats have rigged mizzen halyards to the top of the rudder post to prevent the rudder from dropping downward after a bearing failure. In the first Caribbean 1500, one boat experienced chronic rudder-induced autopilot difficulties. The autopilot would overload and trip off the line. The problem was traced to an inadequate rudder support structure, which allowed the rudder post to move relative to the hull and bind in its bearing. The solution was to pay closer attention to sail trim and thus minimize rudder loading.

While proper sail trim and balance are important for efficient steering under normal conditions, it's even more critical with a steering casualty. Proper trim helps keep the boat on course with minimum rudder activity. Reducing sail area can substantially reduce loads on the damaged steering system with only marginal impact on speed. *Adjusting sails should be right up there with installing the emergency tiller as a first response to a steering breakdown.*

Loss of the rudder. Loss of the rudder itself introduces a whole new batch of challenges. Here, too, adapting the sail plan should be the first response. It may not be possible to steer the same course, but by applying the sail trim techniques discussed in Chapter 22, most boats can be brought to a fairly stable heading. Once the boat has been settled on a course that goes in the proper general direction, there is time to pursue further steps.

The case against jury-rigged rudders. Having read tales of boats sailing long distances using jury-rigged rudders (deck plates or bunk bottoms bolted to spinnaker poles to form a makeshift steering oar), many prospective voyagers consider such a rig as their primary contingency plan. Alas, very few of those rigs prove robust enough to handle the stresses generated in steering the boat. Water pressure rips the board from the pole, stern pulpits prove too weak to handle steering loads, and chafe rapidly destroys the lashings used to suspend the pole. Also, the lack of mechanical advantage makes steering with a makeshift oar exhausting. The vast majority of jury rudder schemes have failed, the efforts eventually abandoned. Valuable time is lost, and lack of success lowers crew morale.

The case for dragging objects on a bridle. In contrast to the jury rudder approach, the technique of dragging objects astern on a bridle has proven to be a simple and effective way to regain directional control after a rudder has been lost. This method has been used in many situations, and the items towed have ranged from buckets or drogues to lengths of anchor chain, dinghy oars, and heavily knotted lines. By rigging the bridle so the drag can be shifted from side to side (Figure 25.1), the boat's direction can be controlled, albeit within broad limits (15-30°). If the bridle is secured to the cockpit winches, it becomes relatively easy to move the bridle's tow point from one side to the other. Dragging gear from the starboard side will make the boat turn to starboard, shifting it to the port side will make it turn to port. The effect can be

Figure 25.1 - Steering by Dragging with a Bridle

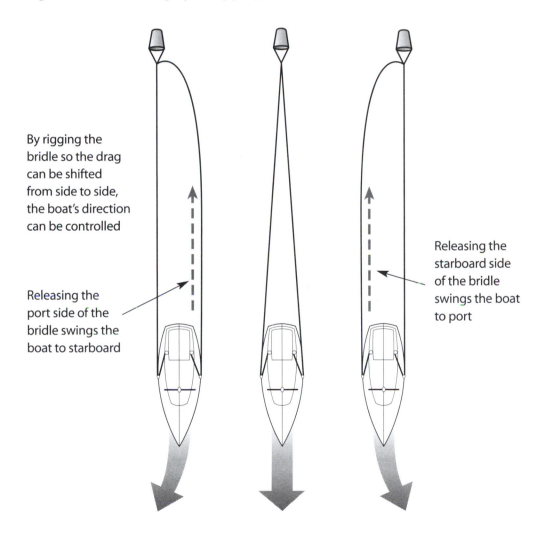

By rigging the bridle so the drag can be shifted from side to side, the boat's direction can be controlled

Releasing the port side of the bridle swings the boat to starboard

Releasing the starboard side of the bridle swings the boat to port

increased by leading the bridle legs through snatch blocks at the widest part of the hull to maximize the lever arm through which the drag force operates.

Most wind vane systems use the vane mechanism to move the boat's rudder, either by turning the normal steering wheel or by manipulating a trim tab attached to the rudder. They are not able to steer the boat if the rudder has been lost. Scanmar, however, has developed an emergency rudder conversion kit for its Monitor servo-pendulum wind vane. Making the conversion involves replacing the servo-paddle with a much larger blade and locking the pendulum in the vertical position. This emergency rudder arrangement is reportedly able to steer the boat in either the wind vane or manual steering mode.

Be flexible – and learn. Coping with a steering casualty may entail changing your destination to an alternate port to which the boat can be sailed more readily, using sail balance and jury-rigged steering devices, and accepting a longer, slower passage.

A steering casualty at sea rarely places the crew or the boat at risk. In coastal waters, where hazards may be more immediate, there is an option not available on the high seas: anchoring to permit repairs or await better conditions. Another option, also available to the steering-impaired boat arriving at its destination, is to tie the outboard-powered dinghy securely alongside and use it to aim the boat. A casualty to the steering system can challenge a passagemaking crew's ingenuity and endurance. Though it may seem at first to be a catastrophic failure that warrants a call for help, in fact *a loss of steering can almost always be dealt with successfully.* Such a casualty provides an ideal opportunity to learn to distinguish situations that are truly life-threatening from those that are merely unpleasant and frustrating.

REFERENCE:
John Letcher, *Self-Steering for Sailing Craft*

CHAPTER 26

TROUBLESHOOTING YOUR ELECTRICAL SYSTEM

Electrical problems, large and small, are among the most common challenges a passagemaker faces. Since many of our systems require electrical power, electrical difficulties can have widespread impact. Backup equipment and contingency plans for completing a trip without the "normal" electrically powered systems are part of any thorough preparation. Awareness of the kinds of problems that may develop can help in both prevention and coping.

If batteries won't charge normally. The electrical casualty that seems to occur most frequently is a loss of normal battery charging, a capability usually provided by the engine alternator. The problem can range from easily correctable situations such as broken or slipping drive belts to less easily repaired conditions such as blown diodes or regulator failures.

Tightening belts. Slipping belts often announce themselves with a squealing noise whenever the alternator has a load placed on it. Tightening the belts normally entails loosening one or more bolts in the bracket supporting the alternator. This allows the entire alternator to slide or pivot so it is farther away from the engine drive pulley, thus tightening the belt(s) that link them. It can be difficult to get the belts pulled tight enough. Using a long screwdriver or bar as a lever sometimes does the trick. Getting the hold-down bolts secured again while the belts are still tight can be even more difficult in the limited space available around most boat engines. As noted in Chapter 4, the belt should be tight enough to prevent turning the alternator by hand. Most engine specifications say the belts should not deflect more than about ½" when pressed by hand. Another thumb rule for belt tension says they should be tight enough that they can be twisted no more than ¼" turn in the longest span between pulleys. Worn or undersize belts cannot be corrected by further tightening. They must be replaced.

About diodes. As the alternator's magnetized rotor spins, it induces a high frequency alternating current in the stationary windings of the stator. A group of diodes converts this into a useful direct current that can flow into the storage batteries. Diodes are most often damaged by placing the battery selector switch in the "off" position while the engine is running. This error is usually inadvertent, and it is frequently corrected within a few seconds, but that is sufficient time to damage or destroy the diodes. One way to avert this problem is to use a battery selector switch that disconnects the alternator field circuit whenever it is placed in the "off" position. This interrupts the alternator output whenever there is no battery to receive the output current. Replacing bad diodes requires specialized tools seldom available aboard.

Alternator output problems. Alternator output problems can also be a result of inadequate field current, since that current determines the alternator's output. This can occur as a result of regulator failure, but it can also be produced by loose or corroded connections in the field circuit. Troubleshooting alternator output problems should include tracing all the circuitry – both the field lead and the output leads – to verify that connections are clean and tight. A good text such as *The 12 Volt Doctor's Alternator Book* can be invaluable in assessing and correcting alternator problems.

One jury-rig fix for an erratic field current is to bypass the regulator's field output. Instead, apply +12 volts DC directly to the alternator's field terminal. This should cause the alternator to produce maximum output. This can quickly lead to overheating and overcharging of the batteries, so it must be done cautiously and only for short periods. A better solution is to wire a couple of 12-volt light bulbs in series with the new field wire to drop the voltage at the alternator. This keeps alternator output at a safer level.

Similar output problems can occur with independent diesel generator sets, and manufacturer's instruction books normally provide troubleshooting guidance for both the engine and the generator ends of the unit.

Backup power sources. "Defense in depth" – having multiple sources from which the batteries can be charged – makes a casualty in any single system less disruptive. Wind generators, towed water-driven units, alternators belted to a freely spinning propeller shaft, and solar cells all provide ways to charge batteries and keep systems running.

Conserving power. Conserving electrical power should be a way of life aboard a passagemaking boat, but any electrical charging problem should be accompanied by immediate steps to further reduce consumption. At any indication that electrical power will be in short supply, institute aggressive conservation measures. Turn off all nonessential power consumers and minimize the use of all others. Be particularly diligent with heavy loads such as autopilots, incandescent lights and electrical pumps. Every amp-hour saved is an amp-hour that won't have to be replaced by an ailing charging system.

Tracing circuits for interrupted power. Most other electrical problems involve interrupted power to equipment, be it a navigation light or a bilge pump. If this happens, carefully trace circuits from the main power source to the inoperative unit, checking all wiring, connections, switches, circuit breakers and fuses along the way. Start by verifying that all circuit breakers and switches are in their proper position. Then check for blown fuses in the circuit. Also look for blown fuses inside a piece of equipment. An accurate wiring diagram for each circuit will be exceedingly helpful in this process, as will a multi-meter that can measure both resistance (to detect open or high resistance connections) and voltage (to detect presence/absence of full operating power). Remember to check the ground side of the circuit – the wiring from the unit back to the negative side of the battery. Broken or erratic ground connections are a common cause of electrical circuit failures.

An unusual drain? An electrical problem merits special attention if it produces an unusual drain on the system and causes battery charge levels to drop faster than normal. The best approach here is to localize the problem circuit. Start by turning off all circuit breakers and switches. If the power drain continues (as indicated by falling battery voltage), look for circuits or equipment that have been connected directly to the batteries rather than through circuit breakers and distribution panels. Once everything has been disconnected and voltage is stable, reconnect the circuits and equipment one at a time, while closely monitoring battery voltage (better yet, the amperage of the load on the battery). When the drain resumes, disconnect the last item reconnected. If the drain stops, it confirms the problem lies in that circuit or piece of equipment.

The next phase is to examine the faulty circuit and everything connected to it, using a similar process of elimination, until the culprit is found. Internal short circuits in motors, pumps and lighting equipment can cause a rapid drain on the electrical system. Undetected, they can lead to complete power failure, and if the current flow continues, it will cause overheating of the wiring which can ignite a fire.

Taking it apart. In the absence of special electrical or electronic skills, disassembling inoperative electrical equipment may not be productive. An exception might be a search for an internal fuse that has failed. If the failure has been caused by age and physical stress (vibration, boat movement), replacing the fuse may be all that is required. If the new fuse also blows, you probably have a significant electrical defect that must be identified and corrected before the unit can be restored to operation.

Another point of view is that if a piece of equipment is already inoperative, there's little to be lost from attempts to disassemble it and find the problem. It may be as simple as a loose/broken wire or bad connection that is visible or easily located. Inspection may disclose an obvious mechanical problem, such as a broken belt between the motor and pump components of a bilge pump. Proceed cautiously to avoid damage to the unit, and record the arrangement of all parts to insure proper reassembly.

Higher voltage systems – use caution! While our discussion has centered on the 12-volt DC electrical system found on most boats, the same principles apply to higher voltage systems (primarily 24 or 32 volts). Working with 110-volt AC systems, whether produced by generators or DC-AC inverters, is not very different, but the hazards are much greater. These systems can inflict deadly shocks and must be treated with utmost respect. Afloat, all 110-volt AC circuits should be protected by Ground Fault Interrupters to reduce the risk of shock injuries.

Electrically powered equipment – ranging from interior and navigation lights to bilge pumps, freshwater pumps, stereo systems, radios, radars and high-tech navigation systems – has made cruising much more enjoyable, as well as considerably safer. These systems depend on the health of the electrical system that fills their unending demand for amps of current. Being prepared to find and able to fix problems in the electrical system are important cruising skills. The principles are relatively clear and simple. The 12-volt circuits are safe to work on. With a few helpful reference texts and plenty of diligence, most cruising skippers will be able to cope successfully with a wide range of electrical difficulties.

REFERENCES:
Edgar J. Beyn, *The 12 Volt Doctor's Practical Handbook* and *The 12 Volt Doctor's Alternator Book*
Nigel Calder, *Boatowner's Mechanical and Electrical Manual,* Second Edition
Charlie Wing, *Boatowner's Illustrated Handbook of Wiring*

CHAPTER 27

ILLNESS AND INJURIES

One significant challenge any voyager may have to face is that of illness or injury among the crew. In the next chapter, Dr. Rob Amsler offers professional guidance for treating medical problems that may occur during a passage. The purpose of this chapter is not to suggest specific treatment but to identify health problems most often encountered and with which the passagemaker must be prepared to deal.

Seasickness. Certainly the most common form of illness encountered in any passage will be motion sickness. Entire books have been written, but our understanding is still imperfect. It seems to originate with mixed signals received in the brain from the systems used to determine balance and orientation: principally the eyes, ears and legs. One way the brain responds to persistent confusion about which way is "up" is to direct the stomach to dump its contents. But before the vomiting begins, the victim experiences symptoms denoting earlier stages of motion sickness. Prompt response to those symptoms may make it possible to limit the condition before it gets out of control. This is especially important because most seasickness medications are primarily preventive. Once the nausea stage has been reached, their effectiveness is greatly reduced.

It's important for everyone aboard to recognize that motion sickness is a body's perfectly natural and normal response to a changed physical environment. It is not a joke, nor is it something to be ashamed of. While the role of diet is secondary, avoiding heavy, greasy and difficult to digest foods certainly makes it easier to control the urge to eject the stomach's contents. Mental attitudes can be very important. Excessive worry about becoming seasick can trigger onset. More than one crew member has, in essence, talked himself into being sick.

Early indications of motion sickness include lethargy and drowsiness, inability to focus attention or concentrate, either a dry mouth or excessive salivation, feeling chilly and/or clammy, looking pale, and reduced manual dexterity or coordination. Whenever any of these symptoms appear, prompt remedial action is warranted. Take medication. Get topside, where the horizon is visible (to reduce conflicting signals the brain receives from the eyes). Or lie down in a bunk and keep your eyes closed, again to minimize conflicting messages to the brain. Some people gain relief from taking the helm, since it requires frequent looks at the horizon, and the compass card gives a continuous visual indication of both direction and the horizontal plane. Standing up and "riding" the boat, rather than collapsing in a passive lump to be tossed about by the sea's motions can also be useful. It helps synchronize the signals the brain receives from the legs with those from the ears and eyes.

There are many nonmedicinal seasickness treatments, ranging from consuming ginger to wearing wrist bands that press on certain points inside the wrist. These remedies are effective for some and useless to others. They seldom make a situation worse, so they may be worth a try.

If seasickness does strike, and medications and preventive tactics don't keep it from reaching the vomiting stage, continue efforts to minimize the effects. Make sure the sick crew member is securely fastened to the boat with a harness, lest a "throwing up" incident turn into a crew overboard situation. Take the victim's diminished capabilities into account in assigning watch and other duties. Most important, keep the victim hydrated. Loss of body fluids through vomiting can quickly develop into dehydration, with the potential for serious lasting effects. Motion sickness victims should continue to take fluids frequently in small amounts, accompanied by bland food such as soda crackers or cooked rice. Even if subsequent nausea causes loss of those foods, the body will have absorbed some of the fluids.

Fortunately, for most people, seasickness is a temporary condition that resolves after 3-4 days at sea. By that time, the brain begins to understand how to cope with the confusing signals it receives from the sensory and balance systems, and the nausea response diminishes. This is commonly known as "developing sea legs." The motion sickness can return if a period of very mild, calm conditions is succeeded by rough weather, but the recovery time is usually much shorter. A small number of people simply cannot acclimate to the ocean's motion and will experience chronic motion sickness. These cases must be treated with great care to prevent the victim from reaching a serious stage of dehydration.

Avoiding dehydration. Seasickness is not the only condition that can cause dehydration during a passage. Hot sun, exposure to continuous winds with their evaporative cooling effect, altered diet and alcoholic or caffeinated drinks (which often have a diuretic effect) can also somewhat dehydrate crew who are not in any way seasick. Keep an abundant supply of fresh drinking water available, and encourage (perhaps even require) the crew to consume healthy liquids on a regular basis. Quite conveniently, all crew members have a simple indicator that reflects their level of hydration: They simply need to observe the color of their urine. When normal pale yellow gives way to darker gold or brown tones, it's a good sign that insufficient fluids are being taken. It is time to drink more water, preferably in small quantities at regular, frequent intervals. Dehydration can induce physical effects such as muscular cramping, weakness and impaired coordination, as well as mental effects that include clouded judgment and irrational decision making. A serious condition, it merits conscientious preventive actions.

Constipation. In conjunction with seasickness and dehydration, the third member of the Unholy Triumvirate of sailing maladies is constipation. This condition can be triggered by the change of diet as a passage begins, compounded by the changed motion. Motion sickness and dehydration contribute to the process, and before long the entire digestive process can be affected. The victim may experience headaches, stomach discomfort and perhaps even abdominal pain, none of which enhance the ability to perform sailing responsibilities. Even when the condition starts to resolve itself and the blockage at last ceases, nature still has one little trick left: An oversize bowel movement can play havoc with the boat's sanitation system, and clearing an obstructed marine toilet does not help anyone's morale! The best preventive regimen is drinking plenty of fluids and eating a high fiber diet that also includes natural laxative foods, such as dried fruit.

Hypothermia. Another commonly experienced condition, as insidious and as potentially harmful as dehydration, is hypothermia. With exposure to steady winds, often while wet from spray, rain and boarding seas, every crew member is a candidate for hypothermia, even while sailing in seemingly benign conditions. Active measures to keep dry and warm are always warranted. Good foul weather gear, protection provided by dodgers and weather cloths, and layered clothing that can easily be adjusted as conditions change will avoid this dangerous condition. Severe hypothermia – a condition with life-threatening possibilities – is generally limited to crew overboard situations and to boats sailing in colder (less than 60°F) waters, but less extreme hypothermia can occur anywhere. The effects – ranging from reduced manual dexterity and sluggishness to impaired judgment, confusion and indecision – can place both boat and crew at risk. If anyone is chilled enough to shiver, he or she is cold enough to need prompt action to stop the further loss of body heat.

Most common injuries. A boat at sea is replete with opportunities for personal injury. Among the most common injuries are cuts, scrapes, bruises, burns and fractures. Cuts can occur anywhere a crew member comes in contact with a sharp piece of gear (cotter pin, broken wire strand, aluminum can, carving knife). Scrapes (abrasions) and bruises (contusions) can occur if a crew member is tossed off balance by a wave, slips or trips and falls on deck or on a companionway ladder. Burns are most common in the galley and around a hot engine, but rope burns can result from runaway lines. Fractures can be inflicted by tripping over deck fittings, falling down ladders, being struck by blocks or booms, or getting hit by a flying object such as a winch handle or a full pressure cooker.

Measures for treating such injuries will be addressed in Chapter 28, but two points deserve emphasis here. The first is that a pervasive attitude of safety-consciousness can prevent most injuries. It's the skipper's job to make sure everyone stays alert for possibly injurious situations. The second point is that a boat's warm and humid atmosphere provides an ideal environment for bacteria. Hence, the risk of infection from even the most minor injury is substantially greater than it would be ashore. Don't overlook any injury, especially if the skin is broken, but take aggressive first aid measures to preclude infection and complications.

When outside help is needed. While independence and self-sufficiency are admirable traits on voyaging boats, few boats have the advantage of including a medical professional in the crew. In an emergency, medical knowledge beyond the first aid level may be needed, and every boat should be prepared to take advantage of assistance available from outside sources. Ways to obtain such assistance have been listed in Chapter 9.

Rarely, a medical situation will be so life-threatening that treatment aboard, whether for lack of facilities or lack of technical skills, will not be possible. In such cases, an emergency evacuation will be needed. The best agency for coordinating such an operation is the US Coast Guard. Within about 200 miles of the US coast, helicopter evacuations can be arranged. Farther offshore, or in situations where helicopter evacuation is not the best alternative, the Coast Guard can activate the AMVER system. Through this program, the Coast Guard can locate and communicate with merchant ships closest to the boat with a medical problem. They can also coordinate a rendezvous to transfer the patient to a ship with better medical facilities or one that can get the patient to a medical facility ashore more rapidly than can the cruising boat.

A word of caution. One word of caution regarding Coast Guard involvement in any emergency. This applies to medical situations, as well as to other cases in which a voyager asks for Coast Guard aid. This caution relates to losing control of the events. On more than one occasion, the Coast Guard has taken command and made decisions in which the skipper had little input and no control. In one instance, with a boat taking on water from an unlocated source, the Coast Guard decided to "save lives, not property" and refused to send the boat emergency pumps they had requested. They chose instead to send a helicopter to evacuate the crew as the boat sank. In another case, the Coast Guard virtually directed a skipper to leave his boat (which had to be sailed to its destination by its two remaining crew members) and embark on a merchant ship that could carry him to a major port for medical treatment. While the Coast Guard can provide invaluable assistance unobtainable from other sources, you must be aware that bringing the Coast Guard into the picture can lead to results other than those you have in mind.

The skipper's focus. A final issue concerning illnesses and injuries relates not to the victim but to the rest of the crew. The primary focus of the boat's leader, whether it be the skipper or one who assumes that role after the skipper has been incapacitated, must be the overall safety of the boat and the crew. Good seamanship must prevail over a perfectly natural tendency to focus attention and concern on the sick/injured crew member. Do not become so preoccupied with the comfort and care of the victim that inadequate attention is given to sail trim, weather prognoses, navigational progress and efficient watchstanding. Boats have been lost when leadership failed and organizational structure disintegrated in the wake of a casualty to a key crew member. Like a play, the boat must go on, and those who sail it must carry out their roles to the best of their abilities.

Against this backdrop of general observations about coping with illness and injury, it's time to focus on specific guidance for handling medical problems. These can range from minor distractions to life-threatening crises, but in most cases, a well prepared and properly outfitted crew and boat will be ready to deal with unexpected medical situations.

CHAPTER 28

MEDICAL AND DENTAL TREATMENT

The medical section of this chapter is derived from the pamphlet *How to Prepare a Medical Kit for Yacht Racing & Medical Tips for the Practicing Sailor* developed and edited by Dr. Robert H. Amsler, Fleet Surgeon, Bayview Yacht Club, Detroit, Michigan. It is included with Dr. Amsler's permission.

Medical tips by symptoms.
The following are to be used in addition to your First Aid book.

Cuts and abrasions
• No matter how much it hurts, scrub it out. If its starts bleeding again, no problem.

• Never close a puncture wound (one that is deeper than it is wide). This includes bites. Wash, put Bacitracin and Band-Aid on wound to keep it clean. Open it periodically or put a sterile wick in it to promote drainage.

To handle a moderately deep wound without suturing:

• Scrub it out and irrigate thoroughly.

• Let bleeding stop or slow to a trickle (use pressure if needed).

• Pull edges together with tape.

• Pad the wound on each side to hold edges together.

• Wrap firmly with Ace wrap.

NOTE: Hold deep wounds together with Ace wraps for at least 10-14 days.

• Ice is always appropriate over the bandage and not on exposed skin.

• Most wounds heal well if immobilized long enough. Use bandages and splints. Keep them on longer than you think you should.

• All deep palm lacerations require antibiotics NOW!

• Ripped nails and nail beds look worse than they are. Cool with ice for 20-30 minutes, then move skin and nail into normal position and tape in place. *Do NOT remove nail.*

Dehydration
To one liter of water, add:

        ½ teaspoon salt (sodium chloride)

½ teaspoon baking soda (sodium bicarbonate)

¼ teaspoon salt substitute (potassium chloride)

2 tablespoons sugar

Drink copiously to replace electrolytes, *or...*

2-glass formula for dehydration —

In glass #1 put:

- 8 oz. fruit juice (rich in potassium)
- ½ teaspoon honey or corn syrup
- Pinch table salt

In glass #2 put:

- 8 oz. water
- ¼ teaspoon baking soda

Drink from both glasses frequently.

Dislocations

• Pull gently with gradually increasing force away from the dislocated joint, and maintain the traction until it pops back into place. No hard snaps, please.

• Use pain medications, ice and Valium to prepare patient for relocation.

Ear problems

• Never put heat on a sore ear.

• Do not put drops in your ear if the ear drum has just ruptured (blood from the ear canal), or if you know a previous ear drum rupture has not healed.

• When using ear drops, err on the heavy side! It is OK to fill the ear canal and then put cotton in the ear.

Eye injuries

• Most eye injuries (flash or sunburn, lacerations, abrasions, foreign bodies) heal in 24-48 hours. Therefore do not use the anesthetic eyedrops more than 3 or 4 times. Use radio to obtain further medical advice if severe pain persists.

• With a visible foreign body, remove it by first anesthetizing the eye using tetracaine drops, and then use a wet Q-Tip to wipe it out. You must then patch the eye.

• Eye infections and injuries heal faster and more comfortably if patched for 24 hours.

• Wear glasses to keep wind off an injured or infected eye.

• If an injury of the eye occurs that is obviously a puncture or cut to the globe of the eye, patch it lightly. No pressure at all. Begin Ciloxan, and use radio to obtain help.

• If eyes do not move evenly after face or head injury, get help as soon as possible.

• If an injured eye looks cloudy or very dilated, seek medical help immediately.

GI problems

• Constipation – the most common gastrointestinal problem – is not good! Do not be afraid to take an enema kit and clean your insides if needed.

• Most vomiting is caused by the body's desire to rid the stomach of its content. If it goes on and on for hours, that is not good. You must start rehydrating and putting electrolytes back in. Stopping vomiting for illness is similar to stopping it for seasickness. Read section on dehydration.

• Diarrhea is as bad as vomiting. You lose a lot of important material needed by your body. If you think it is infection ("tourista"), use Cipro 500mg twice a day for no more than 3 days or Septra DS, one tablet twice a day for 7 days, to kill the bacteria. And be sure to replace with electrolyte package.

• If hemorrhoid or painful bump develops, try to push it back inside the rectal muscle and keep it squeezed in. Don't wait.

• Itchy rectum is usually caused by a fungus when one is sitting in warm areas and moisture lingers in the creases. Use an antifungal cream for quick relief.

Heart fluttering or skipping

• Not all irregular or funny heart beat rhythms are bad, but take action when noticed.

• If there is no pain, no light-headedness, decrease your stimulation. Stop caffeine, get out of sun, rest, cool down.

• If there is chest pain, shortness of breath or dizziness, consider asking for help or seek medical advice. Nitroglycerine spray for chest pain is appropriate. Also take one full strength aspirin immediately.

• If ankles are very swollen and feeling bloated, please decrease all salts. Plain drinking water, minimal foods, especially sweets, and rest. One or two ounces of liquor orally will often start the drying out period.

Sore throat

• Cepastat lozenges will relieve a sore throat or tickle that causes a cough. Use cherry flavor (pediatric strength, because unlike orange, they produce no stomach upset) as often as needed.

• Dr. Amsler's Gargle: crush an aspirin, a pinch of bicarbonate of soda and a vitamin C pill and mix in warm water. Gargle and swallow every 2 hours. (Alternative is one Alka-Seltzer gargled every 2 hours and swallowed.)

• Zinc lozenges, especially with vitamin C, are very effective for colds and sore throat. Suck on 8-10 the first day. Often not needed on second day.

Sprains, strains, contusions and fractures

• Old-time doctors diagnosed bone fractures without X-rays. If an injury (a) is trauma induced, (b) shows point tenderness and (c) is swollen, treat it as a fracture. This allows you to err on the safe side.

• If it's a hand fracture, immobilize it in position of function (as if holding a baseball).

• Fractured ribs feel better with a rib belt, but never sleep with it on.

• Ace wraps are properly and comfortably applied at ⅓ - ½ maximum tension.

Tendon laceration
• Diagnose a tendon laceration by looking for weakness against pressure or an extremity that just won't work.
• Temporary treatment: Splint or wrap in position of comfort. Seek medical attention within 7-10 days (maximum) for proper repair.

Urinary tract problems
• Painless bleeding in the urine can be bad. Start on an antibiotic immediately to stop the infection.
• Severe pain with bleeding usually indicates a kidney stone. Take pain medication and huge quantities of liquids. Plan on knowing pain as never before, but it goes away quickly.
• Never go offshore for extended trips without a catheter. If you are unable to urinate, you will have marvelous stories to tell.

Medications and supplements

Pain and anti-inflammatory drugs and their proper use
• Aspirin and non-steroid anti-inflammatory drugs (NSAID) such as Motrin, Advil, and Aleve have a very similar effect. If truly allergic (not just upset stomach) to aspirin or NSAID, do not take the other.
• Acetaminophen (Tylenol) is an excellent pain medication if taken by itself to maximum strength (1,000mg). Alcohol and acetaminophen do NOT mix and can produce liver problems.
• For moderate pain, take acetaminophen and an NSAID. This combination is just as powerful as Tylenol with Codeine (Tylenol 3) without affecting your thinking process. If codeine makes you nauseous, Hydrocodone products, even though related, often do not have similar effect.

Antibiotics
• Carry two different antibiotics, one from List #1 and one from List #2.
List #1
     Penicillins (Amoxicillin)
     Sulfa (Septra DS)
     Erythromycins (Erythromycin)
List #2
     Cephalosporins (Keflex)
     Quinolones (Cipro)
• If no allergies exist, my best recommendation is Amoxicillin 500mg (3 times a day) and Cipro 500mg (twice a day).
• Avoid sun when on antibiotics. Tetracycline can cause especially strong reaction to sun exposure.

Vitamins

• Strongly suggested! Increased stress burns up vitamin B, increased sun exposure creates free radicals, etc.

• I recommend an antioxidant, multivitamin package that has emphasis on trace minerals, and vitamins E, C and B.

• Theragran-M is very good if extra vitamins C and E are taken.

Anti-motion sickness drugs

See Figure 28.1, compiled by Charles Oman, courtesy of *Cruising World*

NOTE: The following items marked "OTC" are available over the counter; those marked "Rx" require a prescription.

Allergy and cold preparations

• CLARITIN-D (loratadine 5mg & pseudoephedrine 120mg) (Rx) – Use for watery nasal discharge and congestion. Will help decrease allergy symptoms. This is a non-sedating antihistamine.

• AFRIN NASAL SPRAY (oxymetazoline) (OTC) – Temporary relief of nasal congestion associated with colds, hay fever and sinusitis. Do not use for more than 3 consecutive days.

• BENADRYL 25mg (diphenhydramine) (OTC) – A strong antihistamine used for runny nose, itchy watery eyes and hives. CAUTION: THIS MEDICINE USUALLY CAUSES SLEEPINESS. It can be used to induce sleep. (See under "Insomnia.")

• LORCET 10/650 (hydrocodone 10mg/acetaminophen 650mg) (Rx) – Take ¼ to ½ pill every 6 hours to suppress a bad cough. (See under "Pain Medications.")

• CEPASTAT LOZENGES and ZINC LOZENGES with VITAMIN C (OTC) – For coughs and sore throats. (See under medical tips for "sore throat.")

Ear medications

• AMERICAINE (benzocaine otic drops) (OTC) – Place 4 drops in painful ear every 3-4 hours as needed to control ear pain.

• CORTISPORIN OTIC (polymyxin, neomycin, hydrocortisone) (Rx) – Place 4 drops in infected ear 4 times a day to control infection (swollen canal or pus type discharge).

Eye medications

• SALINE EYEWASH (OTC) – Use as an eyewash to remove dirt or foreign material. Use as frequently as desired to moisten dry, irritated eyes.

• TETRACAINE HYDROCHLORIDE 0.5% (Rx) – Place 2 drops in eye to anesthetize it. Use when eye is scratched or when foreign material stuck on eye. Use prior to removing a foreign body to block pain.

• OVAL EYE PADS (OTC) – To cover an injured eye. Covering any injury to the eye generally allows the most rapid healing.

• CILOXAN 0.3% (ciprofloxacin ophthalmic drops) (Rx) – Use these drops for every severe eye injury where the globe has been opened or penetrated or for eye infection.

Heart

• NITROLINGUAL SPRAY (nitroglycerine) (Rx) – Use for angina (chest/heart pain). Very effective when sprayed under tongue. A moderate headache can develop, which is normal. Don't forget to see a doctor once you reach shore to check your heart. Strongly recommend calling on radio for medical advice.

Immunizations

• For local sailing, be sure your tetanus is up-to-date. Usually you should re-immunize every 10 years. For long-distance travel, consult with your physician and ask the Center for Disease Control (Atlanta) about special needs for your selected destinations.

Insomnia/nervousness

• VALIUM 2mg (diazepam) (Rx) – Use for anxiety. DO NOT USE WITH ALCOHOL. May be used for seizure. Can be used for insomnia.

• BENADRYL 25mg (diphenhydramine) (OTC) – A very good and safe, nonaddictive medication for insomnia. Adding 1 Tylenol is a good way to increase the effective strength of Benadryl to aid in sleep.

Pain medications

• TYLENOL 500mg (acetaminophen) (OTC) – Take 2 pills every 4 hours for pain or fever. Excellent for headache and general achiness. DO NOT USE WITH ALCOHOL.

• MOTRIN 800mg (ibuprofen) (Rx or OTC) – Take 1 pill 3 times a day with food. Do not take on empty stomach. This may be combined with acetaminophen or hydrocodone for increased pain relief and inflammation control. DO NOT TAKE WITH ASPIRIN IN YOUR SYSTEM (8 hours as a minimum).

• LORCET 10/650 (hydrocodone 10mg/acetaminophen 650mg) (Rx) – Take 1 pill every 4-6 hours for severe pain. Do not give for head injuries. Use cautiously if sensitive to codeine. CAUTION – CAN CAUSE DROWSINESS.

Rectal

• TUCKS PADS (witch hazel 50%, glycerine 10%) (OTC) – Use as a rectal or vaginal wipe or compress for irritation. Maximum 6 times per day.

• ANUSOL HC SUPPOSITORIES (hydrocortisone) (Rx) – Use 1 suppository 3 times a day for hemorrhoids and anal/rectal irritation.

Seasickness (Also see Figure 28.1, listing anti-motion sickness drugs)

• SEASICK BANDS (OTC) – For many, this is a miracle. Wearing a band on each wrist can be very effective for all types of motion sickness and nausea of pregnancy.

Figure 28.1 - Anti-Motion Sickness Drugs

Generic Name Brand Name (Manufacturer)	Form (OTC/Rx)	Duration Of Action
Dimenhydrinate		
Dramamine (Searle)	tablet (OTC)	4-6 hr
	liquid (OTC)	4-6 hr
	injection (Rx)	4.6 hr
Dramamine (Richardson)	chewable tab (OTC)	4-6 hr
Gravol (Homer)	timed release	6 hr
	capsule; (OTC: B&C)	6 hr
	suppository (OTC: B&C)	6 hr
Meclizine HCl		
Bonine (Pfizer)	chewable tablet (OTC)	6-12 hr
Antivert (Roerig)	tablet (Rx)	6-12 hr
Meclizine (Geneva)	tablet (OTC)	6-12 hr
Cinnarizine		
Stugeron (Janssen)	tablet (OTC: B)	6-12 hr
Cyclizine		
Marezine (Burroughs)	capsule; (OTC)	4-6 hr
	injection (Rx)	4-6 hr
Scopolamine HBR		
Kwells (Nicholas)	tablet (OTC: UK&B)	4-6 hr
Transdermal Scopolamine		
Transderm-Scop (CIBA)	skin patch (Rx, OTC: B&C)	2-3 days
Scopolamine HBR Dextroamphetamine		
Scopolamine + Dexedrine (SKF)	scop + dex tablets (Rx)	4-6 hr
Promethazine		
Phenergan (Wyeth)	tablet (Rx)	6-12 hr
	suppository (Rx)	6-12 hr
	injection (Rx)	6-12 hr
Promethazine & Ephedrine		
Phenergan + Ephedrine (Wyeth)	phenergan + ephedrine (tablets)(Rx)	6-12 hr

OTC = over the counter   Rx = by prescription only
OTC (B&C) = OTC in Bermuda & Canada   OTC (UK&B) = OTC In UK & Bermuda

• DRAMAMINE (dimenhydrinate) (OTC) – Very good for motion sickness, but most people need so much they fall asleep.

• SCOPOLAMINE 0.3mg & DEXEDRINE 5mg (Rx) – According to the US Navy fliers, this combination is #1 to eliminate symptoms of seasickness. Scopolamine 0.3mg: Take 1 or 2 every 6 hours; Dexedrine 5 mg: Take 1 or 2 every 6 hours.

• PROMETHAZINE 25mg & EPHEDRINE 25mg (Rx) – US Navy fliers said this was second best. Promethazine 25mg: Take 1 every 6 hours; Ephedrine 25mg: Take 1 every 6 hours.

Skin

• NIZORAL (ketoconazole cream 2%) (Rx) – To be used for skin fungus. Very good for athlete's foot, jock itch, etc. Use anywhere skin folds on itself and itchy, red skin is present. Very good between buttocks after sitting in wet pants ("rail tail").

• ZINC OXIDE (OTC) – A thick white ointment that sticks to everything, blocks all sun to area and is used to seal off an abrasion. Keep lots of this handy. It even keeps the area you sit on from becoming raw when wet with salt- or freshwater for an extended time.

• WESTCORT CREAM (hydrocortisone valerate 0.2%) (Rx) – This is a steroid cream for skin inflammation (not for infections). Apply thin layer and rub in 2-3 times a day. Exceptionally good for small areas of sunburn such as forehead, nose, lips and chin. Also excellent for itching from poison ivy and bug bites.

• BACITRACIN (neomycin, polymyxin) (OTC) – A very good ointment for burns, infection in cuts, abrasions and ripped finger- and toenails. Put bandage over treated area.

Stomach, constipation and diarrhea

• MYLANTA, MAALOX or GAVISCON (OTC) – Calcium or aluminum hydroxide used to neutralize stomach acid, heartburn, stomach burn. Can be used frequently; often helpful with seasickness.

• TAGAMET 400mg (cimetidine) (OTC) – Use for stomach ulcer or heartburn or stomach pain that does not improve with MYLANTA. Good for heartburn when sleeping.

• DULCOLAX 5 mg (bisacodyl) (Rx) – Use for constipation. Comes in pill or suppository form. Remember to refrigerate suppositories.

• LOMOTIL (diphenoxylate 2.3mg and atropine 0.025mg) (Rx) – Use in addition to fluids and electrolyte replacement for diarrhea. This is an opiate type product and addictive if used for weeks at a time.

Miscellaneous supplies

• Ace wraps	• 4" x 4" telfa pads	• First aid book
• Antiseptic solution	• Sunburn spray (topical ointment)	• 2" adhesive tape
• Assorted Band-Aids	• Vitamins (see Medication Use)	

Water treatment – methods

Heat. Boil water for 10+ minutes. Add a pinch of table salt to each quart of boiled

Figure 28.2 - Offshore Yacht Crew Medical Information

Crew Member Name: _____Date:_____

Age: _____ Weight:_____ Height:_____Blood Type:_____

Address_____

Phone number of medical professionals familiar with your health and history:

Doctor:_____Dentist:_____

Do you have any known chronic illness or disability, or any medical problems that require regular attention or medication? If so, list condition(s) and control methods in use:

Do you currently take any medications? If so, please list:

Please list any allergies:

Food:_____ Medication:_____

Other:_____

What type of allergic reaction do you have?

Do you now or have you in the past had any of the following:

Heart trouble?	Lung trouble?
Stomach ulcers?	Appendectomy?
Gallstones?	Kidney stones?
A hernia?	Dentures?

This information is strictly confidential. In an emergency, it will be used for planning and for radio consultation if assistance is required.

water. When cool, pour from one clean container to another several times to aerate.

Chlorine. Add chlorine bleach per the following table:

Available Chlorine Level in Chlorine Bleach	Drops Added to 1 Quart Clear WaterQuart	Drops Added to 1 Quart Cloudy Water
1 percent	10	20
4-6 percent	2	4
7-10 percent	1	2
Unknown	10	20

Mix thoroughly. Let stand for 30 minutes. A slight chlorine odor should be noted. If chlorine odor is not noted, repeat dosage and wait an additional 15 minutes.

Iodine

Using Tincture of Iodine (2%), add 5 drops to 1 quart of clear water or 10 drops to 1 quart of cloudy water. Mix and let stand for 30 min. (See Chapter 13 for larger quantities.)

Forms for prescription medications

For some forms for prescription medications, see Appendix B.

Offshore dental first aid

This section is from "Offshore Dental First Aid" by Fred J. Botta, DDS, of Elm Grove, WI. It is included with the permission of Dr. Botta, who has embarked on his long-planned life of cruising to distant ports.

Dental First Aid Kit (usually available at a local pharmacy)
• 1 small mouth mirror
• 1 small tweezers
• 1 temporary filling placement instrument
• alcohol swabs (for cleaning instruments)
• cotton balls
• sterile gauze (2" x 2")
• small bottle of clove oil
• temporary filling material such as glass ionomer – a liquid and powder mix that is nonsedative but bonds to tooth surface
• Eugenol and zinc oxide – has sedative effect but does not bond as well
• pain reliever (as discussed in medical section)
• dental floss
• baking soda
• salt (½ teaspoon per ½ glass of water, for mouth rinsing)

Tooth knocked loose

1. Pain reliever if necessary; apply ice pack if swollen
2. Bite on sterile gauze if bleeding
3. Don't chew on injured area; it may make problem worse

Wisdom tooth pain
1. Rinse area vigorously with warm salt water
2. Take pain reliever, but never place directly on affected area
3. Brush and floss regularly
4. Frequently caused by wisdom tooth that does not have enough room to come in

Gumboil (or swelling in jaws)
1. Rinse area with warm salt water
2. Pain reliever if necessary
3. Ice packs to area
4. Don't use hot packs – will worsen situation

Canker sore
1. Rinse area vigorously
2. Apply baking soda to area frequently (don't place aspirin directly on site)

Bleeding gum
1. Rinse area vigorously
2. Apply baking soda to area frequently
3. If it won't stop, apply moist tea bag on area

Broken plate or bridge
1. Save all the pieces
2. Try to keep in mouth if possible
3. Don't try to repair plate or bridge yourself. This will almost certainly lead to greater problems.

Teething pain
1. Cold objects, such as teething ring, help
2. Firm finger massages
3. Teething ointments available from pharmacy
4. Don't leave unsafe objects about that a child may want to place in mouth
5. Don't worry; many have come before you!

Baby teeth
1. Care for as adult teeth
2. Don't think they are not important. They maintain spacing needed by adult teeth.
3. In most cases, damage to baby teeth – if properly attended to – will not cause permanent damage.

Cracked tooth or fillings
1. If painful:

      a. Place on area: cotton soaked in clove oil then dried

      b. Take pain reliever of choice

      c. Dry tooth with cotton and place temporary filling material

2. If not painful:

      a. Clean and dry tooth

      b. Place temporary filling material

3. If swollen, place ice packs on area

4. Don't eat sweet, crunchy or hot foods

5. Don't place aspirin directly on gums or tooth. This will burn the tissue.

Tooth knocked out

1. Find tooth, rinse gently in warm water
2. Gently insert and hold tooth in socket
3. Pain reliever if necessary; ice pack if swollen
4. Bite on piece of sterile gauze if bleeding
5. See dentist as soon as possible. In most cases, the tooth can be reimplanted if done within 24 hours.

Bitten tongue or lip

Apply direct pressure to the bleeding area with a clean cloth. If swelling is present, apply cold compresses.

Objects wedged between teeth

Try to remove object with dental floss. Guide the floss carefully to avoid cutting the gum. Vigorously rinse. If not successful in removing the object, see a dentist at the first opportunity.

Possible fractured jaw

Immobilize the jaw by any means (handkerchief, neckerchief, towel). If swelling is present, apply cold compresses.

With any dental emergency, see a dentist when you reach port. Most dental problems can be avoided with good oral hygiene, healthy diet and regular checkups.

REFERENCES:

Peter Eastman, *Advanced First Aid Afloat*, 3rd Ed.

Michael Beilan, *Medical Emergencies At Sea*

Drs. John Bergan and Vincent Guzzetta, *Sailing and Yachting First Aid*

David Werner, *Where There Is No Doctor*

Murray Dickson, *Where There Is No Dentist*

Paul Gill, MD, *First Aid and Emergency Medicine Afloat: The Onboard Medical Handbook*

CHAPTER 29

DAMAGE CONTROL

Damage control includes all the emergency measures you can take to control a situation that threatens the safety of boat and/or crew. Those situations include fires, flooding, rig failures, and other instances where jury-rigging is needed to restore a boat's ability to proceed safely to its destination. Many damage control measures have already been addressed under steering, sails and engines.

Successful damage control requires a combination of materials and knowledge. Having damage control equipment such as fire extinguishers and patching material does little good if the crew doesn't know how to use that equipment effectively. Conversely, knowing how to control fires and floods won't help if needed materials are not on hand.

Fire. A fire at sea is one of the most dangerous challenges you can face. Flames and toxic smoke produced by combustion of many materials in and on a boat can form a deadly combination. They can spell sudden, swift disaster for both boat and crew.

The 2-minute rule. In a conducive environment, the intensity of a fire will double every 30 seconds. This is the basis for the "2-minute" rule for a boat fire: If you don't get it under control within two minutes, you've probably lost the battle. Thus, on discovering a fire, the crew's speedy response is crucial. *Instant action is essential.* The crew must know what fire-fighting equipment is available, where it is located, how to use it, and which agent to use in the given situation. They must also be prepared to act promptly, without waiting for directions.

Components of every fire. For a fire to start and be sustained, four components are needed: fuel (the material that burns), heat (sufficient to raise the fuel to the point at which combustion occurs), oxygen (the gas that combines with fuel in the combustion process), and the chemical chain reaction that converts fuel to ash and smoke. A fire can be extinguished by eliminating one or more of these four elements.

Four classes of fires. Fires have been separated into four classes, based on the fuel or ignition source. The agent(s) that can be used to fight a fire depend on the fire class.

Class A fires involve normal combustible materials such as wood, fabric, plastics and paper – fires that produce ashes. They can be fought with water, which works primarily by cooling the fuel below its combustion point, or fought with various chemical agents that interrupt the combustion process. Some fire extinguishers are suitable for Class A fires, and will be so labeled. Often an effective approach to a Class A fire is to throw the burning material overboard.

Class B fires involve liquid fuels such as petroleum products, some cleaning agents and solvents, and alcohol. Burning cooking fuels such as propane and compressed natural gas (CNG) are also in this class. The fire is sustained by the vapors generated when the liquid fuel's temperature is raised above its characteristic "flash point"; many flash points are near or below common ambient temperatures. Water is ineffective against these fires, since it tends to float the burning liquid on its surface and spread it. Extinguishers that eliminate the fire's oxygen supply, cool the liquid below its flash point or impede the chemical reaction of combustion are more effective.

Class C fires are those in which electrical circuits are the source of heat that starts the combustion. A short circuit can cause an abrupt outbreak of fire with little warning. Fires caused by overloaded circuits generally develop more slowly. They frequently announce themselves with characteristic odors before they reach the actual combustion stage. Cutting off the power supply is the mandatory first step in fighting any Class C fire. As long as the power is on, the fire will be reignited, and higher voltage (e.g., 110-volt AC circuits) can even be conducted by some fire-fighting agents and cause shock injury to the extinguisher operator. Once power is off, what remains is usually a Class A fire which can be fought with appropriate agents. (Water, though effective, is a poor choice because it will cause further damage to electrical circuitry.)

Class D fires involve burning metals such as magnesium or pyrotechnic materials such as distress flares. They are extremely dangerous because no common extinguishing agents will work on these fires. The only course of action is to jettison the burning material, then fight the Class A and/or B fires it might have ignited. This is another reason to be positive all pyrotechnic material is stowed in isolated but easily accessible locations.

Fire-fighting agents. Common fire-fighting agents include water, which can be used on Class A fires (and Class C after the power has been turned off). It will also extinguish an alcohol fire by diluting and cooling the fuel until it can no longer sustain combustion. Be aware, however, that applying water to a large pool of alcohol will initially complicate the situation. Alcohol is lighter than water, so it floats atop the water and spreads out as the water flows, extending the area of burning surface fuel.

A second common agent is sodium bicarbonate, an effective agent for Class B and C fires. It is the agent usually found in extinguishers labeled "B:C". A more complex dry chemical agent such as monoammonium phosphate works by interrupting the combustion process at the molecular level, so it can extinguish Class A fires as well as Classes B and C. Extinguishers containing these agents are labeled "A:B:C" to indicate their usefulness against all three classes. The effectiveness of these dry chemical agents comes at a price. They are extremely messy. It's very difficult to clean up the powder that remains after the fire is out. Also, most chemical agents have a corrosive effect on electronic circuitry, especially when remaining traces of powder become moist as they absorb water from the atmosphere.

An effective agent that has been around for a long time is carbon dioxide (CO_2). It is a heavy gas that stops a fire by cooling it to some extent; more important, it displaces oxygen-laden air. Without an oxygen supply, the fire dies. CO_2 works best in enclosed spaces where the blanket of gas is not swept away or disturbed by drafts and breezes. If oxygen-bearing air reaches the hot fuel through a disruption of the CO_2 blanket, the fire can reignite. Although not toxic, CO_2 has a suffocating effect on people and animals that can be deadly. One big advantage of CO_2 is its cleanliness. It dissipates in the atmosphere and leaves virtually no residue, so it's well suited for use on electronic and electrical equipment and around the galley, where food may be exposed. Another disadvantage of CO_2 is that it takes a large, heavy container (extinguisher) to hold a useful amount of compressed CO_2 gas.

Foam extinguishers are used on many commercial craft, but are seldom seen on yachts. Intended for Class B fires, foam works by excluding oxygen with a blanket that is less easily disturbed than CO_2. It leaves an enormous mess.

Halon is another agent applied in gaseous form that is highly effective in disrupting the chemical reaction involved in combustion. It is clean and nontoxic unless subjected to extremely high temperatures, but as a member of the chloro-fluorocarbon family its use has adverse impact on the earth's ozone layer. Hence its production has been phased out, and the cost of remaining supplies has escalated. While available, Halon is best reserved for use in the galley and around valuable electronics, where its cleanliness offers a clear advantage, and in the engine room where dry powder can destroy an engine.

New, environmentally friendly agents are being developed by the fire protection industry to replace Halon, and several are now on the market. One, FE-241, is an efficient agent that has only a slight ozone depletion effect, but it is toxic. It's available in fixed systems for automatic or remote operation in unoccupied spaces such as enclosed engine compartments. Another, FM-200, is a bit less efficient but has no ozone effect and is nontoxic so it has broader applications.

Extinguishers empty fast! Whatever type of extinguisher is employed, most people are surprised to learn how little time it takes to completely discharge one of the small, 5-10 pound units commonly carried aboard a boat. If applied in a steady stream, most will empty in 30 seconds or less. Applied properly – with a sweeping motion aimed at the base of a fire – and in shorter bursts, the typical extinguisher may have a one-minute life. All the more reason that the crew must be prepared to act swiftly and catch a fire before it has a chance to get established or grow.

High risk areas. Some parts of a cruising boat present higher risks of fire and should be protected accordingly. The engine space should be equipped with an installed automatic extinguishing system. Designed to discharge if ambient temperatures exceed a set limit (typically 175° F), these units are ideal for potentially catastrophic situations created by a ruptured fuel line or shorted alternator output cable. Since they generally operate in relatively confined spaces, their extinguishing agents can be exceptionally effective. The batteries, if not located within the engine space, merit special consideration. Accidental overcharging can cause batteries to generate significant quantities of highly flammable (potentially explosive) hydrogen gas. Assure adequate ventilation, easy access and proximity to a good extinguisher.

The galley is another high risk area for fires. Propane sniffers to detect fuel leaks, good ventilation, meticulous observation of safe operating procedures and ready access to an extinguisher are essential. The extinguisher must be located where it can be retrieved without having to reach across the stove. Small chemically treated towels/blankets now on the market offer a highly effective way to combat a galley fire. Keep one of these devices handy near the galley to snuff a potentially dangerous flame-up.

The electrical panel is a common spot for wires to overheat, and connections behind the panel can be loosened by seaway movement and engine vibration, leading to shorted circuits. Clean, neat, rational wiring with tight connections, good housekeeping and conservative circuit design can minimize the risk, but it's still prudent to have easy access to the back of the panel and to keep an extinguisher nearby.

Boat maneuvers may help. In fighting a fire, maneuvering the boat can sometimes help. Changing course or speed may reduce the draft that fans a fire, and can also control the direction in which the flames may spread. A course change can affect the direction of blowing smoke, making it easier to find and fight the flames. Since many plastic materials in boats today can produce toxic fumes when burning, keep smoke away from the crew, if possible.

Finally, remember that a fire can change from a small problem to a life-threatening crisis with astonishing speed. Any fire warrants preparing to send a Mayday call and starting to prepare to abandon ship. If there are other vessels nearby, let them know about the situation immediately. They may be able to help if your resources prove inadequate.

Flooding. A second type of damage requiring control is one that produces flooding. A primary tenet of good seamanship is to keep the water outside the boat. A corollary says – if any water gets inside, get rid of it as soon as possible. It's important to distinguish between a leak and a flood. A leak exists when water comes in at a rate that is less than your capacity to remove it. A flood occurs when the water comes in as fast as or faster than you can pump it out. A leak is a nuisance that needs to be corrected promptly, but a flood can be life threatening. In a flooding situation, the first objective of damage control is to turn the flood into a leak (i.e., get the flow under control). The second is to fix the leak.

First steps. As with any general emergency, the first step in a flooding situation is to sound the alarm. Make sure all crew members are aware of the problem and ready to help cope with it. Then start pumping with all available capacity. If the water level starts to fall, you have a leak and can proceed at a measured pace to find and correct the source. If the water level does not fall, you have an emergency, and rapid action will be essential to save the boat.

While pumping, stay alert for pump malfunctions. Electric pumps are easily clogged by the debris that is present in all but the clenest bilges. Clogging can quickly lead to overheating and destruction of the pump or its motor just when it's most needed. Manual pumps are less prone to clogging, and the operator can usually detect obstructions quickly because the pump becomes more difficult to work. Don't overestimate the capacity of manual or electric bilge pumps – and don't underestimate the effort required to remove a substantial quantity of water with a manual pump or a bucket.

In an emergency, remember that the raw water circulating pump on the engine can be rigged to work as an auxiliary bilge pump. Close its sea cock, disconnect the pump's intake hose from the sea cock and immerse it in bilge water. The engine will then be drawing its coolant from the bilge and discharging it overboard through the exhaust system. It doesn't move a lot of water, but every bit helps. Using the engine to pump bilge water involves significant risks. If the suction line draws air or gets clogged with debris, destruction of the raw water pump and consequent overheating of the engine can occur. Other pumps, such as shower sump pumps, also can be rigged for emergency service.

Finding the water source. Once pumping has begun, your next task is to find the source of the water. It could come from a leak in the internal freshwater system. The simplest way to test this is to taste the water. If it's freshwater (and you're sailing somewhere other than the Great Lakes), it's probably coming from a water tank and the maximum volume is that of your tank capacity. Turn off the pressure water pump, and inspect the system. Start with the tanks themselves, and trace the piping to the pump and from there to each outlet – looking for loose fittings, ruptures or disconnects. If it's raining heavily, another source of freshwater in the hull could be a disconnected deck drain.

Being very familiar with the boat and its systems – where the hoses run, sea cock locations and ways to gain access to areas of the hull normally concealed behind cabinetry – will pay big dividends when locating the source of water entering the hull. Many boats that have been lost to flooding have gone down, in part at least, because the crew simply could not find or gain access to the place where the water was coming in.

Floodwater can also come from other parts of the plumbing system, including generator and engine raw water cooling systems. Every below-waterline hull opening should be protected with a sea cock, and closing all sea cocks should stop any water that is coming in through the attached piping and hoses. It's not uncommon for a hose to come loose from a sea cock. This is a result of vibration, sea motion, corrosion failure of hose clamps, or being struck by loose gear as the boat rolls. Closing the sea cock should stop the flood. Very rarely, a sea cock itself will fail, leaving an unprotected opening in the hull. It is for this contingency that a tapered softwood plug of the appropriate size must be stowed immediately adjacent to each through-hull fitting. The plug can be hammered into the broken sea cock to effectively close the opening.

Flooding can be the result of siphoning through an immersed hull opening. This is especially common in head and bilge pump discharge lines not protected by anti-siphon fittings, or on which the anti-siphon fittings have become clogged. Head discharge lines generally terminate low on the hull and are protected with sea cocks that can be closed to stop any siphoning. Bilge pump discharges are frequently at or slightly above the at-rest waterline, and may not be equipped with a sea cock. If such an unprotected outlet is immersed when the boat heels under sail, it's a prime candidate for siphoning. Check this by tacking the boat. If the flooding stops, water may have been siphoning through a discharge immersed on one tack but above water on the other. Periodic checks and cleaning of anti-siphon/vacuum breaker fittings will prevent this.

Several other sources of water inflow that can attain flooding proportions include propeller shaft failures (damage to shaft log, stuffing box or seal, or loss of the shaft itself) and damage at the rudder post (seal failure, loss of post). These can usually be controlled with plugs or reinforced wrappings of canvas or sailcloth. While seldom reaching true flood volumes, water coming down hawse pipes in high seas can drain into the bilge and create astonishing water levels that appear to be a flood.

Perhaps the most serious and frightening cause of flooding is a breach of the hull's integrity, either from collision with another object or from violent sea action during a storm. Fortunately, the likelihood of this is extremely low. Nevertheless, key first steps are the same: Start pumping and locate the source, then work to reduce or eliminate the inflow by stuffing the hole from inside or outside.

Plugging the hole. Once you've identified a flood source, there are many damage control measures that can turn the flood into a leak and then stop the leak. Closing sea cocks or plugging ruptured lines or broken hoses may stop the flow. Vital hoses can be put into emergency service. Wrap them with duct tape, reinforced with wrappings of canvas or sailcloth and backed up further with tight windings of light line. Hull ruptures can be stuffed with plugs. Wind rags around them if necessary to get a better, snugger fit. Larger holes may be stuffed with several plugs, again wrapped with rags to fill gaps between plugs. If the damage is close to the waterline, you may be able to maneuver the boat so the damaged area is above water at least part of the time. Applying an external barrier, such as a collision mat, sail or awning over the outside of the holed area may substantially reduce flooding and buy time in which to devise an internal patch.

Once the flooding is under control, the emergency is relieved. Now there's time to devise more durable repairs. Piping or hoses can be replaced or re-routed to perform essential functions at the expense of less important roles. Stronger patches can be devised, using (for example) cockpit cushions as a gasket against the inner side of a damaged section of hull. Back them up with a strong piece of plywood, like a locker lid from under a bunk. Hold everything tightly in place with shores such as dinghy oars jammed between the plywood and a strong hull part. Underwater epoxy or water-activated fiberglass can be applied to holes, broken piping or damaged fittings to seal them or reduce leakage to a bare minimum. Sealants such as 3M's 5200® can be applied under patches that can be secured in place on wood or fiberglass hulls using drywall or deck screws.

Damage control measures do not have to provide permanent repairs. They simply enable the boat to proceed safely, perhaps at reduced speed, to a safe harbor where final corrective actions can be accomplished. Damage control repairs are never as strong as the original equipment, so all such repairs must be inspected frequently to make sure they're holding up. This is especially true of hull patches, which tend to loosen as the boat works in a seaway.

Effective response to a flooding situation is possible only if your boat carries a suitable kit of damage control materials. If space permits, stow these in a dedicated locker – so the equipment and supplies do not go missing or get "borrowed". Situations in which the damage control gear is needed seem to occur most frequently at night, in storms or when power has been lost, so it's helpful to paint the tools bright orange. Outfit each with a lanyard. You'll want to make your own list of materials needed for your damage control kit, but the list below provides a good start.

Figure 29.1 - Damage Control Equipment

☐ Boards for covering any large ports
☐ Two 12x16" plywood pieces for patching holes
☐ Sturdy self-tapping screws for fiberglass/aluminum boats, deck screws or drywall screws for fiberglass/wood boats
☐ Heavy duty screwdriver
☐ Hatchet, sharpened and preserved, with lanyard attached
☐ Hammer and drifts, with lanyards
☐ Hand drill and assorted drill bits
☐ Two hacksaws, with six blades each (plus carbide blades for rod rigging)
☐ Underwater epoxy
☐ Water-activated fiberglass material (medical supply stores sell this for making casts)
☐ Two tubes of caulking/sealant that will cure under water (such as 3M 5200)
☐ Two caulking guns
☐ Collision mat of synthetic awning material about 4x4' with wide hems and heavy grommets at each corner, into which are rove 10-15' lanyards
☐ Shoring material, preferably at least one 4x4" shore, 6-8' long (if stowage space is very limited, identify pieces of boat that can be used in an emergency)
☐ Six wood wedges that can be used to jam shoring tightly into position
☐ Six to eight spare tapered softwood plugs
☐ Duct tape
☐ Light nylon cord for lashings and seizings

Rigging failure. Another type of damage that demands prompt controlling action is a rigging failure. Spar collapse is usually preceded by failure in one or more elements of the standing rig, so swift response to a standing rig casualty is essential to prevent loss of the spar.

First step. The first step is always to maneuver the boat to reduce or eliminate the stress previously handled by the failed element. If the headstay parts, bear off to put the wind aft, drop the main to ease its load on the mast but keep all headsail halyards tight. Backstay failure calls for prompt heading up, sheeting the main in hard and furling headsails. Shroud or spreader failures require a tack or jibe (whichever will be least stressful) to put the failed element on the lee side, where it will be under minimum load.

Next step. The next step is to devise a substitute for the failed element. Spare halyards make excellent temporary substitutes for broken shrouds or stays. Dinghy paddles and rigid boat hooks can replace broken spreaders. More durable repairs can be made with bulldog cable clamps to create new eyes at the ends of broken wires. A length of anchor chain can be attached to a shroud or stay shortened by repairs to make it long enough to reach the turnbuckle. Multiple turns of small diameter braided nylon or Kevlar line can form Spanish windlasses to tension a rig in place of a fractured turnbuckle. As with all jury rigging situations, creativity is the key.

If a spar is damaged short of complete failure, it can often be splinted and sufficiently reinforced at the weak area to permit the passage to continue. Booms can be splinted with spare propeller shafts, spinnaker poles and boat hooks, all held in place with wrappings of line and wire. Analyze the stress situation carefully to ensure proper placement of the splinting pieces. The splints should lie on the surfaces most subject to tension and compression. Damaged masts have been reinforced with splints cut from dinghy floorboards, wrapped with line and strips of sail and saturated with epoxy.

Mast failures sometimes occur while tacking. This usually happens when lee shrouds, which are hanging slack, disconnected from the end of the spreader. When the boat tacks, they're unable to support the upper mast section and it folds over somewhere near the spreaders. A properly tuned rig doesn't allow too much slack in lee shrouds, but if the shrouds are loose, a quick look aloft before tacking may avert a mast failure.

Dismasting. Probably the worst-case scenario for rig failure is being dismasted. This may result from a parted stay or shroud, or in truly extraordinary circumstances, a severe knockdown or a rollover. If conditions permit, the first step should be to determine how much of the rig can be salvaged. If possible, recover spars, wire, sails and line for a jury rig. If the damaged spar is inflicting further significant damage to the boat, there's little alternative to cutting it loose and abandoning it. Because that means the loss of very valuable resources, it should be done only if absolutely necessary to the safety of boat and crew.

Should it become necessary, this step will be easier if each leg of the standing rig contains at least one easily removed toggle pin. Having the proper tools (high quality cable cutters, tungsten carbide hacksaw blades for rod rigging, appropriately sized drifts and a hammer) in the damage control kit will also facilitate this difficult task.

Jury-rigged masts. Boats have sailed around Cape Horn using jury-rigged masts, with spinnaker poles, booms and even oars lashed to mast stubs to form a primitive sailing rig. Headsails have been set with the tack forward, the clew hoisted to the top of a jury mast and the head trimmed all the way aft, sometimes shortened by having a big fat knot tied in the upper panels of the sail. They may look strange. They probably won't go to windward very efficiently, if at all. But such jury rigs can get a passagemaker out of a jam and safely into a harbor where proper repairs can be made.

Think about the unthinkable. Successful jury rigging is largely a matter of ingenuity and forethought. Using resources in new ways is the hallmark of an accomplished jury-rigger. Before the need arises, you can get a good head start by thinking about the unthinkable. During quiet night watches or dull afternoons broad reaching on gentle breezes, think about how you'd cope with a major equipment failure. How, specifically, would you rig a jury steering system, and what materials do you have that would be useful? If the engine raw water or refrigeration cooling pump were to fail, what do you have that could be used to push or pull water through the lines, and how would you plumb it into the system? If an accidental jibe carries away the traveler blocks, how could you build a substitute system? Contemplating such situations in advance and developing a strategy for handling them will make them far less awesome if they or similar problems eventually occur.

In any jury-rig situation, start with an inventory of your resources – pumps, piping, blocks, lines, shackles, electrical wiring. Next, identify new ways to put these parts together to do what's needed. One Caribbean 1500 Rallier experienced an engine raw water pump failure. This meant he had neither a propulsion engine nor a way to charge his batteries. He found an AC electric motor onboard that he could couple (with some tubing and a pair of hose clamps) to a portable pump. He plumbed this pump into the engine cooling system (more clamps, tubing and pipe fittings). By running the AC pump off the inverter, he could operate the engine. That generated sufficient DC power to charge the batteries and also keep the inverter output sufficient to produce the needed AC power for the pump. It wasn't a pretty lash-up, but it worked! Another boat installed the deck wash-down pump as a substitute for the refrigeration cooling pump. In the first Rally, the boat I was on experienced complete failure of the gooseneck fitting. We removed the boom, stowed it on the foredeck and sailed the rest of the passage (over 500 miles) with a reef in the main that turned the first full-length batten into a flexible boom. We averaged almost 170 miles per day sailing with this jury boom.

Keep in mind that "If it still floats, it's still a boat," and there's a way to get it to a safe destination. Taking what you have and putting it together in a new way will get you to port – perhaps in the opposite direction from your original destination, but someplace where you can make repairs that will enable you to continue your journey.

The essence of good damage control is being prepared to act swiftly to extinguish a fire before it gets out of control, to find the source of water coming into the boat and use plugs/patches to reduce the flow, and to apply creativity to replace a failed component or system. Success requires both knowledge and materials, but inventiveness can often provide new solutions. Thinking about how one could respond to a challenge will make it easier. Keep a positive outlook. A sense of confidence in ultimate success can make the difference.

REFERENCES:
Nigel Calder, *Repair at Sea*
Tony Meisel, *Nautical Emergencies*
Sid Stapleton, *Emergencies at Sea*
John M. Waters, Jr., *A Guide to Small Boat Emergencies*

CHAPTER 30

SUMMARY AND CONCLUSIONS

Our starting point for this book was that, as a passagemaker, you can develop a number of coherent strategies to increase the likelihood of a successful, enjoyable voyage. Other strategies will help you cope with things that can go wrong while sailing long distances across blue waters. The goal is to help you make a passage without surprises. If the strategies for success are less than 100% effective, then the strategies for coping should help prepare skipper and crew to deal with any undesirable developments. Listed in a concise (perhaps deceptively easy) form, our strategies include these points:

Prepare yourself. Start with an awareness of essential differences between coastal cruising and passagemaking. Understand the implications those differences have for the boat, the crew, the degree of preparation required, and the operation of the boat.

Prepare the boat. Select and outfit the boat with care, mindful of specific needs for seaworthiness, crew accommodations, stowage and self-sufficiency.
- Take pains to get to know the boat intimately.
- Inspect the boat in detail from bow to stern, from keel to masthead.
- Trace out systems, locate pipes, hoses and cables.
- Verify the robustness of attachments, backing plates and structural connections.
- Explore nooks and crannies to which access is normally difficult or impossible.

Prepare yourself and your crew. In preparing yourself and your crew for a passage:
- Identify fears that lurk in your minds. Use them constructively to devise tactics that will reduce the risk of encountering the situations feared.
- Develop a reliable team that shares the workload and responsibilities, but remember that solid leadership by the skipper is the essential lubricant without which the voyaging machine cannot run smoothly. The team must be able to function even if the normal leadership is eroded by injury or illness.
- Choose your crew with the greatest care.
- Have an adequate number of crew, given the boat's accommodations, to operate

continuously even under stressful conditions. A blend of skills, interests and experience is usually best.

- Physical and emotional fitness are important, but training the crew to work as a team is paramount.
- Organize the crew into watches and establish standard ways to operate the boat. Consistency in the way actions are performed enhances safety and reduces confusion.
- Establish clearly defined internal and external watch responsibilities so the boat is always under the control of an alert, informed crew member.

Navigation. In the realm of navigation:
- Plan your voyage for the best route and best season. Wait for the weather; don't let the calendar drive decisions.
- Outfit the boat with reliable navigational equipment. Train the crew in its use.
- Follow routines that incorporate prudent navigational practices to minimize risk.

Communication. A good communication strategy can go a long way toward reducing a passagemaker's sense of isolation:
- Include both short range and long distance communication. This can provide today's voyager with information and support only dreamed of a few decades ago.
- Provide for receipt of weather forecasts, facsimile charts and satellite images to anticipate changing weather early.
- Consider use of e-mail and ham radio to keep in touch with friends and families.
- Use high frequency radio to gain direct access to shore-based professional guidance in a medical emergency.

Weather. The weather information available continues to grow as technology improves both quality and quantity of data. A sound weather strategy will take advantage of this trend, because weather affects so many aspects of a voyage:
- *Start early* in the planning process with a focused effort to understand weather patterns and the relationship between weather systems and sea conditions.
- Begin weather awareness well before departure. Continue it by routinely copying periodic forecasts, and assessing weather facsimile charts.
- Make local observations to stay up to date on changing conditions.
- Understand developing weather changes and use evolving patterns to advantage, or to minimize the impact of any adverse conditions.

Heavy weather. Concerns about heavy weather are among the commonest fears of passagemakers. The crew's confidence in their ability to handle heavy weather can be vastly increased by:
- Careful advance planning for potential bad weather.
- Detailed preparation of the boat for rough seas.
- Practicing the tactics and techniques available for coping with adverse weather.

Prevent systems failure. Preventing equipment and system failures beats having to correct those failures. Prevention includes:
- Observant, regular inspections of vital operating systems before and during the voyage to detect symptoms of impending breakdowns.

Medical preparedness. Medical preparedness includes:
- Having appropriate medical supplies aboard.
- Knowing any special crew needs.
- Including medical training among the crew's skills.
- Knowing how to obtain external guidance if a medical problem goes beyond the treatment capacity of those aboard.

Provisioning. Because a boat on a passage must be self-sufficient to a very high degree, careful planning is required to determine provisioning needs, which in turn are influenced by stowage space, refrigeration capacity and reliability, cooking facilities and fuels. Successful provisioning and stowage will:
- Provide adequate food for the whole voyage (with a reserve for emergencies).
- Stow food and other stores securely in a manner that facilitates retrieval.
- Minimize trash generated during the trip.
- Train the crew to keep the boat stowed neatly and to operate the stove and other galley appliances safely.

Crew safety. A strategy to assure crew safety throughout the passage carries a high priority. It includes:
- Carrying both personal and boat safety equipment.
- Ensuring that the entire crew knows how to use each piece of equipment.
- Compliance by all hands, without exception, with basic rules such as wearing and using safety harnesses and PFDs.
- Maintaining a conscious concern for safety aspects of every action during a passage. This reduces risk of injuries.

Sails. Sails are your primary source of propulsion. A strategy to select the best suit of sails for a passage has direct impact on your prospects for success. It includes:
- Sails suitable to serve across a range of expected wind conditions. (This extends to abnormally light as well as unusually heavy winds.)
- Reliable sail handling for quick setting, reducing and dousing of sails.
- Crew understanding of how to prevent flogging, overloading, or other abuse.

Dinghy; personal affairs. There are strategies to deal with peripheral considerations that will reduce stress during the trip and facilitate enjoyment after arrival. Plan for:
- Keeping in touch with a home base and managing personal affairs.
- Selecting and carrying a dinghy to provide transportation in distant harbors.

Coping with adversity. If, despite preventive measures, things go wrong during a voyage, the passagemaker has many established techniques for coping with adversity.

Know how to handle heavy weather. Well before conditions have deteriorated enough to create a "heavy weather" situation, good sail trimming tactics will keep a boat moving at its best speed consistent with crew comfort and safety. If the ride becomes uncomfortable, there's usually a sail trim adjustment that will make things better.

- When heavy weather develops, timely reduction of sail area will minimize risk to boat and crew.
- If the boat's design, the navigational situation and the crew's condition permit, active tactics such as working to weather under minimum sail or running off (perhaps with a drogue to limit speed) can be used.
- In other situations, it may be preferable to adopt passive tactics such as heaving to or deploying a sea anchor until the weather abates. Consider lying ahull under bare poles only as a last resort.
- Remember that a practiced, well organized crew and a properly outfitted, seaworthy boat can survive virtually all heavy weather scenarios.

Propulsion failures. Should the boat's propulsion systems fail, there are tactics to cope with the situation.

- Sail damage can be repaired sufficiently to get the boat to port, provided the boat carries a sensibly stocked sail repair kit. Prompt repair of minor damage will prevent it from becoming major. A little ingenuity with needle, twine, braided webbing and sticky-back sailcloth can accomplish surprisingly effective solutions to sail damage.
- The diesel auxiliary engine is subject to a wide array of malfunctions and failures. Many are relatively easy to identify and correct en route. Logical troubleshooting and a basic set of spare/repair parts can go a long way toward successfully coping with engine problems.
- A similar approach to other systems such as steering mechanisms and electrical circuits can enable a voyager to cope with failures. Think about ways to deal with potential failures before they occur and devise backup arrangements for all vital systems. This can minimize the impact of failures that may otherwise appear overwhelming.

Medical measures. On the medical side, vigorous preventive measures are certainly the best approach. If sickness or injury occurs the crew will have to be prepared, with knowledge and supplies, to cope until help can be obtained.

- A well stocked medical kit, commensurate with crew skills, can enable a sick or injured member to be stabilized long enough to reach a port or arrange external support.
- Knowing how to obtain medical guidance far from shore can be vital.

Damage control. A damage control strategy assures that:
- Your boat is fitted with the equipment needed for fighting fires, controlling flooding, and coping with rig or other structural damage.
- Your crew is trained and ready to use that equipment properly.
- Jury rigging arrangements will protect damaged systems or substitute for equipment no longer operational. These measures are usually the result of applying ingenuity and using equipment in ways not originally intended.

Some conclusions. Assessing these strategies, a few conclusions are evident:

1. *Know your boat, inside and out.* The more familiar you are with where things are, how to gain access to them, and how they operate, the better prepared you are to deal with them when they stop working normally.

2. *You get not what you expect, but what you inspect.* Don't assume that anything is in working order unless you have tested it recently. The difference between gear that is working well and gear still working but on its last legs will not be visible to a cursory inspection.

3. *Know your crew* – both their strengths and their weaknesses. Assign them duties and responsibilities and teach them how to perform them. Have at least two people capable of performing essential duties such as navigating, communicating and handling medical problems.

4. *For every effect there is a cause.* If you detect an unsafe, undesirable or abnormal effect, do not rest until you have determined the cause – and corrected it!

5. *You can't control the weather, but you can learn to understand it and anticipate its developments.* This understanding enables you to take early action to minimize its adverse effects and to exploit the opportunities it presents.

6. *When it's time to use the emergency equipment, it's too late to read the instructions.* Everyone should be intimately familiar with where every piece of safety and distress equipment is stowed. They must also know how to use each item.

7. *Simply having a piece of equipment aboard does not equate to knowing how to use it properly.* For everything from crew overboard recovery gear to radar, from galley stove to damage control supplies, conscious practice to learn to use the equipment correctly is essential. Knowing the procedure for using gear is just as important as having it aboard.

8. *Safety considerations always take top priority.* Before starting any activity, whether routine or an emergency, take a few seconds to consider and discuss safety aspects of the job and take precautions to avoid injuries and damage. The goal of a passage is to get from one place to another safely, as comfortably as possible, and reasonably quickly. The passage should, on the whole, be a pleasant experience, so comfort considerations get rated above speed. At times, speed and progress toward the destination must be sacrificed to enhance the comfort and safety of those aboard as well as the safety of the boat itself. Making the passage reasonably quickly involves using the engine when the wind stops, but be sure to monitor the remaining fuel supply. Keep a reserve for emergencies and for entering port. If the wind blows too hard, or the crew needs rest after days of

rough riding, or you need a steady platform to make an important repair, or you just want to have a quiet dinner to celebrate a milestone accomplishment, be willing to heave to and "park" the boat for a few hours. When a passage extends for a week or so, spending several hours hove to makes little difference in the time spent at sea, but those restful hours can have a remarkable impact on everyone's morale.

9. The transition from coastal cruising sailor to passagemaker brings the sailor to the ultimate level in developing sailing skills. It can be accomplished safely by most sailors willing to devote the time and effort to:
- Prepare thoroughly
- Sail conservatively
- Gradually expand envelopes of experience
- Exercise ingenuity to cope with the challenges that will occur along the way.

Bon voyage! It is hard to match the satisfaction a sailor feels at the end of a successful passage. The challenges of weather, distance and navigation have been met and mastered. There may have been difficult moments along the way, but good preparation avoided any surprises. The problems that arose were handled by a competent and willing crew – another source of satisfaction. It takes a day or so to get the boat cleaned up and rearranged for in-port living, to restock provisions and to get used to the shore-side daily routine. But then there's time to explore the new surroundings, meet the new neighbors, dip into the local culture and enjoy life before starting to think about when and where the next passage will take you.

Here's hoping all your passages are pleasant ones, all your landfalls are at daybreak with clear blue skies, and all your storm sails stay in their bags.

APPENDIX A

Caribbean 1500 Rally Boats By Make/Size (1990-2000)

Able 42: *Arching Sky* (93)
Able 42: *Golden Mean* (94)
Able Apogee 58: *Tara* (99)
Aerodyne 38: *Calvin* (99)
Alajuela 38 Mk II: *Windborne* (99)
Alberg 37: *Tamara* (94)
Alberg 37: *Tania Aebi* (98)
Albin Nimbus 42: *Jarro* (94)
Alden 44: *Puffin* (94)
Alden Boothbay Challenger 46:
    Winborne (94)
Alden Dolphin 47: *Bravo Zulu* (00)
Alden 53: *Laissez Faire* (90)
Alden 54: *Eroica* (96)
Alden 54: *Jessie* (93)
Alden 54: *Troubadour* (92)
Amel 48: *Pegasus* (91)
Amel 48: *Tumbleweed* (90)
Amel Maramu 48: *Boutonniere* (93)
Amel Mango 51: *Huntress* (98)
Amel 53: *Noelia* (00)
Amel 53: *Zafu* (00)
Amel Super Maramu 53:
    Leonore of Sark (97)
Amel Super Maramu 53:
    Tranquility (96)
Antigua 44: *Glenlyon* (94, 98)
Baba 30: *Fridur II* (00)
Baba 40: *Mecca* (93, 97)
Baba 40: *Mezzaluna* (93, 94, 95)
Baba 40: *Perserverance* (90)
Baltic 35: *Rocksteady* (97)
Baltic 43: *Persistence* (00)
Bayfield 40: *My Island Girl* (95)
Bayfield 40: *Symphony* (92)
Beneteau 390: *Sojourner*
    (94, 95, 98)
Beneteau 411: *Majjik III* (00)
Beneteau 430: *Reve D'Icare* (93)
Beneteau 432: *Miss Manhattan* (99)

Beneteau 440: *Vauntcourier* (99)
Beneteau First 405: *French Kiss* (96)
Beneteau Oceanis 39: *Abitibi* (91)
Beneteau Oceanis 400: *Peace* (97)
Beneteau Oceanis 43:
    Nova II (95, 97)
Beneteau Oceanis 44:
    PC Camelot (97)
Beneteau Oceanis 461:
    Marjorie (00)
Beneteau 45F5: *Kavima* (97)
Beneteau 461:
    Bread on the Water (00)
Beneteau 50: *Esprit* (99)
Beneteau 51: *Luna* (99)
Beneteau 53F5: *Relativity* (99)
Block Island 40: *Kate* (94)
Block Island 40: *Spindrift* (95)
Bouganvillea 60: *Anthem* (97)
Brewer 12.8: *Off Broadway* (93)
Brewer Pilothouse 46: *Tempest* (90)
Brewer Pilothouse Cutter 52:
    Night Heron (00)
Bristol 35.5: *Callisto* (98)
Bristol 38.5: *Elan* (95)
Bristol 41.1: *Aeolus IV* (98)
Bristol 41.1: *Dream Weaver* (98)
Bristol 41.1: *Elisa T* (96)
Bristol 41.1: *Elixir* (97, 98)
Bristol 41.1: *Geo Nova* (97)
Bristol 43: *Phantom* (94)
Bristol 45: *Primrose* (96)
Bristol 45.5: *Blue Sonata* (94)
Bristol 47.7: *Spray* (99)
Bristol 53.3: *Sea Gem* (97)
Bristol 54: *Runner* (91)
Bristol: *Recompense* (90)
Bruce Roberts 45: *Baraka* (91)
C&C 33: *Shanti* (96)
C&C 37: *Kapey* (95)

C&C 37: *Wave Dancer* (94, 96)
C&C 37R: *Zio* (98)
C&C 38: *Aku Tiki II* (90)
C&C 38: *Bedouin* (97)
C&C 40: *Hedon* (94)
C&C 40: *Blue Jacket* (00)
C&C Landfall 43: *Dire Wolf* (00)
C&C Landfall 48:
    Between The Sheets (99)
C&C 50: *Roulette* (93)
Cabo Rico 34: *Ra* (97)
Caliber 38: *Blue Devil* (98)
Caliber 38: *Smiles* (98)
Caliber 40: *Valcor* (91)
Cambria 40: *Charade* (90, 92)
Cambria 44: *Phoenix* (93)
Camper Nicholson 35: *Skye* (91)
Camper Nicholson 40: *Journey* (97)
Camper Nicholson 40:
    Mahina Aka (97)
Camper Nicholson 404:
    Guinivere (00)
Cape Dory 40: *Intrepid* (93)
Cape George 36: *Second Wind* (92)
Cape Horn 43: *Blue Moose* (93)
Cascade 36: *Swan* (92)
Catalina 36 MkII: *Refuge* (97)
Catalina 42: *Cathexis II* (92)
Catalina 42: *Defiant* (93)
Catalina 42: *Full House* (91)
Catalina 42: *Miracles* (93)
Cheoy Lee 36: *Tara X* (93)
Cheoy Lee 41: *Pukka* (94)
Cheoy Lee 47: *Cassiopeia* (93)
Cheoy Lee 48: *Sunrise* (92)
Cherubini 44: *Meteor of Lune* (97)
Cherubini 44: *Floatingpoint* (96)
Cherubini 48 schooner:
    Amazing Grace (00)
Clearwater 35: *Orbiter* (90)

Colvin Schooner 53: *Compeller* (96)

Concordia Custom 58:
   Stampede (98)

Crealock 34: *Summer Lady* (94)

Crealock 34:
   Summer Lady (new owner, 97)

Crealock 37: *Another Day* (99,00)

Crealock 37: *Blue Moon* (90)

Crealock 37: *Bon Secour* (00)

Crealock 37: *Daybreak* (00)

Crealock 37: *Iolanthe* (91)

Crealock 37: *Odyssey* (93)

Crealock 37: *Valkyrie* (97)

Crowther Spindrift:
   Blown Away (94)

CS 36: *Dalriada II* (93)

CS 36: *Mike 'n Mic* (94)

CSY 44: *Chesapeake* (96)

CSY 44: *Fair Go* (92)

CT 47: *Bella Luna* (97, 98)

CT 49: *Liberty* (96)

CT 56: *Bountiful* (91)

Cumulant 36: *Ironie* (97)

Dalveel 60 Schooner:
   Rockhopper (98)

Dashew 78: *Beowulf* (00)

Dawn 48: *Velero* (90)

Dean 400 cat: *Manannan* (99)

Deerfoot 62: *Moonshadow* (90)

Deerfoot 72: *Locura* (90)

Dehler 39: *Georges II* (00)

Dragonfly 1000: *Triple Vision* (95)

Dutch Steel Yawl 50:
   Forever Rosie (90)

Endeavor 43: *Obsession* (93)

Endurance 44: *Delphinus* (99)

Ericson 38: *Symphony* (96)

Ericson 38: *Tiramisu* (95)

F&C 44: *Between The Sheets*
   (90, 92, 94, 96)

F&C 44: *Compass Rose* (95)

Fantasia 35: *The Reach* (99)

Fisher 34: *Vaiana II* (00)

Fraser 51: *Wingstar* (00)

Freedom 32: *Panacea* (90)

Freedom 32: *Passion* (95)

Freedom 40: *Maggiemiluv* (90)

Freedom 40/40: *BID 3* (98,99)

Freedom 40/40: *Endymion* (98)

Freedom 44: *Frog Kiss* (93)

Freedom 44: *Wings* (91, 95)

Freedom 45: *Cheers* (97)

Freedom 45: *Genesis* (95)

Freedom 45: *No Problem* (97)

Freedom 455: *Segue* (94)

Frers Maxi 81: *Longhorn* (96)

Frers 36: *Passion* (94)

Fuji 45: *Windward* (92)

Gozzard 44:
   Midnight of Goderich (97)

Grand Soleil 39: *Mustang Sally* (95)

Grand Soleil 46.3: *Azzura* (99)

Gulfstar 41: *Paradise Found* (94)

Gulfstar 44: *Nepenthe* (97)

Gulfstar 50: *Nockabout* (90)

Gulfstar Custom 60:
   Thomasina (91)

Gulfstar Hirsch 45: *Red Wine* (95)

Hallberg Rassey 42: *Asylum* (00)

Hallberg Rassey 45: *Meredith* (94)

Hallberg Rassey 46: *Ayu* (00)

Hallberg Rassey 46: *Meg* (00)

Hans Christian 34: *Windigo* (93)

Hans Christian 38: *Snow Goose* (93)

Hans Christian 41: *Forever* (00)

Hans Christian 41: *Kemo Sabay* (93)

Hans Christian 43: *Sea Hag* (94)

Hans Christian 44T: *Iemanja* (91)

Hans Christian 48: *Togo* (98)

Hans Christian Christina 40:
   Slow Dancin' (99,00)

Helmsman 47: *Mystique* (97)

Heritage 46: *Zafu 3* (97)

Heritage West Indies 46:
   Namaste (96)

Herreschoff 36.5: *Deva* (96)

High Tension 36:
   Three Generations (95)

Hinckley 38: *Dragon* (98,99)

Hinckley 42: *Mir* (90)

Hinckley 49: *Elizabeth* (00)

Hinckley 49: *Pilgrim* (94)

Hinckley 50: *Sophia* (94)

Hinckley Bermuda 40: *Celerity* (93)

Hinckley Bermuda 40:
   Whangaroa (90)

Hinckley Southwester 42:
   Brydie (90)

Hinckley Southwester 42:
   Magic Flute (97,00)

Hinckley Southwester 42:
   Marianne (92)

Hinckley Southwester 50:
   Morning Star (91)

Hinckley Southwester 59:
   Pamina (98)

Hinckley Southwester 59:
   September Song (97)

Horstman 45 Trimaran:
   Desiderata (98)

Hudson Seawolf 44: *Zeelander* (94)

Hunter Legend 45: *Justin* (98)

Hunter Passage 450:
   Eau De Vie (97)

Hunter 54: *Caribbean* (98)

Hylas 42: *Simcha* (94)

Hylas 44: *Zephyrine* (98)

Hylas 46: *Suze* (98)

Hylas 49: *Meander* (95)

Hylas 54: *Archangel* (00)

Irwin 52: *About Time* (00)

Irwin 54: *Egg Crate* (99)

Irwin 54: *Voyager Parrot* (00)

Irwin 65: *Emerald Lady* (93)

Irwin Center Cockpit 41:
   Sound Waves (97)

Island Packet 35: *Cagen II* (94)

Island Packet 35: *C'est La Vie* (95)

Island Packet 35: *Columbine* (97)

Island Packet 35: *Deb II* (92)

Island Packet 35: *Island Time* (95)

Island Packet 35: *Kermac IV* (98)

Island Packet 38: *Haida Maid IV* (99)

Island Packet 38:
   Hope and Glory (94)

Island Packet 38: *La Sirena* (00)

Island Packet 38:
   Swallow (92, 94, 95, 97)

Island Packet 38: *Teal Monday* (93)
Island Packet 380: *Melaka* (00)
Island Packet 40: *Elixir* (98)
Island Packet 40: *Kewaydin* (98)
Island Packet 40: *Relationship* (95)
Island Packet 44: *Antietam* (00)
Island Packet 44:
    Golden Odyssey (91)
Island Packet 44:
    Slow Dancing (92, 93, 98)
Islander Freeport 36: *Jewel* (99)
J 42: *Connie D2* (96)
J 42: *Windtrip 4* (98)
J 120: *Destiny* (99)
Jeanneau 40: *Ciao Bella* (00)
Jeanneau 42: *Intuition* (95)
Johnsen 43: *Sitara* (97)
Kady Krogen 38: *Circe* (98)
Kanter 51: *Arioso* (94)
Kanter 52: *Nautilus* (99)
Kanter 52: *Uliad* (00)
Kanter Atlantic 50: *Destiny* (95)
Kanter Custom 55:
    Charisma (96, 98)
Krogen 38: *Green Sleeves* (95)
Krogen 38: *Liberte* (95, 97)
LaCoste 42: *Nomad* (92)
Lafitte 44: *Aries Won* (92)
Lagoon 37: *Cat'N Around* (93, 94)
Lagoon 37: *Island Flyer* (96)
Lagoon 42: *Island Princess* (97)
Laguna 34: *East Hills Too* (94)
LeComte Fastnet 45:
    Telepathy (92, 95)
Liberty 458: *Antidote* (94)
Little Harbor 42: *Simplex* (92)
Little Harbor 44: *Calypso* (97)
Little Harbor 44: *Fadeaway* (99)
Little Harbor 46: *Tessa* (93)
Little Harbor 53: *Windriven* (98)
Little Harbor 54: *Fleet* (99)
Little Harbor 58: *Rendezvous* (97)
Little Harbor 62: *Rights of Man* (93)
Little Harbor: *Glacier Lily* (90)
Lord Nelson 41: *Nashira* (91)
Luders 36: *Morning Watch* (00)

Mariner 36: *Stolen Moments* (96)
Mason 43: *Denali* (97)
Mason 43: *Sea Shell* (92, 98)
Mason 44: *Bon Accord* (00)
Mason 44: *Chardonnay* (92)
Mason 44: *Esprit Du Vent* (94)
Mason 44: *Last Tango* (91)
Mason 44: *Sovereign* (97)
Mason 44: *Tiger Shark* (97)
Mason 48: *Heritage* (99)
Mikelson 50: *Skol* (00)
Moody 40: *Nautilus* (93)
Moody 425: *Aquavescence* (91)
Morgan 384: *Expatriate* (98)
Morgan OI 416: *Argonauta* (98)
Morgan OI 41: *Caracol* (99)
Morgan 43: *Carpe Diem* (93)
Morgan 44: *Bali Hai* (93)
Morgan 452: *Pelican* (97)
Morgan Classic 41: *Baba Lou* (92)
Morgan 46: *Runnymead* (99)
Morris 36: *Meditation* (94)
Morris 40: *Peregrine* (97, 98, 99)
Morris 46: *Sidekick* (96)
Nauticat 38: *Top Cat* (97)
Nauticat 43: *Black Cat* (99)
Nautilus 40: *Branta* (96)
Niagara 35: *Pals I* (93)
Niagara 42: *Duck Soup* (92)
Nimble 30: *Esprit* (90)
Nonsuch 30: *Windwalker* (90)
Nordic 40: *Chandelle* (92, 93)
Nordic 44: *Isabells* (95)
Nordic 46RS: *Blue Point* (99)
Norlin 60: *Navire* (92)
Norseman 40: *Moonbeam* (00)
Norseman 430 (cat): *Stargazer* (00)
Norseman 447: *Onset* (94)
Norseman 447: *Segue* (00)
Norseman 447: *Zephyr* (92)
OC 42: *Trigger* (96)
Ocean Ketch 62: *Legend* (99)
Offshore 33: *Sycamore* (95)
Offshore Cat ketch 43:
    Connecticut Yankee (91)
Olympic 47: *Centerfold* (95)

Oyster 45: *Yohoho of Sark* (97)
Oyster 46: *Inner Voice* (99)
Oyster 485: *Paper Moon* (94)
Oyster 61: *Lulu* (99)
Pacific Seacraft 31: *Carpe Diem* (91)
Pacific Seacraft 31: *Sea Otter* (92)
Panda 38: *Natural High* (94)
Passport 37: *Free As Air* (91, 00)
Passport 40: *Harmony* (98)
Passport 40: *Imagine* (98)
Passport 40: *Rapture* (98)
Passport 44: *Calypso Rose* (00)
Pearson 36: *MB Three* (90, 92)
Pearson 39yawl: *Nepenthe* (98)
Pearson 40: *Endeavor* (98)
Pearson 40: *Mighty Melissa* (00)
Pearson 419: *Windancer* (94)
Pearson 422: *Briar Rose* (95)
Pearson 424: (sloop) *Jubilee* (99)
Pearson 424: *Euphrosyne* (94)
Pearson 424: *Hi Flite* (99, 00)
Pearson 424: *Sea Duty*
    (94, 96, 97, 99)
Pearson 424: *Sweet Lou* (00)
Pearson 424: *Xanadu* (95, 97)
Pearson Countess 44: *Avatrice* (95)
Pedrick Custom 61: *Twowowie* (91)
Pedrick 80: *Windward Passage* (90)
Peterson 44: *Blue Moon* (90)
Peterson 46: *C'est Si Bon* (98)
Privilege 465: *Change Order* (99)
Prout Snowgoose 37:
    Laura Lee (92)
Prout Escale 39: *Morning Star* (00)
Prout Quasar 50: *Inspiration* (98)
Reliance 44: *Mad River* (93, 94)
Rene d'Antilles 38: *Iskis* (95)
Rhodes 38: *Elixir* (95)
S&S 47: *Palawan* (93)
S2 36: *Lucky Break* (94)
Sabre 36: *Friendly Confines* (96)
Sabre 42: *Valkyrie* (94)
Sabre 42: *Witchcraft* (91, 94)
Sabre 452: *Shalimar* (99)
Saga 43: *Kinship* (99)
Santa Cruz 52: *Aquila* (98, 99)

Sceptre 41: *Weewowie* (96)

Searunner 31: *Mango* (92)

Serendipity 43: *Jam* (95)

Shannon 28: *Arabesque* (92)

Shannon 28: *Viator* (98)

Shannon 38: *Bittersweet* (95)

Shannon 38: *Cygnus* (94)

Shannon 38: *Entity* (98)

Shannon 43: *Tarnhelm* (93, 95)

Shannon 43: *Torch* (99)

Sigma 362: *Savoir-Vivre* (93)

Skye 51: *Keji* (93)

Slipper 42: *Magic* (96)

Slocum 43: *Dakare* (95, 97)

Slocum 43: *Snowdrift* (97)

St. Francis 43 cat: *Obelix* (95)

Stellar 30: *Villa de Coop* (90)

Stevens 47: *After Hours* (92)

Stevens 47: *Nefertari* (94)

Stevens 47: *Noella* (90)

Stevens 47: *Raven* (99)

Stevens 47: *Rising Sun* (96)

Stevens 47: *Sea Chanty* (92)

Stevens 50: *Envoy* (92)

Stevens 50 Custom: *Jolly Moon* (00)

Stevens 50 PH: *Envoy* (98)

Sundeer 60: *Reunion* (97)

Swan 42: *Corban* (96)

Swan 44: *Juluca* (97)

Swan 44: *Moondance* (93)

Swan 46: *Mary Blair* (98)

Swan 48: *Caribe* (98)

Swan 48: *Hinano* (98)

Swan 48: *Spectra* (95)

Swan 48: *Taino* (97)

Swan 48: *Yocahu* (97)

Swan 55: *Swanaire* (97, 98)

Swan 56: *Mensae* (00)

Swan 65: *Talina* (97)

Swan 68: *La Reverende* (97, 98)

Sweden 36: *Hobo* (90)

Tartan 37: *Astri IV* (95, 97)

Tartan 37: *Manatee* (93)

Tartan 37: *Midnight Wave* (92, 94)

Tartan 37: *Orion* (00)

Tashiba 36: *Caravela* (00)

Tashiba 36: *Surprise* (94)

Tashiba 40: *Shangri-La* (96)

Tashiba 40: *Solace* (97)

Tashiba 40: *Trinity* (95)

Tashiba 40: *Valkyrie* (98)

Tashiba 40: *Wanderlust* (97)

Taswell 43: *Windwalker* (98)

Taswell 49: *Boomer* (98)

Taswell 49: *Cherubino* (93)

Taswell 49: *Promise* (99)

Taswell 49: *Tai-Pan* (92, 94)

Taswell 58: *Gray Lady* (96, 98)

Tatoosh 51: *White Eagle* (98)

Tayana 37: *Ambrose Light* (95)

Tayana 37: *Calloo Callay* (90)

Tayana 37: *Esperanza* (97)

Tayana 37: *Marieusz* (00)

Tayana 37: *Pyewacket* (99)

Tayana 37: *Whisper's Echo* (97)

Tayana 37-2: *Revision II* (98)

Tayana 42: *Archipelago* (96)

Tayana 42: *Canvasback* (90, 94)

Tayana 42: *Gamelan* (97)

Tayana 42: *Kampeska* (98)

Tayana 42: *Lady J* (96)

Tayana 42: *Perseverance* (98)

Tayana 42: *Sea Whisper* (97)

Tayana 47: *Grand Jete'* (00)

Tayana 47: *Serafe* (92, 94)

Tayana 48: *About Time* (96)

Tayana 48: *Far Niente* (94, 95)

Tayana 48: *Tonica* (98)

Tayana 52: *Amadeus* (93)

Tayana 52: *Cat's Cradle* (94)

Tayana 52: *Sojourner* (90)

Tayana 52:

   Sojourner (new owner, 94, 95)

Tayana 52: *Stargazer* (98)

Tayana 52: *Summer Swell* (90)

Tayana 52: *Tiara* (97, 98)

Tayana 52 Aft Cockpit:

   Endless Summer (99)

Tayana 55: *Boutoniere* (94)

Tayana 55: *Magic Dragon* (97)

Tayana 55: *Tioga* (96)

Tayana 65: *Bravado* (99, 00)

Thompson 60 tri:

   Pacific Challenge (95)

Trintella 44: *Azulea* (95)

Trintella 53: *Feisty* (99)

Union 36: *Interlude* (99)

Ushant Rogger 41:

   Nancy Jeanne (96)

Vagabond 47: *Arabesque* (93, 94)

Vagabond 47: *Jade Queen* (92)

Valiant 37: *About Time* (92)

Valiant 40: *Blue Yonder* (96, 98)

Valiant 40: *Calypso* (98)

Valiant 40: *Chianti* (99)

Valiant 40: *Columbine* (95)

Valiant 40: *Culmination* (93)

Valiant 40: *Danseang* (90)

Valiant 40: *Dawn* (96)

Valiant 40: *Initiative* (94)

Valiant 40: *Perfect World* (95)

Valiant 40: *Promise* (94)

Valiant 40: *Windwalker* (99)

Valiant 42: *August Crow* (99)

Valiant 42: *Blue Moon* (97)

Valiant 42: *Pegasus* (96)

Valiant 47: *Square Peg* (94)

Waterline 444: *Kaien* (93)

Wauquiez 35.5: *Whistler* (93)

Wauquiez 43: *Second Wind* (96, 00)

Westerly 38: *Rainbow* (97)

Westerly Fulmar:

   Next One Comes Along (94)

Westsail 42: *Vikara* (92)

Westwind 42: *Mariah* (93)

Whitby 42: *Harmony* (92, 93, 95)

Whitby 42: *Janus* (91)

Whitby 42: *Rita T* (96)

Whitby 42: *Solana II* (90)

Whitby 42: *Windswept* (91)

Windship 52: *Godspeed* (95, 96)

Bermuda Cruising Rally Boats 1993-2001

Alberg 37: *Tamara* (94)

Allied Seawind 30: *Italic* (95)

Allied Seawind 30: *Reveille* (96)

Amel Super Maramu 53:
  Drifter (99)

Baba 30: *Pintail* (94)

Baba 35: *Fantasia* (00)

Beneteau 390: *Chartwell* (94)

Beneteau First 42S7: *Valkyrie* (99)

Beneteau Oceanus 400:
  Tiramisu (99)

Beneteau Oceanus 440:
  American Pie II (96)

Beneteau 461: *Galatea* (98)

Bristol 35.5: *Amira* (01)

Bristol 35.5: *Mekeia* (98)

Bristol 38.8: *Horizon* (01)

Bristol 45.5: *Blue Sonata* (94)

Bristol 47: *Spray* (98)

C&C 34: *Shadowfax* (94)

C&C 34: *Just Amazing* (93)

C&C 37: *Persuasion* (99)

C&C Landfall 48: *Latitude* (01)

Caliber 38: *Blue Devil* (98)

Caliber 40: *Dawn Treader* (98)

Caliber 40: *Explorer* (97)

Caliber 40: *Sea Hew* (00)

Caliber 40 LRC: *Starsong* (99)

Cape Dory 36: *Monarch* (98)

Cape Dory 36: *Paper Clipper* (95)

Cape Dory 36: *Sojourner* (95)

Cape Dory 38: *Acadia* (97)

Catalina 34: *Full Moon* (00)

Catalina 34: *Immunity* (95)

Catalina 42: *Full House* (93)

Cheoy Lee 41: *Encore* (94)

Comet III 36: *Touche* (98)

Compac 35: *Rosajeanette* (97)

Coronado 35: *Ciel Bleu* (95)

CS 33: *Ynys-Fon* (94)

CSY 37: *Proteus* (95)

CSY 44: *Dreamer II* (99)

Cuttyhunk 41: *Bounty* (97)

Dean 400 cat: *Manannan* (98)

Deerfoot 63: *Great Escape* (93)

Edel 35 cat: *Cat Morgan* (95)

Ericson 30: *St. Somewhere* (93)

Freedom 35: *Pyxis* (95)

Freedom 39 PH schooner:
  Resolute (98)

Freedom 44: *Airborne* (95)

Gemini 34: *Gemini* (93)

Gozzard 44: *Troubadour* (01)

Hans Christian 33:
  First Light (96, 97)

Hans Christian 33: *Sojourn* (98)

Hans Christian 38: *Gypsy Rose* (98)

Hans Christian 41: *2nd Wind* (98)

Helmsman 47: *Mystique* (97)

Hinckley Pilot 35: *Windstream* (93)

Hunter 37C: *Valhalla* (01)

Hunter 37.6: *Wind Dancer* (96)

Hunter 40.5: *Razzmatazz* (97)

Hunter 410: *Offline* (01)

Hunter 42: *Dream Catcher* (96)

Hunter 45: *Guten Tag* (98)

Hunter Passage 450:
  Eau-De-Vie (97)

Hunter 54: *Caribbean* (98)

Irwin 52: *Wind Dancer* (96)

Island Packet 35: *Tillbedjare* (96)

Island Packet 38: *Fully Involved* (97)

Island Packet 38: *Gold Star* (93, 96)

Island Packet 38:
  Hope and Glory (96)

Island Packet 40: *Relationship* (95)

J 40: *Solstice* (94)

Jeanneau 42.2: *White Silence* (01)

Jeanneau Voyager 11.2:
  Endurance (94, 96)

Joubert/Nivelt 40: *Caribbean* (93)

Kanter 51: *Arioso* (93)

Lancer 44: *Destiny* (94)

LeComte 45: *Telepathy* (95)

Little Harbor 46: *Toot* (94)

MacGregor 65: *Caledonia* (95)

Mason 43: *Anna* (99)

Morgan 44: *Contessa* (01)

Morgan OI 41: *Misty Maiden* (01)

Morgan 67: *Mahle* (98)

Morgan Out Island 51:
  Growltiger (98)

Morris 36: *Meditation* (94)

Neptune 33: *Gipsy* (93)

Niagara 35: *Explorer II* (94)

Nordic 40: *Betelgeux* (99)

Nordic 44: *Gratitude* (98)

Oceanic 43: *Passat V* (96)

Oyster Heritage 37: *Meltemi* (97)

Oyster 48.5: *Whiteflash* (97)

Pacific Seacraft: *Green Dolphin* (00)

Passport 40: *Myosotis* (98)

Pearson 365: *Broken Arrow* (94)

Pearson 365: *Long Winded* (95)

Pearson 38: *Fantasea* (94)

Pearson 424: *Sea Duty*
  (93, 94, 95, 96)

Peterson 46: *Katrajena* (98)

Rival 36: *Van Der Mer* (00)

Sabre 36: *Sailin'Whalen* (00)

Sabre 36: *Wind Sprint* (98)

Sabre 38 MKII: *Jerawyn* (97)

Sabre 425: *Bad Boy* (97)

Schock 50: *West Marine* (96, 97)

Stevens 47: *After Hours* (94)

Stevens 47: *Wischbone* (94)

Sundeer 60: *Reunion* (97)

Tartan 37: *Moonshadow* (96)

Tartan 37: *Windfall* (94)

Tartan 372: *Ful Phyl* (94)

Tartan 41: *Vector* (93)

Tayana 37: *Sirena* (95)

Tayana 42: *Endless Summer* (96)

Tayana 42: *Fidelitas* (94)

Tayana Vancouver 42:
  Bambooshay (97)

Trintella 49: *Paragon* (99)

Vagabond 42: *Shenandoah* (96)

Valiant 40: *Tootsie* (94)

Whitby 42: *Rita T* (95, 97, 98)

Whitby 42: *Manana V* (99)

World Cruiser 50: *Topaz*

APPENDIX B

The following forms for prescription medications which are mentioned in "Medical and Dental Treatment" (Chapter 28) can be copied and provided to your family physician. This will make it easier for him or her to issue the prescriptions. You can insert your name and address. The doctor needs only to add the quantity and sign it. The forms and medical information were provided by Dr. Robert H. Amsler, fleet surgeon of Bayview Yacht Club, Detroit, who has served as a presenter in West Marine Passagemaker Seminars.

Name _____ Date _____

Address _____

Original Rx No. _____ Phone by _____ Refill ___ times ☐ Deliver ☐ Will Call

℞   DIPHENOXYLATE 2.5MG / ATROPINE 0.025 MG   # _____

TAKE TWO PILLS IMMEDIATELY WITH TREATING DIARRHEA, THEN ONE EVERY SIX HOURS AS NEEDED TO CONTROL IT.

Doctor _____ Medicaid No. _____

Dr.'s Address _____

DEA No. _____ Pharmacist _____

Name _____ Date _____

Address _____

Original Rx No. _____ Phone by _____ Refill ___ times ☐ Deliver ☐ Will Call

℞   DEXEDRINE 5 MG   # _____

TAKE ONE OR TWO EVERY SIX HOURS WITH SCOPOLAMINE 0.3 MG TO SUPPRESS SEASICKNESS.

Doctor _____ Medicaid No. _____

Dr.'s Address _____

DEA No. _____ Pharmacist _____

Name _____ Date _____

Address _____

Original Rx No. _____ Phone by _____ Refill ___ times ☐ Deliver ☐ Will Call

R̷   PROMETHAZINE 25 MG   # _____

     TAKE ONE EVERY SIX HOURS WITH EPHEDRINE 25 MG TO SUPPRESS
     SEVERE SEASICKNESS.

Doctor _____ Medicaid No. _____

Dr.'s Address _____

DEA No. _____ Pharmacist _____

Name _____ Date _____

Address _____

Original Rx No. _____ Phone by _____ Refill ___ times ☐ Deliver ☐ Will Call

R̷   SCOPOLAMINE 0.3 MG   # _____

     TAKE ONE OR TWO EVERY SIX HOURS WITH DEXEDRINE 5 MG TO
     SUPPRESS SEVERE SEASICKNESS.

Doctor _____ Medicaid No. _____

Dr.'s Address _____

DEA No. _____ Pharmacist _____

Name _____ Date _____

Address _____

Original Rx No. _____ Phone by _____ Refill ___ times ☐ Deliver ☐ Will Call

R̷   EPHEDRINE 25 MG   # _____

     TAKE ONE EVERY SIX HOURS WITH PROMETHAZINE 25 MG
     TO SUPPRESS SEVERE SEASICKNESS.

Doctor _____ Medicaid No. _____

Dr.'s Address _____

DEA No. _____ Pharmacist _____

Name _____ Date _____

Address _____

Original Rx No. _____ Phone by _____ Refill ___ times ☐ Deliver ☐ Will Call

℞   DIPHENHYDRAMINE 25 MG   # _____

TAKE TWO PILLS THREE TIMES A DAY FOR ALLERGIC REACTION.

CAN ALSO BE USED TO INDUCE SLEEP BY TAKING PRIOR TO BEDTIME.

Doctor _____ Medicaid No. _____

Dr.'s Address _____

DEA No. _____ Pharmacist _____

Name _____ Date _____

Address _____

Original Rx No. _____ Phone by _____ Refill ___ times ☐ Deliver ☐ Will Call

℞   CIPROFLOXACIN 0.3% OPHTHALMIC SOLUTION

USE TWO DROPS EVERY 15 MINUTES FOR FIRST SIX HOURS THEN TWO DROPS EVERY

30 MINUTES FOR REMAINDER OF FIRST DAY, THEN TWO DROPS EVERY FOUR HOURS.

Doctor _____ Medicaid No. _____

Dr.'s Address _____

DEA No. _____ Pharmacist _____

Name _____ Date _____

Address _____

Original Rx No. _____ Phone by _____ Refill ___ times ☐ Deliver ☐ Will Call

℞   TETRACAINE HYDROCHLORIDE 0.5%

USE TWO DROPS IN EYE TO ANESTHETIZE IT WHEN REMOVING EMBEDDED FOREIGN

OBJECTS OR FOR SEVERE EYE PAIN. MAY REPEAT FOUR TO SIX TIMES AS NEEDED TO

CONTROL PAIN. (MAXIMUM 24-36 HOURS)

Doctor _____ Medicaid No. _____

Dr.'s Address _____

DEA No. _____ Pharmacist _____

Name _____ Date _____

Address _____

Original Rx No. _____ Phone by _____ Refill ___ times ☐ Deliver ☐ Will Call

℞   CORTISPORIN OTIC

PLACE FOUR DROPS IN INFECTED EAR FOUR TIMES A DAY
FOR FOUR DAYS TO STOP INFECTION.

Doctor _____ Medicaid No. _____

Dr.'s Address _____

DEA No. _____ Pharmacist _____

Name _____ Date _____

Address _____

Original Rx No. _____ Phone by _____ Refill ___ times ☐ Deliver ☐ Will Call

℞   HYDROCORTISONE RECTAL SUPPOSITORY 25 MG

USE ONE SUPPOSITORY TWO TO THREE TIMES A DAY TO REDUCE HEMORRHOID
SWELLING AND RECTAL IRRITATION. KEEP COOL.

Doctor _____ Medicaid No. _____

Dr.'s Address _____

DEA No. _____ Pharmacist _____

Name _____ Date _____

Address _____

Original Rx No. _____ Phone by _____ Refill ___ times ☐ Deliver ☐ Will Call

℞   KETOCONAZOLE 2% CREAM
30 GRAMS

APPLY TWICE DAILY TO SKIN FOR FUNGAL INFECTION

Doctor _____ Medicaid No. _____

Dr.'s Address _____

DEA No. _____ Pharmacist _____

Name _____ Date _____

Address _____

Original Rx No. _____ Phone by _____ Refill ___ times ☐ Deliver ☐ Will Call

℞   CIMETIDINE 400 MG   # _____

TAKE ONE AM AND ONE PM FOR HEARTBURN THAT DOES NOT GO AWAY.
USE IN CONJUNCTION WITH ANTACIDS.

Doctor _____ Medicaid No. _____

Dr.'s Address _____

DEA No. _____ Pharmacist _____

Name _____ Date _____

Address _____

Original Rx No. _____ Phone by _____ Refill ___ times ☐ Deliver ☐ Will Call

℞   HYDROCORTISONE VALERATE 0.2%

30 GRAMS
APPLY TO SKIN TWICE DAILY FOR INFLAMMATION.

Doctor _____ Medicaid No. _____

Dr.'s Address _____

DEA No. _____ Pharmacist _____

Name _____ Date _____

Address _____

Original Rx No. _____ Phone by _____ Refill ___ times ☐ Deliver ☐ Will Call

℞   BISACODYL 5 MG   # _____

TAKE ONE OR TWO AT BEDTIME FOR CONSTIPATION

Doctor _____ Medicaid No. _____

Dr.'s Address _____

DEA No. _____ Pharmacist _____

Name _____ Date _____

Address _____

Original Rx No. _____ Phone by _____ Refill ___ times ☐ Deliver ☐ Will Call

℞   NITROGLYCERINE SUBLINGUAL SPRAY

ONE SPRAY UNDER TONGUE FOR HEART PAIN. IF NO RELIEF, MAY REPEAT IN FIVE
MINUTES. THIS WILL CAUSE A HEADACHE.

Doctor _____ Medicaid No. _____

Dr.'s Address _____

DEA No. _____ Pharmacist _____

Name _____ Date _____

Address _____

Original Rx No. _____ Phone by _____ Refill ___ times ☐ Deliver ☐ Will Call

℞   HYDROCODONE 10 MG / ACETOMINOPHEN 650 MG   # _____

TAKE ONE PILL EVERY SIX TO EIGHT HOURS FOR SEVERE PAIN.
IBUPROFEN MAY BE TAKEN WITH THIS.

Doctor _____ Medicaid No. _____

Dr.'s Address _____

DEA No. _____ Pharmacist _____

Name _____ Date _____

Address _____

Original Rx No. _____ Phone by _____ Refill ___ times ☐ Deliver ☐ Will Call

℞   AMOXICILLIN 500 MG   # _____

TAKE ONE PILL EVERY EIGHT HOURS TO SUPPRESS INFECTION.

Doctor _____ Medicaid No. _____

Dr.'s Address _____

DEA No. _____ Pharmacist _____

Name _____ Date _____

Address _____

Original Rx No. _____ Phone by _____ Refill ___ times ☐ Deliver ☐ Will Call

℞   SEPTRA DS 14 MG   # _____
        TAKE ONE PILL EVERY 12 HOURS TO SUPPRESS INFECTION.

Doctor _____ Medicaid No. _____

Dr.'s Address _____

DEA No. _____ Pharmacist _____

Name _____ Date _____

Address _____

Original Rx No. _____ Phone by _____ Refill ___ times ☐ Deliver ☐ Will Call

℞   KEFLEX 500 MG   # _____
        TAKE ONE PILL EVERY SIX HOURS TO SUPPRESS INFECTION.

Doctor _____ Medicaid No. _____

Dr.'s Address _____

DEA No. _____ Pharmacist _____

Name _____ Date _____

Address _____

Original Rx No. _____ Phone by _____ Refill ___ times ☐ Deliver ☐ Will Call

℞   CIPRO 500 MG   # _____
        TAKE ONE PILL EVERY 12 HOURS FOR SERIOUS INFECTION.

Doctor _____ Medicaid No. _____

Dr.'s Address _____

DEA No. _____ Pharmacist _____

Name _____ Date _____

Address _____

Original Rx No. _____ Phone by _____ Refill ___ times ☐ Deliver ☐ Will Call

R̶x   ERYTHROMYCIN 330 MG   # _____

       TAKE ONE PILL EVERY EIGHT HOURS TO SUPPRESS INFECTION.

Doctor _____ Medicaid No. _____

Dr.'s Address _____

DEA No. _____ Pharmacist _____

Name _____ Date _____

Address _____

Original Rx No. _____ Phone by _____ Refill ___ times ☐ Deliver ☐ Will Call

R̶x   IBUPROFEN 800 MG   # _____

       TAKE ONE PILL THREE TIMES A DAY FOR PAIN. ALWAYS TAKE WITH FOOD.

Doctor _____ Medicaid No. _____

Dr.'s Address _____

DEA No. _____ Pharmacist _____

Name _____ Date _____

Address _____

Original Rx No. _____ Phone by _____ Refill ___ times ☐ Deliver ☐ Will Call

R̶x   DIAZEPAM 2 MG   # _____

       TAKE 1/2-1 TWICE A DAY FOR ANXIETY. DO NOT USE WITH ALCOHOL.

Doctor _____ Medicaid No. _____

Dr.'s Address _____

DEA No. _____ Pharmacist _____

INDEX